Research Methods and Youth Sport

This is the first book to focus entirely on physical education and youth sport, it guides the reader through the research process, from first steps through to completion of a dissertation or practice-based project, and introduces key topics such as:

- formulating a research question
- qualitative approaches
- quantitative approaches
- mixed-method research
- literature review
- case studies
- survey, interviews and focus groups
- data analysis
- writing the dissertation.

Each chapter includes a full range of useful pedagogical features, including chapter summaries, practical activities, case studies, dialogues with active researchers and guidance on further reading and resources. With contributions from some of the world's best-known researchers in the field, this book is indispensible reading for all students and professionals working in physical education, youth sport, sports coaching and related subjects.

Kathleen Armour is Professor of Education and Sport, and Head of the Department of Sport Pedagogy at the University of Birmingham, UK. Her research interests are in teacher/coach career-long professional development, physical activity and health pedagogies, and the role of sport in the lives of disaffected/disengaged youth.

Doune Macdonald is Professor and Head of the School of Human Movement Studies, University of Queensland, Australia. Her research interests have addressed the challenges of curriculum reform and its impact, and more recently broader questions of physical activity, health and young people.

Research Methods in Physical Education and Youth Sport

Edited by Kathleen Armour and
Doune Macdonald

 Routledge
Taylor & Francis Group

LONDON AND NEW YORK

First published 2012
by Routledge
2 Park Square, Milton Park, Abingdon, Oxon OX14 4RN

Simultaneously published in the USA and Canada
by Routledge
711 Third Avenue, New York, NY 10017

Routledge is an imprint of the Taylor & Francis Group, an informa business

British Library Cataloguing in Publication Data
A catalogue record for this book is available from the British Library

Library of Congress Cataloging in Publication Data
Research methods in physical education and youth sport / edited by Kathleen
Armour and Doune Macdonald.
        p. cm.
    1. Physical education and training–Research–Methodology. 2. Sports for
children–Research–Methodology. 3. Sports sciences–Research–Methodology.
I. Armour, Kathleen M. II. MacDonald, Doune, 1959-
GV361.R48 2012
613.710721–dc23   2011026328

ISBN: 978-0-415-61884-7 (hbk)
ISBN: 978-0-415-61885-4 (pbk)
ISBN: 978-0-203-80717-0 (ebk)

Typeset in Garamond
by HWA Text and Data Management, London

Printed and bound in Great Britain by
CPI Antony Rowe, Chippenham, Wiltshire

Contents

Illustrations

Figures

Tables

Boxes

Part I
Planning the research process

1 What is your research question – and why?

Kathleen Armour and Doune Macdonald

Who we are as researchers revolves around the questions that we ask.
(Brustad, 2009: 114)

[I]n research, as in life, what one finds depends on where one looks and how one looks – and the tools and methods that are used are determinative of these findings.
(Spencer Foundation Task Force, 2009: 28)

Pseudo-inquiry is ubiquitous: both the sham reasoning, making a case for a conclusion to which you are unbudgeably committed at the outset, and, especially, fake reasoning, making a case for a conclusion to the truth value of which you are indifferent.
(Haack, 2008: 34)

Introduction

Despite the fact that this is a research *methods* book, you should not assume that research begins with methods; it does not. Research begins with *questions* and researchers often care very deeply about both the questions and the potential answers. The identification of a viable research question is not, however, a straightforward process; the selection of questions is influenced by myriad factors including personal background, interest and skills, personal preference, available funding, sociopolitical factors and current trends. The primary purpose of this chapter, therefore, is to focus on how and why research questions are developed, and to encourage you to identify two or three questions against which the methods chapters that follow can be considered.

The secondary purpose of the chapter is to introduce the approach and structure of this book. Countless research methods books are available and, like many others, this book introduces a wide range of methods and methodological issues. In this text, however, we have taken a different approach. Each chapter has (at least) two authors: one senior, experienced researcher and one emerging researcher who was engaged in learning about the research method/issue addressed at the time of writing. Authors have approached the writing of their chapters in a range of ways, but one of the tasks we set them was to ensure that, where feasible, the voices of each author could be heard. Hence, in many of the chapters, the senior author presents material on a method or approach, and the junior author offers comment on issues encountered while trying to use the method in their research. In this way, we hope that readers who are relatively new to some of these methods will be able to gain valuable insights into the research process in *practice* as well as in theory.

About us

Kathleen Armour, co-editor of this book, is Professor of Education and Sport and Head of the Department of Sport Pedagogy at the University of Birmingham in the UK. She has been working in the academic field of education, sport and physical education for about 25 years. Her research interests are all located in the academic spaces where sport and education meet, so she has been influenced strongly by research in the wider education field. In the last 10 years, Kathy has been involved in large, multidisciplinary teams of researchers undertaking longitudinal evaluations of government- and corporate-funded interventions. This collaborative research activity has given her new insights into the challenges and opportunities of working across traditional disciplinary boundaries. Kathy has also been active in trying to raise the profile and quality of educational research in physical education and sport coaching, and she is founder and lead convenor of the new Sport Pedagogy Research Network within the European Education Research Association. Most recently, Kathy has been appointed to the REF (Research Excellence Framework) panel for sport-related research, which is part of a periodic national assessment of published research undertaken in all subjects across all universities in the UK. It is interesting to consider the impact of such assessments on the research process, researchers' careers ... and the kinds of research questions that are valued.

Doune Macdonald, co-editor of this book, is a Professor of Health and Physical Education (HPE) and Head of the School of Human Movement Studies at the University of Queensland. She has been working as an academic in the field of HPE for about 25 years, having taught HPE in primary and secondary schools after her undergraduate degree. Over this time, she has had a range of research interests in the areas of HPE teacher education, curriculum and equity, and more recently in sociocultural questions around young people and physical activity. Several of these projects have been multidisciplinary and longitudinal, necessitating careful project planning, communication and management. She has worked with more than 15 research higher degree students who have been integral to her applied and commissioned research, grants and publications. Being a head of school, or chair of department as it might be known elsewhere, has given her insights into the changing context in which research is now being conducted in universities and the myriad of challenges that may arise for research students and early career academics.

What is research?

Research can be defined in many different ways, but at its heart is the notion of investigation – finding out – for a purpose. At its very simplest, a dictionary definition tells us that research is a 'methodical investigation into a subject in order to discover facts, to establish or revise a theory, or to develop a plan of action based on the facts discovered'. All research takes place within a broad social and political context, and this means that definitions shift, albeit subtly. For example, in the forthcoming assessment of research to be undertaken in universities in the UK, there is a strong emphasis on research 'impact'. The draft definition of research for these purposes is: 'a process of investigation leading to new insights *effectively shared*'. Different forms of research have purposes that can have a major influence on the ways in which the research process is conceptualized and questions formed. For example, critical theorists form their research questions from the fundamental standpoint of questioning 'the assumption that societies such as the United States, Canada, Australia, New Zealand, and the nations in the European Union ... are unproblematically democratic and free' (Kincheloe and Maclaren, 2005: 303). Researchers working in this tradition have the core purpose of using research 'as a form of social or cultural criticism' (ibid.: 304). Similarly, those engaged in participatory action research (PAR) have the stated objective of producing 'knowledge and action directly useful to a group of people' in order to 'empower people at a deeper level through the process of constructing and using their knowledge' (Nieuwenhuys, 2004: 210). What we need to take from all this is that researchers in different traditions tend to ask different questions for different reasons.

The range of situations in which we might engage in research is vast. At one end of the spectrum, it could be argued that we are engaged in a form of research much of the time in our daily lives, i.e., we investigate – sometimes in great detail – choice of university, holiday destination or buying a house. In this book, however, we are interested in formal research, which is 'the systematic gathering, presenting and analysing of data' (Burton and Bartlett, 2009: 3) with a view to expanding knowledge and solving problems. Importantly, and this point cannot be overstated, once we engage in research at the formal level, we are usually shifting from researching mainly undertaken for our own purposes to producing research findings which we intend to share with others. The intention is to develop new knowledge that could influence policy, theory and/or practice in the field in which we work. This means that we have a clear responsibility to ensure that research is undertaken rigorously, using the most appropriate design, methods, analysis, reporting and dissemination strategies, all of which must be compliant with increasingly exacting ethical standards. A critical understanding of the research process, and the strengths and weaknesses of different traditions and methods is therefore the hallmark of a professional approach to research.

Professional responsibility

Once researchers enter the public realm, it could be argued that they have a professional responsibility to the potential users of their research. For example, we would argue that physical education researchers have a professional responsibility to those teachers, pupils and policymakers they are seeking to inform. By this, we mean that researchers should address not only the questions in which they have a personal interest, but also those questions that matter to teachers, schools, parents and policymakers. In other words, research at this level should be more than a personal hobby; indeed, in order to attract funding, research has to focus on areas of public interest. Following on from this, it is logical to suggest that researchers also have a professional responsibility to ensure that the research they conduct is fit for purpose, making best use of the range of appropriate methods and using the best research knowledge – and methods – available. Without this quality control imperative, poor research can enter the public domain and could have a negative impact on some users.

Research funding

This last point raises the issue of research funding and research questions. How can researchers retain an interest in their own questions, while simultaneously seeking funding and perhaps changing their questions in order to attract funding? What is the point of funding and do we need it? O'Sullivan (2007: 254) poses the following question:

> As a scholar, you decide whether your interest in a particular research agenda is driven by access to research funding or whether the questions of interest are of keen significance and importance. Is it possible to do both?

One response to this is that doing both is not optional; rather it is essential, although it is also important to recognize that researchers tend to do different things at different stages in their careers. It is unlikely, for example, that a cell biologist will be allowed to enter a PhD programme and work entirely alone on a topic of choice that is not part of a larger, funded research programme. On the other hand, it is possible that a researcher in the social sciences, including aspects of physical education and coaching, will have more freedom, working with a supervisor and perhaps without any external funding. We have argued elsewhere, however, that the field of physical education has not been served well by the predominance of lone, essentially part-time researchers who are also academics with large teaching and administration commitments (Armour, 2010; Macdonald, 2009). The field has suffered from a lack of funding to support large, sustained research teams that are common in the natural sciences, and this has restricted the ability of physical education researchers to ask 'big' research questions and to answer them effectively and robustly. It could be argued that this has resulted in a quantity and quality of research knowledge that is unable to inform practice with confidence.

Research purposes

It is important to recognize that research is undertaken at different points in a career for different reasons – e.g., study for university credit, a research degree, a commissioned project – and that the reason will, to some extent, guide how the experience unfolds. In particular, underpinning reasons shape the purpose of your research and the questions you want to ask matched to the time available. For those undertaking an undergraduate honours project or a research degree (such as a Master or Doctor of Philosophy), it is important to consider what you might want from your research experience. Are you looking for this research experience to take you into a university career, or are you developing a skills set that will be most useful to industry (e.g. working as a coach, being promoted to advanced teacher status)? If it's the former, your research project is very much a building block upon which your career trajectory may be built. The presumed goal of undertaking an MPhil or PhD is for you to demonstrate that you can operate as an independent researcher and, preceding this, an honours project may signify your readiness to undertake a higher degree.

Research also has a number of formalized terms that describe its purpose. Traditionally, universities talk in terms of basic and applied research, where *basic* or *pure* research is an activity in which academics are free to engage driven by the pursuit of truth for its own sake. This kind of research often has the goal of generating theory and discovering 'fundamental facts'. *Applied* or *field* research uses a rigorous system of inquiry to apply new knowledge to everyday problems. It is most likely that your research project will fall into this latter category if you work with teachers, coaches, students, athletes, parents, or policies to understand and refine practice. As was noted earlier, commissioned research occurs where organizations such as government agencies, sporting groups, school systems etc., want a particular research project undertaken and they pay researchers to do this under contract. These projects will, to some extent, delimit some of the questions asked, perhaps the methods employed, budget, timelines, and opportunities for publishing the findings.

Much large-scale, commissioned research in the field of physical education and sport takes the form of evaluations. The research is usually undertaken to assess the effectiveness of an intervention such as a new programme or policy. Even in this case, however, the research process is less straightforward than it might at first appear. For example, Weiss (1998) has identified clashes between the needs of researchers and those of corporate or government sponsors in evaluation research. Researchers tend to want more time than is available (Rossi *et al.*, 2004) and are keen to identify both positive and negative impacts of the intervention. Sponsors, on the other hand, might, for a variety of reasons, prefer to hear only the positive outcomes of the research. Sponsors might also have very fixed views about methods, making it difficult for researchers to design appropriate studies, and they might believe that research can always identify the kind of direct and simple lines of causation that are needed to demonstrate a programme has 'worked'. This is particularly problematic in the social sciences because expectations tend to be rooted in natural science models of research. Nonetheless, where unrealistic expectations of research exist, negotiation with sponsors can clarify misunderstandings and some compromise may be required. Challenges of this type are rarely insurmountable: they are simply part of the reality of the research process; research questions are never asked – or answered – in a vacuum.

Contribution to knowledge

Another way to think about research questions is to consider the purposes of research and the types of knowledge to which it contributes. Gall, Gall and Borg (2007) suggested the following ways in which research might contribute to knowledge:

> *Description* – involves using a range of instrumentation (e.g. pedometers, surveys) to describe natural or social phenomena. You may be interested in whether a coach is giving equal feedback to boys and girls, or how teachers are following a new physical education syllabus.
>
> *Prediction* – allows us to forecast when something might occur in the future based upon current information. For example, given the trends for participation in junior soccer, when might the competition schedule need to change or more coaches be required?
>
> *Improvement* – looks at the effectiveness of interventions designed to improve practice. Education and sporting systems are constantly adjusting their approaches, resources, pedagogies etc., to improve learning and performance outcomes. Research can inform the efficacy of the interventions.
>
> *Explanation* – to some extent subsumes the above purposes, in that explaining a phenomenon means you can describe it, predict how it will play out and intervene to change the consequences. Often, explanations for phenomena, such as boys' stereotypical behaviours in sport, are framed as theories and, in the example used here, feminist theory may be helpful.

Clearly, each of these different types of contribution to knowledge will require different kinds of research questions. We invite you to consider the contribution that you are interested in making though your proposed research.

Shifting research contexts

Potential issues around funded research were signalled earlier. It was also noted that research never takes place in a vacuum, and this means that wider social, political and economic factors will, inevitably, impact on the research questions that can be asked and the findings that will be 'heard'. As John Evans (2009: 107) has pointed out:

> That we story our lives into existence and, just as critically, have them storied into existence for us by powerful others more capable of making their views and values heard, perhaps goes without saying ...

In the context of universities, philosophers and educational sociologists have been arguing for some time that with the drive to increase the rate of knowledge production, commissioned research is likely to continue to grow such that 'Knowledge is and will be produced in order to be sold' (Lyotard, 1984: 4–5). Marginson (1997) identified the period from the 1980s as a time of fundamental change with respect to the research activities of universities. There was a shift from a situation in which there was reward for non-market, basic research and the production of knowledge for its own sake, to one of social, political and economic turmoil in which universities were encouraged to become entrepreneurial and research became a commodity that could be exchanged. Universities can now be regarded as corporate players in university–industry partnerships, operating within circuits of economy and power (Slaughter and Rhoades, 1990). This is evidenced by the UK, New Zealand and Australian research assessment processes where research impact is measured, and both research income and published output are key indicators of success.

You might question whether any of this is relevant to you as an inexperienced researcher. Well, the answer is it might be relevant, particularly if you develop an interest in a particular line of research and want to pursue it. Certainly, it is appropriate (and arguably necessary) to discuss the principles that underpin research that is undertaken at a specific moment in time, and also to have some awareness of the wider context in which you are working. It might also be helpful for you to remember that even at the highest levels, research is a complex, often messy and always value-laden activity. Cohen and Manion (1989) argue that research is distinguished by being a form of systematic and controlled empirical inquiry that is self-correcting in order to reduce error and withstand public scrutiny. At the same time, Sparkes (2002: 220) reminds us that the ways in which we construct, view and judge research are always shifting:

> There are no fixed standards, historical or contextual, on which to base our judgments. Therefore, just as with our enquiries we construct reality as we go along with these enquiries, we also construct our criteria for judging them as we go along.

The shift towards entrepreneurialism and accountability is a good example of a wider structural influence that can impact upon the kinds of research that are valued. Indeed, reinforcing a point made earlier, Grundy (1996: 4) argued that for some academics, there may be 'tension between the academic researcher's responsibility to mount a critique without fear or favour and the temptation not to "bite the hand that feeds us" '. This is a major concern for the future integrity of research.

Back to those questions

As should be clear by now, research is political: it reflects who you are and your interests and priorities and/or the practices that you wish to understand and, possibly, seek to change. Therefore, it is important to reflect on the source of your motivation to undertake research in a particular area and for a particular purpose. A good starting point is to ask the following questions:

- What do you hope to contribute through your research?
- What is your key interest, and why?

- What are the personal, local, national and international imperatives that may impact upon the questions you could – or should – ask (think of the obesity issue)?
- If applicable, which research questions are likely to be funded – and by whom?

Framing your research question

It should be apparent by now that while framing research questions is a vital early step in any research process (Lewis and Munn, 2004), researchable questions are not always easy to articulate. The quote by Haack (2008) that opens this chapter is blunt – and deliberately so. Novice researchers often come to research to find out 'that' something 'is' or 'is not' the case. In other words, they don't have questions; they have answers – and strong beliefs – for which they are seeking support. This is not a good way to start! At the same time, it is of course the case that we come to any research process with prior observations, ideas and experiences – and these are not to be denied. Instead, these ideas need to be interrogated such that genuine questions can be identified to which the answers would be of interest and value. Cheek (2000: 408) cites the work of Schutt (1996) on this point, arguing that 'A good research question will be *feasible* within the time and resources available, it will be socially important, and it will be scientifically relevant.' At a more specific level, it could also be argued that a 'good' research question should be clearly worded and have a single focus.

The identification of a 'good' question is only the beginning of a more complex set of questions about design and process. For example, in much biosciences research, a question will be defined further in the form of a set of hypotheses to be tested. Tenenbaum *et al.* (2009: 117) point out that 'A hypothesis is not an entity by itself, but rather an entity which reflects knowledge accumulation, an essential product of scientific inquiry.' On the other hand, the generation of hypotheses in the traditional sense is not a requirement in all types of research. As ever, the approach to be taken has to reflect the questions a researcher is asking.

Once a research question has been identified, it may need further refinement as potential research designs and methods are considered. For example, you could have a general area of interest in a decline in student participation in conventional sports such as volleyball and netball. The questions that you identify will provide a more specific focus for inquiry and will form the foundation of effective research design. It is also the research questions that delimit what you are able to seek to know after you have collected, analysed and synthesized your data. So, in a school setting, an apparently straightforward research question could lead to a range of potential methods and strategies, of which one, some or all may be appropriate depending on the research scale and context:

- *Research question*: Why are so few students signing up for the end-of-term volleyball competition?
- *Research design and process*: Depending on the research design, some of the following data collection possibilities could follow:

- checking school records of participation to establish whether there are clear participation trends and how they compare to the trends for other sports;
- seeking student 'voice' on the issue by surveying or interviewing students to ascertain why they do – or do not – participate in certain sport competitions and what factors are attractive or otherwise with respect to volleyball;
- gaining some insights from the volleyball teachers/coaches by interviewing them to establish their perspectives on practices and participation;
- ascertaining wider teacher/coach perspectives on the issue by interviewing them about the ways in which the curriculum supports the development of students' volleyball competence and about the perceived value of volleyball as an activity;
- finding out more about the structure of volleyball and its youth development opportunities by conducting a document/web analysis and interview or survey.

Clearly, the data from these research processes will be analysed in ways that are appropriate to the question asked: for example, statistical analysis of trends, coding or thematic analysis of interview transcripts, case reports providing holistic analysis of individual interviewees etc. It might be useful at this stage to consider the different ways in which your potential research question could be explored, and to check whether it is feasible, socially relevant and scientifically important.

Good questions – good design – good research

It is interesting to consider the destination of research, i.e., where the process is heading and, if successful, what it will look like when we get there. The following descriptors from the UK research assessment process are informative. Published outputs from research undertaken in universities are graded on three key criteria: 'originality, significance and rigour'. There is no expectation that an undergraduate research project would routinely meet these criteria. On the other hand, doctoral theses are judged on very similar criteria:

- *Originality* is a characteristic of research that is not merely a replication of other work or simply applies well-used methods to straightforward problems, but which engages with new or complex problems or debates and/or tackles existing problems in new ways. So, for example, a review of existing research can demonstrate originality if it analyses and/or synthesizes the field in new ways, providing new and salient conceptualizations. Originality can also lie in the development of innovative designs, methods and methodologies, analytical models or theories and concepts.
- *Significance* is the extent to which research outputs display the capacity to make a difference, either through intellectual influence within the academic sphere or through actual or potential use beyond the academic sphere, or both.

Significance can be judged in different ways according to whether the research is basic, strategic or applied.

- *Rigour* can be judged in many ways, and can helpfully be associated with methodological and theoretical robustness and the use of a systematic approach. It includes traditional qualities such as reliability and validity, and also qualities such as integrity, consistency of argument and consideration of ethical issues. It certainly entails demonstrating a sound background of scholarship, in the sense of familiarity and engagement with relevant literature, both substantive and methodological.

In terms of the publication of research, an established specialist journal in our field, the *Journal of Teaching in Physical Education*, published in the United States, asks reviewers of research-based articles to comment on:

- *Relevance/significance of the study* – including questions such as whether the theoretical framework is logically explained. Is the rationale for the study clear? Does the literature review provide the most relevant and current scholarship on the issue? What significant, unique or valuable knowledge will readers learn from the study?
- *Methodology and presentation of results* – including foci on whether the research questions are specific enough so that the theoretical framework/construct logically leads to the selection of appropriate variables/phenomena for the study. Is the research design explicitly explained? Are participants clearly specified? Has their consent been gained? Are there sufficient data sources to address the research question(s)?
- *Discussion and interpretation* – including questioning whether the findings make a unique contribution to the body of knowledge. Are interpretations of the results based on the data and related to the literature? To what extent have the results answered the research questions? Are practical implications of the findings presented when appropriate?
- *Clarity of information presentation and writing* – which prompts assessors to comment upon, for example, whether the writing allows a clear, accurate and concise presentation of information. Is the general arrangement of the sections logical? Is the tone of reporting academically appropriate? Is the reference list accurate?

These two sets of criteria are helpful in reminding us that phases of the research process, from identifying researchable questions and appropriate designs, through to undertaking rigorous data collection and analysis, and providing well-written reports, are all integral to the production of high-quality research. This point applies no matter what the scale of the project being undertaken.

At the beginning of the chapter, we cited a short quote about research questions from Brustad, a highly experienced researcher. We will close this section by providing a longer extract from the passage from which his comment was drawn:

The most useful revelation that I gained from three years of work as the editor of the *Journal of Sport and Exercise Psychology* pertained to how the so-called 'gatekeepers' of knowledge (reviewers, associate editors and editors) arrived at judgements about 'good' and 'not-so-good' research during the manuscript review process. I was surprised to see how frequently studies with 'airtight' methodologies were placed in the 'not-so-good' research category as a consequence of what the reviewers regarded as an uninspired, uninteresting, or uninsightful research question. It seems to me that, for many researchers, concern for methodology serves as a psychological 'safety net' that provides a false sense of security that can lead to dull research questions.

(Brustad, 2009: 114)

Organization of this book

Some of the (English-speaking) world's best-known authors in the field of physical education and sport agreed to lead a chapter in their area of expertise, supported by one or more emerging scholars. This pairing approach, as outlined earlier, adds richness to the chapters because the emerging scholars (students and early career researchers) offer engaging and sometimes intimate insights into their research experiences. As they share their deliberations, case studies, problems – and solutions! – readers will get a taste of what may be in store for their own research journey. The authors are drawn from the UK, Europe, North America, Australia and New Zealand, giving the text a breadth of international perspectives alongside the breadth of author experience.

The book has five parts and we suggest that during your reading of this chapter, you attempt to draft some potential 'researchable' research questions. You can then test these questions against the methods and approaches covered in each section/chapter.

Part I: Planning the research process

Following this first chapter on an introduction to the context of research and asking research questions, the next three chapters provide you with signposts that give directions for what to think about as you start the research process, how the process may feel, and where you should be aiming in the production of 'good' research.

Part II: Methodology: the thinking behind the methods

This part comprises six chapters that focus on identifying some of the often unspoken assumptions that lie behind research. Engaging in early critical thinking about theoretical perspectives, ethical issues, qualitative and/or quantitative approaches, and the place of participants' voices can assist with the coherence of your project. Together, Parts I and II emphasize that doing research is a highly personal experience, and who you are is integral to the questions you ask and the methods you choose.

Part III: Selecting the most appropriate method(s)

This is the longest part of the book. Twelve chapters are dedicated to advice on undertaking reviews of literature and the most common data collection methods in our field. The methods cover both quantitative and qualitative techniques and, importantly, allude to the strengths, weaknesses, challenges and potential contributions of these methods.

Part IV: Data analysis – consider it early!

The chapters in this part provide an overview and insights into key considerations in qualitative and quantitative data analysis strategies. Data analysis is, of course, a vital step in the research process and the point made in these chapters is that it should be considered early, i.e., at the research design stage.

Part V: Communicating your research

The two chapters in this part link back to the key messages from Chapters 1 and 2. The research process is not complete until you have fulfilled the professional responsibility to share your findings, using whatever media are appropriate. The chapters offer advice on effective writing and managing the writing process, so that you too may feel the pleasure and reward of bringing a project to completion.

References

Armour, K. M. (2010) 'The physical education profession and its professional responsibility … or … why "12 weeks' paid holiday" will never be enough', *Physical Education and Sport Pedagogy*, 15, 1: 1–14.

Brustad, R. J. (2009) 'Validity in context – qualitative research issues in sport and exercise studies: a response to John Smith', *Qualitative Research in Sport and Exercise*, 1, 2: 112–15.

Burton, D. and Bartlett, S. (2009) *Key Issues for Education Researchers*, London: Sage.

Cheek, J. (2000) 'An untold story? Doing funded qualitative research', in N. K. Denzin and Y. S. Lincoln (eds) *The Sage Handbook of Qualitative Research*, 2nd edn (401–20), London, Sage.

Cohen, L. and Manion, L. (1989) *Research Methods in Education*, Beckenham: Routledge.

Evans, J. (2009) 'In praise of body knowledge and stories we need to tell: a response to John Smith', *Qualitative Research in Sport and Exercise*, 1, 2: 107–11.

Gall, M., Gall, J., & Borg, W. (2007) *Educational research: an introduction*, Boston: Pearson/Allyn & Bacon.

Grundy, S. (1996) 'Building professional research partnerships: Possibilities and perplexities', *The Australian Educational Researcher*, 23, 1: 1–16.

Haack, S. (2008) *Putting Philosophy to Work*, New York: Prometheus Books.

Kincheloe, J. L. and Maclaren, P. (2005) 'Rethinking critical theory and qualitative research', in N. K. Denzin and Y. S. Lincoln (eds) *The Sage Handbook of Qualitative Research*, 3rd edn (303–42), London: Sage.

Lewis, I. and Munn, P. (2004) *So You Want To Do Research! A Guide For Beginners on How to Formulate Research Questions*, Glasgow: The SCRE Centre, University of Glasgow.

Lyotard, J-F. (1984) *The Post-modern Condition: A Report on Knowledge*, trans. G. Bennington and B. Massumi, Minneapolis, MN: University of Minneapolis Press.

Macdonald, D. (2009) 'Evidence-based practice in physical education: Ample evidence, patchy practice', in L. Housner, M. Metzler, P. Schempp and T. Templin (eds) *Historic Traditions and Future Directions of Research on Teaching and Teacher Education in Physical Education* (199–205), Morgantown, WV: West Virginia University.

Marginson, S. (1997) *Markets in Education*, Sydney: Allen and Unwin.

Nieuwenhuys, O. (2004) 'Participatory action research in the majority world', in S. Fraser, V. Lewis, S. Ding, M. Kellett and S. Robinson (eds) *Doing Research with Children and Young People*, London: Sage, 206–221.

O'Sullivan, M. (2007) 'Research quality in physical education and sport pedagogy', *Sport Education and Society*, 12, 3: 245–60.

Rossi, P. H., Lipsey, M. W. and Freeman, H. E. (2004). *Evaluation. A Systematic Approach*, 7th edn, London: Sage.

Schutt, R. (1996) *Investigating the Social World: The Process and Practice of Research*, Thousand Oaks, CA: Pine Forge.

Slaughter, S. and Rhoades, G. (1990) 'Renorming the social relations of academic science: technology transfer', *Educational Policy*, 4(4), 341-361.

Sparkes, A. C. (2002) *Telling Tales in Sport and Physical Activity: A Qualitative Journey*, Champaign, IL: Human Kinetics.

Spencer Foundation Task Force Report (2009) *The Preparation of Aspiring Educational Researchers in the Empirical Qualitative and Quantitative Traditions of Social Science: Methodological Rigour, Social and Theoretical Relevance, and More*, Chicago, IL: Spencer Foundation.

Tenenbaum, G., Razon, S., Thompson, B., Filho, E. and Basevitch, I. (2009) 'The judgement of research quality: a response to John Smith', *Qualitative Research in Sport and Exercise*, 1, 2: 116–24.

Weiss, C. H. (1998) 'Have we learned anything new about the use of evaluation?' *American Journal of Evaluation*, 19(1): 21–33.

Further reading

Thomas, J., Nelson, J. and Silverman, S. (2011) *Research Methods in Physical Activity*, 6th edn, Champaign, IL: Human Kinetics.

2 Research principles and practices

Paving the research journey

Doune Macdonald and Louise McCuaig

> For me, research is for people who have ever asked why something is or isn't, and as a result are motivated to understand and investigate phenomena in depth. The movement of ideas from genesis to submission may take years; along the way, publishing and presenting your work at conferences and seminars allow you both to self-check and to receive feedback from others to ensure that you are on track. To see your project start to take its place in the world of research and to know that you have contributed to the development of new knowledge – well, nothing tops that!
>
> (Joseph Occhino, research student in sports coaching, 2011)

> [At] least you're doing something for the community to try and help us … and it's good to go share with other people.
>
> (Participant in Alison Nelson's work with young indigenous Australians, 2009)

Introduction

Conducting research can be a complex, challenging, sometimes frustrating, and hopefully rewarding experience, as we see in the quotes above. Doing research in physical education and youth sport, as with any social process, is overlaid by a research context that is frequently political, of public interest, and potentially attracts a range of opinion. Much of this complexity can be attributed to physical education and sport sitting at the intersection of differing expectations and priorities related to physical activity, physical fitness, sporting success, health, body weight and citizenship, to name a few. As indicated in this book, this also generates research that draws on a range of theories and methods and must speak to a range of audiences. Whatever question you choose to explore, the quotes above indicate the excitement that may be felt as your research work contributes to knowledge or the appreciation expressed by research participants who perceive that you are trying to make a difference. Similar contributions are what may define your research journey.

This chapter discusses five guiding principles to assist you in navigating your research activities, whether that research be related to teaching, coaching, children, adults, the story of one, or the patterns of thousands. These principles have been distilled from our own experiences as researchers and enriched by conversations with our colleagues at the University of Queensland.

So, who are we?

About us

Doune Macdonald: One of the great things about a career in education, whether in schools or universities, is that you see your students grow into independent and successful professionals in their own right. Students interested in undertaking research degrees have arrived to work with our group from a variety of backgrounds: experienced teachers and coaches looking to extend their knowledge; early career teachers and health professionals seeking a career change; international students looking for adventure! I had the pleasure of teaching Louise McCuaig, co-author of this chapter, in her undergraduate programme, where her outstanding teaching and organizational skills and musical, sporting and dance talents shone in her year group.

Louise McCuaig: At the conclusion of my undergraduate degree I embarked on a wonderful 14-year teaching career in Queensland schools, a career that was characterized by an increasing interest in health education and the capacity of health and physical education (HPE) teachers to transform their practice into a more egalitarian and caring one, reflective of social justice agendas underpinning contemporary HPE. Subsequently, I returned to my alma mater and undertook a doctoral study exploring the role of caring teachers, teacher education and HPE in the social and moral education of young people. This work has inspired my current projects concerning health literacy in schools and across the lifespan, health education teacher education and student transitions.

Each of our principles will be explained and then explicated in frank conversations between Louise and her colleagues, both research higher-degree students and early career researchers, undertaking a breadth of research in the field. Although Louise's conversations have been with students doing research higher degrees, we anticipate that their perspectives are transferable to your research context. While some of the principles will be elaborated in more detail in later chapters, we hope that here they provide a compass that can help guide your research activities and experiences in positive ways.

Principle 1: Follow your interests and strengths

It may be that your research project will take many months, if not years, and for this reason alone you should have a strong personal interest in the project. As suggested in Chapter 1, it may be that the topic is a prelude to a line of research that may take your career in a particular direction. Sometimes people have a broad range of research interests or simply cannot decide on a research question. A survey of coaches working with junior elite athletes to ascertain their perspectives on gender may be of equal interest to you as a project interviewing Muslim girls about their attitudes to physical education (PE) and sport. How might you decide? Some things to consider when refining your research topic and questions are:

- *Do you want to work with people in your data collection or do you prefer to work with literature, policies, artefacts etc.?* Worthwhile projects can be undertaken without interacting with people. For example, you might carry out a systematic review of literature (see Chapter 11) or a policy analysis (see Chapter 22).
- *If you'd like to work with participants, would you prefer them to be teachers, coaches, administrators, young people, children, parents or community organizations?* Participants are usually found in particular organizations, such as children and young people in schools. Some researchers are keen to work with children and schools while others do not feel this affinity.
- *What methods will you be most comfortable with, e.g. physiological measures, psychometric tests, surveys, interviews, field notes, photography?* While different academic traditions on which you are drawing, such as sports psychology, history or pedagogy, tend to have a 'usual' set of methods, you should not feel limited to these. As will be described in Chapter 9, multi-methods can often be most fruitful. That said, you may have an aptitude or a background in using particular methods that can assist you in this decision.

As an HPE teacher of some 15 years, Louise had been challenged by the diversity of health issues young people faced and the capacity of schools, teachers and programmes of health, sport and physical education to respond authentically and appropriately to these needs. Her experiences and passion for young people's health and well-being provided a sustained motivation that facilitated her navigation of the challenging experience of a research journey. As Crotty (1998: 13) points out, 'we typically start with a real-life issue that needs to be addressed' and many of these issues stem from the intrigue, successes and frustrations we experience in working as practitioners with young people, parents and colleagues. Not surprisingly, Louise employed a qualitative approach to her doctoral research so that she could explore the stories of teachers who were charged with creating the healthy citizens of tomorrow. However, others such as Louise's colleague, Bonnie Pang, undertake a research journey as a result of interests and opportunities emerging out of their undergraduate experiences. Bonnie participated in her first research project as an undergraduate student contributing to a collaborative project between Chinese University Hong Kong (CUHK) and the University of Queensland (UQ) entitled 'Comparative study of children's sport participation and physical activity pattern in Australia and Hong Kong'. Having enjoyed the research experience, Bonnie followed with a research master's degree which highlighted the importance of taking into account cultural and gender factors in relation to young Chinese people's participation in physical activity. Bonnie's supervisor then suggested that her dual Australian–Hong Kong citizenship and experiences provided the perfect foundations for a doctoral study on a similar topic within an Australian context (and in which she is currently engaged). Unlike Louise, who 'fell' into a research project as a result of her daily experiences as a practitioner in the profession, Bonnie has had a more strategic, research-focused trajectory. Nonetheless, she is just as passionate about her hopes to share her research findings with students, parents and teachers, so that these stakeholders will have a greater appreciation for and commitment to diversity in PE, sport and physical culture.

Both Bonnie and Louise agree that undertaking a research project has been facilitated by the opportunity to build on their theoretical and methodological interests and strengths. For example, Bonnie's field notes reveal her capacity to connect with her participants: 'Because I look young, I'm female and I'm Chinese, they might feel less distant with me. And when I said I know how to speak Cantonese, Mandarin and English, several of their eyes sparkled! I guess this is a strength as they find me more alike to than different from them.' Bonnie's cultural knowledge of her participants' lives and parental expectations also facilitated her ability to recruit participants for her study. Given this knowledge, Bonnie devised a strategy to:

- inform parents of the explicit relationships between this research and their child's knowledge of healthy citizenship;
- explain how her findings related to their child's academic studies;
- highlight her academic qualifications as a Chinese researcher.

Here, Bonnie demonstrates the importance of reflection as a means of identifying personal strengths and understandings, according to the specific cultural contexts, in order to conduct research appropriately and build the necessary rapport.

Principle 2: Manage the research process carefully

Time can slip away very quickly in any research process. There is a wealth of literature in which to get buried, participants who are difficult to recruit, misplaced data, and the need to relocate lost references. Right from the start of your project it is essential that you are clear about your milestones, processes and expected outcomes. Mapping out a realistic timeline is important for keeping you on track and balancing your reading, data collection and analysis, and writing. While revising timelines is appropriate as events unfold, many projects have deadlines, such as those defined by scholarships, funding bodies or semester deadlines. Therefore, it is helpful to become practised at working within time frames.

During the research process you will gather substantial materials that need to be digested, stored and periodically retrieved. This requires effective management skills, including:

- *Begin with accurate and systematic referencing.* Using a computer program such as Endnote to catalogue journal articles, book chapters, reference notes etc. can assist in keeping accurate and retrievable records. Take great care when noting/ entering details of your references. It can be very frustrating trying to find the page numbers for a passage you want to quote two years down the track!
- *Manage notes and data files efficiently; don't try to rely on memory.* Researchers have their own approaches to managing information but it is worth starting with carefully labelled files or artefacts stored in such a way that you can readily find them. Regular backing up of data, if you are working on a computer, is essential. Time spent in setting up and complying with a system that works for you will not be time wasted.

- *Write memos.* Throughout the research process, you may have fleeting insights into questions or observations – so-called 'ah-ha' moments. Have an easy way of noting these ideas as well as those incidental thoughts or observations you have in relation to literature or data.
- *Write regularly.* It can be tempting to leave writing until the end: the end of reading, the end of the data collection process, the end of the week … Writing is never premature because organizing your thoughts through writing can help you to focus, clarify and share your progress, allowing for input and refinement.
- *Leave ample time for polishing your research report.* The end of the research process might be marked by a report, a thesis or a manuscript for publication, and each requires time to complete it to a high standard.

As Louise discovered, the most important principle guiding the research process is the old adage that prevention is better than cure. Adopting a proactive approach to the management of your research activities not only ensures you are organized, it also provides you with the necessary breathing space when things don't go to plan. As many health, sport and physical education researchers work with children, schoolteachers or coaches, organizing interview schedules as early as possible can provide the necessary latitude for the inevitable cancellations, miscommunications and opportunities to re-interview. Anthony Leow's experiences during his own doctoral research serve to highlight the need for a proactive approach. Anthony's project explored the uptake of health promotion policies by schools and their teachers, and it was the unexpected changes to interview schedules that were particularly challenging. For example, participants regularly had less time to be interviewed than Anthony had planned for, were unwilling to have interviews digitally recorded, or were absent from their workplace when Anthony arrived after a long-distance drive to interview them.

Anthony devised a three-step contact process when liaising with interviewees. First, at the onset of interview confirmations, he sent an email to thank the interviewee for agreeing to the interview. One week before the interview, he sent a reminder email and asked the interviewee whether it was still OK to go ahead with the interview. Two days before the interview, a courtesy call was made to the interviewee to confirm the timing and place for the interview. In instances when an interviewee was unreachable, a note was left for them to call Anthony back. So far, this method and attention to organization detail have proved effective in managing the interviewees.

Additionally, Louise and Anthony both found that the interview experience itself demands focus and organization. Anthony classified his questions on the interview schedule according to their importance – e.g. 'must know', 'good to know' and 'peripheral information' – and asked the critical questions first in the event that the interviewee was called away before the end of the scheduled interview time. In short, Anthony believes that flexibility is an essential attribute of researchers, who must expect the unexpected and be thoroughly prepared in the event that alternative options are required. This proactive approach extends to the most mundane of tasks, such as those outlined by Doune above, because a lost reference, misplaced interview data or unheeded deadline can compromise the quality and efficiency of your work.

Principle 3: Work ethically

> In the widest sense, the subject matter of ethics is the justification of human actions, especially as those actions affect others.
>
> (Schwandt, 2001: 73)

Given the social nature of the research enterprise and, in particular, the likelihood of working with children and young people, it is important to work with your research colleagues and participants in the research process in ethical ways. There are spectacular research horror stories, ranging from the fabrication of data through to experimentation being conducted on humans in the name of science. To enshrine ethical behaviours in research practice, organizations worldwide have created codes of ethics for research (e.g. Australian Association for Research in Education Code of Ethics, 2005). The four principles of the AARE Code are:

1 The consequences of a piece of research, including the effects on the participants and the social consequences of its publication and application, must enhance the general welfare.
2 Researchers should be aware of the variety of human goods and the variety of views on the good life, and the complex relation of education with these. They should recognize that educational research is an ethical matter, and that its purpose should be the development of human good.
3 No risk of significant harm to an individual is permissible unless either that harm is remedied or the person is of age and has given informed consent to the risk. Public benefit, however great, is insufficient justification.
4 Respect for the dignity and worth of persons and the welfare of students, research participants and the public generally shall take precedence over the self-interest of researchers, or the interests of employers, clients, colleagues or groups.

While working ethically will be addressed in more detail in Chapter 6, with a focus on working with research participants, here we touch on some broad issues.

- *Working ethically in data collection.* Before you start your data collection, it is likely that you will have to submit an application for ethical clearance. These pro formas are intended to prompt researchers into briefing participants appropriately and managing data collection and storage in such a way that participants come to no harm. However, these applications are usually made early in the research process and your research may need to be cleared again if it changes too much from its original design. Moreover, as the research journey unfolds, the researcher is likely to encounter ethical dilemmas. For example, what do you do if a young person reveals in an interview that they are involved in substance abuse? It is worthwhile taking the time to read a code of ethics so that you have guidance for your research journey.
- *Working ethically in data representation.* One key driver of research is to make an original contribution to knowledge, hence the data and their representation

need to be original (i.e., not plagiarized) and authentic (i.e., not falsified or embellished). Further, and perhaps more complex than this, is the expectation that data will be represented faithfully, and this is not as easy as it sounds. Are the statistics selected to treat the data the most appropriate or are they those that support the hypothesis? Are the excerpts taken from interviews carefully selected in line with what the participants said or have they been chosen to support your prior assumptions? How has your biography shaped your reading of the data?

- *Working ethically with colleagues.* Most universities make it explicit that a research student 'owns' their research work. On the face of it, this sounds like a straightforward statement. Things become more complex, however, when the student researcher joins a research team or the student is working on a project commissioned by an outside agency that is paying for the work to be undertaken. Who then owns the ideas? It may be important to talk these issues through with your advisor and/or your research office so that you are clear about both your rights and your responsibilities. Authorship of publications arising from your research can also become problematic. Again, check ethical guidelines. The AARE guidelines, similar to most, suggest that 'All those and only those who have made substantial creative contributions to a product are entitled to be listed as authors of that product.'

Some of the most challenging aspects of working ethically emerge when researchers engage in work with indigenous, marginalized or at-risk populations. Our colleague Alison Nelson conducted her research on the place and meaning of physical activity and health in the lives of urban Indigenous young people. As a non-Indigenous female researcher, Alison encountered a range of issues, including the challenge of staying connected to the Aboriginal and Torres Strait Islander community affected by her research. Alison was regularly in touch with two or three key people who had links to the community and they enabled her to touch base regularly, ask questions and seek advice without the need for formal meetings. In particular, Alison adopted a multi-pronged approach with at least one person who was involved in the main research site who could help with day-to-day operationally related questions and an Aboriginal academic who could help with the more theoretical issues. As Alison was also employed part-time within her research context, her rich engagement with this community increased her willingness to trust her own reading of situations, particularly in relation to participants' readiness to speak with her. Here a positivist may raise questions about 'bias' and 'validity' of the data analysis process given Alison's investment in data collection and analysis (see, for example, Chapter 8).

A significant challenge for Alison in her research context was that of trying to ensure that the theory and methodology used in her study enabled the participants' voices to ring true, as opposed to constraining them to fit within specific theoretical paradigms. Anti-racist researchers would argue that to collect data and for the researcher to theorize without involvement from the participants are simply another form of colonization (Dei, 2005), and so it was important for Alison to be wary of theorizing the data in abstract ways devoid of their context (Du Gay, Evans and Redman, 2000). This sentiment also underpinned her efforts in both representing research to participants and the wider community and meeting academic requirements for reporting. Research is reproduced and interpreted by many different audiences and adopting anti-racist research approaches can encourage researchers to seek collaboration with participants in the ways in which they are represented and also to respect the rights of participants to withhold information (Dei, 2005).

In the process of her research, Alison came to the conclusion that while written text was the most pragmatic form of representation for academic requirements, it was not the most suitable for the participants. In order to increase young people's access to the ways in which their stories were being reproduced, a digital story comprising participants' comments, artwork and photographs was provided for each participant so that they could approve or withdraw their contributions. Digital stories also afforded the participants a tangible outcome from their involvement in the research. In their final interview, the young people were asked how they felt about Alison (as a white woman) representing them in research papers. Responses varied from 'I don't really care' to 'I reckon that will be all right' to the opening quote in this chapter that indicated Alison's research was welcomed by her participants, mitigating some of her ethical concerns.

Tina Skinner's ethical dilemmas were of a different nature in her experimental work to investigate the effect of caffeine dose and timing on exercise performance. As she was asking athletes to ingest 6–9 mg kg^{-1} caffeine (equivalent to the caffeine content in approximately 4–6 cups of espresso coffee) and take up to nine venipuncture blood draws within each testing session, she notes how important it was for her to fully explain the procedures and potential risks of participation to her 'subjects', in addition to highlighting the participants' opportunity to withdraw from the study at any time, without question or prejudice. She was asking athletes to be tested for 5 hours, six times, across a period of 4–6 weeks. Given this demanding testing protocol, Tina was conscious of scheduling sessions to allow minimal disruption to the athletes' work, training and lifestyle commitments—even if this did mean some sessions started at 3 am! Tina was also aware she was asking the athletes to risk infection associated with blood sampling and potential adverse effects of high caffeine doses such as gastrointestinal distress. She therefore understood the importance of adherence to all health and safety guidelines, including documentation and follow-up with all participants regarding potential adverse effects related to her research. Even though appropriate precautions and risk assessments were completed, and despite having had several uneventful blood draws, one of her participants lost consciousness during a blood draw. Tina immediately contacted the first aid officer to attend to the athlete and even though he was cleared by medical services, Tina watchfully waited until the next of kin arrived. Following required protocols, she then completed the injury and incident report forms and followed up with the athlete the next day.

Principle 4: Build a support network

Research can be a lonely journey. While you may have peers who are also taking a similar journey and advisors/supervisors who may be working alongside you, it is important to build some networks of people who can support you in various ways. Research undertaken on learning communities suggests that people learn best when they are inducted into a particular culture that is welcoming and supports their individual growth (Wenger, 1998). You may need to be proactive in building a support network by using some of the following strategies:

- *Schedule regular communication with your advisors/supervisors.* Advisors for your project or thesis are often very busy and they may need you to manage their involvement. That said, they also have an ethical responsibility to induct beginning researchers into the field. It may be wise to develop a regular pattern of communication and to identify clear goals and targets for meetings. Sending out an agenda prior to a meeting can help you to optimize the meeting time and will ensure your advisors are prepared for the discussions.
- *Talk with other students and build semi-formal groups.* Talking through your ideas with trusted peers is invaluable. Articulating the complex ideas or conundrums in your research often results in the refinement of ideas or even in finding solutions. Both the research journey and the outcomes are likely to be more rewarding if you have someone who can listen to your incidental musings and problems. If there is no tradition for periodic meetings with colleagues to discuss research issues, start a group. Such groups can be helpful for discussing key publications in the field (known as a 'journal club'), understanding a theorist, practising presentations or offering critical perspectives on data analysis and interpretations. These semi-formal gatherings can also be a good place to learn to listen carefully and frame insightful questions.
- *Engage widely within and beyond your field.* Undertaking research is a time of intense learning and you assemble, digest and apply ideas from a range of sources, some of which are unexpected. Take time to learn from a range of sources across the university, the media and/or your professional community. It may be that you devote some time to attending public lectures, building a Facebook discussion or emailing someone (anywhere in the world) who is undertaking similar research. Reaching out usually enriches your knowledge and can generate unexpected support.

Here, one of the most useful strategies to employ is the willingness to pursue a range of mentors and colleagues who may offer varying degrees of input, intimacy and guidance for you and your research. It is important to emphasize the word 'pursue' as the network won't come to you and will be reliant upon your initiative, energy and needs. Some mentors, such as master's or doctoral advisors, will make a very intimate and sustained contribution to your work, while others, such as international leaders in your particular research space, may merely provide you with one golden lead, invitation to a pertinent conference or words of encouragement. Erin Flanagan was an undergraduate student of Louise's who recently returned to conduct her own study on the micro-politics of HPE staff rooms. She found it difficult to create a balance between the independence and freedom of managing her teaching, administrative and research work and her need for structure, guidance and constructive criticism. Erin resolved these tensions by securing additional support from another doctoral advisor who had expertise in the specific methodological and theoretical approaches she was adopting. As aspiring academics, Louise and Erin both found it useful to have an experienced colleague who became a general mentor. This relationship does not have the burden of supervision responsibilities and so presents different opportunities for career guidance, empathy and insight from previous experiences.

In the initial stages of her research journey, Erin found that much of what was required of her as a doctoral student was established through informal conversations with others, particularly fellow doctoral students. Informal conversations often enabled access to information and support in a non-intrusive or burdening fashion. These informal relationships can serve to increase your sense of connectedness and decrease your sense of isolation, through opportunities to share, empathize and draw insight from others' research experiences. Having been inspired by their work, Louise expanded her network of support through emailing local and international scholars to garner their insights, clarify personal interpretations and/or seek guidance. Every academic she has contacted in relation to her research has responded with a generosity that was both motivational and instructive.

Emma Beckman began building a support network through undertaking an Erasmus Mundus Master's programme in Europe after her undergraduate degree. This international experience fed her interest in undertaking research with paralympic athletes that would maximize participation for all athletes regardless of disability. It also gave her an international network upon which she drew for her subsequent PhD. She learnt early the importance of gaining the support and respect of those working in the field internationally and having the confidence to approach lecturers who worked in her area of interest and to ask questions of them. For example, a simple conversation about biomechanics led to a research trip to the Paralympic Winter Games in Torino, where she was able to assist in data collection with sledge hockey athletes. Back in Australia while completing her PhD, she built on the support network by making links with those researching domestically in her area through attending local and interstate conferences and obtaining accreditation with all of the relevant organizations in her field. Working with community organizations as a volunteer also helped establish links that became vital in her recruitment of research participants.

Principle 5: Disseminate discerningly

> When the research's over, don't turn out the lights.
>
> (Willinsky, 2006: 439)

The research process is not complete until you have shared your findings and their implications with others. This process of dissemination is an important aspect of being recognized as a scholar and, it could be argued, is an ethical outcome of the research process. As noted in Chapter 1, the definition of research in the UK within the forthcoming national research assessment exercise includes 'sharing findings' as an integral part of the concept.

Those undertaking research associated with university degrees should be mindful of the increased expectations and accountability that may be associated with their research project and outcomes. As noted and illustrated in Chapter 1, several countries have ranked research journals according to perceived quality, and individuals and groups of researchers have their work appraised in terms of the quality and quantity of publications (e.g. book chapters, journal articles), grants and research student activity. This surveillance and accountability can add pressure to your experience and those with whom you are working through 'the system's' expectations for timeliness, producing publications for high-ranking journals, generating funds from outside the university and tightly managing budgets. While this context is considered pernicious by some, a wise researcher would be cognisant of the 'rules of the game' so that they can make informed choices about their work.

Despite the pressures mentioned above, different projects have messages that should be heard by different audiences (see Chapter 25). Often one project has multiple audiences for its research findings and implications. For example, teachers and coaches may be interested in particular aspects of your project that are different from those messages for principals and different again from messages for education/ sport systems or other researchers. Further, different audiences access information in different ways and in different places. Typically, dissemination may occur through the following conventional channels alongside other avenues such as blogs that, to date, do not carry the same academic weight as other output channels:

- *Conferences.* These often attract researchers working in universities, sports organizations and leaders in schools or school systems. Abstracts (summaries of the proposed presentation) are called for several months prior to the conference, are reviewed and then presenters are notified of acceptance or otherwise. Communication of research at a conference may be via an oral presentation as a stand-alone paper, as part of a cluster of papers often called a symposium or as a poster display.
- *Workshops and seminars.* You may have messages suited to more interactive or practice-oriented audiences such as teachers, coaches or parents who may be interested in how they can do things differently. Teachers may attend these seminars as part of their required professional development.
- *Research journals and books.* These avenues are the most challenging forms of dissemination, as most published work passes through a rigorous peer review process and requires several months of communication and refinement. Journals (and book publishers) are ranked using complex esteem measures, and early career researchers need to be informed as to what these are and whether they are relevant to their proposed publication plan.
- *Professional publications.* Teaching and coaching bodies, schooling systems, sports organizations and the like often have print or web-based publications that present short and practical research reports written in a genre that is engaging for their readerships.

It is important to strike an appropriate balance between dissemination through conferences, research and professional publications. For presentations, you need to keep your ideas fresh but, more importantly, for publications, you must avoid repeating or plagiarizing your own work because it is likely that the publishers own the copyright for what you have written. For those undertaking a longer study such as an MPhil or PhD, it is important to consider what pattern of dissemination will enhance your research experience and curriculum vitae.

If you are planning a career in academia, publishing in academic journals is a non-negotiable expectation. For many universities, this one dimension of dissemination can be the most significant criterion against which the quality and effectiveness of your research are judged. One of our most passionate students in the field of coaching, Joseph Occhino, argues that as a 'researcher in training' it is imperative that you actively pursue opportunities to practise journal writing style under the guidance of your advisor(s). Joseph argues that this is a very good way to get your research into the wider academic community (if it is of the right level and quality) and begin to build a name and reputation for yourself as an expert within the field. However, Louise and Joseph both warn that publishing in academic journals is not for the faint-hearted. Multiple rejections, confusing feedback, conflicting journal guidelines and the length of 'in press' time all serve to test the most experienced and reputed researchers. Additionally, the specific groups for whom the research has been produced and the stakeholders that you may wish to 'speak to' may not have ready access to academic journals. As Joseph recommends, researchers can use other avenues of publishing, such as magazines, blogs, newspapers and professional newsletters to obtain a quicker and more effective communication of findings and implications to those in the field. Nonetheless, it remains important to consider any potential copyright breaches. It is also important not to release raw research findings into a community that may act upon them. This is where the peer review process, although far from perfect, can act to protect the interests of the public and potential users from poor-quality research, which, at worst, could do harm if recommendations from it were to be implemented.

For both Joseph and Louise, conferences are one of the most enjoyable aspects of working in research – and the opportunity to meet and visit with colleagues across the globe is certainly a bonus! Nonetheless, conference attendance must result in tangible outcomes; conferences are expensive to attend in both time and money and, although enjoyable, they are also hard work and often very tiring. Joseph has been fortunate enough to attend conferences in Japan and Belgium, where he had the opportunity to connect with like-minded colleagues and share his interests, ideas and findings, and, as indicated in the opening quote of the chapter, derive direction and a sense of achievement.

Conclusion

This chapter has provided some principles and practices to consider as you go about your research journey, however long it may be. Running through the points made is the importance of asking questions of your research advisors/supervisors, colleagues, participants or even funding agencies, to keep your inquiry on track. Further, if you hit a road block, try to identify what it is as quickly as possible and seek assistance if required. It may be that you need support for simple things, such as interpreting a theorist or accessing software, through to recruiting participants or overcoming writer's block. Louise and her colleagues have illustrated their successful navigation of the research journey with reflections on managing themselves, their data and their relationships. Each of their stories highlights the individuality of their research experience, although each also suggests the careful planning that typifies most worthwhile journeys.

Key terms

Research management   Prior to starting a project, attention should be given to intended outcomes, timelines, resources required, budget, data management, and expectations for supervision and dissemination.

Ethical research   Researchers must be vigilant of the effects of research participation and dissemination on the welfare of participants and its contribution to public good.

Support network   Regular, formal and informal communication, either face-to-face or remotely, with peers, more experienced researchers, supervisors, content experts etc. can provide varying input, intimacy and guidance that may assist the quality of both the research experience and outcomes.

Research dissemination   Research processes and findings may be shared via publication in academic journals, conference presentations or posters, professional newsletters or various electronic media.

References

Australian Association for Research in Education (2005) *Code of Ethics* <http://www.aare.edu. au/live/> (accessed 16 December 2010).

Crotty, M. (1998) *The Foundations of Social Research: Meaning and Perspective in the Research Process*, St Leonards, NSW: Allen & Unwin.

Dei, G. J. S. (2005) 'Critical issues in anti-racist research methodologies: An introduction', in G. J. S. Dei and G. S. Johal (eds) *Critical Issues in Anti-racist Research Methodologies* (1–28), New York: Peter Lang Publishing.

Du Gay, P., Evans, J. and Redman, P. (2000) 'General introduction', in P. Du Gay, J. Evans and P. Redman (eds) *Identity: A Reader* (1–5), London: Sage in association with The Open University.

Schwandt, T. (2001) *Dictionary of Qualitative Inquiry*, London: Sage.

Wenger, E. (1998) *Communities of Practice: Learning, Meaning and Identity*, Cambridge: Cambridge University Press.

Willinsky, J. (2006) 'When the research's over, don't turn out the lights', in K. Tobin and J. Kincheloe (eds) *Doing Educational Research: A Handbook*, Rotterdam: Sense Publishers.

3 Positioning yourself as a researcher

Four dimensions for self-reflection

Juan-Miguel Fernández-Balboa and Nathan Brubaker

> In order to more fully understand this reality, we must take into account other dimensions of a broader reality.
>
> (John Archibald Wheeler (1911–2008), North American physicist)[1]

Introduction

In this chapter we take a different approach from many others in this book. As a student and, perhaps, future researcher in physical education (PE) and sport, it is important for you to understand that research, far from being a matter of meticulously applying certain methods to finding out the solution(s) to a particular problem, entails many factors that affect not only the processes, purposes and outcomes of research studies but also the researcher him/herself. The researcher's 'position' is one of these factors.

The term 'position' has many interpretations. It can be understood as (a) one's point of view or ideological perspective (e.g. technocratic, critical, neo-liberal, democratic); (b) one's location in the power hierarchy (wherein one can have more or less influence on decision making); or (c) a concrete place in the ongoing developmental process that goes from beginner to master and beyond. There is yet another way of looking at this concept: that of being in different dimensions – i.e., hypothetical self-contained separate realities coexisting with one's own.[2]

Have you ever looked at a picture in which there is a vertical white figure in the middle that, at first sight, resembles a vase or jar, but when you look again you see that this is just the space between two silhouetted profiles facing one another (see Figure 3.1)?

This is the crux of our question. Both the vase and the faces had been there all the time; yet on looking at the figure for the first time, you may have seen just one of these elements (people seldom see both simultaneously). It could be argued that initially you could see this picture only partially because the rest is in a different 'dimension'; only after you penetrated that other dimension did what was 'missing' appear.

Something similar could be said regarding your position as a researcher. No matter where you are in your development as a researcher (be it as beginner or expert), there are different dimensions into which you can enter depending on your level of consciousness at a particular moment. In this chapter, we will theorize about four such dimensions.

Figure 3.1 Perceptual coexisting dimensions (Source: extracted 11 Feb 2011, from http://2. bp.blogspot.com/_mXL5SHlStcE/S0tnt9ZlT-I/AAAAAAAAAK0/vY6cQnJdGFs/s320/ image.png).

Before we begin, however, we wish to clarify two things. First, that far from considering ourselves experts in this matter, we approach this writing as explorers going into new (at least to us) territory. Second, that although this book addresses itself mainly to those researching in physical education and sport, or those intending to do so in the future, you will notice that, beyond this point, we present our ideas generically.

We invite you to join us in this journey of (self-)discovery and engage in your own (self-)inquiry using your memory, knowledge and intuition to establish the links between the ideas we present here and your own position as a researcher. We trust that, in doing so, you will expand your possibilities for understanding and approaching research in purposeful and satisfying ways.

About us

Juan-Miguel Fernández-Balboa was born in Barcelona, Spain in 1956. He received his undergraduate degree in physical education from the National Institute of Physical Education in Barcelona (Spain, 1983) and his doctorate in education from the University of Massachusetts Amherst (USA, 1989). After teaching at North American universities for 20 years, reaching the rank of full professor, Juan-Miguel is now at the Universidad Autónoma de Madrid (Spain). His research interests revolve around socio-critical thinking, critical pedagogy, ethics and critical evaluation.

Nathan Brubaker was born and raised in Vermont, USA. He received his undergraduate degree in physical education and history from the University of Vermont and his master's and doctorate in pedagogy, concentrating in philosophy for children, from Montclair State University in New Jersey. After teaching in public schools for 10 years, Nathan is now assistant professor of elementary education at James Madison University in Virginia. His research interests include negotiating authority, teaching for critical thinking, democracy and social justice, and self-study of teacher education practices.

Stages of development as a researcher

Human beings are always (re)searching. From the moment they are born, people intuitively (informally) look for answers to particular questions. But within formal (institutional) research, the awareness of *being* a researcher tends to emerge as people become students in undergraduate or graduate programs and are assigned 'research papers.' That is the starting point, developmentally speaking, for those who choose to pursue research in a particular field of study. Their awareness of becoming (being) researchers continues to evolve as they 'mature' along the continuum of experience and expertise – a continuum that never ends, for there is always something more one can learn, regardless of how long and how much one has researched.

For the sake of simplicity, let us assume that, after those first research papers, there are two main developmental stages in the continuum (each with their own associated degrees): (a) beginner to expert and (b) expert to master. It could be said that the first stage is characterized by little awareness of oneself as *researcher*; that is, usually one just *does* 'research.' Then, as one pursues further study, one becomes increasingly immersed in research and begins to identify with it, adopting what could be called a 'researcher's identity.' Over time, doing things as generally expected, mastering the written and unwritten codes of the discipline, and overcoming diverse challenges and barriers of methodology and research design, those who still can and wish to continue doing research may reach the level of experts. In this second developmental phase, with somewhat more knowledge and experience, researchers become able to undertake their own research paths and even have their own research projects and assistants. Soon enough, for the most part, the rewards of perseverance (perhaps more so than of intellectual capacity) begin to solidify in the form of accomplished publications, invited presentations, research proposals granted, reputed jobs and titles, an established name in one's field etc., and the 'master' level is achieved.

Four dimensions in research

So far, what we have described is quite obvious. From our perspective, however, what is not so evident (or, at least, is not spoken about as much) are the different dimensions researchers may enter (consciously) within those developmental stages. In an attempt to shed some light on these, we will explore four such dimensions as follows: survival, success, significance and spirituality.[3] Contrary to the stages mentioned above, we do not consider these dimensions to be developmental. Instead, as with the example in Figure 3.1, dimensions in research can be understood as alternative perceptual spaces that, based on one's viewpoint, can be experienced. As such, these may be encountered separately or simultaneously; and, depending on the circumstances, one may lose sight of any of them and recover them when those circumstances change. Such is the nature of these dimensions.

The survival dimension

Regardless of whether one is a novice or a master researcher, survival – by which we mean the act and process of continuing despite adverse circumstances and diverse challenges – is always a struggle. The meaning and degree of survival may be different depending on one's resources and wisdom; but the symptoms of being in this dimension are easily recognized, regardless of the developmental stage one occupies: stress, exhaustion, lack of balance, frustration, fear etc. For novices, survival may also imply wondering what it means to actually be a *researcher* and to have really made it as such. Moreover, at this stage, conducting research with the total presence of mind or holistic awareness that extends beyond just doing research may not be possible, for this depends on the ability to establish a distinction between research *as an exercise* and *as a way of life*; this, in turn, requires a solid experiential base that novices have typically not yet acquired.

Surviving the early experiences of research, often with limited resources and support, means having to devote a lot of time and energy to becoming familiar with the body of knowledge of one's field or discipline, learning the 'institutional ropes,' understanding the appropriate research paradigms and methods for future research undertakings and gathering and analyzing data (often for more experienced researchers or tutors) – sometimes with little autonomy.

On their part, proficient researchers, in order to further or sustain their career, also struggle to survive in their own way: for example, trying to meet deadlines, find resources, improve visibility, keep up with strong pressures and the demanding pace of publications and grant applications. What may happen, though, is that this dimension may not be as freely acknowledged by proficient researchers as it was by novices, since giving the impression of struggle may be viewed as a sign of weakness at the expert level.

Nevertheless, this dimension has positive and negative aspects. On the positive side, researchers at both stages have an opportunity to strengthen their will power, develop courage and fortitude, sharpen their skills, gain new knowledge and expand their experience. On the negative side, both for newcomers and seasoned researchers, the 'Go, go, go!' pressures in which they are immersed, each in their own way, not only leave them with little time for critical reflection; but also, for some, turn out to be too much to bear. Obviously, not everyone makes it in research. Perhaps this is why the phrase 'publish or perish' (Wilson, 1942) has so much meaning among researchers – for some do 'perish' even after, apparently, having done what they expected was necessary to survive (Hynes, 1997). On the other hand, those who persist in the face of such challenges may be able to enter other dimensions.

The success dimension

Experiencing the tensions and struggles of survival may be the key to realizing success. Think of it this way: What would the latter be without the former? Success can be experienced at any of the two developmental stages as well. For a beginner, success may mean learning new methods, mastering new skills, accomplishing pre-established goals, getting published for the first time, or receiving the first invitation to present their discoveries. Similarly, success for the veteran may entail, among other things, discovering a breakthrough concept, being granted a substantial sum of research money, publishing in a highly reputable journal, receiving international recognition and/or being offered a leadership position at a research institution.

At both levels, success may be experienced as a pleasant and rewarding process to the extent that researchers are able to maintain balance between their professional commitments and other aspects of their life (e.g. family, friends, hobbies, spirituality, health). Here, researchers may be passionate about their work as they feel and see that they contribute to their respective fields and find intrinsic and altruistic satisfaction in their undertakings. Here, it could also be said that researchers, besides being in the *success dimension*, are also in the *significance dimension* (see the next section of this chapter).

There is a shadowy side to success, too, as some researchers become obsessed with their work; and, in the angst 'to discover that new, unique idea that will propel them instantly to fame and fortune' (Goswami, 2008: 366; our translation), enter a fierce, narcissistic race for personal power and prestige. In these cases, researchers may lose sight of their initial vocational purpose – for example, to contribute to the field and to society – and undertake research for ulterior motives.

When this happens, other aspects of life may be neglected, and life balance may be lost. Some researchers may even find that they will never be able to achieve all that they thought was possible. Either way, if the pressures become too high, feelings such as emptiness and disappointment can result and the first signs of burnout emerge. This process may lead the researcher to return, once again, to the survival dimension. Emerging from it again will depend on whether they are able to view the process as an opportunity for growth or as a struggle without remedy.

But not all depends solely on the researcher's attitude. There are hidden factors that also distort the idea of 'success,' accentuating the sense of crisis. Let us examine these briefly. Far from being completely autonomous, researchers are strongly influenced by the context(s) in which they live and work. Some theorists (e.g. Bourdieu, 2007; Fernández-Balboa and Muros, 2006; Foucault, 1994; Merleau-Ponty, 1967) argue that researchers are affected by conditioning forces (i.e. habitus, ideologies and dominant discourses) that determine, to a great extent, what to think and do and how to perceive oneself. In relation to this, Goswami (2008) affirms that the very axioms of the Newtonian paradigm (i.e. objectivity, material monism, reductionism, causal determinism, continuity and locality) lead to a curious paradox: the more one pretends to know reality in scientific terms, the less likely one is to know oneself. This lack of self-knowledge is perpetuated by institutional traditions, themselves caught in dualistic, technocratic, political, materialistic and ideological traps (Douglas, 1986).

One aftermath of these traps may be found in what Erich Fromm (1947) termed 'authoritarian conscience.' This is a common – albeit unconscious – behavioral pattern, produced within the dominant socio-institutional system, where punishments or rewards are respectively imposed or granted depending on degree of submission to the system. Thus, the higher the degree of submission, the more external 'rewards' one receives. This, of course, could be regarded as the antithesis of critical reflection and the development of new knowledge. Under these circumstances, researchers subject to an 'authoritarian conscience' may lose their sense of self to some degree and replace it with what 'the order of things' (institutionalized neo-liberalism and material scientism) dictates (Foucault, 1994; Goswami, 2008). They may also develop a neurotic syndrome characterized by a constant search for external recognition, the weakening or paralysis of originality and spontaneity, and the emergence of guilt and fear – aspects that can only be appeased through even greater accomplishments or/and renewed submission to the authority (Fromm, 1947). Despite their growing reputations, this could lead apparently 'successful' researchers to feel confused, dissatisfied and insecure.

As the ego, in its never-ending need for expansion, keeps demanding more and more after every new achievement (Tolle, 1997), the solution is not to delve even deeper into one's work, for this would be like trying to put out a fire by throwing more wood into it. Although not an academic researcher, Tolstoy (1983) in his book, *Confession*, spoke of a similar situation and pointed to a healthier alternative:

> At the time we were all convinced that we had to speak, write, and publish as quickly as possible and as much as possible and that this was necessary for the good of mankind. Thousands of us published and wrote in an effort to teach others, all the while disclaiming and abusing one another. Without taking note of the fact that we knew nothing, that we did not know the answer to the simplest question of life, the question of what is right and what is wrong (pp. 20–1) ... I was talking like a person being carried along in a boat by the waves and the wind; without really answering, such a person replies to the only important question – 'Where are we to steer?' (p. 22) ... I knew ... that it was wrong. Therefore ... I [now] judge not according to progress but according to my own heart. (p. 23)

What Tolstoy's words lead us to is yet another dimension – that of significance.

The significance dimension

As we have said before, some researchers experience success not so much in terms of ego building and reputation seeking, but more in terms of an intrinsic satisfaction and balanced sense of contribution to the greater good and society. Hence, without ceasing to experience success, they also find significance in who they are and what they do, much like Tolstoy did in the end.

Viktor Frankl (1984) found significance in his life and work during his dismal years of internment in Nazi concentration camps. There, he investigated the meaning of life in regard to what distinguished those who survived in those horrific conditions from those who died. Eventually, as a result of his research from those years and thereafter, he developed *logotherapy* – a type of existentialist analysis focusing on a 'will to meaning' as the most powerful and primary motivating force in human beings (see Frankl, 1986). This 'will to meaning' is, precisely, what opens the gate to the significance dimension.

The shift we see in these two examples toward a greater purpose transcends, though does not deny, performance-oriented research and the financial and/or professional rewards it may yield. As for Tolstoy and Frankl, researchers – novices and masters alike – can pose significant questions in terms of what their work means to themselves, their professions and the world. This focus, in turn, unveils the strengths and flaws, the possibilities and limits, of science itself, while enabling researchers to, more often than not, avoid the institutional and paradigmatic traps we have disclosed above. This does not make them immune to those traps, but makes them less prone to falling into the 'less desirable' aspects of success and survival. In our experience, the focus on significance acts as a beacon that helps regain balance.

A focus on significance in research also means acting not so much according to what is considered institutionally *good* (in terms of knowledge gains, accolades etc.), but instead in terms of what is deemed to be ethically *right* (Fernández-Balboa, 2009). Entering this dimension thus implies a keen redefinition of what one sees and seeks as well as of who one is. In other words, in finding significance in one's research, it may be possible to begin to surrender personal narcissistic ego (Fromm, 1964), become more generous and humble, and widen focus of attention to alternative meanings. Magnin (2006) argues that new ethical and epistemological meanings also emerge as the incompleteness and the 'absence of fixed representation' of science are unveiled, for it is precisely this that 'starkly highlights the questions of foundation and meaning [and] forces man [sic] to accept his contingency and finiteness. This is where we touch upon moral issues' (p. 148).

The significance dimension, then, is an alternative ontological and epistemological perspective that, without negating the inherent value of the self, 'involves both recognition of otherness and an inclination toward unity' (Magnin, 2006: 150). As we understand it, the acknowledgement of a fundamental 'otherness' is precisely the key to the significance dimension, as the search for meaning in one's life and work (being mutually linked) continues. Once this dimension is entered, researchers can fathom a 'further field,' located beyond technical and performance-oriented questions, whereupon they dare to explore matters related to ethical, social and political responsibility, for the sake of others' well-being. This might include matters such as social justice, critical thinking, increased thoughtfulness, improved reasoning, greater social/political/cultural awareness and understanding, community and world peace, environmental sanity and widespread health. All in all, it could be affirmed that the conditions for a 'superior' consciousness have been set (Natsoulas, 2000). Perhaps this is what the Dalai Lama meant when asserting that, 'scientists … have a special responsibility. Besides [their] own profession, [they] have a basic motivation to serve humanity, to try to produce better, happier human beings.'[4]

Needless to say, one does not have to be an expert researcher to enter the significance dimension. Beginners and experts alike, although perhaps in different ways and to varying degrees, can do so. Notwithstanding being in this dimension, researchers may not only experience success and survival in all their facets, but may also even enter another: spirituality.

The spirituality dimension

Having an insight is something mysterious. Have you ever wondered where it comes from? Stop and ponder the origins of your inspiration – of a breakthrough you had, your strength to continue struggling, your newfound sense of purpose. If you believe that all this comes from your brain, think again, for there may be more to it. In fact, some scientists argue that inspiration stems from a much bigger source called 'universal consciousness.'[5] John Hagelin, director of the Institute of Science, Technology and Public Policy at Maharishi University of Management (USA), explains that consciousness, far from being chemically created by the brain, is 'an ocean of existence at the basis of everything … [and that] the self, in the big sense, is universal; knowing that, knowing it through experience, is called "enlightenment".'[6] Likewise, Peter Russell (2002), in a blend of physics, psychology and philosophy, holds that consciousness is as fundamental to the cosmos as space, time and matter – a universe similar to that described by many mystics.

Similarly, Gregg Braden, a computer geologist and well-known author, suggests that there is a hyper-connectivity of all things and beings within 'an underlying fabric of all Creation.' In his own words:

> Almost universally, ancient texts in spiritual traditions suggest that everything in our world is connected in ways that perhaps we are only beginning to understand. This subtle field of energy is, in fact, described by Western scientists as a net or a web that creates what they call 'the underlying fabric of all Creation.' This field of energy has been here from the very beginning. It is an intelligent field – an intelligence that responds deeply to human emotion.[7]

We suspect that realizing this – or something akin to it – is the key that opens the gate of the fourth dimension: spirituality. To enter this dimension, one does not need to be a great physicist, a bio-geneticist or a computer scientist, nor does one need to be an accomplished researcher. We believe that all researchers can access spirituality as they begin to perceive and feel themselves not as separate entities but, rather, as essential parts of that intricate 'underlying fabric' of consciousness or that ungraspable source of the Universe itself (Capra, 1975; Russell, 2002; Wilhelm and Jung, 1962). Albert Einstein put it thus:

> The human mind is not capable of grasping the Universe. We are like a little child entering a huge library. The walls are covered to the ceilings with books in many different tongues. The child knows that someone must have written these books. It does not know who or how. It does not understand the languages in which they are written. But the child notes a definite plan in the arrangement of the books – a mysterious order, which it does not comprehend, but only dimly suspects.[8]

What these accomplished minds are saying, essentially, is that entering the spiritual dimension depends upon realizing that in this 'mysterious order,' as the late physicist Carl Sagan suggested, 'we are a way for the Cosmos to know itself.'[9] This begins by acknowledging the possibility that far from being the main actor of the play, the researcher is a mere instrument of a much higher 'creative intelligence' (Marina, 1993) – more like a flute through which a 'Great Flutist,' the true protagonist, creates an amazing symphony of endless possibilities (Capra, 1975). Einstein seemed to know this well when he asserted:

> Everyone who is seriously involved in the pursuit of science becomes convinced that a spirit is manifest in the laws of the Universe – a spirit vastly superior to that of man [sic], and one in the face of which we, with our modest powers, must feel humble ... admiration of the illimitable superior spirit who reveals himself in the slight details we are able to perceive with our frail and feeble mind.[10]

Hence, when you have a real insight – a new idea – you might feel that you are in the spiritual dimension if you recognize the hand of 'a spirit vastly superior' and are humbly overtaken by its beauty and awe-inspiring nature; otherwise you may just remain in the success dimension. The difference, therefore, consists of where you place the source of that insight – wholly within you or partially in something much more awesome than you.

Researchers who place the source of inspiration within themselves may find it difficult to understand, as Hagelin suggests, that the Universe is 'an ocean of pure potentiality' conscious of itself.[11] Such difficulty, in turn, may be fostered by the traditional split between science and religion and by the false association of spirituality only with the latter. This paradigmatic distortion is beginning to change. The Dalai Lama, for one, has expressed that 'Today, in ... the 21st century, science and spirituality have the potential to be closer than ever.'[12] Certainly, there are scientists who do not believe this is so (e.g. Dawkins, 2006) and, instead, wield science as an irrefutable proof of the non-existence of God.[13] Others, such as geneticist Francis S. Collins (2007), the leading researcher in the Human Genome Project, appear to be able to reconcile these extremes by appealing to the rigorousness of science, on the one hand, and the belief in a transcendental God, on the other. Arguing that faith is an entirely rational choice with principles that are complementary to science, Collins advocates the merging of the two perspectives, saying:

> The God of the Bible is also the God of the genome. One can worship [it] in the cathedral or in the laboratory. [Its] creation is majestic, startling, intricate and beautiful (p. 227) ... and cannot be at war with [itself]. Only we, imperfect humans, can initiate such battles. And only we can end them. (p. 233)

In view of all this, whether you believe in any form of religious being or not, it is interesting to consider the role of spirituality as a dimension of research and a potential source of insight.

Conclusion

Carl Sagan once affirmed that 'we make ourselves significant by the courage of our questions and by the depth of our answers.'[14] Given that conceptions of who one is and why one exists greatly determine an individual's research – and vice versa – we might argue that research speaks volumes about personal identity and life meaning. We might also argue that some of the most courageous questions a researcher can ask have to do with his or her own personal and professional 'realities.' Some of these fundamental questions are: Who am I? Why do I exist? What is the ultimate purpose of my work?

In conclusion, we ask you to consider the possibility that the four dimensions of research offer a way of engaging in self-reflection as praxis (Fernández-Balboa, 1998). Regardless of field of research or developmental stage, these dimensions provide a valuable and viable framework for researchers to expand their realities and perceive a whole new range of possibilities for finding out some of the answers to the questions they have.

Key terms

Researcher identity   The distinct personality of a researcher.
Dimension   Time–space when/where a researcher lives and acts and which is determined by his or her degrees of freedom.
Survival   The act or process of being able to remain in existence.
Success   The achievement of something desired, attempted or planned.
Significance   The state of being significant and expression of meaning.
Spirituality   A state in which one connects with a higher, non-tangible, inspiring force.

Acknowledgements

With deep gratitude, we wish to acknowledge the insightful suggestions provided by the two editors of this book, Kathleen Armour and Doune Macdonald, as well as by Alvaro Sicilia Camacho, David Kirk and Eva Palencia Granado. Also thanks to those who participated in the Physical Education and Sport Pedagogy seminar at the University of Bedfordshire, where the first author trialed the main ideas in this chapter.

Notes

1 http://www.brainyquote.com/quotes/keywords/dimensions_2.html
2 http://en.wikipedia.org/wiki/Parallel_universe_(fiction)
3 Based on Warren's (2003) categorization, although without adhering to any religious denomination.
4 See http://www.mindandlife.org
5 See Wilhelm and Jung (1962).
6 See http://www.youtube.com/watch?v=WScObbwFGSY
7 See http://www.youtube.com/watch?v=wMGXk3KPXrM
8 See http://www.simpletoremember.com/articles/a/einstein
9 See http://www.youtube.com/watch?v=XGK84Poeynk&feature=related

10 See http://www.simpletoremember.com/articles/a/einstein
11 See http://www.youtube.com/watch?v=WScObbwFGSY
12 See http://www.youtube.com/watch?v=5o6_KB7tDbc
13 See http://www.youtube.com/watch?v=DMqTEfeqvmM&feature=fvw
14 See http://www.youtube.com/watch?v=AUF38eHqdxs&feature=fvw

References

Bourdieu, P. (2007) *Autoanálisis de un sociólogo*, Barcelona: Anagrama.

Capra, F. (1975) *The tao of physics: An exploration of the parallels between modern physics and Eastern mysticism*, Boulder, CO: Shanbhala Publications.

Collins, F. S. (2007) *¿Cómo habla Dios? La evidencia científica de la fe*, Madrid: Temas de Hoy, S.A.

Dawkins, R. (2006) *The God delusion*, New York: Houghton & Mifflin.

Douglas, M. (1986) *How institutions think*, Syracuse, NY: Syracuse University Press.

Fernández-Balboa, J. M. (1998) 'The practice of critical pedagogy: Critical self-reflection as praxis,' *Teaching Education*, 9(2): 47–53.

Fernández-Balboa, J. M. (2009) 'Bio-pedagogical self-reflection in PETE: Reawakening the ethical conscience and purpose in pedagogy and research,' *Sport, Education & Society*, 14(2): 147–64.

Fernández-Balboa, J. M. and Muros, B. (2006) 'The hegemonic triumvirate – ideologies, discourses and habitus in sport and physical education: Implications and suggestions,' *Quest*, 58(2): 197–221.

Foucault, M. (1994) *The order of things: An archaeology of the human sciences*, New York: Vintage Books.

Frankl, V. (1984) *Man's search for meaning*, New York: Simon and Schuster.

Frankl, V. (1986) *The doctor and the soul: From psychotherapy to logotherapy*, New York: Vintage Books.

Fromm, E. (1947) *Man for himself*, New York: Rinehart.

Fromm, E. (1964) *The heart of man: Its genius for good and evil*, New York: Harper and Row.

Goswami, A. (2008) *La ventana del visionario*, Madrid: La Esfera de los Libros, S.L.

Hynes, J. (1997) *Publish and perish: Three tales of tenure and terror*, New York: Picador.

Magnin, T. (2006) 'Moral philosophy: A space for dialogue between Science and Theology,' in J. Staune (ed.) *Science and the search for meaning: Perspectives from international scientists* (137–62), West Conshohocken, PA: Templeton.

Marina, J. A. (1993) *Teoría de la inteligencia creadora*, Barcelona: Anagrama.

Merleau-Ponty, M. (1967) *The structure of behavior*, Boston: Beacon Press.

Natsoulas, T. (2000) 'Consciousness and conscience,' *Journal of Mind and Behavior*, 21(4): 327–52.

Russell, P. (2002) *From science to God: A physicist's journey into the mystery of consciousness*, Novato, CA: New World Library.

Tolle, E. (1997) *The power of now: A guide to spiritual enlightenment*, Vancouver: Namaste Publishing.

Tolstoy, L. (1983) *Confession*, New York: W.W. Norton.

Warren, R. (2003) *The purpose-driven life*, Philadelphia, PA: Running Press.

Wilhelm, R. and Jung, C. G. (1962) *The secret of the golden flower: A Chinese book of life* (R. Wilhelm, trans.), San Diego: Harcourt Brace.

Wilson, L. (1942) *The academic man: A study in the sociology of a profession*, New York: Oxford University Press.

4 What counts as 'good' research?

Stephen Silverman and Eve Bernstein

Introduction

Reading, using and carrying out research are similar to setting out on an adventure that takes time and requires preparation and skill. Taking part in this journey can be compared with the experience depicted in the documentary movie *Deep Water*. In this documentary, Donald Crowhurst participates in the 1968 Golden Globe Race, a widely covered event where individuals sail alone around the world. Crowhurst was one of a small number of participants in the race, hoping to win it and the £5,000 prize that would help save his business ventures and bring him fame. The one problem, however, was that Crowhurst was not an experienced sailor, and his boat was not equipped to sail safely around the world. As a result, he used deception to misreport his location while sailing, and eventually his venture had a tragic ending. While research rarely has these consequences, understanding what makes good research is critical to a successful career as a researcher and to reading research and applying it to professional practice. If you are not prepared to assess what you read and to use that information, you will be lost in a sea of research reports and will be unable to use research for your intended purposes.

About us

Steve Silverman is a professor of education and department chair at Teachers College, Columbia University. For over 30 years, he has conducted research on teaching in physical education with a focus on skill and attitude, to gain an understanding of how to enhance student learning. He has also written extensively about research methods and is the co-author of three highly successful research methods books (Locke et al., 2007; 2010; Thomas et al., 2011). Steve has supervised many doctoral students who are now successful teacher-educators and researchers. His work is based on the belief that having a research base to understand effective teaching can provide a basis for future research and professional practice.

Eve Bernstein was one of Steve's doctoral students, having received her EdD in curriculum and teaching in physical education from Teachers College, Columbia University. She has extensive teaching experience in secondary and primary schools as well as at the university level. She holds a professional teaching licence, K-12 in physical education, from New York State. In 2009, Eve joined the Family Nutrition and Exercise Science Department at Queens College, City University of New York, as an assistant professor. She primarily instructs graduate students in physical education. Her research interests focus on how students perceive, and how teachers structure, competitive activities in physical education class.

Why is it important to understand what is 'good' research?

Those who are planning to be professionals in the field of physical education and sport do not need to have an experience of being lost in an endless ocean, as Donald Crowhurst was, as they plan research or look for research to help them solve problems in their professional life. There is a vast array of literature in the field, and it is expanding every day. The amount of literature can be overwhelming. It is necessary to develop skills that will aid in evaluating research to determine whether it is 'good' for planning other research, getting a firm grounding in the field, or to use research to learn more and apply the findings to the day-to-day tasks of teaching or working with children. We must note, however, that how you develop this skill will depend on your intended purpose – planning and doing research; reading, understanding and applying research findings; or both. In the remainder of this chapter, we will discuss issues that are related to understanding 'good' research and how one develops these skills in order to conduct it. While in this chapter we will focus on becoming a researcher, if you are a master's student who wants to use research for professional practice, understanding these issues will give you a better insight into the research process and the production of research.

Methodological issues in research

Much of this volume focuses directly on research methods and provides in-depth treatments of specific methodological topics. We will not repeat any of that discussion. As you read the specific chapters that follow, you should note that what makes 'good' research depends on the questions being asked and methodologies employed. It is hard to use one fixed standard to evaluate all research. The standards for 'good' research must be contextualized by multiple factors, including where the research is conducted, who the participants are, how much time is needed in the research site and with the participants, how the methods will be adapted to allow the research questions to be answered and the contemporary standards in the field of study and for the chosen methodological approach. Just as in dating and looking for a life partner, the evaluation factors must be matched with the situation. Not all people are the same, and each research situation has different demands.

As you read research and possibly think about planning research, some questions to consider are:

*   *What were the research questions?* Were the questions important and interesting? Did the researchers provide you with the context of the research questions and the practical or theoretical background to understand why these questions were important?

- *Where was the research conducted?* Is this an appropriate site to answer the questions? How was/were the site or sites selected? If multiple sites are used, do they help answer the research questions by increasing participants or broadening the context of the study? If you are interested in applying the results to teaching or other work with children, is this research site similar enough to where you work to apply its findings?

- *Who were the participants?* Were they appropriate in composition – age, gender, and other characteristics – to answer the research question? Were they selected in a way that enhances answering the research question (i.e., very narrow or widely representative of a group, depending on the goals)? Were there enough participants to answer the question using the method? Does it appear that the researcher treated the participants with respect and did not use coercion to get them to participate?

- *Did the researchers get good data that allow them to answer their questions?* This is what most people focus on when they think about whether the research is 'good' or not; however, the answer is not a simple yes or no. Questions to ask are:

  - *Did the researchers do a pilot study to test and refine methods and ascertain that they can get good data?* Do they provide information from the pilot study or their own previous research to suggest that they have taken the necessary steps to make sure they get good data? For example, in a qualitative study that employs interviews, did they pilot and refine their semi-structured interview questions so that they increased the likelihood of yielding good data? In a quantitative study, did they pilot the experimental intervention to make sure it is appropriate and practical for the situation? In all cases, did the researchers explain the methodological decisions they made, so that you understand how the decisions improved the study or made it feasible to complete it?

  - *Did the researchers collect data using accepted practices?* For example, in a qualitative study, did the researchers have prolonged engagement in the research site and use multiple methods to collect data? Or, in a quantitative study, did they use instrumentation for which they can provide information on the reliability and validity of the scores obtained from data collection? Do they provide detail (or references to other sources that provide the detail) that substantiate how the methods helped provide good data? If they ventured into highly original methods, did they provide a rationale for using those methods and provide a detailed description to help you judge the methodological quality?

- *Is the analysis appropriate to answer the questions?* Does the analysis provide answers to the questions? Does it answer them in a parsimonious way, or does it appear that the researchers may have analyzed in ways that do not directly answer the question? Do the researchers show attention to detail (e.g., awareness of their bias/position and triangulating data in qualitative studies or using appropriate follow-up techniques in statistical analyses)?

- *Is the rest of the report written in ways that logically follow the method?* Do the results follow the method and provide support to answer the questions? Is anything obviously left out, and if so, do they explain why? Are the conclusions appropriate to the results or is the discussion overblown, so that it leaves you worrying about the objectivity of the authors?

All research requires trade-offs; how we evaluate those trade-offs depends on the factors discussed above. As an example, all research takes time. The questions you ask as you read and assess quality will need to consider the questions the authors asked and the method they used. Some studies will require more time than others. For example, a small study looking at a focused instructional intervention might take less time than a large-scale qualitative study that involves in-depth interviews and multiple observations. Likewise, a large-scale validation study may require hundreds of participants, while a descriptive study may require far fewer. As you read research – and plan your own research projects – you should consider the trade-offs and whether they appear to be appropriate for the study you are assessing. Not all trade-offs are bad, and having an inflexibly high standard that no study can meet will not allow you to judge 'good' research, since most will fail to meet your standard.

From the examples highlighted in the paragraph above, about time and participants, it should be clear that each study demands that you assess whether it is 'good' research based on the research focus and method. While it would be nice to have one, simple, specific list to guide you, this might not work well for all studies. There certainly are some excellent lists that provide more detail to evaluate method (e.g., see the discussions of qualitative and quantitative approaches to research in Locke et al., 2010). Remember that many factors must be used to evaluate each study and you will be well served throughout your career.

Assessing research quality

Examining the methods used in a study, as we noted above, is one way to assess research quality. On a daily basis, however, researchers and practitioners use many other ways to decide whether a study is 'good' or has the potential to be good. How you go about assessing quality may depend on your motive for reading research. For example, if you are a primary school physical educator, you may want to find research that helps you teach children. If you are a graduate student who is doing a paper, you may want to find research that helps you review a topic. And, if you are planning research, you may want to find studies that provide results and theory to frame and design your project.

We believe there are many factors that will influence whether or not a published paper is 'good.' As with interpreting methodological issues in research, other factors in relation to your intended use need to be considered. Sometimes a paper is good enough for your purposes, sometimes part of the paper can be valuable, and still sometimes the paper cannot provide information for the purposes you intend. In this section, we discuss a number of issues to consider when you evaluate the quality of a paper. Of course, you need to read the research paper and examine the method. The issues that follow will give you a head start in assessing the research in ways that are beneficial for your purpose.

Has the research undergone review?

The research process can help you decide whether it is just the researchers who think the research is good or whether others who have read the research concur. Research is research only when it is made public and submitted for review, as encouraged in Chapter 2. This review process occurs in at least three different ways.

The first occurs after researchers complete a study. Often, the first step of disseminating the results is to present the paper at a research meeting or conference, such as the American Alliance for Health, Physical Education, Recreation and Dance, the Australian Association for Research in Education, or the British Educational Research Association. For each association where research is presented at its annual meeting, there is a review process that determines which papers will be presented. Typically, two or three other researchers read an abstract, which can range from a couple of hundred to a couple of thousand words, and rate it on a number of factors. Each submission is judged against the others, and a program chair determines which abstracts have the highest scores; these accepted abstracts then appear on the program. Although the research has been reviewed for presentation and others think it has merit, papers that are reviewed for conference presentation have the liability that those reading the reviews do not have all the details that are found in a full paper. The review provides some assurances of quality, but depending on how the conference review process is organized and how many papers are accepted, the quality of the review may vary greatly.

A second way in which to disseminate research is by publishing it in a journal. The review process for most research journals (e.g. the *Journal of Teaching in Physical Education*, *Physical Education and Sport Pedagogy* or the *Research Quarterly for Exercise and Sport*) is more involved and more rigorous than that for conference presentations. Once the paper is submitted to the journal, the editor selects reviewers, or referees, who have expertise in the topic of the study, the research methods, or both. These two or three reviewers go through the paper and comment, often in great detail, on many areas of the paper. These areas can range across the question being asked and the focus of the study, the case made for doing the study, the methods, the results, the interpretation of the results, the quality of the discussion, and how the manuscript is organized and written. The referees provide comments that are both general (e.g., 'The method is sophisticated and directly answers the questions being asked') and specific (e.g., 'This sentence is hard to follow. You need to break it up and then provide more specificity'). When the editor receives all the reviews back, they make a decision on whether the paper is accepted, rejected, or requires a revision before a decision can be made. Typically, one or more revisions are required before a paper is accepted and a back-and-forth occurs between the author, editor and reviewers until the editor accepts or rejects a paper. A paper that has gone through a couple of rounds of revisions and has multiple referees' and an editor's approval for publication is stronger than one that has not gone through this review.

The third way in which research is reviewed prior to publication is when it is funded. Research that is given a grant is often not considered as having been peer reviewed since this occurs before the study is conducted. The grant, however, that is provided by a governmental or other organization that is known to support quality research has probably been 'pre-approved' for its quality (Locke et al., 2007). As with a manuscript review for a journal, the grant proposal is often reviewed and revised one or more times before funding is provided. These reviews are often quite rigorous and suggest that the resultant study has much merit.

In which journal has the research been published?

Journals vary in quality and the perception of quality. Those perceptions are an indication whether you can expect 'good' research to appear in that journal. There are different ways of perceiving journal quality. These may be very specific to the research focus and your advisor's and your perspective on the journals in the field, or some form of external indicator may help you judge the quality of a journal and the research published in it. We will discuss each of these ways of evaluating journals. Each person has different approaches to evaluating research journals based on past experiences with a journal, how they plan to use the information, and whether a topic is a familiar one, or one in which they know very little.

General perceptions of journal quality

All experienced scholars have a hierarchy for journals. Some are considered to publish consistently good research; in others, the perception of papers vary; and in still others, while there is an occasional good paper, the overall quality of the published research is not that good. Often, these perceptions come from reading many papers and asking the methodological questions posed earlier. This generally occurs over a number of years, and the stratification of journal quality will become more nuanced the longer someone has been forming and modifying their perceptions in terms of methodological considerations.

At this point you may be thinking 'If it's going to take years, I'll never be able to develop my own perceptions.' We understand if you feel this way, but are not suggesting that you start from the beginning. One good way to get a good start on forming your perceptions of journal quality is to talk with your advisor and other faculty members who have similar interests to yours. You also can talk with graduate students who are more advanced than you and have a head start on forming their hierarchy.

Before you approach others about their perceptions of journals, do some preparation. First, make a list of journals in your field. Look at each of the journals' mission statements to get an idea of the focus. Look at who the editor is and who is on the editorial board for this volume and previous volumes of the journal. If the journal publishes a yearly list of reviewers, look at the list and see who they are. Do you recognize the reviewers' names or their institutions for being places that have good reputations for research in the field? Then look at a few issues of each journal and read some of the articles that interest you. You will probably notice that some journals favor certain methodological approaches in the papers they publish, some have a broader or narrower range of topics addressed, and some have clearly higher levels of editing and production.

When you talk to your advisor and others about journal quality, ask them which journals they think publish good research and which are perceived as publishing lesser-quality research. In the ideal case, since you have done the preparation we suggest, this will be a discussion and not a lecture. Ask questions! Share what you noticed, and see if those perceptions are shared by others.

Once you have had this discussion, you can form your own list. You may have more than one list – these journals in sport pedagogy, these others in kinesiology, and others again in education. The lists may overlap. They will change as you mature in the field and as various journal editors change; they will also change depending on how you want to use a specific journal. Refereed journals vary in quality, and your perceptions will vary and change with time.

Quantitative indicators of journal quality

Over the last decade or so, it has been more common for researchers and others to use quantitative indicators to determine the quality of research published in journals. This tendency is based on the need to get beyond perceptions and to use 'hard' data. While we think these quantitative indicators are one way to look at journal and research quality, we also know that they tell only part of the story of journal quality and, as we discuss below, should be used cautiously.

One indicator that is assessed when looking at quality is the acceptance rate for a journal. This is the number of papers accepted and published as a proportion of all the papers submitted to the journal. For most journals, this changes slightly from year to year, but hovers in a relatively consistent range. A journal that has a higher acceptance rate probably doesn't publish research of as high quality as one that has a lower acceptance rate. For example, it should be evident that a journal that accepts 90 per cent of the submitted papers does not provide the same level of review and scrutiny as one that accepts only 20 per cent of papers after revisions and the full review process.

Another indicator used to evaluate journals is the impact factor and the five-year impact factor (Thomson Reuters, 2010). The impact factor is the number of times articles from a journal, when considering the total number of articles published, have been cited in other journals over the previous two years. The five-year impact factor, which has only been reported by the Institute for Scientific Information since 2008, is the same measure over a five-year period. Journals with high impact factors are thought to be better, and those with low impact factors are thought to be of lesser quality. Impact factors can range from about zero, for journals that have few papers cited in other journals, to values in the 20s or above for a very few journals that are cited frequently.

It would be nice if it were as easy as looking at the impact factor to evaluate research. There have been a number of criticisms of impact factors as a primary method of evaluating research (Joint Committee on Quantitative Assessment of Research, 2008; Kulinna et al., 2009; Larivière and Gingras, 2010; Lawrence, 2003; Sammarco, 2008). For example, papers may be cited in other journals because of methodological problems, and the range of impact factors in one field may not be the same as in another field; even among sub-areas within a field the range may be different. Just as our individual perceptions of journals may vary based on a variety of factors, the perception of the value of an impact will vary greatly among individuals. It is just one piece of evidence, along with everything else we present in this chapter, for you to use in determining good research.

How research will be used and journal quality

How you use the various ways we discuss of evaluating research will depend on your purpose (Locke et al., 2010). For example, if you are interested in papers that present findings that you can use as a teacher, you may ignore some of the aspects we discuss and then decide if the findings can be applied to your situation. If you are planning a research study and a paper presents a new technique for collecting data, such as an instrument to measure children's attitudes or a way of structuring focus groups, you may attend particularly to those aspects of the paper. If you are an instructional leader who is looking at ways to improve the curricular offerings in a school, you may pay most attention to the arguments made in introductory sections of research papers.

Using research for your own purposes and determining what is good for those purposes is legitimate. If you know why you are making decisions, and what you are paying attention to, and what you are ignoring, this strategy will help you assess research and get the most from it. While many who publish research would hope everyone who reads their papers reads every word, you should use research based on your needs and your evaluation of whether a specific paper meets those needs.

Case study of determining what is 'good' research

Suppose you are a teacher who wants to apply research to improve teaching or, as discussed here, a doctoral student, as Eve was, starting a literature review. How could you determine what constitutes 'good' research for your own use? In Eve's case, as she started thinking about her doctoral studies, the first thing she considered was who to study with, since an advisor with similar research interests and a record of research productivity is essential to getting a good start as a researcher. Eve worked on research projects early in her graduate experience, in order to get a head start on understanding the research literature and the publishing process.

As Eve was focusing in on a specific research question, Steve helped her refine her topic and question. His knowledge of the literature and various journals helped Eve save time during her initial exploration of her topic. Eve's research question focused on competitive activities that are presented in middle school physical education class. Once she had an idea of the focus of her own research, she conducted an intensive search for research papers in various electronic databases. These databases were relevant to physical activity and physical education such as ArticleFirst, Dissertation Abstracts, ERIC, Medline, Web of Science, and SPORTDiscus. She found she was inundated with search results until she used the strategies discussed above to narrow articles down to include those that are 'good' research. She focused her search on peer-reviewed articles. From her previous classes and seminars, and from discussions with

Steve and other graduate students, Eve had both a framework for evaluating articles and a hierarchy of journals in her field. She used her perception of each journal as an initial benchmark to review quality, but read each relevant article and assessed its quality. The journals most relevant for her work tended to be from physical education and education, and published articles that focused on teaching, student motivation and attitude, as well as task presentation.

As Eve read each article and assessed its quality, she focused on methodology and asked herself the questions we present in the first section. Then she asked if the method the authors used was sufficient to answer the research questions and whether the article could be applied to her own work. In the search that Eve conducted, she found articles that used both quantitative and qualitative methods. She paid attention to all the articles that she read, since each could help inform her research questions and the rationale for doing the study. Since she was interested in student perceptions of competitive activities and her questions lent themselves to qualitative methods, such as interviews and focus groups, she spent more time reading and evaluating methods in the qualitative research papers.

Finally, when reading each article, Eve asked whether she could trust that the authors took the steps needed to ensure that their research was sound. Did they pay attention to detail? Did they provide references to back up their statements, report any limitations of the study and, finally, report appropriate techniques to confront any biases that might have occurred during analysis? With each study, it was important to Eve that the authors discussed issues of trustworthiness and credibility, including whether they triangulated data and used an audit trail to record methodological issues. In addition, since her research would occur in middle schools, she was particularly observant of the research setting presented in each article. She noted as she read that authors who provided detail about the setting made it easier to assess whether the results could inform her work. Eve took great care in reading articles and understanding how the research was conducted so that she could incorporate appropriate methods into her pilot studies. Each of these elements was important for her to consider when finding reputable and appropriate articles. And each gave her a different angle for assessing quality.

Conclusion

Crowhurst set sail without having some of the tools necessary to launch a successful voyage. Having a plan to prepare to assess research in systematic ways will aid you in your work – and save time and effort. If you are starting a research career or want to use research to assist you in answering professional questions, actively pursuing an interest in what makes 'good' research, while challenging, will be the first step to ensure smooth sailing and a successful journey.

Key terms

'Good' research   Research that has been judged on a number of factors to be sound for the purposes intended by the reader.

Journal quality   The regard of a journal by the academic community.

Refereed journal   A journal in which each published article has undergone a blind review by referees who comment on whether it is of appropriate quality for the journal. This process often involves multiple rounds of review.

Impact factor   A statistic from the Institute for Scientific Information that indicates how often a journal is cited in articles in other journals.

References

Joint Committee on Quantitative Assessment of Research (2008) *Citation Statistics*, Berlin: International Mathematical Union.

Kulinna, P. H., Scrabis-Fletcher, K., Kodish, S., Phillips, S. and Silverman, S. (2009) 'A decade of research literature in pedagogy,' *Journal of Teaching in Physical Education*, 28: 119–40.

Larivière, V. and Gingras, Y. (2010) 'On the relationship between interdisciplinarity and scientific impact,' *Journal of the American Society for Information Science and Technology*, 61: 126–31.

Lawrence, P. A. (2003) 'The politics of publication,' *Nature*: 422: 259–61.

Locke, L. F., Spirduso, W. W. and Silverman, S. J. (2007) *Proposals That Work: A Guide for Planning Dissertations and Grant Proposals*, 5th edn, Thousand Oaks, CA: Sage.

Locke, L. F., Silverman, S. J. and Spirduso, W. W. (2010) *Reading and Understanding Research*, 3rd edn, Los Angeles, CA: Sage.

Sammarco, P. W. (2008) 'Journal visibility, self-citation, and reference limits: Influences in impact factor and author performance review,' *Ethics in Science and Environmental Politics*, 8: 121–5.

Thomas, J. R., Nelson, J. A. and Silverman, S. J. (2011) *Research Methods in Physical Activity*, 6th edn, Champaign, IL: Human Kinetics.

Thomson Reuters (2010) 'Journal Citation Reports,' retrieved from <http://admin-apps.isiknowledge.com.ezproxy.cul.columbia.edu/JCR/help/h_impfact.htm> (accessed 9 March 2011).

Further reading

Pyrczak, F. (2008) *Evaluating Research in Academic Journals: A Practical Guide to Realistic Evaluation*, 4th edn, Glendale, CA: Pyrcak Publishing.

Part II
Methodology: the thinking behind the methods

5 Thinking about research frameworks

Richard Tinning and Katie Fitzpatrick

Introduction

You might think that doing research is rather like cooking: you just follow a set of procedures rather as you follow a recipe. There is, however, an important difference. In research, the methods themselves are underpinned by certain assumptions about the world, including the nature of reality and the nature of knowledge. In this chapter, we want to discuss some of these things that are usually hidden, so that you can better understand what we call the research process.

About us

First you need to know something about ourselves as the 'we' in this chapter.

Professor Richard Tinning is a teacher educator who has been working in Physical Education Teacher Education (PETE) and physical education (PE) research for over four decades. He has supervised many student research projects, including honours, masters and PhD theses. Over the past decade, he has worked in a school of human movement (HM) studies and taught research methods to undergraduate HM students. Some of these students pursue careers in health and physical education (HPE) teaching; others in sport and exercise science or health promotion. His particular interests are in the nature of knowledge and truth and the claims made by various research frameworks to both knowledge and truth.

Dr Katie Fitzpatrick is an experienced HPE teacher who, in 2004, left secondary school teaching to take up a position as lecturer in health and physical education at the University of Waikato. Her recently completed PhD thesis, titled 'Stop Playing Up! A critical ethnography of health, physical education and (sub)urban schooling', won the New Zealand Association for Research in Education (NZARE) Sutton Smith award for the best doctoral thesis of 2010. She is currently a research fellow at the University of Auckland.

The approach used in this chapter

This chapter is about the research process and the frameworks that can be used to facilitate that process. We want to encourage you to think about research in ways that are open to multiple ways of knowing, multiple ways of finding out what is known, and multiple ways of representing that knowledge. In order to ground this explanation in something tangible, we are going to use Katie's PhD thesis as a point of departure for discussing the many possible ways of approaching research.

But before we can begin our conversation about Katie's thesis, we must make two things explicit. First, we assume that researching physical education and youth sport is essentially researching a particular form of socio-cultural practice. For the sake of simplification, we will categorize our research as social science and, at the same time, recognize that it is not like researching chemistry or geology because we are dealing with humans and their interactions in a particular context. It is by nature messy. Second, we are also going to limit our discussion to empirical forms of research. By 'empirical', we mean research in which we use our senses (mainly our eyes and ears) to collect information regarding a particular issue or question. This empirical form of research is different in nature from research in which logic and argument are the sole 'evidence'.

Frameworks and paradigms

While you might be directed to a certain research topic by your advisor or supervisor (see Chapter 1), you will probably also find yourself directed to use a certain research framework. In this case, and throughout this chapter, when we talk of research frameworks, we are talking about conceptual structures and particular patterns of thinking. According to Wiktionary, a framework has a number of different meanings including:

1   (literally) The arrangement of support beams that represent a building's general shape and size.
2   (figuratively) The larger branches of a tree that determine its shape.
3   (figuratively, especially in computing) A basic conceptual structure.
4   (literally) The identification and categorization of processes or steps that constitute a complex task or mindset in order to render explicit the tacit and implicit.

The meaning most relevant in this discussion is 'a basic conceptual structure'. Importantly, a research framework is much more than a set of techniques for gathering data and analysing those data. It will be based on certain assumptions and it will represent a particular way of thinking about knowledge and reality. Accordingly, in the process of learning to do research, a graduate student will become socialized, acculturated or indoctrinated (choose your own preferred term) in particular ways of thinking. These ways of thinking, sometimes called paradigms, will include not only disciplinary knowledge, but also theories, metaphors and rhetorical devices. Unfortunately, in the research world, the terms 'framework', 'paradigm' and 'theory' are usually loosely defined (if at all) and are sometimes even taken as synonymous. This is especially confusing for newcomers.

Here is what Wikipedia says about the word 'paradigm':

The word paradigm … has been used in linguistics and science to describe distinct concepts.

Until the 1960s, the word was specific to grammar: the 1900 Merriam–Webster dictionary defines its technical use only in the context of grammar or, in rhetoric, as a term for an illustrative parable or fable. In linguistics, Ferdinand de Saussure used *paradigm* to refer to a class of elements with similarities.

From the 1960s onward, the word has referred to a thought pattern in any scientific discipline or other epistemological context. The Merriam–Webster Online dictionary defines this usage as 'a philosophical and theoretical framework of a scientific school or discipline within which theories, laws, and generalizations and the experiments performed in support of them are formulated; broadly: a philosophical or theoretical framework of any kind.'

It is the more contemporary (i.e., after 1960) meaning related to thought patterns that we are concerned with in this chapter. Notice that at the end of the Wikipedia explanation it says 'a philosophical or theoretical framework of any kind'. Think for a moment about Newtonian physics. Isaac Newton, in devising his laws of motion, was applying a particular way of thinking about motion and about the world. When Albert Einstein came along later with his theory of relativity, he introduced a different paradigm or theoretical framework to science.

There are also paradigms or frameworks that operate in the social world. For example, we can think of communism as a paradigm or thought pattern that resulted from a particular view of the relationship between humans and capital. More recently we can think of neo-liberalism as a paradigm or pattern of thoughts and beliefs that, among other things, advocate small government, the responsibility of the individual and unfettered deregulation of the economy.

So paradigms are frameworks that orient and represent particular *ways of thinking*. They are grounded in certain assumptions about nature and reality. That is, they have different *ontological* starting points.

In the discussion that follows, we reveal how research frameworks inform or shape one's research and how such frameworks are always underpinned by certain epistemological and political orientations that inevitably have practical consequences. While this discussion is essentially philosophical in nature, we hope to show that it is as important to the research process as the more technical knowledge that is necessary for the practical conduct of a research project.

In this book, you will be introduced to some different frameworks for doing research. Basically there are different frameworks (paradigms, if you prefer) and different research *methods* within each framework. There are many different ways in which research can be classified. One popular way is to categorize it as either positivist, interpretive or critical. We present a brief account of these categories here in the recognition that they are often in some tension and sometimes overlapping. In other words, these categories are not like categories in science that tend to be based on strict taxonomic criteria.

The *positivist* research tradition or paradigm, which is dominant in the natural sciences (such as biology, physics, medicine), begins with the assumption that there is a real world 'out there' that can be objectively measured. Positivistic research tends to use quantitative data (but this is not a necessary and sufficient attribute to deem a research project as positivist). Research in this frame tends to be concerned with seeking confirmation or refutation of a theory and/or law, and hence causality. One of the best examples of a programme of physical education research studies in the positivist tradition is that of the Ohio State doctoral programme under the leadership of Daryl Siedentop (see, for example, Siedentop, 1981). Chapter 13 of this book, on the measurement of physical activity, contains examples of research methods in the positivist paradigm.

Coming from a different set of assumptions about knowledge and reality is the *interpretivist* paradigm. For the interpretivist, reality is constructed by the individual – people experience things differently and hence the research process should try to uncover the meaning that individuals ascribe to an event, experience or happening. Typically (but not always), this research relies on qualitative-type data. For example, although social science research is often qualitative, the extensive use of surveys in social science relies on the quantitative data that may or may not be derived from qualitative responses to questions. Common theoretical 'tools' usually associated with the interpretive paradigm include phenomenology, ethnography, narrative inquiry and life history.

Another orienting framework of research is known as the *critical* paradigm. The issues of concern for researchers who position their work within the critical paradigm are those related to social justice and equity. This work is avowedly political in the sense that it sets out to make a difference to people's lives by exposing and challenging inequities and power relations. Topics of focus might include gender, sexuality, ability, social class and/or ethnicity. Critical-oriented research most often, but certainly not exclusively, uses qualitative data. Among the many theoretical tools used in critical-oriented research are critical theory, poststructural theory, feminist theory, postcolonial theory, critical race theory, critical ethnography and queer theory.

Ideas, theories and theorists

In one sense, research is about ideas. In its simplest form, research takes an idea and investigates it. The idea could be rather general such as 'Physical education promotes health' or 'Sport builds character'; or it could be more specific such as 'The obesity crisis is a social construction.' An idea might be articulated in the form of a specific theory such as 'Educational streaming disadvantages average students' or 'Kinaesthetic feedback facilitates learning of motor skills.' In the process of our investigations we will often engage with more general theories, usually named after their authors: Freud's psychoanalytic theory; Einstein's theory of relativity (this probably will not be of much use in researching youth sport or PE); Marx's theory of capital; Foucault's theory of power/knowledge; Maslow's theory of motivation; Gidden's structuration theory; Bourdieu's theory of habitus; or Piaget's theories on active learning.

It is important to recognize that for a doctoral thesis, theorizing is a necessary, but usually not sufficient, dimension. Although a philosophical thesis might contain no empirical data, in this chapter we are limiting our attention to empirical research. *Empirical research* refers to research that uses information gained through observation, experience or experimentation. Thinking about something, even in sophisticated ways, does not constitute empirical research. While interpretive and critical research is generally associated with the positivist paradigm, it is important to understand that it can also be empirical if based on the use of the senses to collect data (e.g. in observation or experience). The nature of data (quantitative or qualitative) does not distinguish empirical from non-empirical research.

We do, however, contend that empirical research should be adequately theorized lest it become mere empiricism. *Empiricism* refers to the belief that all knowledge must come from the experience of the senses and the senses only. This rules out theorizing and thinking (e.g., applying logical and critical thinking) in the process of gaining knowledge.

Theory helps us to better understand the social contexts we are studying and moves us on from simply describing what we see and hear. Theory also enables the researcher to reflect on how the very social context itself frames what they pay attention to during the research process. The use of social theory is increasingly part of the research landscape in PE and youth sport. Importantly, a scan of the sociocultural research literature of our field reveals that different theoretical frameworks or perspectives are relatively less or more successful in contributing to our understandings. Sometimes, but not often, the results of such research are used to inform policy making that, in turn, may contribute to improved social justice and equity.

But how do you choose a theoretical framework that will be more, rather than less, generative in terms of understanding and explanations? Obviously, our choices will be limited by the theories we understand, or at least have some knowledge of. Mats Alvesson offers some useful advice in this regard:

> It is important that researchers primarily use theories they grasp well and for which they feel an emotional preference ...
>
> Very few researchers can successfully move between theories with different paradigmatic roots ...
>
> It is my experience that it is necessary to concentrate within a particular theory, in order to be able to exploit its interpretive powers.
>
> (Alvesson, 2002: 133)

There are also 'hot' theorists whose work could provide a generative theoretical frame for an educational or youth sport research topic. For example, Judith Butler, Michel Foucault, Anthony Giddens, Basil Bernstein, Graeme Turner, Raewyn Connell and Valerie Walkerdine represent major theorists whose ideas are 'hot' in some sections of educational and youth sport research literature. On the other hand, it would probably be difficult to find many contemporary researchers in PE and youth sport still using Marx or Marcuse or Horkheimer. And whatever happened to the significance of Piaget, Bruner, Skinner, Erikson or Vygotsky?

Most often we will use theories that build on the work of others. It useful to think of *big* theorists (such as Marx, Habermas, Bourdieu, Bernstein, Derrida, Foucault, Giddens, Mead, Skinner, Vygotsky, Maslow, Piaget, Gilligan or Butler) and what we might call 'derivative theorists' whose work is informed by, or based on, the work of the big theorists. All of the research work in physical education and youth sport is derivative. Importantly, calling it 'derivative' is not meant to be pejorative. It is simply a recognition of the debt that they owe to the originators of particular theories. For example, much of the contemporary research related to TGfU (Teaching Games for Understanding) (see Kirk and MacPhail, 2002) draws on adaptations of ideas from the original theorizing of psychologists Lev Vygotsky and Jean Piaget. In the sport and exercise psychology field, motivation is a key topic of study (see, for example, Weinberg and Gould, 1999). Theories of motivation all 'evolve' from Abraham Maslow's (a big theorist) original 'A theory of human motivation' published in 1943. Interestingly, however, in both these examples there is no specific reference to the original big theorists' ideas, which exist only as 'ghosts' in the background (Nicholson, 2010).

It is important to recognize that theorists tend to work within a particular paradigm. So when you choose a particular theory or theorist's work to be the framework for your research you are, necessarily, also choosing a particular research paradigm.

Finally, becoming what you are

There was an old sage (are there ever any young ones?) who said that who you are is the product of the people you hang around with and the books you read. While this might overplay the effect of environment on behaviour and identity, it is relevant for this discussion. Think of the people with whom you hang around as an undergraduate or graduate student and the books you read in the process. Hanging around within an honours or doctoral programme, reading what you must read, in some way or another influences the you that you become. Theorizing can reflexively make you a different person! You might become what you read.

In what follows, we engage in a conversation focusing on the research process that constituted Katie's PhD project. In this conversation, we are guided by a number of questions that relate to the process of inquiry more generally.

Katie's thesis

'Stop Playing Up! A critical ethnography of health, physical education and (sub) urban schooling'

Abstract

This thesis explores the place of health and physical education in the lives of Otara youth in New Zealand. Situated in the southern suburbs of New Zealand's largest city, Otara, South Auckland is known for its cultural diversity, as well as for poverty and crime. It is home to large numbers of indigenous Maori and migrant Pasifika (Pacific Island) youth. Based on a year-long critical ethnography of a multi-ethnic high school, this thesis explores how these young people engage with and respond to the school subjects of health and physical education. It also discusses broader issues in their lives, including the social geographies within which they reside, and how they understand their bodies, sexuality, health, gender and physicalities.

The subjects of health and physical education are compulsory in most schools internationally – in New Zealand they are directly linked in curriculum policy documents and in school practice – but share a somewhat uneasy relationship and differing historical positions. Considered low status in schools, these subjects are also conflated with narrow body and health norms, possibly problematic for young women, and/or are wedded to the social and cultural world of sport. Curriculum policy documents established in the last 10 years offer the possibility of critical and social approaches to these subjects, but examples of critical practice remain rare. Health and physical education are thus compulsory, contentious, contradictory and complex subjects within contemporary schooling.

Critical ethnographies of schooling are relatively scarce compared with conventional ethnographic accounts, but critical ethnographies of health and PE are almost unheard of. The use of such a methodology in this study enabled an in-depth account of Otara youth in the subjects of health and PE at school. It also provided a platform for storied accounts of how one teacher, Dan, enacted a critical and culturally connected pedagogy of health and PE with the young people in his classes.

This thesis explores the complex potential for health and PE as key sites of learning for Pasifika and Maori youth. It examines health and PE as subjects that are both politically fraught and spaces of hope.

Katie's research was informed by the critical paradigm. She drew heavily on the work of French sociologist Pierre Bourdieu as her interpretive framework – particularly Bourdieu's concepts of field, capital and habitus. In addition, Katie drew on the work of a number of scholars across such diverse fields as gender studies, critical race theory, youth studies, social geography and critical pedagogy. Methodologically, Katie drew on the work of scholars in critical ethnography and post-structuralism and engaged issues relating to method (how to do the research) and methodology (epistemological and reflexivity issues).

Richard: So, what did you want to know when you began the study?

Katie: I taught high school health and PE at low socio-economic, working-class, multi-ethnic schools in New Zealand. When I began my doctoral study, I wanted to find out more about the students at these schools, what they thought about and experienced in health and PE classes, and how their wider lives intersected with school and affected their life choices. My initial focus was fairly broad and I tried to be open to 'newness' and not let my assumptions and past experiences dictate what I looked for. I was, however, interested in understanding the social conditions that students dealt with day to day, and how inequities concerned with social class, racism, gender and sexuality were playing out for them. I wanted to know why so few young people from these communities ended up in professions or at university.

Richard: Why did you or do you think this is important to know?

Katie: As a high school teacher, I was concerned about how many students, particularly those from working-class and non-European backgrounds, dropped out of school or failed to fulfil their own aspirations about study and careers post school. National statistics in New Zealand show that youth from working-class, Maori and Pasifika backgrounds underachieve in education, drop out earlier and enter tertiary education in disproportionately low numbers compared with their European contemporaries. My teaching experiences alerted me to the social realities of students' lives, how so many things (poverty, working nights, family commitments etc.) got in the way of their educational achievement, but there was little research reporting the perspectives of the youth themselves. Committed to health and PE, I also wanted to ascertain if these subjects were reinforcing educational underachievement for these youth or challenging it, and I wanted to know what meaning it held for them.

Richard: How did you go about finding out what was already known about these issues?

Katie: This is an interesting question because there are many ways to attempt to 'know' about a problem/issue. The statistics tell a particular story about class and ethnicity patterns in relation to educational achievement in New Zealand. While these figures are overwhelming, they give no sense of the stories beneath them. With the statistics in mind, I read the work of researchers who aimed to explain and elucidate the relationships between class, ethnicity and educational success. Such studies in New Zealand focus on racism, cultural differences and class patterns, but few include youth perspectives and many ignore the unique aspects of particular localities/communities. While discussing class/ethnicity, this work also fails to comment on the intersection of these in relation to other issues such as gender/sexuality. I began to feel uncomfortable about how this literature positioned students in negative ways by focusing on their underachievement, at the expense of a more complex account of their lives and schooling. I wondered if there were different ways of looking at these young people in and beyond school.

Two bodies of research helped me to expand my thinking. The first was post-colonial writing. Put very simply, post-colonial writers refocus discussion on how individuals and communities speak back to their social positioning and resist colonial (and other) power relations. They highlight the importance of identity, particularly the complex interplay of identity positions, and seek to challenge essentialist and generalist accounts of marginalization. The second was post-structuralist and feminist writing in health, PE and sport. Both of these areas of research made me aware that there were different and more hopeful ways to view the youth in my study and, beyond that, many similarities between youth cultures in New Zealand and other globalized places.

Richard: What was actually do-able in terms of your study?

Katie: Well, I had to be realistic. I knew that I couldn't personally change the social statistics with one study and I knew that it was important to understand the social context first. I come from a Pakeha (European) background while the youth in my study are almost all Maori and Pasifika. Ensuring the research was do-able first meant forming relationships and trust. It would have been pointless for me to try to gain an understanding of the experiences of these young people if I hadn't first gained their trust and built ongoing relationships. I decided early on that gaining deep personal insights was what I wanted (rather than broad, sweeping generalizations) and I knew this would take time.

Richard: What ethical considerations did you need to consider?

Katie: Ethics was a key consideration for me. In line with a critical ethnographic approach, consideration of power issues and inequities extends to the research itself, including processes, representation and my relationship with participants. The ethical issues of this study are too many to discuss here, but I'll reflect on a few of the key concerns that I attended to throughout. First was my responsibility to the students and the school. Allowing a researcher to be in the school for an entire year required a large amount of trust. I needed to be aware constantly of respecting that trust and not reporting on aspects of the school that were outside the research brief and what the school had given me permission to do. This was a juggling act, as I didn't want to ignore important insights and experiences, but I needed (and wanted) to respect and protect the school (which was itself subject to marginalizing practices and school hierarchies). A second concern was my European/Pakeha background. Because of my different age, cultural background and ethnicity, there was potential for misinterpretation and miscommunication. I tried to be aware of own assumptions during the year and checked with students throughout the study about meanings. A third issue was anonymity. I planned from the beginning to use pseudonyms for students' names, but many of the young people insisted that I use their real names when writing up the study. I decided against this in the end because many of the young people had told me deeply personal stories, accounts of crime, and had discussed family members/ friends not involved in the study. The potential harm of revealing their stories outweighed their request for their names to be used.

In a general sense, I also thought through ethical concerns by relationship. Soyini Madison (2005) argues that relationships are central to ethnographic research. In forming reciprocal relationships with others, we are responsible to those people, their communities and, in this case, their school. Listening to their concerns, discussing ethical decisions with them and ensuring that they benefit from the research became part of the process.

Richard: What counted as evidence in answering your questions?

Katie: In ethnography, almost anything (within ethical bounds) counts as evidence because the researcher is immersed in the context and seeing, feeling, listening and being with the participants, and in the cultural space. Paul Willis describes an ethnographer's task as seeking to 'understand the social creativity of a culture' (Willis, 1977: 121). In order to attempt this, the researcher must attend to all the 'goings on'. While this is not possible, conversations, actions, movements, what is said and not said all matter. Evidence can be constructed more formally (interviews) and less formally (experiences, observations, conversations, note taking).

Richard: So what methods, strategies and techniques did you use to collect the data?

Katie: I don't like this question. As a result of my theoretical framework and ontological beliefs, I don't view data as 'collectable'. The word 'data' itself comes from a scientific perspective that assumes there are 'knowable' realities and that we can 'collect' evidence to prove this. In my study, the social relations between myself and the students within the school formed the research evidence/stories/writings. We made the 'data' rather than reported or collected them. Having said that, I did use particular methods or approaches to record and reflect on what was going on, what students said and did, and what I was experiencing. My central method was simply to be present in the school for extended periods of time (a whole year). This is a crucial part of any ethnography, getting deeply familiar with the context and forming relationships with people. I hung out in school all day, participated in health and PE classes and wrote down what I saw, felt, heard and thought (this is, of course, highly personal and subjective). I then set up what I termed 'research discussions' with groups of students from the classes I was part of and with whom I formed strong connections. These were like focus groups with varying numbers of students and a range of topics (relationships, friendships, racism, school, health and PE, what makes good teaching, drugs, gangs, the community, future aspirations ...). These continued two or three times per week all year with different student groups. At the end of the year, I conducted more structured interviews with some of the students and teachers I knew well. Throughout the year, I also kept a research journal in which I recorded class activities, conversations, thoughts, feelings and so on.

Richard: I take your point on not viewing data as 'collectable' in the sense that they are out there waiting for your collection. As you have said, you 'made' the data in and through the social relations you formed with the students. And yes, even the word 'data' has a particular positivistic loading. It fits better with some frameworks than others. What methods, strategies, techniques and theories did you use to analyse and understand the data?

Katie: This was a key concern. The study generated a large amount of empirical material from interviews, research conversations and note taking/journalling. Because these texts were cumulative (i.e., I worked with them over the whole year and earlier conversations influenced later ones), I was very familiar with them. I did all the transcribing myself and this helped me to 'know' it even better. The writing itself became a form of analysis because I used narrative to tell stories about the students' lives and experiences. Using many of their own words, I wrote storied accounts for many of the students, as well as for my experiences during classes and the school day. These stories, I then realized, were accounts of how issues of gender, sexuality, ethnicity, culture and school intersected in students' everyday experiences. I used these stories to highlight key issues (focusing more at one time on gender, another on class etc.) to show how these 'big picture' issues of inequity were realized in their lives. After a great deal of shifting around, I came up with chapter themes, each of which told a story about how students' experiences, perspectives and actions reflected, mingled with and/or resisted wider societal and political contexts. One chapter dealt with class and place, another with racialization in sport and PE, another with gender/sexuality in school, and so forth. I employed a range of theories and literature in each of these chapters to theorize and explain the stories, and relate them to other research. Drawing on theory helped me to unpack the experiences and student views, but it also helped me to reflect on how I generated the data – i.e., what I attended to and what influenced what I saw, heard and felt. The work of Pierre Bourdieu became central to the research analysis in addition to other post-structural, post-colonial and socio-geographic theories.

Richard: What about representation, how did you tell the story of your research?

Katie: This is linked to my last answer. The writing voice for me was inextricably linked to the analysis. I wanted to avoid a 'traditional' thesis format (literature review, methods, data, analysis, conclusion) so I wove the literature, analysis and evidence into each of the chapters. I used narrative to tell students' stories and record what happened during health and PE classes and I also used poetry. I was aware throughout the writing process of making my voice audible (i.e. being reflexive) without making me the research topic. I centralized students' voices and stories but tried to show how I was interpreting and theorizing their experiences and how my relationships with them affected the outcomes.

A final word

In this chapter, we have attempted to share with you some of our thinking about how research frameworks affect the research process. For Katie, there was an alignment between her view of the world, her political disposition, and her choice of theory and research methodology. The theories she engaged were compatible with her overall critical framework. Katie did exactly what Mats Alvesson (2002) recommended, that is, she used theories that she felt an emotional connection to and she developed a sophisticated understanding of them.

It is important to note that, even if you're not aware of it, you already have views of the world, assumptions about your research topic and prior experiences that are underpinning your approach. Attempting to 'excavate' or 'expose' those assumptions and challenge your thinking is the first step. As you read and write, try to position yourself and your work in relation to some of the theoretical terms and ways of thinking we mention above.

Key terms

Framework   'A basic conceptual structure'. A research framework is much more than a set of techniques for gathering data and analysing those data. It will represent a particular way of thinking about knowledge and reality.

Paradigm   A particular framework that orients and represents *ways of thinking*. In research, a paradigm provides the framework in which it is possible (and acceptable) to think about the research process.

Empirical research   Research that uses information gained through observation, experience or experimentation.

Empiricism   The belief that all knowledge must come from the experience of the senses and the senses only.

Ethnography   A research genre that is often employed for gathering empirical data on human societies and cultures. Its aim is to portray culture such that the reader can understand or make sense of human society and culture. Ethnographic methods are used across a range of different disciplines, primarily by anthropologists, but also frequently by sociologists and educational researchers.

References

Alvesson, M. (2002) *Postmodernism and Social Research*, Buckingham: Open University Press.

Kirk, D. and MacPhail, A. (2002) 'Teaching games for understanding and situated learning: Rethinking the Bunker–Thorpe model', *Journal of Teaching in Physical Education*, 21: 177–92.

Madison, D. S. (2005) *Critical Ethnography: Method, Ethics and Performance*, Thousand Oaks, CA: Sage.

Nicholson, B. (2010) 'Ghost-busting: Exposing the invisible hand of Vygotsky and Piaget within HPE's constructivist literature', paper presented at Australian Association for Research in Education Annual Conference, Melbourne, 30 November–4 December.

Siedentop, D. (1981) 'The Ohio State University supervision research program summary report', *Journal of Teaching in Physical Education* (introductory issue): 30–8.

Weinberg, R. and Gould, D. (1999) *Foundations of Sport and Exercise Psychology*, 2nd edn, Champaign, IL: Human Kinetics.

Willis, P. (1977) *Learning to Labor: How Working-Class Kids Get Working-Class Jobs*, New York: Columbia University Press.

Further reading

Gratton, C. and Jones, I. (2004) *Research Methods for Sport Studies*, London: Routledge.

Sparkes, A. (1992) 'The paradigms debate: An extended review and a celebration of difference', in A. Sparkes (ed.) *Research in Physical Education and Sport: Exploring Alternative Visions*, London: Falmer Press.

Wright, J. (ed.) (1997) *Researching in Physical and Health Education*, Wollongong, NSW: University of Wollongong.

6 Conducting ethical research

Jan Wright and Gabrielle O'Flynn

The Year 5 children erupted into the room with its strange machines and people. Fitness testing! Eyes alighted on scales, lung capacity tester [Vitalograph], exercise bikes, benches, and before teachers organized queues, the boys were blowing, poking, questioning, pushing. The girls tended to huddle, apprehensive, eyeing each other … Perhaps one was viewing them through pre-programmed eyes but most of the boys seemed boisterously competitive, while the girls were more hesitant, even anxious, with some reluctance to try hard … In no other test were the differences more noticeable that in the simple weighing of the children. The boys seemed either indifferent, with the odd self-conscious body-hugging from both the skinny and the really chubby, while most easily bounced on and sent the machine's arm swinging. The girls moved up in tight groups, and while one stepped on, the others gathered to read the result even before the tester.

(Burns, 1993: 78)

Introduction

This scenario was often repeated in nationwide fitness testing of children. It is less likely to be repeated now, and we invite you to consider why this is so. What are the ethical issues evident in this scenario? By the end of this chapter, it should be apparent that the practices in the opening scenario do not conform with key tenets of ethical research as they are currently conceived.

Over the last decade, there has been a growing awareness of, and discussion about, moral issues implicit in research. National governments and research institutions, including universities, have instituted in some cases legislation and in others a more voluntary system of guidelines for ethical research. For the new researcher (and often for the experienced researcher), these may seem onerous and possibly intrusive. However, there are always moral issues in human research; researchers intrude into people's lives, asking them to do things that, for the most part, they would not otherwise do; collecting information that that they might not otherwise give. With children and young people, this is even more the case. In this chapter, we will try both to assist new researchers to understand ethical research and to provide a guide to the various aspects of ethics applications. We will use 'stories' from our own and our colleagues' experiences to illustrate some of the dilemmas and strategies for managing the application process. The stories will, however, go beyond the technicalities prior to conducting the research to the ethical/moral dilemmas that can confront researchers while conducting their research.

About us

On what basis of experience do we write this chapter? Professor Jan Wright has been conducting research with young people in the area of physical education and physical activity for over 20 years. Dr Gabrielle O'Flynn completed her PhD on the place and meaning of health and physical activity in the lives of young women. Since completing her thesis, she has conducted health and physical activity research with young and older women. Jan's and Gabrielle's work has been informed by post-structuralist and other social theories that are concerned with the operation of power. This means that it is difficult to avoid thinking through issues of the power relations between participants and the researcher and the responsibilities that go with that. From this perspective, one of the first questions is: What are our responsibilities to our participants in relation to protecting them from harm? Harm can take many forms and in the kinds of research conducted in the area of physical activity, emotional harm as well as physical harm can be a very real risk.

What is ethical research?

If you are in the academic community, in most countries you cannot conduct research involving human subjects without meeting the requirements of a university ethics committee or research ethics board, which itself is usually subject to national or state guidelines. Research ethics boards have been established in institutions to manage the balance between the potential benefits and harms of research.

Applying for approval to ethics boards can seem onerous, but it can be very beneficial in helping researchers think through research choices, such as sample or participant selection, forms of data collection, and even the nature of interview and survey questions. Every researcher needs to identify the possible harms and potential benefits to participants and their organizations (for example, clubs and schools) of their research. This is about responsibility and rights. How these are interpreted is often a point of contention. Researchers and research students want to address a knowledge problem that they think is very important. However, to do so may mean collecting data from people who do not, or whose parents do not, share the researcher's point of view. Parents, for example, may see that their children's time completing a survey or participating in an interview is time out of class, time away from learning. They may regard some questions as intrusive, or see a topic as irrelevant or even harmful to their child. The task of the researcher is then to ensure that research will do no harm, and to convince the ethics committee and the participants that the research is worthwhile and will both have some benefit for them personally and contribute to the greater good. This can sometimes be a challenge. In the areas of health, education and sport, research is usually conducted to make a difference in the quality of children's and young people's lives. This more general benefit, however, may not be immediately obvious to participants.

Protocols and expectations vary from university to university and sometimes within universities, so it important to find and read the guidelines carefully for any particular institution. For example, in Canada, all research including undergraduate interviews for a term paper need to be scrutinized by the University Research Education Board (Haggerty, 2004). In the United States, ethical approval is sometimes contingent on completing training offered by the CITI Program (Collaborative Institutional Training Initiative; https://www.citiprogram.org/Default.asp?), a subscription service offered to affiliated institutions, which provides research ethics education.

When completing the ethics application form, it is often very useful to seek assistance from supervisors and from others who have gone through the process. The ethics application can be interpreted by ethics boards as an indication of the researcher's capacity to do the research, so it is worth taking care over the application and asking another person to read through it before submission, right down to the spelling. Templates for consent forms and information sheets are often available on institutional websites and again it can save considerable time if examples of completed ethics forms are available from those who have already gained approval for their research for similar projects. Further information about the meanings of sections of the application form is available below.

Conducting research in schools

Much of the research that involves children and young people, and much of the physical activity, will take place in school contexts. This poses an additional set of expectations in relation to ethics. Schools and school systems do not see their major purpose as providing a site for research. Some schools and some systems are much more accommodating than others, but all will want to see what the benefits of the research will be for their school, for their system, or for children and young people more generally. Schools and education systems will be particularly concerned that the research does not distract teachers and students from the main purpose of the school – that is, student learning. Some forms of research conducted in schools, such as case study research, also raise issues of reputation of schools or systems. Should the identities of the schools be revealed? The state system of education with which the authors are most familiar, for example, is very reluctant to support research that looks like it might compare schools from one system with another (e.g., the state with the Catholic or independent systems). In case study research, confidentiality is often very hard to guarantee when the rich context of the case study or the ethnography is important to the quality of the analysis. This will sometimes restrict the kind of research that can be done. In these cases, there are a number of strategies, including: a collaborative approach where the participants are more involved in planning the research and may also be involved in writing it up; ensuring that in the reporting of the research, individuals are not characterized in ways that would cause them harm; in instances where none of this can be avoided, a thesis may be withdrawn from public access for a stipulated amount of time.

Conducting research in schools can be a tricky road to negotiate. An example is provided in one of the case studies below and the following is an email response from an experienced classroom researcher (see Chapter 7) who was asked how he manages entry into schools:

> [D]ifferent school systems have different requirements for entry – but in most cases, personal contacts can expedite the process – viz. if you are a good citizen and have worked in the school before and have good relationships with the admin and teachers, you usually don't have much of an issue in the first instance … thereafter, it depends upon how intrusive your stuff is … as an example, many [schools] have issues with video, but less with direct observation.
>
> (Peter Hastie)

Gabrielle believes the intention in conducting research is always to improve the lives of children and young people. However, this intention does not always guarantee the absence of harm. It also does not guarantee that the community will share the benefits of the research, or perhaps the individual participants we want to involve in the project. As researchers, we need to consider putting ourselves in the shoes of potential participants and asking, 'What *effect* will participating in the research project have on my life, my learning, my anonymity and my sense of self?' In relation to schools, it involves asking, 'What *impact* will the research have on the school's daily business? What immediate *benefits* are there for the school or the students?' This reflection process should be part of the formal ethics approval process. It should also be a continuous part of *how* we research.

How to successfully seek approval for ethical research

The basis for the following section is the various application forms and guidelines from universities in the United Kingdom, the United States, Australia, Ireland and Scandinavia. They are very similar in what they require. This is because there are some widely agreed key concepts that always need to be attended to when conducting ethical research that protect participants and are indicative of the balance between benefit and harm. All university ethics applications ask questions about these key issues, and the success of an ethics application (i.e., having the application accepted first time round) is contingent on understanding what these concepts imply and how to address them in research planning. This means explaining your actions clearly and explicitly. As mentioned, while some of these requirements may seem onerous or obvious, there is a history as to why such questions are asked, a history in which research has not always respected the benefits and especially the potential harm to participants. One powerful illustration of this is described below under 'Informed consent'.

There are often several sections to an application form: one dealing with the researchers and their 'competence' to do the research; one about the research design; and another about the participants and their protection from harm. The section dealing with researchers is about the capacity of the researchers to undertake the research. This may seem strange in an ethics application, but committees need to be assured that participants will not have their time wasted in research that may not be completed or where the researchers do not have sufficient experience to conduct themselves responsibly. For research students, this often means that a supervisor may be expected to take responsibility for the ethical conduct of the research by being named as the chief investigator or principal researcher. Some applications ask for evidence of experience in conducting research. In this section, there may also be questions about funding sources.

The section about the research itself usually requires an explanation of the purpose of or rationale for the research and a description of the research design, including, in some cases, how the data will be analysed. This section can be a good opportunity for thinking through questions such as 'Why am I conducting this research? Who will benefit? What contribution do I make and to what or whom?' It can also be useful for thinking through why decisions have been made about the research design: why these people; why this method of data collection? While it may seem unnecessary for the research methodology to be scrutinized by a research ethics board, the quality of the research is part of the balance between harm and benefit for participants. As an example, the following rationale is provided in the guidelines from the ethics committee at the authors' university:

> In order to assess the ethical acceptability of a research proposal, the Human Research Ethics Committee needs to consider a number of features of the research methodology and procedures. These include:
> * whether the research question is one likely to advance understanding or knowledge;
> * whether the research methodology used to address the question is likely to achieve the stated aims;
> * whether the value of the research justifies the risks, discomforts, inconvenience or intrusion of privacy that may be experienced by research participants.
>
> (University of Wollongong, 2008: 8)

If the research involves 'specific communities', 'vulnerable populations' (children, adolescents, economic disadvantage, people with physical/intellectual disabilities), there is usually an expectation that there is a very good reason for the research to involve this group and that some additional care has been taken in planning the research. With some indigenous communities, such as Aboriginal people in Australia and Canada or Native Americans/First Nations people in the United States, there are national guidelines that must be addressed. Again an example from the authors' university:

> If the research involves specific communities, when describing the research design you should mention whether you have discussed (or will discuss) the proposal with members of the community and whether community members will be involved in oversight of the project – such discussions are required for research involving Aboriginal people and Torres Strait Islanders (see the NHMRC [2003] 'Values and ethics: guidelines for ethical conduct in Aboriginal and Torres Strait Islander health research'). It is also helpful to indicate whether some members of the research team have particular skills or experience which may make them

more sensitive to the ethical issues which may come up in the research, or better able to identify and respond to potential problems.

(University of Wollongong, 2008: 8)

In preparing an ethics application, researchers may be asked to detail the possible risks and benefits. Risks can include the risk of emotional upset because of sensitive questions (for example, questions which might ask about body image), discomfort if students are to be measured in any way, or the embarrassment of failing to complete particular physical tasks or skills, particularly in front of peers. This section offers the opportunity to think through possible harms and how these might be minimized. In some cases, if questions may cause emotional distress, it may be a requirement to have access to counselling or a debriefing process.

Confidentiality and anonymity

The protection of the privacy of the individuals (and sometimes institutions or organizations such as schools and sports clubs) is an important expectation in conducting research. That is, the identity of research participants or institutions will not be revealed – without explicit written approval. Babble (2010: 67) distinguishes between anonymity and confidentiality. He defines anonymity as the situation when not even the researcher knows the identity of the participants, as is the case in an anonymous survey. Confidentiality is then the non-disclosure of the participant's identity publicly.

In the collecting and processing of the data (for example, audiotape transcription, entering data into a statistical package), procedures must be in place so that the information provided by participants or collected about participants is protected. In the case of qualitative data, pseudonyms are usually assigned or chosen by participants. For quantitative data, numerical codes are often allocated to replace names. Researchers have been provided with information in a context of trust and it is important not to abuse that trust.

Confidentiality extends to how the research will be published and presented. As well as changing names of individuals and sites, other identifying information should be handled with care. Preserving confidentiality when the context of the study is important is not a straightforward issue; however, a rich description of the site – e.g., 'a large primary school in an inner-city neighbourhood with large immigrant population' – can often serve as well. If photographs are to be used in publications (including the thesis) or presentations, then written consent must be provided by the participants and their parents (if participants are categorized as children) and by all people in the photographs, whether or not they are participants in the research.

Informed consent

The requirement of informed consent is a concept which can be traced back to research that took no account of the rights of research participants. In the following quote, Haggerty (2004) describes how the atrocities conducted by German physicians in the name of 'science' prompted the drafting of a code that emphasized the importance of voluntary, informed consent from competent subjects:

> Contemporary concerns about research ethics would undoubtedly be quite different were it not for the almost incomprehensible cruelties of a group of German physicians in Nazi Germany. Drawing their 'research subjects' from the concentration camps, these physicians subjected Jews and Gypsies to 'experiments' that included immersing them in freezing water, and injecting them with poison, diseases, and even gasoline – in an effort to learn how the body responds to such extreme manipulations (Annas and Grodin, 1992). Twenty Nazi doctors were ultimately indicted for their actions, and appeared before the Nuremberg War Crimes Tribunal in 1946. This tribunal condemned the sheer barbarity of these experiments and repeatedly emphasized that the experiments were conducted without the consent of the participants. In an effort to establish the basic principles that must be adhered to in conducting research on human subjects the tribunal drafted the famous Nuremberg Code. The requirement that researchers must secure the consent of research subjects, and that this consent must be voluntary, competent, informed, and comprehending is the very first item on that code.
>
> (Haggerty, 2004: 404)

What does informed consent require of the researcher? Usually, ethical guidelines are quite explicit about what is required. The research will need to be explained to participants in terms that are understandable by the people being researched (and, for children, by their parents). In some cases, this may mean translating the information into the language spoken by the participants or their parents and also presenting it orally. The information provided to participants needs to include: the aim of the research; the methods used and what these require of the participants; the benefit and risks; the fact that the participation is voluntary and that the participants can withdraw from the research (and, if possible, withdraw their data from the research) at any time without negative consequences to themselves. This last requirement means that research needs to be planned from the beginning to take this contingency into account.

Working with children

Children are regarded as a particularly vulnerable population and there are usually specific expectations about how they need to be protected in the research context. For example, in some cases children are deemed not to be able to provide informed consent (the age of consent varies from country to country) and so parents or guardians must provide consent. The capacity of children to provide consent is debated in the literature and researchers committed to participant child research argue that children should be involved in the project and are quite capable of providing informed consent. If children are to be full participants in the research, it is a good idea to fully inform them of the nature of the project and ask them to sign a consent form if they are willing to participate, even when only parental consent is required by the institution.

There are a number of other issues when conducting research with children, such as protection legislation. In most countries, researchers are expected to report on any cases of abuse and neglect. In some countries, researchers are required to submit to police checks before conducting research with children. The following list from Loughborough University on instances when a criminal check will be required is indicative also of the kinds of situations in which extra care is needed when researching with children:

a.   Investigators with unsupervised access to child participants (i.e., if an investigator is likely to be alone in a room with one or more children/young people).
b.   Taking physical measurements from child participants.
c.   Requirement for child participants to remove any clothing.
d.   Recording child participants on video.
e.   Testing of new equipment.
f.   If requested by the sponsor of the research.
       (http://www.lboro.ac.uk/admin/committees/ethical/gn/wwccop.htm)

Researchers should organize their data collection so that they are not out of sight of others when collecting data from children. However, there may be instances for the child's privacy when this needs to be the case.

Case studies

This section of the chapter presents three case studies. The purpose of each is to examine the ethics process – both in relation to formal ethics approval and as a continuous part of *how* we research. As defined in this chapter, ethics relates to reducing harm and making explicit the benefits of the research. Harm relates to direct injury (physical or psychological). It also relates to the *impact* the research process may have on an individual's life or sense of self, and on a school's core business, including the time and expectations involved in participating.

Each case study is an example of research in the areas of health, education and sport which has been conducted in the context of schools. In examining the ethics process, each case study presents possible situations (or dilemmas) that might occur for researchers in the fields of physical activity or physical education. Each highlights particular ethical conundrums, with the intention to offer some insight into how such dilemmas might be overcome or worked through.

As a starting point, the first case study examines Lou's experience. For Lou, the formal ethics approval process was quite seamless and smooth. Once he received the tick that he had completed the formal 'ethics training', and that his research was 'non-invasive', he seemed to have no trouble undertaking his physical education research in schools. To facilitate Lou's smooth ethics process, most of the university faculties he was employed in had developed reciprocal relationships with local schools. Consequently, he did not always need to seek approval from state education bodies; and in some cases, parents' general consent for their child's participation in research by the university was received at the commencement of the school year, resulting in Lou not needing direct parental consent.

Many researchers do not have access to the same university and school relationships as Lou. This means that in addition to acquiring formal ethics approval from an affiliated university, approval from state or district education bodies – such as the district department of education or, in Australia, religious education offices – is also required. This may mean more uncertainty about how and when the research can be conducted.

Case study 1

Working in schools: when things run smoothly

Lou's research involved working in schools to examine the affective and social domains of physical education lessons. His experience with conducting research within higher education spanned multiple universities in the USA. At each of the universities, it was required that all lead researchers complete some type of ethics training, which was commonly online. In addition, each university had a standard ethics application process that was completed and reviewed by a committee. Most of Lou's work was defined as 'exempt' and 'non-invasive'. The process was therefore quick and involved few points of clarification from the review panel.

Once ethics was approved, it was time to obtain consent from all participants and begin the collection of data. For Lou, informed consent was conducted in two ways. The first was the need for school board and sometimes school district approval. Once this was granted, Lou was allowed to gain consent from the students and teachers who were part of the study. This sometimes required consent from parents or guardians for underage students. The second process to obtain consent involved the school, and parents/guardians providing consent at the beginning of the year; this basically stated that research could be conducted with students as long as the university had given approval.

What does Lou's story tell us? It is not the 'horror' ethics story that we might expect. His story demonstrates that it is advantageous to have good relationships with schools already set up through the university. However, it is worth noting that such relationships sometimes have their own disadvantages. While Lou could access schools easily, it did not mean that he could undertake the research that he always intended. This is described in Lou's comment:

> As an untenured junior faculty member, I [wanted to conduct] research that could be turned over in a quick and efficient manner. [This] focused much of my research attention on the development of exempt projects with schools that had university partnerships. This in turn caused a dilemma between what I would term high-quality research (which could be non-exempt and longitudinal) and feasible research to keep your job.

The added layer of applying for approval from state education or district bodies is, for many, just a hoop to jump through. The process can be quite seamless, especially if one's research supports the department's broader agenda, aims and perspectives. But what if your research challenges the department's policies and practices? And what if, unlike Lou, you do not have access to established university–school relationships? Many researchers working from a sociocultural perspective may fall into this category. The next case study examines this dilemma. It is an example of when research challenges, or runs counter to current policy. What is interesting here is the way in which Rob navigates the situation. He wants to do his research, but it may not take the shape that he had originally intended.

Case study 2

Working in schools: when things run not so smoothly

Rob's research involved examining 'curriculum change' in health and physical education (HPE). He worked with teachers to develop and implement units of work based on a new syllabus document. For Rob, getting approval from a state education authority was challenging. While he had no trouble with the feedback from the university ethics review, one of the problems with the state education body was that he had to wait over two months to receive a response. As part of this process, Rob thought it would make him look 'organized' and 'thorough' if he submitted a draft of the unit plan he would be using in his work with teachers. It had taken considerable time and effort to develop a plan that emphasized and would achieve his research purpose. However, according to the state education ethics review, his unit did not reflect 'best practice' in programming, did not 'reflect the main messages' promoted in planning the rollout of the new syllabus, and contained 'busy work' and activities that didn't 'explicitly link with the outcomes of the syllabus'.

At the time, Rob recalls thinking:

> Had the curriculum officer really taken to my application with a red pen like it was an assignment that she wasn't impressed with? None of the ethics bodies had any concerns about my information sheets, or the justification for the research, or the plans for disseminating the findings. Was it really within their jurisdiction to decide whether my reading of the syllabus was legitimate? And how long would it take to turn all of this around? Would my PhD timeline be irreparably damaged?

How did Rob resolve this situation? Basically, he more or less complied with all of the requests for changes to the draft unit plan. This was partly because he desperately needed to get the approval to continue his research without damaging his PhD timeline. It was also because he felt that it was not negotiable – he had to accept the changes or risk not undertaking his research. Rob went on to adopt the changes and conduct his research. The process became part of his interpretation and analysis of the context of curriculum change in HPE for a successful PhD. On reflection, his story demonstrates the difficulty of conducting research that challenges the status quo. It demonstrates how various stakeholders can interpret research in schools so very differently – interpretations that are not just related to the research method, but also to the application of the syllabus and learning materials designed. From the state education body's perspective, students' learning and time must explicitly relate to the syllabus. This presents a possible challenge for research that pushes the boundaries of a 'syllabus' and endeavours to promote innovation.

Our final case study examines a situation when the 'ethical' issues emerged throughout the process of the research. Here, Gabrielle describes experiences she faced when conducting her PhD research on the place and meaning of health and physical activity in the lives of young women.

Case study 3

Talking with young women: interviewing or intervening?

Interestingly, the ethics application process for my PhD was quite straightforward. From memory, there were no major concerns or misunderstandings. Approved with a tick, I set out to recruit and talk with young women about health and physical activity in a longitudinal project. So why I am writing this story? What is there to learn? Well, this tick of approval didn't guarantee that 'ethical' conundrums would not emerge. It seemed that the more the 14 young women talked about health and physical activity, the more uncomfortable I felt about the whole process. Here I was, interview after interview, providing a context for the young women to examine their bodies, selves and lives in relation to the very problematic notions of health and thinness I set out to analyse. For example, one young woman regularly asked me 'How do you stay so thin?' and others would point to and grab the parts of their bodies (tummies, arms and thighs) which they wanted to 'tone up'. Was I producing a context for the young women to scrutinize their bodies? And what about the production of guilt and dissatisfaction with their bodies? I know I was feeling guilty for intervening into their lives! And then there were the tensions around writing about the young women from a critical perspective. As I wrote about them I couldn't help wonder how they would feel if they read my critical representation and reading of their talk.

These may seem like minor 'ethical' conundrums. At the time, however, they were extremely important to how I experienced the research process. I was deeply concerned about the impact the interview process had on the young women's sense of selves and their bodies.

So how would I deal with this in future research? As a starting point, I would consider the balance between the potential harm and benefit of the research. I would weigh up the important understandings and knowledge gained in talking with young women about their bodies and health. On reflection, I think I would ask the 'why' question more often. I would probe the young women to think about why they feel their bodies are too fat, flabby or in need of toning. This could open up the possibility for the young women to reflect on their own meanings and understandings of their bodies.

In terms of writing about the young women, an obvious starting point is to maintain confidentiality through the use of pseudonyms and removal of identifiable information. But what about harm that could be done if a participant read the interpretation of her talk? To overcome this, there are ways of representing participants' talk that remove the focus from specific individuals. These include the use of plays, narratives and stories or composite fictions (Richardson, 2000). Such approaches are useful in reducing the harm in writing about an individual, especially when writing from a critical approach that uses case studies and longitudinal research. Some researchers may criticize such methods of representation, saying that these are not 'authentic' representations; however, as has been argued for many years by quantitative researchers, stories and narrative representations provide the advantage of allowing us to highlight themes across the data. They also provide the opportunity for us to read our own lives against narratives and to reflect on the ways particular discourses operate in our own lives.

Conclusion

Meeting all of the requirements of research ethics committees may at times seem burdensome. These requirements, however, have evolved to protect participants, and particularly participants who may be vulnerable. In the past, researchers have not always taken on their moral responsibility and have perhaps been motivated rather too much by their own desire to increase knowledge or enhance their own research record. Ensuring that research benefits are maximized and research risks are minimized and managed is an integral part of becoming a morally responsible researcher. It is important to include sufficient time to plan ethically appropriate research and to have research approved by institutional ethics committees and boards. Carefully reading guidelines and using the experience of colleagues and peers can help avoid a lengthy process of rejection and revisions. However, as Gabrielle's example points out, our moral obligations to ethical issues do not stop with institutional ethics requirements. Researchers need to be constantly alert to how participants respond to data collection and to anticipate any possible harms, emotional, social and physical.

In returning to the opening scenario, what was contraindicated ethically? In our view, it was ethically questionable that the children were weighed publicly and in a manner in which they could read and comment on the measurements of other children. There is also a question for us about the need to weigh children and, if they need to be weighed, how they are provided with information about their weight. These are issues of emotional harm and moral responsibility for the welfare of the children being tested.

Key terms

Confidentiality   The purposeful non-disclosure of the participant's or school's identity or personal information in any public documents, including journal articles, book chapters, books, theses or websites.

Benefits and harm/risks   These relate to the balance between the advantages of the research for the wider community, with the potential risks of harm to the participants. Harms can range from the basic incursion on the individual's or school's time and daily routines, to physical or psychological duress to participants.

Informed consent   Involves the researcher providing accessible and user-friendly information about the research project to the participants. It involves the researcher acquiring signed consent from each participant acknowledging that they have read and understand the information provided. The information provided should clearly communicate the purpose of the project, the methods used and what is required of the participant, the benefit and risks, that participation is voluntary, that participants are free to withdraw from the project at any time without penalty, and how the results of the project will be used.

Morally responsible research   Refers to the purposeful and mindful approach of a researcher to consider and reduce the potential risks of harm to participants. Such considerations should take place during all stages of the research project, including during the research design, implementation and publication.

References

Annas, G. and Grodin, M. (eds.) (1992) *The Nazi doctors and the Nuremberg Code: Human rights in human experimentation*. New York: Oxford.

Babble, E. R. (2010) *The Practice of Social Research*, 12th edn, Belmont, CA: Wadsworth, Cengage Learning.

Burns, R. (1993) 'Health fitness and female subjectivity: what is happening to school health and physical education', in L. Yates (ed.) *Feminism and Education* (78–94), Melbourne: La Trobe University Press.

Haggerty, K. D. (2004) 'Ethics creep: Governing social science research in the name of ethics', *Qualitative Sociology*, 27(4): 391–414.

National Health and Medical Research Council (2003) 'Values and ethics: Guidelines for ethical conduct in Aboriginal and Torres Strait Islander health research', <http://www.nhmrc.gov.au/publications/synopses/e52syn.htm> (accessed 22 October 2010).

Richardson, L. (2000) 'Writing: A method of inquiry', in N. K. Denzin and Y. S. Lincoln (eds) *Handbook of Qualitative Research* (923–49), 2nd edn, Thousand Oaks, CA: Sage.

University of Wollongong (2008) 'Guidelines for completing the initial application for approval to undertake research involving human participants', <http://www.uow.edu.au/research/rso/ethics/UOW009383.html> (accessed 22 October 2010).

7 Qualitative approaches

Peter Hastie and Peter Hay

Before when we went to physical education classes, they, Sergei, Anatoliy, Sasha, Pavel and some other boys, would usually grab and have all the balls and are playing by the time when we are done changing in the dressing rooms. When we come in we just end up sitting here on the benches. Sometimes we listen to music on the cell phones but mostly we talk to each other. Only few of us end up playing at all.

(Sinelnikov and Hastie, 2008)

Introduction

The scenario presented above might seem at first glance just a story from some Russian girls about how they don't really enjoy physical education. However, a closer look presents a number of different questions that might be asked. First, why are the boys first to class? Why don't the girls participate when they do eventually arrive? What do students perceive the purpose of physical education to be? And where is the teacher in all this discussion?

If we view research as a method of problem solving, then Viktoria's quote has provided us with a beginning springboard from which to dive into the intricacies, micropolitics, and social meanings of Russian physical education. To achieve a quality result, however, we need specific tools, to understand the beliefs, values, feelings, and motivations that underlie behaviours and their consequences. Qualitative research allows for these understandings because it is particularly focused towards the complex, messy and at times unpredictable contributions to and outcomes of social interactions. This requires a form of inquiry that recognizes this complexity and involves the interpretation of multiple, integrated sources of information. The purpose of this chapter, then, is to describe and explain the mechanisms of doing qualitative research in order to best make sense of the social realities of interest.

About us

Peter Hastie is a professor in the Department of Kinesiology at Auburn University in the USA. His research focuses on two particular lines of inquiry, both of which are particularly amenable to qualitative research methods. In sport education research,

Peter has used qualitative research extensively in order to gather primary data from teachers and students about their experiences of participating in sport 'seasons'. In research on classroom ecologies, extensive use of field notes and interviews were used to understand the detailed processes through which teachers and students negotiate physical education lessons and activities. In both these examples, the challenge facing any researcher is to find innovative and robust approaches to research that are true to the data and that also lead to compelling narratives for readers who may wish to use the findings in the context of their own practice.

Peter Hay is a lecturer in pedagogy in the Department of Human Movement Studies at the University of Queensland, Australia. He was a secondary school teacher in health and physical education (HPE) before returning to university to teach and to undertake his PhD. Peter's research, which is mainly qualitative in nature, is in the areas of curriculum and assessment policies, practices and technologies in HPE and education more broadly. Additionally, he seeks to understand both the manner in which students' abilities are constructed in different educational contexts and the implications for students' engagement in learning. Peter would identify key challenges in qualitative research as collecting, analysing and presenting data that accurately and coherently capture the complexities of agency and structure – and their interplay – in health and physical education contexts.

Qualitative research: What is it, what can it do, what can't it do, and when could I use it?

According to Patton (2002), qualitative research is a process of inquiry that seeks to understand phenomena in real-world settings where the researcher does not attempt to manipulate the phenomenon of interest. Qualitative researchers take a naturalistic approach to the subject matter because they focus on the ways in which people make sense of their experiences and the world in which they live (Denzin and Lincoln, 2005). In particular, qualitative research is an *interpretive* form of social inquiry that attempts to understand phenomena through accessing the meanings that participants assign to them.

Qualitative research therefore differs from *quantitative* research, which attempts to gather data by objective methods in order to provide information about relations, comparisons and predictions, without 'contamination' by the investigator. While it is quite possible and often desirable for qualitative and quantitative researchers to work in the same setting and on the same broad problems, they will nonetheless be asking different types of questions. Historically, these differences were presented in terms of one approach 'versus' the other, leading to vitriolic debates between proponents of each methodology (for good examples, see the first sections of the text by Miles and Huberman, 1984). More recently, there has been growing evidence of compromise and a realization that there is room – indeed a need – for both forms of inquiry. Essentially, neither 'good' research nor 'poor' research is confined to either side of the divide. Instead, and particularly in the absence of adequate training, there are examples of poor research in both paradigms (Denzin and Lincoln, 2005). As noted in Chapter 1 of this book, it is the research question that should determine which research approach is most appropriate.

Patton (2002) defined the task of qualitative research as an effort to understand situations in their uniqueness, as part of a particular context, and the interactions that happen in that context. In the worlds of physical education and sport, such contexts include pupils in schools, student teachers in their physical education teacher education programmes, teachers of physical education in schools, players, coaches and parents in youth sport and adult participants in community and performance sport.

While qualitative research can come in many forms, all qualitative research studies share some key characteristics. First, in all modes of qualitative research, the researcher is the primary instrument for data collection and analysis. Second, research in this genre often involves fieldwork; that is, the researcher goes to people at their site of practice in order to observe behaviour in its natural setting. Third, qualitative research uses inductive research strategies; rather than testing existing theories, this research serves to build abstractions, concepts, hypotheses or theories. Fourth, qualitative research offers rich description of the phenomena under investigation.

In general, qualitative researchers spend their time in ways that are very different from those of researchers working in more quantitative paradigms. For example, qualitative researchers:

- often spend extensive time in the settings that they study (this is known as *fieldwork*);
- generally rely on themselves as the main instrument of data collection (which presents issues of *subjectivity*);
- employ expressive language and use 'voice' – of both themselves and the participants – in presenting descriptions and explanations of findings (hence they need to be proficient writers);
- conduct an ongoing analysis of the data (rather than conducting analysis only towards the end of the research);
- are judged as researchers in the criteria of believability, trustworthiness and the internal logic of their interpretations.

Qualitative research is particularly useful when seeking to understand people's beliefs, values, feelings and motivations. It is particularly useful, therefore, for describing and/or answering questions about the perspectives of the groups under study; for example, on occurrences, contexts, events or practices in their natural settings. Perhaps for this reason, qualitative research has been described as a set of methods that illuminate the 'invisibility of everyday life' (Erickson, 1986: 121). There are examples of research projects that use a range of qualitative techniques in this book: for example, case studies (Chapter 16) and action research (Chapter 19). The important point to note is that the range of options is very broad. Ethnography, for example, is a long-term investigation of a group (often a culture) that is based on immersion and, optimally, participation in that group (see Chapter 5). Narrative inquiry is the process of gathering information for the purpose of research through storytelling (some examples can be found in Chapter 18) and phenomenology is concerned with understanding the 'lifeworlds' of groups or individuals (see Husserl, 1970: 127).

Qualitative research in physical education and sport

Physical education and sport are inherently social activities. As sites of social interaction, marked by relationships, institutional expectations, unique learning contexts and different engagement modes, physical education and sport settings provide challenging and complex sites for investigation. Qualitative research methodologies offer generative tools for understanding and explaining these sociocultural complexities. The rich and multifaceted contexts of physical education can be understood through different *theoretical perspectives*. These perspectives not only influence the research focus, but also impact upon the qualitative methods to be used and data analysis procedures (Macdonald et al., 2002). For example, researchers operating within a 'positivist perspective' may employ systematic observations and structured interviews to ascertain causal relationships between certain teaching or pedagogical strategies and student learning behaviours. In contrast, research within a 'post-structural' paradigm may draw on participant observations and semi-structured interviews to understand the influences of discursive resources and power relationships on students' opportunities for participation and recognition in physical education.

Given the centrality of the researcher in the process of qualitative research, it is essential to recognize, acknowledge and account for the influence of the researcher's personal values, beliefs and experiences on the research process and its outcomes. Such an understanding is described as researcher 'reflexivity' and is a very strong feature of socially critical, post-structural and feminist research. Reflexivity involves consideration and, in some instances, articulation of researchers' values, beliefs, investments and life experiences and the potential influence of these on the collection and interpretation of data and in communicating research findings. Given the centrality of the researcher in the qualitative research process, this form of critical reflection and engagement is an essential step in ensuring that findings, conclusions and recommendations are transparent, allowing research audiences to understand how conclusions have been derived. Remember, the researcher is 'present' to some extent in all forms of research. In qualitative research, however, this presence is built into the research process in explicit ways.

Doing the fieldwork

When designing a qualitative research project, there are five practical steps to be considered in planning the fieldwork: (i) gaining entry to the research setting; (ii) contacting and selecting participants; (iii) collecting the data; (iv) enhancing validity and reducing bias; and (v) leaving the setting.

Gaining entry

Qualitative research is typically done in real-life settings (e.g., schools, sports fields or teachers' staff rooms), and the researcher is the primary instrument of data collection. This means that negotiating access to the research setting is a fundamental requirement. This may require extensive negotiation (and often some compromise) with the various gatekeepers to these settings (e.g., school principals and school boards, local authorities, parents, coaches and coaching authorities). Decisions about whether to support or deny access requests can be at least partially dependent on personal characteristics and the ways in which the researcher is perceived by gatekeepers. It is important to remember that access to a research site is not a right, and that potential research participants are busy with their own lives. Gaining participants' permission to conduct research can therefore be a protracted process. Trust is something that is earned, not simply given, and being a good citizen within the research setting is critical.

Contacting and selecting participants

The goal of participant selection in qualitative research is to ensure the deepest possible understanding of the person, issue or setting being studied. As a consequence, this often requires the identification of specific participants, rather than a random sample. In some cases, such as a study of a particular physical education class, the participants might include all those involved in the setting at a given time (teacher, pupils etc.). Likewise, in a coaching setting, the coach, assistant coaches, support staff and players may all be recruited to a study. In other cases, purposive *sampling* is employed, where certain participants are selected because they have specific characteristics linked to the research question. Examples of purposive sampling in the field of sport pedagogy might include: specific extreme or deviant cases (such as outstanding sport successes, notable sport failures, highly active students or very inactive students), or criterion cases, which means selecting all cases that meet a particular criterion (such as low-skilled girls or children who are rarely selected to play on a sports team).

A question often asked is how a qualitative researcher can be confident that there are sufficient numbers of participants for a study. Two indicators are relevant here. The first is the extent to which the selected participants represent the *range* of potential participants in the research setting. This can be determined before embarking upon data collection. The second indicator is more difficult, and can only be determined as the study progresses. Glaser and Strauss (1967) use the term *data saturation* to indicate the point when the collection of new data does not shed any further light on the issue under investigation; that is, the point when you probably don't need to recruit any more participants. However, it should be noted that the notion of data saturation is challengeable in regard to being too easily and superficially claimed. Consequently, rather than claiming there are no more purposeful data, we might be better to state that our ability to interpret any new possible meanings on the topic has been mostly exhausted.

Collecting the data

The two predominant forms of data collection in qualitative research are interviews and observation. Interviews are particularly useful in qualitative research because, as Weiss (1994) notes, they give us access to the views of others through what he terms a virtual window on a particular experience. Weiss suggests that 'through interviewing we can learn about places we have not been and could not go and about settings in which we have not lived' (p. 1). Interviews are not, however, only about gathering data in the form of simple recollections about people, places and events. Instead, some types of interview allow us to obtain in-depth data about participants' thoughts, feelings and activities within the context under investigation.

Observation

With respect to observation, the term most commonly used in qualitative research is *naturalistic observation*, because the process involves observing participants in their natural habitats in the context of the research (classroom, sports club, training ground etc.). Observation can be undertaken with the researcher as a participant or non-participant in the activity or setting being observed. Observations may be *covert* where the participants do not know they are being observed or, more commonly in physical education and youth sport, *overt*, meaning that the participants are aware they are being observed. In both cases ethical clearance is required to conduct the investigation.

When conducting observations, the researcher will record descriptive as well as reflective notes about personal thoughts on what was seen, heard and experienced during the session. These notes are referred to as *field notes*, and should be written up as soon as possible following the observation. It is critical that field notes include the date, site, time and topic on every set of notes. They should also be formatted to have wide margins for the purposes of the analysis that will follow and, where appropriate, should include drawings or diagrams (such as the location of players during a practice).

Interviews

When planning for interviews, a researcher has to reconcile two key questions. The first is whether to conduct interviews with individual participants or with groups (sometimes called focus groups). The advantage of group interviews is that they provide for direct evidence about similarities and differences in the participants' opinions and experiences. At the same time, they provide less depth and detail about the opinions and experiences of any single participant. The advantages of individual interviews are that they allow for close communication between the interviewer and the participant. The interviewer in this case is also able to control the direction of the interview. In this way, it is possible to obtain concentrated amounts of data on precisely the topic of interest (Morgan, 1997). However, in some cases (especially with young people), we have found that group interviews are preferable because of the social support peers provide to each other during an interview and the development of a positive attitude toward interviews because the students were accompanied by their friends.

With respect to the number of people being interviewed, this will be determined by the research question, the type of interview selected and the size of the project. A large, funded project with a team of researchers will obviously allow for greater numbers of interviews. It is important to remember that it is not necessary in group interviews for the group to reach any kind of consensus; nor is it necessary for everyone to disagree. One of the key advantages of group interviews is that they can be time efficient for both the researcher and the participants.

The second question is whether to use fixed-item, structured interviews or less structured approaches in which the interviewer has degrees of freedom to take the interview in different directions as determined by the responses of the participants. The fixed-item style is most useful when looking for very specific information, as it keeps the data concise and reduces researcher bias. Structured interviews are best used when you are investigating a topic that is very personal to the participant. If you wish to find as much information as possible about your topic, the less structured interview is the preferred option. Take note, however, that the data sets of less structured interviews are much larger than those with structured interviews, and so are more demanding to analyse.

There is a range of different questioning techniques, depending on the degree of structure required and whether it is necessary for all participants to answer exactly the same questions. Structured interviews (where each participant is presented with exactly the same questions in the same order) are most suitable for studies where the goal is to compare/contrast participant responses to a specific event or situation. The list of questions and their order is called an *interview schedule*. Unlike the structured interview, semi-structured or unstructured interviews begin with more general questions or topics. In addition, while some questions may be designed and phrased ahead of time, many of them are created during the interview in response to the participant's emerging responses.

Regardless of the number of interviews to be conducted, or the degree of openness in the interview questions, there are a number of rules that all interviewers should follow. Table 7.1 includes some important dos and don'ts about interviewing.

Table 7.1 Some important dos and don'ts when interviewing

Do	Don't
Follow up on answers that are not clear and ask for clarification, as this facility is one of the key advantages of an interview.	Use leading questions that are phrased in such a way as to suggest desired responses.
Listen more and talk less.	Interrupt unnecessarily (unless the responses are moving totally off topic).
Be tolerant of silence – give your participant time to think.	Be judgemental about or react to opinions or responses unless your engagement in a two-way conversation is a feature of the research design.
Note your impressions of the participant's non-verbal behaviour.	Make unwarranted assumptions about non-verbal behaviour.

Other sources of data

Aside from observations and interviews, there are a number of other sources of information that can prove to be invaluable data for a qualitative researcher. All forms of documents, such as official records, letters, newspaper accounts, diaries, portfolios and reports can be analysed. Indeed, many research projects in physical education have used teacher and student diaries as rich sources of data. One specific form of document is the interactive journal, which is a log book in which participants are asked to make comments about particularly meaningful events or interactions that have occurred in the context being studied: for example, a physical education lesson or a coaching session. In physical education research, interactive journals can serve as a comfortable medium for students to express thoughts and ideas that may not otherwise have been expressed during group discussions or interviews (Oliver, 1999). In these journals, students make entries after each lesson outside class time and, importantly (and what makes the journal interactive), the researcher collects and reads them, and then makes notes or writes questions in the journals for students to address. This format allows for an ongoing dialogue between the participants and the researcher and has been used to good effect in studies where students are experiencing new approaches to physical education such as sport education (e.g., Sinelnikov and Hastie, 2008) or one focused on girls' bodies and physical activity (Oliver and Lalik, 2004).

Critical incidents

Aside from diaries and interactive journals, another procedure used to investigate those features of a particular context that participants find significant or important is the critical incidents technique. Most commonly, participants are asked to complete two tasks. The first is to write about 'one thing that happened during your lesson/practice/match today that you found important. It may have been important because it made you excited, made you bored, made you worried, or because it was something you learned that was really new' (see O'Sullivan and Tsangaridou, 1992). The second task is to try to explain *why* the incident described was important.

Drawings

One qualitative technique used increasingly to explore the lived experiences of children is that of drawings. In this technique, the participants are provided with the means to draw – paper and coloured pencils or electronic equipment – and are then given a broad, yet focused task. As an example, in the study by Mowling, Brock and Hastie (2006), the students were given the following instructions: 'I want you to think of soccer and draw whatever comes into your head.' The general tenet is that children tend to depict in their drawings what they know about the stimulus. That is, they tend to grab hold of the aspects most important to them in certain situations. It has been argued that in interviews, children and young people might give responses that they feel the interviewer wishes to hear, whereas drawings assist their verbal communication by creating a more comfortable environment and providing a personal template from which to speak. This last point implies that participants are asked to comment on their drawings and, indeed, this is a vital stage in the process. Whenever drawings are used as a research tool, it is critical (consider it a requirement) that students are interviewed about their drawings to elicit their descriptions and interpretations of the people, places and events taking place.

Enhancing validity and reducing bias

In all forms of research, reliability and validity are critical concerns. While there is some debate as to whether these two terms are as appropriate for qualitative research as they are for quantitative research, the intent is the same. Remember, reliability relates to the extent to which the results of a study could be reproduced using the same methods, while validity is the extent to which the research succeeds in measuring that which it was intended to measure. It has been argued that in qualitative research more appropriate terms to describe these issues are *credibility*, *dependability*, *transferability*, and *confirmability* (Lincoln and Guba, 1985).

Credibility relates to the extent to which the data are an accurate representation of the context. In qualitative research, there are two threats to credibility. The first occurs when the researcher brings some *preset interpretations* to the study and imposes them upon it. Bias is impossible to eliminate – indeed, a researcher's personal beliefs and values are reflected not only in the choice of methodology and interpretation of findings, but also in the choice of a research topic. Nonetheless, if your study is being driven by *what you want to know*, rather than by *what you already know*, then you are starting from a position of acknowledgement that multiple perspectives/ interpretations are possible. The second threat to credibility is researcher effect, which results from the impact of the researcher's participation on the setting or those being studied. This threat can be managed by developing a good rapport with participants, developing less obtrusive observations and spending time in the field, thereby reducing the 'novelty' effect.

The technique known as *triangulation* can also be used to promote the credibility of qualitative research. Triangulation refers to the use of several different methodologies (such as observations, interviews and document analysis) to address one question. This approach has a number of advantages. For example, if only one method is used, there is a strong temptation to believe in the findings and this may result in the researcher drawing unwarranted conclusions (see Chapter 9 in this book). On the other hand, two or more methods may result in data that offer different perspectives on the same issue, which, at the very least, will avoid the tendency to jump to premature conclusions and may result in some congruence in the data. In essence, triangulation means that the use of different methods in concert compensates for their individual limitations.

Dependability requires that a researcher accounts for the ever-changing context within which research occurs. Consequently, a qualitative research paper should describe not only the changes that occurred in the setting, but also how these changes affected the ways in which the researcher approached the study.

In terms of *transferability*, a qualitative research paper needs to include a thorough description of the context, as well as the assumptions that were central to the research.

In this case, the reader who wishes to 'transfer' the results to a different context is then responsible for making the judgement about whether such transfer is appropriate. A paper by Oliver and Lalik (2004) provides one example of research in physical education that discusses these issues.

Confirmability (otherwise known as trustworthiness) refers to the degree to which the research results and interpretations can be corroborated by others. To enhance trustworthiness, a qualitative research report or paper must include descriptions of the ways in which the researcher checked and rechecked the data throughout the study. It is also good practice to include examples of negative cases that contradict the main findings.

Leaving the setting

One important question that is unique to qualitative research is when the researcher should leave the site of data collection. This question arises because the collection and analysis of the data are often concurrent, and also because in research conducted over periods of time, bonds formed with study participants may complicate the leaving process. This is a particular issue in some long-term ethnographies (see *Writing the new ethnography* by Lloyd Goodall, 2000). In some cases, while time constraints associated with a project (e.g. when writing a thesis) may dictate the time of departure, a more appropriate time is when you have a sufficient amount of accessible data. That is, if you come to a point where further observation or interviews (or indeed any other forms of data collection) are not adding to the findings or are repeating what was already found in the previous efforts, you can consider you have reached the point of data saturation and can legitimately leave the setting.

An illustrative qualitative research project

Title

'Evidence for the social construction of ability in physical education' (Hay and Macdonald, 2010).

Purpose

This research was provoked by the conceptual and theoretical musings of John Evans (2004), who had critiqued traditional and contemporary understandings of pupils' 'inherent ability' in physical education and offered an alternative 'social construction' perspective. Evans suggested that the embodied dispositions of a person (what they looked like, how they behaved, what they believed etc.) could be perceived by others as abilities when 'defined relationally with reference to values, attitudes and mores prevailing within a discursive field' (2004: 100). He observed that a person's identification as 'able' served as a form of cultural capital that could be traded for other capitals such as high achievement grades in a subject.

The purpose of this research was to examine the empirical veracity of this perspective and to understand the social, interpersonal and personal factors that might be involved in the construction of students' abilities. Additionally, the researchers sought to understand the effects of this potential construction process on different students in terms of their understanding and awareness of their own abilities and their engagement in physical education as a course of study in upper level secondary school (ages 16–18, which shall be referred to here as 'senior physical education').

Theoretical perspective

John Evans's proposition was based in a certain theoretical perspective. He was rejecting meritocratic assumptions of inherent abilities and drawing attention to the privileging and marginalizing consequences of ability recognition for children and young people in physical education. In this regard, his conceptualization of socially constructed abilities was informed by a *socially critical theoretical perspective*. As such, the research endeavour was similarly informed by this theoretical perspective. A critical perspective focuses on problems of social inequity and injustice produced through practices of social control. It thus focuses on power relationships and assumes the disproportionate access of individuals, groups and communities to resources within social contexts (Macdonald et al., 2002). Consistent with these theoretical assumptions the following research questions framed the project.

- How are abilities 'socially constructed' in senior physical education?
- What factors (in social fields and in relation to individuals' possession of physical, cultural and social resources) are involved in the construction process?
- What impact does the construction process have on the students' perceptions of themselves and their engagement in the learning context of senior physical education?

Consistent with the broad critical perspective orienting this research, French sociologist Pierre Bourdieu's theoretical concepts of field, habitus and capital (e.g., Bourdieu, 1990) were used to aid in the analysis of the data and articulation of the processes of interest.

In any research endeavour (qualitative or quantitative) a particular theory can prove to be helpful for framing the research design, informing data analysis and communicating the findings. Over-reliance on a specific theory can be problematic, however, where the theory constrains the possible interpretations of collected data, or even where certain possible interpretations of collected data are overlooked or dismissed because of their inconsistency with the theoretical status quo.

Participant recruitment

The process of participant recruitment was an important element of the research design. The research contexts were two demographically distinct schools – one a low socio-economic government school and the other an 'elite' co-educational private school.

Six Year 11 students (Year 11 being the penultimate year of schooling in Queensland) were identified by the senior physical education teacher in each school in three broad and loosely defined ability categories: high, middle and low. The teachers were not provided with an explanation of the ability categories (nor was it requested by them) and were asked to select an even number of male and female students. The identified students were invited to participate in the project, unaware that their selection had been made on the basis of the teacher's perceptions of their abilities.

Methods

A text analysis of the Queensland senior physical education syllabus was conducted to ascertain the 'official' curriculum and assessment expectations of the subject and the official expectations of student engagement and performance in senior physical education. This provided a reference point for the prevalence and influence of other factors (such as the teacher's own beliefs and school-specific cultures) on the context in which students' abilities were being constructed. The text analysis involved a structural overview of the syllabus; description of the key foundations of the subject; content and assessment expectations; and identification of official ability discourses.

Semi-structured interviews with teachers and students – and, where possible, parents – were conducted at five specific junctures across two consecutive senior physical education units (each unit is about 10 weeks in length) in relation to the school's physical education curriculum and assessment plan. The semi-structured interviews were focused on three broad lines of inquiry: socio-biographical information; contextual experiences; and perceptions of self and others. The first juncture questions for each participant were the same. The subsequent four interviews were structured by three levels:

1   Questions that all participants were to answer, providing some common reference points for comparative analyses of perceptions, beliefs and expectations of the participants within and across the two contexts;
2   Questions specific to each particular participant, generated following the previous interviews (including the responses of other participants) and informed by the weekly participant observations;
3   Latitude for questions arising during the interviews in order to pursue a particular line of inquiry deemed significant at the time.

The interviews were recorded using a digital audio recorder, transcribed in full and then given to each participant to confirm their accuracy and meaning.

Participant observations of one lesson per week at each context were undertaken according to the observation protocols of Sarantakos (1998). Observations focused particularly on the extent and nature of the interactions between teachers and students, the assessment processes employed by the teachers (as indicated by them) and the interaction between student participants and other students in the class. Observations were not made on the same days each week, to ensure that the interactions between teachers and students were observed in a variety of contexts. The observations were first recorded as 'jotted' field notes and then 'direct observation' notes (Neuman, 2003), compiled immediately following the observation period. The notes were ordered chronologically and served as a detailed description of what was seen, heard and noted in the field.

In consideration of the credibility of the research, efforts were made to negotiate the observer effects and biases of the methods. In the first instance, this meant that the researcher spent concentrated time in the two classes in order to foster a productive rapport with the participants and to gradually become less conspicuous to them. The value of these endeavours was evident in the extensive – indeed effusive – responses by participants in the later interviews. The triangulation of data provided by the use of text analysis, semi-structured interviews and participant observations was the primary regulator of observer effects. In this regard, the inherent limitations of each individual method (such as teacher-biased explanations about assessment approaches) were somewhat mitigated by the other methods (the official assessment requirements of the syllabus, and the observed assessment practices of the teachers).

Analysis

The data were coded with the assistance of NVivo, a qualitative analysis software package. During this process, the interview transcripts and observation notes were examined line by line through open coding. Coding refers to the classification of research data into categories or themes. Gibbs (2002) describes this process as 'identifying and recording one or more discrete passages of text or other data items that, in some sense, exemplify the same theoretical or descriptive idea' (p. 57). This process was *informed* by the principles of a constructivist version of grounded theory (Charmaz, 2003), an approach that 'assumes the relativism of multiple social realities, recognizes the mutual creation of knowledge by the viewer and the viewed, and aims toward interpretive understandings of subjects' meaning' (p. 250). The coded data were analysed in relation to ability categorization, vertical differentiations of fields, structuring elements of fields and participant dispositions.

The socially critical perspective through which these aspects of physical education practice were examined was sensitive to the factors involved in individual constructions of ability and the varying degrees of power individual students possessed within the contexts of their senior physical education experiences. The implications of each ability construction in terms of the students' perceptions of themselves, engagement in the field and understanding of futures were captured and communicated in a manner that might not have been possible through other research perspectives or endeavours.

Trustworthiness of the data collection and analysis techniques was promoted through member checking and external reviews. Member checking involved sending the raw interview transcripts to each participant so that they could check the accuracy of the transcript and make any response clarifications they deemed necessary. External reviews involved providing researchers external to the project with excerpts of interview transcripts, applied coding characteristics and associated analysis comments, to allow them to reflect upon and corroborate (or otherwise) the appropriateness of the analyses and interpretations.

Outcomes and implications

The research findings provided evidence in support of Evans's (2004) 'social construction' of ability proposition. Students' abilities were observable as a complex construction dependent on the constitution of the field of physical education practice (e.g., expected physical education practices, the teacher's values, beliefs and expectations, the dispositions and relational connections of the other students) and the students' possession of valued physical, cultural and social resources (which Bourdieu described as 'capital'). Within this construction process, high-ability students were privileged in terms of learning and achievement possibilities, while low-ability students were marginalized in terms of access to contexts in which valued resources might be acquired and/or displayed, resulting in their enduring low-ability identification.

The findings offered an alternative perspective to prevailing notions of ability and challenge educators to reconsider how the potential of students in and beyond physical education is viewed. For example, abilities may be reconceived or recognized differently through changes in teacher beliefs and expectations, changes in assessment practices and curricula content, or through increasing students' access to the resources important to the recognition of ability in senior physical education.

To assist others to understand, interpret and 'transfer' the results and implications of the research to different contexts, the reporting and dissemination of the research featured rich explanations of the context in which the research was conducted, as well as overt statements accounting for the theoretical perspectives and methodologies foundational to the design, implementation and analysis of the research. Finally, Bourdieu's social theory was used to draw connections between the site-specific outcomes of the research and general processes involved in the social construction of abilities.

Conclusions

Qualitative research is about exploring issues, understanding phenomena and answering particular types of research questions. Qualitative research techniques are used to gain insight into people's attitudes, behaviours, value systems, concerns, motivations, aspirations, culture or lifestyles. While interviews and field notes are the most common data collection techniques in qualitative research, other sources may include interview transcripts, open-ended survey responses, emails, notes, feedback forms, photos and videos. The nature of qualitative research means that, compared with quantitative research, datasets tend to be less structured – more messy – and this means that data analysis techniques are also different (see Chapter 23).

Key terms

Researcher as the primary instrument   In contrast to quantitative methods where the intent of the researcher is to be removed from investigation, in qualitative research it is the investigator who is responsible for analyzing and interpreting data into credible findings in order make sense of the phenomenon under study.

Interviews and observations The two most common forms of data collection in qualitative research.

Fieldwork A general term given to the collection of primary data or information which is conducted in situ.

Natural or real-world settings The places where the phenomenon under investigation is occurring naturally; removing participants from their setting could lead to contrived findings that are out of context.

Interpretive research Research in which the meaning-making practices of the human participants are at the centre of the investigation, and where the researcher does not start with concepts determined a priori but rather seeks to allow these to develop from various interactions with those participants.

References

Bourdieu, P. (1990) *Sociology in question*, Cambridge: Polity Press.

Charmaz, K. (2003) 'Grounded theory: Objectivist and constructivist methods', in N. K. Denzin and Y. S. Lincoln (eds) *Strategies of qualitative inquiry* (249–91), Thousand Oaks, CA: Sage.

Denzin, N. K. and Lincoln, Y. S. (2005) *The SAGE handbook of qualitative research*, Thousand Oaks, CA: Sage.

Erickson, F. (1986) 'Qualitative methods in research on teaching', in M. C. Wittrock (ed.) *Handbook of research on teaching* (119–61), New York: Macmillan.

Evans, J. (2004) 'Making a difference? Education and "ability" in physical education', *European Physical Education Review*, 10(1): 95–108.

Gibbs, G. R. (2002) *Qualitative data analysis: explorations with NVivo*, Buckingham: Open University Press.

Glaser, B. and Strauss, A. (1967) *The discovery of grounded theory: Strategies for qualitative research*, New York: Aldine Publishing Company.

Goodall, H. L. (2000) *Writing the new ethnography*, Lanham, MD: AltaMira Press.

Hay, P. and Macdonald, D. (2010) 'Evidence for the social construction of ability in physical education', *Sport, Education and Society*, 15(1): 1–18.

Husserl, E. (1970) *The crisis of European sciences and transcendental phenomenology*, Chicago: Northwestern University Press.

Lincoln, Y. S and Guba, E. G. (1985) *Naturalistic inquiry*, Newbury Park, CA: Sage.

Macdonald, D., Kirk, D., Metzler, M., Nilges, L. M., Schempp, P. and Wright, J. (2002) 'It's all very well, in theory: theoretical perspectives and their applications in contemporary pedagogical research', *Quest*, 54(2): 133–56.

Miles, M. B. and Huberman, M. (1984) *Qualitative data analysis: A source book for new methods*, Thousand Oaks, CA: Sage.

Morgan, D. L. (1997) *Focus groups as qualitative research*, Thousand Oaks, CA: Sage.

Mowling, C. M., Brock, S. J. and Hastie, P. A. (2006) 'Fourth-grade students' drawing interpretations of a sport education soccer unit', *Journal of Teaching in Physical Education*, 25: 9–35.

Neuman, W. L. (2003) *Social research methods*, Boston: Pearson Education.

Oliver, K. L. (1999) 'Adolescent girls' body narratives: Learning to desire and create a "fashionable" image" ', *Teachers College Record*, 101: 220–46.

Oliver, K. L. and Lalik, R. (2004) 'Critical inquiry on the body in girls' physical education classes: a critical post-structural perspective', *Journal of Teaching in Physical Education*, 23: 162–95.

O'Sullivan, M. and Tsangaridou, N. (1992) 'What undergraduate physical education majors learn during a field experience', *Research Quarterly for Exercise and Sport*, 63: 381–92.

Patton, M. Q. (2002) *Qualitative evaluation and research methods* (3rd edn), Thousand Oaks, CA: Sage.

Sarantakos, S. (1998) *Social research*, South Yarra: Macmillan.

Sinelnikov, O. A. and Hastie, P. A. (2008) 'Teaching sport education to Russian students: An ecological analysis', *European Physical Education Review*, 14: 203–22.

Weiss, R. S. (1994) *Learning from strangers: The art and method of qualitative interview studies*, New York: Free Press.

Further reading

Resources for qualitative research: <http://www.qualitativeresearch.uga.edu/QualPage/index.html>

Qualitative research methods: A data collector's field guide, available from: <http://www.fhi.org/en/rh/pubs/booksreports/qrm_datacoll.htm>

8   Quantitative approaches

Beverley Hale and Dudley Graham

I'm a third year and I've got my data. What do I do with them?

Introduction

Many students have asked this question as part of a tutorial with one of the research methods and statistics team at our university. If they have to ask such questions, it may be already too late for them to conduct the best possible quantitative research.

About us

This chapter is co-authored by two lecturers in research methods and statistics.

Dudley Graham is a senior lecturer at the University of Chichester, teaching undergraduate research methods modules across a variety of sports science degree programmes. His role includes the supervision of undergraduate projects in the different fields within sports sciences. A key issue that Dudley has to deal with throughout his modules is students' ability to plan a logical research design to answer research questions. His own research interests lie within the field of sports biomechanics, focusing on cricket.

Dr Beverley Hale is an applied statistician who has been teaching research methods and statistics on sport and health-related degree programmes for many years. In a recent research project, Beverley found that understanding the relationship between methods of data collection, data analysis and how to interpret the results in order to discuss the key research question is a recurring difficulty for sports students. If you have these concerns, this chapter will help you decide whether your draft research questions can be investigated adequately through a quantitative approach.

While we focus here on methods of quantitative data collection, Chapter 24 will assist with decisions about the appropriate statistical analyses to make sense of data. It is important that the analysis procedures are considered as part of the research design, so there will be some reference to statistical analysis in this chapter, together with links to Chapter 24.

Why use quantitative methods?

Quantitative methods commonly address questions that relate to performance levels, teaching or coaching methods – anything, in fact, that can be measured or coded into numbers. An advantage of the quantitative approach is that large amounts of data can be summarized to provide a broad picture of a particular situation. Various graphs and descriptive statistics enable large volumes of data to be summarized so that patterns can be identified.

The questions below have a specific focus, and could be investigated through quantitative methods.

- Can a revised training programme decrease 100 m sprint times?
- Is there evidence that exercise before mathematics tests improves pupils' test marks?
- Is there a relationship between anxiety and performance in cricket?

Some of the words in these questions need careful definition before a research design can be finalized. A closer look at the questions reveals that the first two have defined measurements that should be collected – finish times in 100 m races and marks from mathematics tests. The final question is harder to pin down. For example, what kinds of measures would be indicative of 'performance' (once the meaning has been defined)? These research questions are developed in a later section of the chapter to demonstrate how to handle such difficulties.

Two common types of quantitative research are experiments and questionnaire-based studies. Experimental designs include control of the environment so that it is possible to link cause and effect. No other research design includes sufficient controls to be able to show causal relationship. Problems can arise with experimental research that does not control the environment adequately, so published studies need to be scrutinized thoroughly before any claims to causal links can be accepted.

Questionnaire research does not have the controls in place that are attributed to experimental work. Questionnaires provide a cross-sectional 'snapshot' of a group of people at a given time. For example, a questionnaire could be constructed to provide feedback for teachers on how a particular guest speaker was received by their pupils. In these circumstances, the questions have a very limited focus, apply to a once-only event and what needs to be asked is quite clear. Most questionnaires contain closed questions that require the respondents to fit themselves into predetermined categories by ticking boxes.

Research questions that require predictions of future outcomes (such as the prediction of marathon run times from times in 10 km training runs) or an evaluation of difference conditions (for example, cycling time trial times at sea level and at high altitude) require quantitative methods. Statistical procedures to evaluate the strength of relationships or the size of group differences can be applied in specific circumstances and are explained in Chapter 24. It is sometimes possible to make general statements about a larger group, or population, based on the statistical findings from a particular sample, but only if suitable sampling has been undertaken.

With the exception of single-subject designs, quantitative approaches do not allow for individuality, because the procedures absorb the individual into a group. If a research question requires the evaluation of individual experiences or opinions, then quantification of data may cause loss of information that could compromise the value of any findings.

The most important point to extract from this initial introduction is the degree of careful thought that is required to design a research project. Time spent planning is rarely wasted, and researchers should allow time to consider all the factors that could affect their work. The identification of any necessary control or manipulation of these factors is important for the production of trustworthy research. Despite a carefully considered research design and protocol, there might still be problems with the method. A pilot study (a type of dry run) is an excellent way to detect problems and ensure that everything works as intended.

Planning a quantitative study

Research terminology is important. Use of quantitative methods is often linked to a scientific approach, with the requirement of precise, concise communication. The interrelationship of research design, protocol and method is crucial for trustworthy research. Methodology can be viewed as the science of method. It is the philosophical perspective of the researcher, declared as a system of methods for gathering data. A mixed methodology suggests a researcher who has interwoven qualitative and quantitative methods in some way (see Chapter 9). The research design is the way in which particular methods have been selected and ordered so that a specific research question can be answered, and is governed by the methodology. The application of the particular research methods and the stages through which the participants will progress in order to generate the required data are known as the 'protocol' in some fields of sports research, although other fields prefer the term 'research method' to cover both the particular method and how it is applied.

Relationship between research questions and possible quantitative methods

Consider the research questions you wrote in response to the introductory chapter. Which ones lend themselves to the collection of measurement, or require you to compare responses from different groups of people, or seek to find relationship, or develop a causal link? Any of these situations suggests that quantitative methods would be appropriate. It is very important to begin with a clearly defined question as it identifies what is necessary to illuminate and evaluate the situation. The selection of research methods must be influenced by the question, and not the other way round. 'I'm not good at statistics so I want to do qualitative research' – or vice versa – does not give rise to a good research design. Be aware that although a 'research question' has been posed, it is unlikely that a definitive answer will be found. At best, the research will provide *an* answer, but it is likely to reveal more questions as well.

The research methods should ensure the collection of reliable and valid data; that is, the data must measure what is required to shed light on the research question, and the methods should gather those measurements in a way that could be repeated if necessary. So, for example, to investigate the third question posed earlier in this chapter (Is there a relationship between anxiety and performance in cricket?), it is imperative to justify the reason for the research and to reach a decision about appropriate definitions of anxiety and performance, articulate the definitions clearly in a method, and adhere to those measurements throughout the piece of research.

Cricketers waiting to start a match are often subject to anxiety before they play. A coach's role is to help the players harness anxiety so that they are able to play their best. Anxiety is a psychological construct that needs to be carefully defined. It cannot be measured with a simple instrument like a tape measure. Various questionnaires have been developed to assess both the type and intensity of a sportsperson's anxiety, and a suitable choice would need to be made from those available. Measurement of performance could be a count of the number of runs that batsmen score, or wickets for bowlers. If there is a relationship between anxiety and performance it must not be interpreted to infer causation, as there are numerous confounding variables, including other players, which could affect the chosen measures of performance but cannot be quantified as part of the research design.

The importance of sampling

It is important with quantitative approaches that the sample used is representative of the population of interest, because the aim of much quantitative research is to conduct statistical analysis in order to generalize from the sample to the population. There is widespread belief that the best sample is a random sample, but this is rarely possible or desirable for physical education (PE) and sport research. To obtain a truly random sample, the names of everyone in the population of interest must be available because each individual should have an equal chance of selection through a process equivalent to pulling names from a hat. This is possible in a school or club setting, but is unlikely to be achievable with less specific populations, for example, female competitive gymnasts. A further drawback of random sampling is that it is unlikely to lead to a representative sample unless the sample size is very large.

A common approach in sport-related research is to use a volunteer or a convenience sample. Such samples will almost certainly not be representative of a population, and may lead to inappropriate conclusions. It is vital to read papers critically, to evaluate whether the conclusions are defensible, and likewise to consider whether a volunteer sample is adequate for any intended research. Representation of a particular population is often better achieved through purposive or stratified samples. Further discussion of sampling methods applicable to PE and sport can be found in Thomas, Nelson and Silverman (2005).

Experimental designs

Experimental research designs require controls so that the effects of independent variable(s) upon the dependent variable are isolated. The *independent variable* is *manipulated to affect the dependent variable* if you are looking to test for cause and effect. The *dependent variable is what is measured to identify the anticipated effect*, and its scores are therefore dependent upon, or predicted from the independent variable. For example, to determine the effect of a revised training programme on 100 m sprint times (our first research question posed earlier) the runners' sprint times form the dependent variable. The training programme (original or revised) is the independent variable, because we think running speed *depends* on the training regime. It is important not to change the runners' diets or the type of running shoe they use at the same time as revising the training programme; to do so would mask any training effects.

There are two main types of experimental designs: the repeated measures design and the independent groups design. Within both designs, there are at least two conditions in the independent variable that have potentially differing effects on the dependent variable.

The most efficient use of a sample is to repeatedly measure the same participants by using them in all the experimental conditions. This approach evaluates change within the same group of people and helps remove the issue of individual differences between participants' abilities; the change within each person is analysed to seek differences between the conditions. The effects of the treatments in the independent variable need to be reversible for there to be the opportunity to collect data from both conditions. The effect of different boot designs on downhill slalom skiing speed could be examined by a repeated measures design.

A repeated measures design is inapplicable if permanent changes occur in the participants' characteristics, either physically or mentally, as a result of experimentation. For example, competitive participants have a tendency to improve their performance simply by completing a task twice. The effect of different boot designs on downhill slalom skiing speed could be masked as skiers become familiar with the slalom course and adopt a strategy to improve their speed. Any improvement in speed might be the result of a learning effect rather than a change in boot design.

If a learning, or order, effect is possible, an experimental design may attempt to counterbalance the effects and distribute them across both conditions. The most common method is a crossover design. In the skiing example, that would mean that half the participants use boot design A and then boot design B, while the other half uses design B followed by design A. In Figure 8.1, Condition a illustrates the simple cross-over design while Condition b shows a three-condition crossover design. Another way to control for learning effects is to try to eliminate them completely through sufficient familiarization with the testing procedure before the first condition to minimize additional learning between experimental tests.

Condition a			Condition b			
Group 1	A	B	Group 1	A	B	C
Group 2	B	A	Group 2	B	C	A
			Group 3	C	A	B

Figure 8.1 Condition a: simple crossover design; Condition b: three-group crossover design

Independent group designs are used when a researcher wishes to compare (at least) two mutually exclusive groups, or if the effects of the independent variable are irreversible. The most obvious example of this is the assessment of difference between the sexes. The strength of this design is that there can be no learning or order effects because participants are measured only once. The most critical weakness is that there may be many unknown differences between the sample groups that could obscure the effect of interest.

Irreversible effects, for example the use of nutritional supplements to increase muscle mass, render participants permanently changed or at least altered for the time frame of the research project. In these cases, a more complex research design needs to be adopted to isolate the effects of the independent variable. One approach is to include a control group. Participants in the experimental group are measured before and after the course of supplementation and the control participants are measured at the same times, but without the supplementation in between. The dependent variable is the change in the participants' muscle mass from before to after the experiment.

It is important that the control group is as similar as possible to the experimental group before the participants are exposed to the experimental treatment. A large sample size makes the groups more representative of the wider population, and therefore more likely to be similar. A viable alternative for sport-related research, where sample sizes are usually small, is to allocate participants to groups in a way that increases the likelihood of similarity. Assessment of the participants during familiarization trials, or within initial baseline measurement, makes it possible to systematically assign them to groups using what is known as the ABBA method. Following baseline measurements, participants are ranked in order according to their scores: the first participant is assigned to group A, the second and third participants are assigned to group B, the fourth participant to group A, and so on until all participants are assigned.

Knowledge of the group to which they have been assigned can affect participants' behaviour and influence the outcome of an experiment. Decreased motivation to complete experimental tasks with the required effort can result if participants know that they have been assigned to a control group. To avoid this, a single blind placebo design could be used. Participants are not informed of the group to which they have been assigned and both groups experience a treatment or intervention. (This is known as single blind. If the person conducting the experiment, perhaps a research assistant, does not know either, then the procedure is known as double blind.) It is important that the placebo appears as similar as possible in every characteristic to the full experimental process, but that it does not have any effect on the dependent variable; for example, a sugar pill that looks exactly like the nutritional supplement administered to an experimental group.

In the discussion about experimental designs we mentioned potential problems, or errors. A systematic error is something that is not controlled within the design, sample or method, but consistently skews the results of the experiment. It potentially reduces the validity and reliability of the study. An example of this is a poorly calibrated speed gun which consistently overestimates throwing velocity by 3 mph. Systematic errors can be corrected if identified, because the level of reliability is high, but the level of precision is low. Random errors occur by chance because the measurement process is insufficiently precise. An example of this is the use of stopwatches to time races, where the operator might press the stop button a fraction too early or too late. A more reliable measurement of time can be obtained from light timing gates, which use a light beam to start and stop a timing clock. However, there is still potential for random error as some participants may break the beam with their hands while others might break it with their bodies.

Physical education and youth sports research requires much of the work to be conducted in the field. Working within the athletes' natural environment helps to increase the ecological validity of the research, but reduces the ability to control the environment. Ecological validity is a measure of how much the experiment approximates the real-life situations under investigation. The greater the degree of control you apply to your experiment, the more you reduce ecological validity. Field and Hole (2010) provide further guidance for experimental design that helps to address the issues highlighted in this section.

Questionnaires

Psychological research, where variables cannot be directly measured, lends itself to questionnaire-based methods. The process of questionnaire development requires careful planning because it is hard to determine precisely which questions to ask. If the proposed research requires the development of a specific questionnaire, then allow time for piloting and initial validation. Several iterations of the questions will be necessary to guarantee that the data provided in response will be sufficient to meet the aims of the research. There must be confidence in the data collected if meaningful conclusions are to be drawn. Wording of the questions has to be such that they are accessible to everyone within the intended population, and they need to be piloted to check this. Each question must address one issue only. Questions that use a connective word, such as 'and', often include two ideas, lack clarity and cause the respondent to answer only half of the question. Consider the clarity of the following questions to see what we mean:

- At what age did you start to play football seriously?
- When did you start to play serious football, and what caused you to do so?

Gillham (2000), Munn and Drever (1999) and Foddy (1995) are helpful texts for questionnaire design, and how to order the questions. Oppenheim (2000) provides clear assistance with the reliability and validity of questions.

Questionnaires that have been validated as suitable for measuring psychological factors are available to the PE and sports communities. For example, the BREQ-2 measures exercise regulation (Markland and Tobin, 2004; questionnaire available online) and could be used to compare motivations to exercise between active and sedentary adolescents. The credibility attached to previously validated questionnaires is advantageous because research can proceed with confidence to build on existing knowledge. It is vital that those intending to use such questionnaires check the literature and familiarize themselves with the validation procedures and the contexts (for example, age groups or specific sports communities) in which the questionnaire is considered valid. Further validation is necessary before a well-respected questionnaire about motivations for exercise in adults can be used to research school pupils' motivations to exercise. If modifications are required to make the transfer to a different context, then revalidation of the modified questionnaire is important.

Questions that require a respondent to tick a box, or several boxes, to indicate categories that apply to them are known as 'closed questions' because the individuals completing the questionnaire have no option to choose their own responses. Responses to closed questions are coded for quantitative analysis. It is important to remember that coded data are not truly numeric, and that statistical analysis tools are limited. Chapter 24 provides an explanation of how different types of data limit analysis procedures.

The main problem with questionnaire research is that the response rate is usually low (less than 30 per cent). The preparation for questionnaire research must consider sampling and how to keep respondent numbers as high as possible.

Case studies

Can a revised training programme decrease 100 m sprint times?

Prior to the revision of a training programme, coaches must assess the athletes' baseline performance, before any changes are made. Field tests, using race times from 100 m sprints before and after the revision of the programme, could be compared to evaluate any changes in race times. This approach would provide ecological validity because the stresses and strategies that accompany competitions would affect the data collected. The ability to attribute any decrease in sprint time to the revised training programme would be compromised due to a lack of controls to the environment. An additional investigation of changes to technique as a result of the alterations to the training programme would enable further evaluation of the effects of the programme, but would require more controlled conditions. An assessment of running gait could be undertaken on an athletics track, but without the presence of other competitors or spectators, in order to avoid obstruction of recording equipment. This limited development of what appears to be a relatively simple research question illustrates how both experimental and field research would be applicable. Often complex research designs are required to answer what appear to be relatively simple research questions.

Is there evidence that exercise before a mathematics test improves pupils' marks?

'Wake Up! Shake Up!' (Mitchell, 2002) concluded that activity early in the morning increases primary school pupils' concentration. To investigate whether findings from published research can be applied to mathematics lessons in a particular secondary school setting the following study was designed.

Initially, it was proposed to design a study that compared mathematics test marks of two independent groups of pupils, one group who had a PE lesson first thing in the morning and a group who did not have PE. A class was identified who had PE first thing in the morning on one day a week, but there was a problem finding a comparable group. This second group needed to be in the same year, and attend the same classes with the same teachers. The pupils needed to be of the same ability so that it was possible to isolate the effect of early morning PE on test marks. Working within the constraints of a timetabled secondary school meant that the researchers were unable to change classes around to ensure that all pupils in the experiment were taught by the same teachers. The researchers returned to the drawing board.

The potential positive effect of PE first thing in the morning would not remain with the pupil to affect the next testing day, so it was decided that each pupil could act as their own control, through the use of a crossover design. Sometimes pupils would have PE before a mathematics lesson, and sometimes they would not. Data would be collected under both situations, on days of the week when morning mathematics lessons were preceded by PE and when they were not.

Despite being in different groups for specific lessons, each pupil consistently attended the same classes on the chosen day of the week throughout the term. This situation meant that the same teachers would be in contact with the pupil on each testing day, although all the children were not taught by the same teachers, except for mathematics. As the study was designed to look at changes within individual children rather than a comparison between different pupils, the lack of consistency of teachers was deemed less important (although undoubtedly this point could be argued).

A series of mathematics progress tests were used as the dependent variable. The mathematics teacher agreed to plan half the tests for days when mathematics followed a PE lesson, and half for days when mathematics was at a similar time, but there was no PE. The mean test marks for PE days were compared with mean marks from tests when there was no PE in order to determine whether exercise improved mathematics marks. In addition, the Strengths and Difficulties Questionnaire (SDQ, available from www.sdqinfo.org) was used to get an indication of the pupils' behaviour, hyperactivity and social skills in lessons following PE and those without PE. The inclusion of this questionnaire enabled data about pupils' behaviour and social integration to be included in the study. These variables were selected following a decision that academic achievement was an important facet of learning, but not the only one.

Twelve- to 14-year-old pupils were sampled because they had already been in secondary school for at least a year. The selection of this age group limited the applicability of findings, but ensured that each child in the class followed the same diet of subjects across the school day. These pupils were below the age of consent, which gave rise to a variety of ethical consideration, including the need for parental consent. (Ethical issues relating to research are considered in Chapter 6.)

The research design included repeated measurement of mathematics marks and SDQ subscales, therefore statistical procedures needed to pair data to allow for comparisons of change within each pupil. Choice of statistics was influenced by the statistical levels of quantitative data that were collected. This case study is revisited in

Chapter 24 to explore the implications of design, sample and data collection on the data analysis and interpretation of results.

Key points from the chapter

Research design and research method should be selected to ensure the collection of data that are both valid and reliable for the research question(s) posed.

The importance of sampling must not be underestimated. The sample affects the results and conclusions drawn from quantitative research, and impinges on the interpretations and generalizations that can be inferred from the results.

Experimental research requires careful planning. The role of experimental research is to isolate effects and evaluate causal links. Poor control of the environment or injudicious selection of variables can mask potential effects. Conversely, it is possible to 'over control' and design an experiment that is certain to confirm a theory because the potential to behave any other way has been removed: a biased experiment.

Questionnaire research is prone to validity issues. Preparation of questions and testing for reliability and validity are vital parts of the development process; upon them rest the success or failure of the piece of research.

Key terms

Experiment   A quantitative research design using tight controls so that cause and effect can be determined.

Questionnaire   A document containing a series of limited-response questions which the research participants complete.

Reliability   The ability to measure the same phenomenon consistently when the conditions of measurement are kept constant.

Validity   The ability of a variable to measure what it sets out to quantify.

Variable   A measurement which has the potential to differ from person to person, or on different measurement occasions. There are two types of variables in quantitative research: *independent variables* do not change within an experiment; *dependent variables* are the measurement(s) of interest in the research and are thought to be affected by the independent variable.

References

Behavioural Regulation in Exercise Questionnaire (BREQ-2) available online from <http://www.bangor.ac.uk/~pes004/exercise_motivation/breq/breqdown.htm> (accessed March 2010).

Field, A. and Hole, G. (2010) *How to Design and Report Experiments*, London: Sage.

Foddy, W. (1995) *Constructing Questions for Interviews and Questionnaires: Theory and Practice in Social Research*, Cambridge: Cambridge University Press.

Gillham, B. (2000) *Developing a Questionnaire*, London: Continuum.

Markland, D. and Tobin, V. (2004) 'A modification of the Behavioral Regulation in Exercise Questionnaire to include an assessment of amotivation', *Journal of Sport and Exercise Psychology*, 26: 191–6.

Mitchell, R. (2002) 'Wake Up! Shake Up!' campaign available online at <http://www.wakeupshakeup.com> (accessed March 2010).

Munn, P. and Drever, E. (1999) *Using Questionnaires in Small-scale Research: A Teacher's Guide*, Edinburgh: Scottish Council for Research in Education.

Oppenheim, A. N. (2000) *Questionnaire Design, Interviewing and Attitude Measurement*, New edition, London: Continuum.

Strengths and Difficulties Questionnaire available online at <www.sdqinfo.org> (accessed March 2010).

Thomas, J. R., Nelson, J. K. and Silverman, S. J. (2005) *Research Methods in Physical Activity*, 5th edn, Champaign, IL: Human Kinetics.

9   Is mixed methods the natural approach to research?

Stephen Gorard and Kyriaki Makopoulou

The authors are pleased to announce the death of mixed-methods research.

Introduction

In this chapter, we argue that mixed methods are so obviously the natural approach to research that we have no real need of the epithet 'mixed'. If researchers do, or should, naturally use whatever methods they need to answer their research questions, then there is no methods schism. This means that there are no separate elements to be 'mixed'. Stephen Gorard has been saying this, or something like it, for a decade or more. Kyriaki Makopoulou wanted to know why. This chapter tries to capture some of the discussion between them in the hope that this will provoke similar discussions for readers.

About us

Stephen Gorard is an established researcher in education who routinely uses a range of designs including trials, comparative, longitudinal and case study; with a range of techniques for data collection and analysis including historical archives, documents, focus groups, a variety of interviews, participant observation, surveys, modelling, secondary sources and meta-analysis. He uses every one of these with every other, and has done so since completing his PhD in 1996, in response to the variety of projects on which he has worked. He has never believed in the artificial separation of techniques into qualitative and quantitative work, finding that this acts as a barrier to understanding. His recent and current research includes investigation into the links between family behaviour, poverty and success at school, the socio-economic determinants of participation in science subjects, and the role of enjoyment in learning. He also publishes regularly on the conduct and quality of social science research.

Kyriaki Makopoulou is an emergent researcher in sport pedagogy. Kyriaki joined the School of Education at the University of Birmingham in September 2008, having been a research associate at Loughborough University since 2005. She was trained in the University of Athens between 1996 and 2000, in a faculty with a powerful orientation towards quantitative, experimental research designs. Research methods modules were designed with the intention of training students to develop objective data collection tools and, upon graduation, she was, perhaps naively, convinced that good research derives from a good hypothesis. She discovered qualitative research while studying for a master's degree in the UK, and was fascinated by the power of personal experiences. Drawing upon qualitative methodologies, her recent research focused on the nature of physical education (PE) teachers' engagement in career-long professional learning and its impact upon practice.

What is mixed-methods research and when might it be appropriate?

Stephen Gorard poses the question: 'What does it mean to mix methods?' The chapters in this book so far imply that what is being mixed are 'qualitative' and 'quantitative' approaches, although there is of course a range of different kinds of methods that could be mixed (Symonds and Gorard, 2010). Mixing visual and oral datasets is mixing methods, for example, and it is not clear why everything involving numbers is counted as one approach, and everything else including smells, drawings, acting, music and so on is treated as an alternate monolith called 'qualitative'. Yet even if we use this very simple idea of just two 'Q' categories, it can still be argued that mixing methods is clearly the natural approach in social science research. It is so natural that for me it does not even seem like there is any mixing, because I do not separate the qualitative and quantitative approaches in the first place. In fact, I would argue that this natural synthesis of different kinds of data is what we all do in our everyday lives whenever we are faced with a task with an outcome that is important to us.

Education is an important applied field and the results of research, if taken seriously, can affect the lives of real people and lead to genuine expenditure and opportunity costs. It is instructive to contrast how we, as researchers, sometimes behave when conducting research professionally with the ways we behave when trying to answer important questions in our personal lives. When we make real-life decisions about where to live, where to work, the care and safety of our children and so on, most of us behave very differently from the way we do as 'researchers'. If, for example, we were intending to purchase a house by paying most of our savings and taking out a mortgage for 25 years that is equal in size to many times our salary, then we would rightly be cautious. We would have many crucial questions to answer from the beginning, and would only go ahead with the transaction once assured that we had sufficiently good answers from what is, in effect, a serious piece of research. It is worth considering this example in some detail because it illustrates fundamental issues in a very accessible way.

When purchasing a house, we will believe that the house is real even though external to us, and that it remains the same even when we approach it from different ends of the street (else why would we buy it?). Thus, we would not start with 'isms' or paradigms. We would not refuse to visit the house, or talk to the neighbours about it, because we were 'quantitative' researchers and did not believe that observation or narratives were valid or reliable enough for our purposes. We would not refuse to consider the interest rate for the loan, or the size of the monthly repayments, because we were 'qualitative' researchers and did not believe that numbers could do justice to the social world. In other words, in matters that are important to us personally, there is a tendency to behave logically, eclectically, critically, and sceptically. We collect all and any evidence available to us as time and resources allow, and then synthesize it quite naturally and without considering mixing methods as such. I have long argued that academic research should be considered in the same way. For me, this means no Q words, no paradigms and no isms.

I do not believe that types of data or methods of data collection and analysis have paradigmatic characteristics, and so for me there is no problem in using numbers, text, visual and sensory data synthetically (Gorard, 2010a). The methods of analysis for text, numbers and sensory data are largely the same, consisting of searching for patterns and differences, establishing their superficial validity and then trying to explain them. Other commentators and methods resources may try to claim that there is a fundamental difference between looking for a pattern or difference in some measurements and in some text or observations. This unnecessarily complex view is based on a number of widely held logical fallacies that get passed on to new researchers under the guise of research methods training (Gorard, 2010b). There are no 'qualitative' and 'quantitative' paradigms; working with numbers does not mean holding a view of human nature and knowledge that is different from when you work with text. As noted earlier, my position is that the whole schism is nonsense, and so mixing is not needed since there is nothing separate to mix.

In the sociology of science, the notion of a 'paradigm' is a description of the sets of socially accepted assumptions that tend to appear in 'normal science' (Kuhn, 1970). A paradigm is a set of accepted rules within any field for solving one or more puzzles – where a puzzle is defined as a scientific question to which it is possible to find a solution in the near future. An example would be Newton setting out to explain Kepler's discoveries about the motions of the planets. Newton knew the parameters of the puzzle and so was working within a paradigm. A more recent example might be the Human Genome Project, solving a closely defined problem with a widely accepted set of pre-existing techniques. Such puzzles can be distinguished from the many important and interesting questions that do not have an answer at a particular stage of progress (Davis, 1994). The 'normal science' of puzzles in Kuhnian terms is held together, rightly or wrongly, by the norms of reviewing and acceptance that work within that taken-for-granted theoretical framework. A paradigm shift occurs when that framework changes, perhaps through the accumulation of evidence, perhaps due to a genuinely new idea, but partly through a change in general acceptance. Often a new paradigm emerges because a procedure or set of rules has been created for converting another more general query *into* a puzzle.

Yet, instead of using 'paradigm' to refer to a topic or field of research (such as traditional physics), which might undergo a radical shift on the basis of evidence (to quantum physics, for example), some commentators now use it to refer to a whole approach to research including philosophy, values and method (Perlesz and Lindsay, 2003). The most common of these approaches are qualitative and quantitative, even though the Q words only make sense, if they make sense at all, as descriptions of data. It could be argued that these commentators use the term 'paradigm' to defend themselves against the need to change, or against contradictory evidence of a different nature to their own. In such cases, the idea of paradigm functions to defend them because they (pointlessly) parcel up unrelated ideas in methodology. Thus, the idea of normal science as a collection of individuals all working towards the solution of a closely defined problem has all but disappeared in the social sciences. Instead, we have paradigm as a symptom of scientific immaturity.

The result of a defensive use of the term 'paradigm' is that the concept has become a cultural cliché with so many meanings it is now almost meaningless. Many of the terms associated with paradigms – i.e. the isms such as positivism – are used almost entirely to refer to others, having become intellectually acceptable terms of abuse and ridicule (see also Hammersley, 2005). Yet, surely most of us could agree that 'Research should be judged by the quality and soundness of its conception, implementation and description, not by the genre within which it is conducted' (Paul and Marfo, 2001: 543–5). The paradigm argument that reinforces the differences between the Q word approaches is a red herring and, I would argue, unnecessarily complex.

One common argument for difference between the Q word approaches is their scale (e.g. Creswell and Plano Clark, 2007). It is argued that qualitative data collection necessarily involves small numbers of cases, whereas quantitative relies on very large samples in order to increase power and reduce the standard error. Yet even this is misleading for two main reasons. First, it is not an accurate description of what happens in practice. The accounts of hundreds of interviewees can be properly analysed as text, and the account of one case study can properly involve numbers. The supposed link between scale and paradigm is just an illusion. Second, issues such as sampling error and power relate to only a tiny minority of quantitative studies, where a true and complete random sample is used, or where a population is randomly allocated to treatment groups. In the much more common situations of working with incomplete samples with measurement error or dropout, convenience, snowball and other non-random samples and the increasing amount of population data available to us, the constraints of sampling theory are simply not relevant. It is also the case, as I have argued elsewhere, that the standard error/power theory of analysis is fatally flawed in its own terms, even when used as intended (Gorard, 2010b). It is based on the logical error of mistaking the probability of encountering the data observed given a true hypothesis (for example, what significance tests calculate) for the probability of the hypothesis being true given the data observed (what significance testers actually want, and usually pretend that they have calculated).

Qualitative research, so its proponents argue, is supposed to be subjective and thus closer to a social world (Gergen and Gergen, 2000). Quantitative research, on the other hand, is supposed to help us become objective (Bradley and Shaefer, 1998). This distinction between quantitative and qualitative analysis is exaggerated, largely because of widespread error by those who do handle numbers (Gorard, 2010b) and ignorance of the subjective and interpretivist nature of numeric analysis by those who do not (Gorard, 2006). What few seem to recognize is that the similarities in the underlying procedures used are remarkable (Onwuegbuzie and Leech, 2005). Few analytical techniques are restricted by data-gathering methods, input data, or by sample size. Most methods of analysis use some form of number, such as 'tend', 'most', 'some', 'all', 'none', 'few' and so on (Gorard, 1997). Whenever one talks of things being 'rare', 'typical', 'great' or 'related', this is a numeric claim, and can only be so substantiated, whether expressed verbally or in figures (Meehl, 1998). Similarly, quantification does not consist of simply assigning numbers to things, but of linking empirical relations to numeric relations (Nash, 2002). Personal judgements lie at the heart of all research – in our choice of research questions, samples, questions to participants and methods of analysis – regardless of the kinds of data to be collected. The idea that quantitative work is objective and qualitative is subjective is based on a misunderstanding of how research is actually conducted.

Response from an emergent researcher

Kyriaki Makopoulou writes: I would like to probe the 'objective' versus 'subjective' issue further as there is a lot of confusion surrounding it. Giacobbi et al. (2005: 23) write:

> While mixing methods from different paradigms is possible, desirable, and often productive, the underlying assumptions of various paradigms (i.e. constructivists versus positivism) may contradict one another (Krane and Baird, in press; Lincoln and Guba, 2000). In other words, a constructivist may use quantitative data but will adopt a subjective epistemology, while a positivist who uses a post-experiment interview will do so under an objective epistemology.

Debates on objective versus subjective research are also implicated in discussions about research quality. Quantitative researchers consider concepts like validity, reliability, generalizability and objectivity to be essential criteria in assessing research quality (Healy and Perry, 2000). From a qualitative perspective, these terms are not always adequate to encapsulate the range of issues that affect quality in qualitative research (Seale, 1999) and new concepts and criteria have been developed. For example, it is claimed that qualitative research should be 'trustworthy', replacing the notion of research validity. When the definitions of these apparently different terms are unpacked, it is clear that they share (more or less) the same meaning. From the perspective of those who champion different paradigms they do differ, however, in the degree of claimed neutrality.

Researchers adopting a positivistic approach aim to consciously avoid personal involvement that might bias a study. This means that researchers try to detach themselves from the 'object' of inquiry – in essence, depersonalize their research – with the aim of capturing and communicating the 'truth' in an 'objective' manner. Schwandt (2000) defined 'bias' as the tendency for researchers to impose a priori theoretical frameworks or interpretations on the data, marginalize or exclude opposite or alternative perspectives, and draw unjustifiable inferences or generalizations. Many qualitative researchers, although acknowledging that any factors influencing findings in an unethical way should be eliminated, accept a degree of involvement as an inevitable part of the inquiry and treat claimed neutrality as 'deluding' or 'misleading'.

Greenbank (2003) captured this as the debate between those advocating a value-neutral and those arguing for a value-laden approach to (educational) research. Seale (1999: 3) talked about a clash of two moments.

This debate is prominent and persisting, although I also support this chapter's position that researchers should not 'tie' themselves to a particular paradigm. The key argument is that dualistic thinking (either–or) is problematic in an ever-evolving world that necessitates multidimensional insights and solutions to complex problems. For decades, it has been acknowledged that a rigid, unreflective adherence to a research paradigm might encourage researchers to take fundamental assumptions for granted (Patton, 1978), thereby preventing them from learning from other researchers working within apparently contrasting research perspectives (Bailey, 2007). This chapter's position is that engaging in such a discussion in the first place is restrictive. Should researchers in their search for 'warranted' evidence (Gorard, 2002) therefore strive for neutrality in the process, or should they acknowledge a degree of involvement? Or should debates about the degree of neutrality be abandoned altogether and replaced by discussions on research designs that are robust, rigorous and transparent? If so, what would such a research design look like?

There is another apparent constraint in endeavours to 'mix' methods. In most cases, quantitative studies (especially experimental designs) begin with a *research hypothesis*, which is the expected result (Thomas et al., 2010), and which is tested to be supported or refuted. Qualitative studies, on the other hand, set out to explore answers to *research questions*. In most forms of research, both hypotheses and questions should be developed following a thorough, in-depth review of the available literature. The logical question that follows from this, however, is: What is the starting point of a study that is not framed by the 'paradigmatic war'? Should researchers pose questions and/or hypotheses?

Some ideas on how to conduct mixed-methods studies

Stephen Gorard responds to the questions posed by Kyriaki Makopoulou: If we consider just some of the ways in which methods can be mixed within one study or programme it becomes obvious, to me, that these questions should be reconsidered. A programme of research conducted by one team, or a field of research conducted by otherwise separate teams, will incorporate most methods of data collection and analysis. Figure 9.1 is a simplified description of a full cycle for a research programme. The cycle is more properly a spiral that has no clear beginning or end and in which activities (phases) overlap, can take place simultaneously, and iterate. Starting with draft research questions, the research cycle might continue with a synthesis of existing evidence (phase 1).

Ideally, this synthesis would be an inclusive review of the literature both published and unpublished, coupled with a re-analysis of relevant existing datasets of all kinds (including data archives and administrative datasets), and related policy/practice documents. It is impossible to conduct a fair appraisal of the existing evidence on almost any topic in applied social science without drawing upon evidence involving text, numbers, pictures and a variety of other data forms. Anyone who claims to be

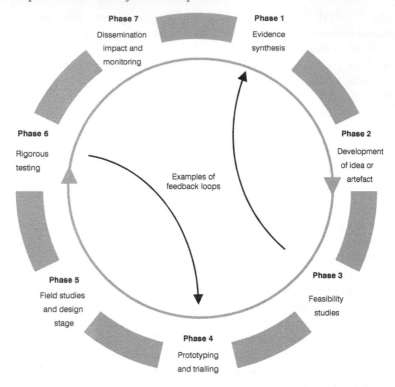

Figure 9.1 An outline of the full cycle of social science research and development

conducting even the most basic literature review without combining numeric and textual data is surely misguided. One way (of many) to combine disparate datasets is via Bayesian synthesis, where the in-depth evidence and perhaps professional judgements provide a subjective a priori probability for a research claim, with numeric data used to adjust this base a posteriori (Gorard et al., 2004). It can be argued that this relatively straightforward method of generating a result is fair and inclusive, and requires little technical expertise. It also illustrates that, by definition, the outcomes will be subjective. Indeed, no matter how transparent and technically sound a process of analysis might be, the result will always be subjective for the reasons Kyriaki Makopoulou suggests above. We might argue, therefore, that conducting this kind of synthesis is one way to persuade those who purport to be 'quantitative' researchers that their work is not quite as objective as they claim, even when only a single method is used.

Where a project or programme continues past phase 1 in Figure 9.1, every further phase in the cycle tends to require a mixture of methods. The overall research programme might be envisaged as tending towards an artefact or 'product' of some kind. This product might be a theory (if the desired outcome is simply knowledge), a proposed improvement for public policy, or a tool/resource for a practitioner. In order for any of these outcomes to be promoted and disseminated in an ethical manner, however, they must have been *tested*. If there is no testing, the dissemination can only state (ethically) that the product or output seems to be a good idea, but that we have no real idea of its value. A theory, by definition, will generate testable propositions. A proposed public policy intervention can be tested realistically and then monitored in situ for the predicted benefits, and for any unwanted and undesirable side effects. Therefore, for the minority of programmes that continue as far as phase 6 in Figure 9.1, rigorous testing would usually involve a mixture of methods and types of evidence in just the same way as phase 1.

Even where a purely numeric outcome is envisaged as the benefit of the research programme (such as a more effective or cost-efficient service), it is pointless knowing that the intervention works if we are not also aware that, for example, it is unpopular and therefore likely to be ignored or subverted in practice. Similarly, it would be a waste of resource, and therefore unethical, simply to discover that an intervention did not work in phase 6 and so return to a new programme of study in phase 1. We would want to know *why* it did not work, or perhaps how to improve it, and whether it was effective for some regular pattern of cases but not for others. So in phase 6, as in phase 1, the researcher or team who genuinely wants to find something out will, quite naturally, use a range of methods and approaches including measurement, narrative and observation.

The key point to be made here is that a research design, such as case study, longitudinal research or randomized controlled trial is completely independent of individual methods of data collection and analysis. Research design, including the pre-specification of success and failure criteria, is one important defence against the inevitable researcher bias in any study. Replication, syntheses and critical judgements are others. The best examples of each design are likely to use all and any available data collection methods irrespective of type and without consideration of invented epistemological schisms.

A range of simple ways in which data can be mixed are given in Gorard with Taylor (2004). One of these suggested ways is termed 'new political arithmetic', but is really just a sequence of related questions answered by different kinds of data. Typically, large-scale data (perhaps already existing from official sources) is used to define a problem, pattern, trend or difference. It is also used to select a representative subset of cases for in-depth research to investigate the reasons for the problem, pattern, trend or difference. The in-depth work is, therefore, generalizable in the sense that this term is traditionally used, and different datasets are used to define the pattern and its determinants. Again, what an example such as this makes clear is that all research answers a question, so the notion of a formal hypothesis is not necessary to describe the process. It follows, therefore, that the concern raised earlier by Kyriaki Makopoulou – hypothesis or research question – can be addressed quite easily. A question can be converted to a hypothesis simply by assuming one answer to the question, and vice versa, so that a hypothesis immediately generates the question 'Is it true?' For example, the question 'Are men and women different in this regard?' is the same as the hypothesis 'Men and women are different in this regard,' which can be true or false. Any claim about a fundamental difference between the two, as made by Thomas et al. (2010) for example and cited earlier, is just plain wrong.

Some examples of real-life studies

What happens currently in practice in sport pedagogy research? As part of the preparation for this chapter, Kyriaki Makopoulou hand-searched the articles in two journals – *Sport, Education and Society* and *Physical Education and Sport Pedagogy* – over three years (2008 to 2010). Both are based in the UK, but international in remit and content, and we use these to give us an idea of the range of methods and types of work being conducted in the field. The journals contained 135 peer-reviewed articles, of which 28 (21 per cent) had no empirical evidence. This is rather less than the proportion of 'thought pieces' we have found in more generic reviews (e.g. Gorard et al., 2007). Of the remainder, 72 (67 per cent) were described as 'qualitative' and made no use of numeric evidence at all. Therefore in this admittedly limited sample, over two-thirds of research involves no numbers. (It should also be acknowledged that some other journals in the field have a bias towards publishing quantitative research.)

The preponderance of qualitative research in the two journals selected, both of which have a social science base, is in line with more generic reviews both in education and most social sciences more widely. It is astonishing but apparently true. Around 21 per cent (23 papers) used numeric evidence only and these were largely based on sampling theory derivatives (often incorrectly). This leaves only 12 papers (11 per cent) that used both numeric and some other form of evidence, usually interviews. What this suggests is that 'mixed-methods' papers, if that is what these were, are a minority at least for the authors, editors and readers of these two journals. Similar studies have found even smaller proportions. Examining the methodologies employed in published dissertations in the United States, Silverman and Manson (2003: 291) found that a combination of both qualitative and quantitative methods was used in 8 per cent of dissertations. Similarly, Ward and Ko (2006) investigated articles published in the *Journal of Teaching in Physical Education* by methodology from 1981 to 2005 and reported that of the 68 per cent of articles that were research studies, only 6 per cent were mixed methods. Likewise, a review conducted in 2003 found that out of 485 published papers in three leading sport psychology journals, only 5 per cent adopted a mixed-methods approach (Giacobbi et al., 2005).

Two decades ago, Schempp (1989) identified a strong research tradition influenced by the natural and biological sciences in the PE and sport pedagogy research field. If it were true then, it is clearly not so now. For some time, the number of studies drawing upon so-called 'qualitative' methodologies has dominated output. Meanwhile, qualitative and quantitative methodologies are still viewed as two fundamentally distinct approaches, perhaps appropriate for answering different kinds of research questions, but underpinned by diverse philosophical and epistemological standpoints. This means that in the few examples of apparent mixed-methods work found in our search of the journals, qualitative and quantitative methodologies are not really being 'mixed' in the field of sport and sport pedagogy.

A clear example is the study by Lee et al. (2007) from the sport psychology field. This drew upon five other studies to develop and validate a questionnaire, but the paper is a report of a survey study with a small focus group thrown in, almost as an addition. It displays many of the common weaknesses of standard quantitative research. The data they use for the factor analysis are not interval in nature. The factor analytic model explains very little of the variance in the dataset, and the majority of variance is just ignored in the analysis, with no reason given. The authors just omit uncorrelated items (but see Gorard, 2010c). The use of significance tests is completely unjustified as there is no randomization involved, and so the probabilities they quote are meaningless, but also misleading. A further example, Morgan and Hansen (2008), is very similar. The different kinds of data are dealt with separately rather than synthesized, and numeric analysis predominates, but is of the usual poor quality. For example, their model only explains 32 per cent of the variance, they imply an unjustified causal model from mere association, and they conduct their significance tests at the level of individuals when the only randomization is of schools. If these examples are really mixed methods rather than just two isolated streams of data dealt with in the same report, then they do not appear very natural (or very good). There is a way to go yet, before evidence outweighs paradigmatic clutter.

Kyriaki Makopoulou, meantime, is developing a new research proposal on continuing professional development (CPD) for PE teachers (PE-CPD). Her intention is that with guidance from colleagues, including Stephen Gorard, it *will* be a mixed-methods study in the full sense of the term. The research cycle began from phase 1, by drafting a set of research questions to guide an 'inclusive' synthesis of available evidence:

- What is currently known about CPD practices that have positive impact on teachers and pupils? What needs to be known to inform CPD policy and practice?
- What kind of evidence can provide a robust basis for CPD policy and practice?

The synthesis suggested that a significant shift in CPD research is required: towards experimental or quasi-experimental research designs that measure impact on pupils as well as teachers. However, it was also noted that recent efforts to test the relative effectiveness of different CPD types yielded disappointing results (Garet et al., 2008). Even more problematically, collecting numerical data alone in the form of pre- and post-test measurements provided disappointing findings as researchers were unable to offer insights into how and why the interventions failed to work. In other words, as Stephen Gorard pointed out earlier, these studies lack explanatory power for practice.

The analysis undertaken in preparation for the proposed PE-CPD study (including the review of the relevant literature and policy documents) showed that in order to advance scientific knowledge and to impact CPD policy and practice, a mixed-methods approach to CPD research – one that is advocated as 'natural' in this chapter – is required. To address this gap (and moving into subsequent phases of Stephen Gorard's cycle suggested above), the proposed study will employ an experimental design and use mixed methods to investigate the relative effectiveness of two different forms of CPD for both teacher and pupil learning. In particular, a CPD programme will be designed, delivered and evaluated rigorously to assess impact on teachers and pupils. The proposed study will employ a three-arm experimental design. One treatment will be the usual three-day block workshop. A second treatment will involve the same amount of involvement in CPD but with shorter meetings spread across a longer period of time. The third group will be a control with no treatment.

The next phase in the research cycle is to conduct a feasibility study, involving a mixture of methods. This is a vital and ethical practice to ensure, before implementing the CPD intervention with the wider PE population, that we can be sure how, why, when, for whom and under what circumstances it works. As Stephen Gorard stressed above, it would be 'unethical ... to discover that an intervention did not work in phase 6 and so return to a new programme of study in phase 1'. In the CPD literature, feasibility studies are defined as studies that measure the impact of a CPD intervention delivered by the same provider in one area. The proposed CPD intervention will be implemented in one local authority in England. A thorough investigation of the PE teachers is required to ensure that the PE-CPD intervention has meaning and relevance to the participant teachers, and can be tailored (personalized) to their needs and expectations.

In all subsequent phases of the project, a mixture of methods will be employed to ensure that the research team has a holistic picture of the nature and impact of the CPD intervention. For example, to measure impact on pupil learning, a traditional achievement test will be developed to measure pupil learning in terms of health-related components and aligned with the expectations outlined in the attainment section of the national curriculum for physical education. However, it is also important to explore pupils' experiences of health-related exercise in PE and explore the ways pupils construct meanings and how they believe that their experiences will influence their participation in physical activity.

Conclusions

An analysis of papers published in two social science-based journals in the field of physical education and sport pedagogy suggests that researchers do not routinely adopt mixed-methods approaches, nor synthesize data of different types. The tendency to publish quantitative and qualitative research undertaken in this field in different journals must surely reinforce the notion of two researcher 'camps', each intrinsically hostile to the approach of the other, but often without the skills to be appropriately and helpfully critical for each other. This might be one explanation for the finding that much so-called qualitative research tends to lack the rigour found in the best examples, and too much so-called quantitative research is needlessly complex and prone to serious error. Combining approaches, therefore, as long as we combine the best of each approach rather than the worst, holds the promise of providing better answers to important research questions. Recognition of the danger of obscuring research design with polarized paradigmatic clutter could also lead to substantive improvements in single-methods studies.

So what does all this mean in practice for new researchers? We realize that asking new researchers to reject traditional methods, teaching and resources is challenging. Perhaps one way to think about this is to ensure that you ask questions about the track record of any person giving methodological advice. You may find that those who argue most strongly for the importance of the Q word paradigms also conduct the weakest research, using an impoverished set of designs and techniques repeatedly. This should, at the very least, raise some questions about their critical understanding of the wider research landscape and the potential for 'mixing' methods. So, we argue that if a researcher really cares about finding something out that is as robust as possible, they should consider ignoring the traditional two-camp research methods resources and behave in research as they would in real life. In real life, the use of mixed methods is natural – so natural, in fact, that we do not generally divide data in the first place. The question to be asked, therefore, is why research should be any different.

Key terms

Quantitative research Traditionally meant to involve measurement, and be systematic, objective and generalizable. In fact, of course, simply using measurement does not necessarily guarantee any of these things.

Qualitative research Traditionally meant to involve particular cases with no generalizability, and with greater subjective understanding. Again, simply not using numbers does not necessarily guarantee any of these things.

Mixed-methods research Traditionally meant to combine quantitative and qualitative approaches. As this chapter suggests, it is simpler not to think in quantitative and qualitative terms in the first place.

Research design The template used to convert the research questions into a project, using elements such as the time sequence, comparator groups, and presence or absence of interventions. Design is independent of the methods of data collection or analysis.

References

Bailey, R. (2007) 'The problem with paradigms', invited paper presented at the 12th Annual Congress of the ECSS, 11–14 July, Juvaskyla, Finland.

Bradley, W. and Shaefer, K. (1998) *Limitations of Measurement in the Social Sciences*, Thousand Oaks, CA: Sage.

Creswell, J. and Plano Clark, V. (2007) *Designing and conducting mixed methods research*, London: Sage.

Davis, J. (1994) 'What's wrong with sociology?', *Sociological Forum*, 9, 2: 179–97.

Garet, M.S., Cronen, S., Eaton, M., Kurki, A., Ludwig, M., Jones, W, Uekawa, K. et al (2008) *The Impact of Two Professional Development Interventions on Early Reading Instruction and Achievement*. Washington: Department of Education.

Gergen, M. and Gergen, K. (2000) 'Qualitative inquiry, tensions and transformations', in N. Denzin and Y. Lincoln (eds) *The Landscape of Qualitative Research: Theories and Issues*, Thousand Oaks, CA: Sage.

Giacobbi, P. R., Poczwardowski, A. and Hager, P. (2005) 'A pragmatic research philosophy for sport and exercise psychology', *The Sport Psychologist*, 19: 18–31.

Gorard, S. (1997) 'A choice of methods: the methodology of choice', *Research in Education*, 57: 45–56.

Gorard, S. (2002) 'Fostering scepticism: the importance of warranting claims', *Evaluation and Research in Education*, 16, 3: 136–49.

Gorard, S. (2006) 'Towards a judgement-based statistical analysis', *British Journal of Sociology of Education*, 27, 1: 67–80.

Gorard, S. (2010a) 'Research design, as independent of methods', in C. Teddlie and A. Tashakkori (eds) *Handbook of Mixed Methods*, Los Angeles: Sage.

Gorard, S. (2010b) 'All evidence is equal: the flaw in statistical reasoning', *Oxford Review of Education*, 36, 1: 63–77.

Gorard, S. (2010c) 'Measuring is more than assigning numbers', in G. Walford, E. Tucker and M. Viswanathan (eds) (389–408) *Sage Handbook of Measurement*, Los Angeles: Sage.

Gorard, S. with Taylor, C. (2004) *Combining Methods in Educational and Social Research*, London: Open University Press.

Gorard, S., Roberts, K. and Taylor, C. (2004) 'What kind of creature is a design experiment?', *British Educational Research Journal*, 30, 4: 575–90.

Gorard, S., with Adnett, N., May, H., Slack, K., Smith, E. and Thomas, L. (2007) *Overcoming barriers to HE*, Stoke-on-Trent: Trentham Books.

Greenbank, P. (2003) 'The role of values in educational research: the case for reflexivity', *British Educational Research Journal*, 29(6): 791–802.

Hammersley, M. (2005) 'Countering the "new orthodoxy" in educational research: a response to Phil Hodkinson', *British Educational Research Journal*, 31, 2: 139–55.

Healy, M. and Perry, C. (2000) 'Comprehensive criteria to judge validity and reliability of qualitative research within the realism paradigm', *Qualitative Market Research*, 3(3): 118–26.

Kuhn, T. (1970) *The Structure of Scientific Revolutions*, Chicago: University of Chicago Press.

Krane, V., & Baird, S.M. (in press) 'Using ethnography in applied sport psychology', *Journal of Applied Sport Psychology*.

Lee, M. J., Whitehead, J. and Ntoumanis, N. (2007) 'Development of the attitudes to moral decision-making in youth sport questionnaire', *Psychology of Sport and Exercise*, 8: 369–92.

Lincoln, Y.S., & Guba, E.G. (2000) 'Paradigmatic controversies, contradictions, and emerging confluences', in N.K. Denzin & Y.S. Lincoln (eds) *Handbook of qualitative research* (2nd ed., pp. 163-188), Thousand Oaks, CA: Sage.

Meehl, P. (1998) 'The power of quantitative thinking', speech delivered upon receipt of the James McKeen Cattell Fellow award at American Psychological Society, Washington DC, 23 May.

Morgan, P. J. and Hansen, V. (2008) 'The relationship between PE biographies and PE teaching practices of classroom teachers', *Sport, Education and Society*, 13(4): 373–91.

Nash, R. (2002) 'Numbers and narratives: further reflections in the sociology of education', *British Journal of Sociology of Education*, 23, 3: 397–412.

Onwuegbuzie, A. and Leech, N. (2005) 'Taking the "Q" out of research: teaching research methodology courses without the divide between quantitative and qualitative paradigms', *Quality and Quantity*, 38: 267–96.

Patton, M. (1978) *Utilization-Focused Evaluations*, London: Sage Publications.

Paul, J. and Marfo, K. (2001) 'Preparation of educational researchers in philosophical foundations of inquiry', *Review of Educational Research*, 71, 4: 525–47.

Perlesz, A. and Lindsay, J. (2003) 'Methodological triangulation in researching families: making sense of dissonant data', *International Journal of Social Research Methodology*, 6, 1: 25–40.

Schempp, P. G. (1989) 'Building the science of teaching in physical education: A crack in the foundation', *Research Quarterly for Exercise and Sport*, 59: 197–9.

Schwandt, T. D. (2000) 'Three epistemological stances for qualitative inquiry: Interpretivism, hermeneutics, and social constructionism', in N. K. Denzin and Y. S. Lincoln (eds) *The Handbook of Qualitative Research*, 2nd edn, (189–213), Thousand Oaks, CA: Sage.

Seale, C. (1999) 'Quality in qualitative research', *Qualitative Inquiry*, 5: 465–78.

Silverman, S. and Manson, M. (2003) 'Research on teaching in physical education doctoral dissertations: a detailed investigation of focus, method and analysis', *Journal of Teaching in Physical Education*, 22: 280–97.

Symonds, J. and Gorard, S. (2010) 'The death of mixed methods?: or the rebirth of research as craft', *Evaluation and Research in Education*, 23, 2: 121–36.

Thomas, J. R., Nelson, J. K. and Silverman, S. J. (2010) *Research Methods in Physical Activity*, 5th edn, Champaign, IL: Human Kinetics.

Ward, P. and Ko, B. (2006) 'Publication trends in the "Journal of Teaching in Physical Education" from 1981 to 2005', *Journal of Teaching in Physical Education*, 25, 3: 266–280.

10 Listening to young people's voices in physical education and youth sport research

Eimear Enright and Mary O'Sullivan

While thinking about how to frame this chapter in a way that compels readers to think differently about how they engage with and respond to young people in research, an old Paul Simon song comes on the radio; its timeless lyrics conveying people's ability to hear without listening. Serendipity …

Introduction

People have the ability to hear without listening. This is an important distinction and one which those who seek to access young people's voices in physical education (PE) and youth sport research need to seriously consider. Hearing describes the physiological process of perceiving sound; listening, however, is a psychological process. Listening has been defined as *the process of receiving, constructing meaning from, and responding to spoken and/or non-verbal messages* (International Listening Association, 1995). This distinction between hearing and listening helps us to think about how we design research with young people, and specifically how we choose to interpret, represent and respond to young people's experiences, perspectives, feelings and identities. In this chapter, we discuss methodological concerns of relevance to the design and conduct of research with young people in physical education and youth sport. Access, ethical practices, the importance of context, research relationships, representation and the interest in participatory approaches to hearing young people's voices in research are among the topics considered. Our intention is not only to prompt you to engage in a meaningful and sustained way with the various methodological and ethical implications of undertaking research with young people, but also to give you the confidence to gain first-hand experience of research with young people.

About us

Eimear Enright: I believe that what defines both my teaching and my research is a commitment to engaging with young people's voices and listening to their stories with the intent of responding to what they say. The purpose of my doctoral research was to work with a group of disengaged teenage girls to understand and to help them transform self-identified barriers to their physical education engagement and physical activity participation. The study took place over three years in a designated disadvantaged city-centre girls' school and was framed methodologically, theoretically and philosophically by a feminist participatory action research (PAR) orientation (Enright and O'Sullivan, 2010). My study was premised on a conviction that young people have unique perspectives on learning and life, that their voices deserve not only to be heard but also to be acted on, and that these young people should be partners in any efforts at reimagining physical education. I truly believe that young people should have greater responsibility for their own learning, through more imaginative and flexible pedagogies, and I believe that in order to create these pedagogies of possibility, young people need to be listened to and actively engaged in their construction. I constantly seek therefore to support students repositioning as active participants in educational research and in their own learning. I do not hold this commitment lightly. Experience has taught me that it is not a straightforward or easy task to truly listen to what young people are saying. Things get in the way.

Mary O'Sullivan: Much of my early research career was focused on researching teaching and teacher education. I was always interested in the views of teachers and pre-service teachers and what they understood as the purpose of physical education and how they saw their role in creating experiences that would be challenging and meaningful for the young people they were teaching. As this work progressed, I became focused on the importance of designing curricular experiences of value to students. Ben Dyson and I (Dyson, 1995) worked with 8- to 10-year-old children to gain their perspectives on the alternative physical education programme in their primary school (the programme focus was adventure education). There followed a series of studies with several doctoral students in which we used a variety of pedagogies to engage adolescents differently in their physical education and sport experience (Kinchin and O'Sullivan, 1999; Bush, 2002; Pope, 1998). This early research was about conversing with young people to gain an understandings of their lived experiences of PE and sport in school. In recent years, I have become keen to explore strategies that might not only allow students to tell stories of their lived physical education experiences but, in the process of their doing so, might also allow them to shape their own experiences and challenge their beliefs and practices around physical education and sport. My recent collaboration with Eimear Enright is a lovely example. Eimear had the young people become co-researchers and active partners in the research agenda. This approach to research, while hugely satisfying, takes a particular commitment to long-term engagement with young people, demands researcher courage to trust young people to take responsibility for their own learning, and requires the researcher to be open to having their own values and practices challenged and revised. This is not an easy role to assume for a researcher, especially one who is new to research.

While both of us have different backgrounds and experiences, we share a commitment to listening to young people's voices, with a view to having those voices inform physical education practice and policy. Our shared key questions in undertaking research with young people are:

- What kinds of strategies might we use to support young people as active participants in the research process?
- What methods can best help us to help young people share their experiences, opinions, feelings and perspectives?
- How can we actively listen to young people with a view to facilitating change?
- How might we conduct research with young people that engages them and effects change that impacts positively on their lived experiences?

Participatory methods and methodological sensibility

This chapter encourages researchers who are conducting research with young people to go beyond simply conversing with young people about what their experiences in physical education and youth sport are like. Rather, we want researchers to consider young people's authentic involvement in opportunities for decision making, investment and participation around issues of direct interest to their lives, that is, their lived experiences in physical education or sporting contexts in school and in their community. This is Rudduck and McIntyre's (2007) concept of authentic 'participation' in the research enterprise. Researchers might also consider ways to engage young people as co-researchers and as a result of this engagement have a more central role in shaping their own and others' experiences and policies around physical education and sport. The important difference in conducting research with this emphasis is that you focus on developing conditions that allow young people's voices a more central role in the research, rather than merely reporting research undertaken with young people. The challenge then is to get buy-in from young people. Long and Carless (2010) outlined four reasons why young people's voices can go unheard, two of which are central to the theme of this chapter. One reason is the power differential with the adult researcher, where young people don't feel they can provide a story that is different from the 'expected' one. A second reason relates to the researcher's ability to hear a story that is beyond their own preconceptions and may even steer the young person to an 'acceptable story'. The challenge for researchers then is:

> to extend our thinking on devising innovative and effective practices and methodology in encouraging young people to share their stories that allow for the enhancement of understanding of young people's needs and experiences in physical education and youth sport settings, which in turn can be used to inform and formulate policy.
>
> (O'Sullivan and MacPhail, 2010: 7)

We have found that participatory methods can go some way towards helping us address this challenge and engage in the necessary task of carefully listening to young people's stories. Participatory methods are those that facilitate participants in finding their own language to articulate what they know and help them put words to their ideas and feelings and share understanding of their worlds, thereby giving participants more control over the research process. Most often, participatory methods are practical activities, which are considered engaging, enjoyable and relevant ways for participants to engage in research and generate data. Examples of participatory methods include: student-led photography; social mapping exercises; student-led tours; role-play exercises; drama; music; dance; diary keeping; collage; model making; storytelling; print journalism; and radio production (Gallacher and Gallagher, 2008). Some examples of participatory methods used in physical education and youth sport research have included: photography; development of personal biographies; free writing; body drawing; journal writing; drama; scrapbooking, student drawings; poster design; and timelines (Enright and O'Sullivan, in press). Participatory methodologies have been praised for: supporting the active participation of young people in shaping the research process (Clark and Moss, 2001; O'Kane, 2000; Punch, 2002); facilitating access to different types of knowledge and different understandings of complex questions (Kesby, 2000); helping young people in 'learning to derive meaning from themselves and the world around them' (Kincheloe, 2007: 745); promoting enjoyment and relevance for students (Barker and Weller, 2003; O'Kane, 2000; Punch, 2002); and encouraging student empowerment (Allard, 1996).

'Participatory' goes beyond the mere choice of methods to decisions around how, and by whom, the research process is shaped, the findings are shared, and who learns and benefits from the process. The researcher's methodological sensibility therefore is every bit as important as the chosen methods. We understand methodological sensibility as an awareness and appreciation of the rationale for the use of certain methods and a keen intellectual and ethical perception regarding when and how particular methods may be best used to help research participants share their experiences, perspectives and feelings (Enright, Barnes and Gallagher, 2010).

Our methodological sensibility is based around three core tenets. The first of these relates to our understanding of young people's positioning within the research process and is grounded in what has come to be known as the new social studies of childhood (James, Jenks and Prout, 1998). The new social studies of childhood represent an epistemological shift away from understanding of children and young people as incompetent, incomplete adults and/or passive subjects, towards an understanding of children and young people as 'being', meaning that:

> the child is conceived of as a person, a status, a course of action, a set of needs, rights or differences – in sum, as a social actor … this new phenomenon, the 'being' child, can be understood in its own right. It does not have to be approached from an assumed shortfall of competence, reason or significance.
>
> (James, Jenks and Prout, 1998: 207)

Grounding our work in this theoretical understanding means that the children and young people we work with are recognized as active participants in and fellow architects of the research process.

The second core tenet of our methodological sensibility is our acknowledgement of, and belief in, our responsibility to attempt to address the power inequalities and differentials between researchers and their participants (Alderson, 2000; Christensen and Prout, 2002; Hill, 2005; Mayall, 2000). Alderson suggests that, when undertaking research with children, 'a key question is: how can adults get beyond the power constraints and expose the intricacies of power in relations between adults and children?' (2000: 254). We speak to this power issue with reference to a case study later in this chapter.

The third fundamental element of our methodological sensibility relates to our appreciation of 'reflexivity', where we seek to not only critically interrogate our researching selves, both in the field and beyond it through our writing, but also help the children and young people we work with to engage in a critical and reflective way with the questions we ask of them and those they ask of themselves. Engaging in participatory research can help children and young people develop a critical capacity and question taken-for-granted assumptions in a way that they may not have the opportunity to do through other methods.

'Listening' to young people's voices

Drawing on the definition of listening provided in the introduction to this chapter we have organized this section under three headings: receiving; constructing meaning; and responding.

Receiving young people's voices

Hill (2005) has commented that the main difference between research with children and research with adults relates to ability and power. In terms of communicative ability, some children and young people are less verbally competent, less able to understand and articulate abstract concepts. This is more relevant when working with younger children but it may also, of course, be true for people regardless of age, for whom the language used is not their first language, or for those with intellectual disabilities. This understanding and acknowledgement behove those of us who seek to speak with and listen to children and young people to ensure that our language and methods are adapted to the communicative ability and preferences of our research participants.

The power issue relates to social status and lived experience. Many children are not accustomed to having their perspectives requested, listened to and acted on by adults. Indeed, the relationship between many children and the adults in their lives is often characterized by tight hierarchical patterns of engagement, which may or may not be supportive. Difference in social status cannot be avoided and should not be ignored. Children and young people can feel pressurized into participating in research and/or giving responses that they perceive will be acceptable to the adult researcher.

The following case study is adapted from Eimear's doctoral thesis and speaks to this issue quite well. One of the methods Eimear used when working to understand and transform her students' relationships with physical education and physical activity was photovoice (see also Chapter 20). Photovoice has been described as a powerful participatory action research method where individuals are given the opportunity to take photographs, discuss them collectively, and use them to create opportunities for personal and/or community change (Wang, 2003). The young people in Eimear's study were asked to make photographs of their lives and given some prompts to focus some of their image making. These prompts included: 'where I spend my leisure time'; 'my physically active life'; 'physical activity facilities nearby'; 'physical activity in the lives of my family and friends'; and 'the things that are important to me'. The students' photographs were then discussed in individual and group contexts where the students and Eimear engaged in dialogue regarding what these participatory research artefacts represented.

Case study 1: People talking without speaking ...

Students have years of learning what constitutes a teacher-pleasing response and in the beginning of this study many of the participants gave me the type of responses that they thought would please me. Most of the participants, for example, had over-reported their physical activity participation in participation diaries they kept in the first eight weeks of the project. This misrepresentation only became evident during the photovoice discussions, as is illustrated by this exchange between Jade and me (my emphasis):

Eimear: You didn't get any pictures for the third prompt, your physically active life.

Jade: Yeah [laughing] ... that's because I don't do anything.

Eimear: You said in your diary that you go swimming and running and ...

Jade: Yeah, cos that's what I thought ye wanted to hear like, for the diary ... but in the photographs is what I do, who I am.

Jade had been reporting what she 'thought [we] wanted to hear' as opposed to what she was actually doing; quite a patent example of the 'researcher/teacher/observer effect'. Examples such as this highlight the epistemological benefits of engaging with students using participatory methods. Participatory methods allowed us to access knowledge that students are often unwilling to share through other methods. Written text is privileged in school culture. Taking photographs was perceived as a temporary escape from conventionalised routines of everyday schooling. The students acknowledged that it would be more difficult to 'tell lies' (Kelly) through photographs and because the photovoice task was not 'real homework like essays or writing stuff' (Debra), they did not feel that they had to tell lies. Photographs therefore became 'a more transparent representation of the life experiences of participants' (Dodman, 2003: 294), conveying their 'real flesh and blood life' (Becker, 2002: 11). Jade's example also reminds us of the absolute necessity of triangulation and of spending significant time with our research participants. It took time for us to gain Jade's trust and for her to feel safe enough to tell us her truth.

(adapted from Enright and O'Sullivan, in press)

Both the communicative ability and power issues may be partly addressed through the use of participatory methods within a context of genuine respect for young people's perspectives and ideas, as illustrated by the dialogue between Jade and Eimear. In order to 'receive' young people's authentic voices, the research needs to start from their perspectives, and time is necessary for the development of a trusting relationship between the adults and young people involved. While we found that participatory methods helped us to 'receive' young people's voices in ways that other methods might not, it is important to note that participatory research methods do not have to be – and we would argue should not be – used in isolation. We used participatory methods in conjunction with other ethnographic techniques, namely interviews/discussions and observation. Participatory methods therefore supported and enhanced, rather than replaced, more traditional data collection methods in our research.

Constructing meaning from young people's voices

The reliability, validity and ethical acceptability of research with young people can be improved by using methods that facilitate students in shaping the research agenda and are deemed by young people as relevant and interesting methods to engage with their realities (Thomas and O'Kane, 1998). Youth research participants can be involved in all stages of the research process, including analysis/interpretation. A participatory approach to interpretation and analysis can encourage a rethinking of constructs and causality. This means going back to young people several times to discuss the findings, their interpretations, and whether your interpretations of what they said are aligned with theirs. A participative approach to coding with the research participants in Eimear's doctoral study ensured that the young people were actively involved in coding the transcripts of conversations she had with them (Enright and O'Sullivan, in press). This resulted in unpacking and rebuilding the codes and constructs as the student researchers and Eimear worked together to ensure that how Eimear was constructing meaning from the young people's voices was indeed meaningful to them. In this way, she worked to ensure she was representing them and their ideas as accurately as words would allow, and tried to avoid retelling their stories in a way that was not authentic to them. This approach to analysis and interpretation enhanced the construct validity and ensured that our constructs were valid and our causal analysis meaningful. In terms of expert validity, the use of participatory methods can challenge the very notion of what expertise is and where it resides by 'recognizing and elevating deep and varied local knowledges' (Fine, 2008: 223).

Responding to and with young people's voices

There are several questions we might ask of ourselves and our research when it comes to responding to and with young people's voices. First, do the children and young people involved with the research know about the findings? At a very minimum, we recommend that the young people involved as participants in the research project be provided with an accessible summary of the major findings and outcomes. Second, how do we represent young people's voices in our work? Third, do we represent and address all voices? Finally, are there opportunities for the young people to communicate the findings? When young people are actively involved in the presentation of research findings and have the opportunity to share their related experiences, this can have a greater impact on audiences. Fine offers a novel conception of generalizability which speaks quite well to this point. She defines provocative generalizability as:

> a measure of the extent to which a piece of research provokes readers or audiences, across contexts, to generalize to 'worlds not yet', in the language of Maxine Greene; to rethink and reimagine current arrangements. To what extent [can this research] instil in audiences a sense of urgency, pressing the question, what must we do?
>
> (Fine, 2008: 227)

Young people, the primary stakeholders in their own youth sport and physical education experiences, have a greater capacity to provoke audiences to rethink and reimagine current youth sport and physical education provision. Engaging them in research dissemination can work to help them influence decisions made by adults, in a direction that is meaningful to them. Supporting students in adopting this role is not, however, without challenge. The following case study is an adapted extract from Eimear's PhD and highlights some of the problems associated with involving young people in disseminating research findings.

Case study 2: People hearing without listening ...

It is common practice to share research findings at conferences; the protocol to do so involves submitting a formal abstract of the intended presentation. One of the abstracts the student researchers I worked with wrote and submitted to a conference received the following reviews:

> Reviewer 1: I can tell that you are very excited about your after-school physical activity club, and I applaud your efforts! I am very concerned about girls' physical activity levels, and am glad to see that you took the initiative to create your own club! However, [name of research group] is a research organization, and you are not reporting research. Your presentation would be more appropriate [elsewhere].

> Reviewer 2: Your work is valuable and could make a contribution to the field. It could be a valuable presentation [elsewhere]. Nonetheless, [name of research association] is a prestigious research conference. To be accepted ... your proposal would need to have a stronger theoretical framework, detailed and rigorous methods, and strong results that contribute to the field.

Initially my reaction to these reviews was frustration. I was immediately reminded of a quote from bell hooks:

No need to hear your voice when I can talk about you better than you can speak about yourself. No need to hear your voice. Only tell me about your pain. I want to know your story. And then I will tell it back to you in a new way. Tell it back to you in such a way that it has become mine, my own. Rewriting you I write myself anew. I am still author, authority. I am still colonizer the speaking subject and you are now at the centre of my talk.

(hooks, 1990: 343)

I wondered if the abstract would have been rejected if I had rewritten it *for* the students, if I had become the 'speaking subject' and the students the 'centre of my talk'. I thought not. On further reflection, however, I began to question what I had done to help the conference reviewers to understand and receive this work as quality physical education research and realized I too may have been at fault. I failed to help them hear the students' voices. This incident highlighted for me the importance of not only practising pedagogy, research and theory building that repositions students as architects of research and curriculum, but also of advocating for this approach and helping others to listen to young people's voices.

In many ways, the above case highlights an important responsibility we have as youth researchers and more specifically participatory youth researchers. Those of us who are passionate about the potential of physical education and youth sport need to help others to open themselves and their work, be it research or teaching/coaching, to being transformed by young people, their interests, discourse and priorities. We need to educate the physical education and youth sport community to respect and engage with the politics and the possibilities of young peoples' voices. We have a responsibility to communicate in a way that helps others to truly listen to young peoples' voices.

Conclusion

Participatory research challenges conventional notions about what constitutes knowledge and how knowledge/data should be produced and shared. Listening to young people's voices using participatory methods is a valuable approach, however challenging for you as a researcher. It not only allows you to gather interesting data to answer a question of interest to you, but also provides you with an opportunity to interact with young people in a more authentic way and gain important insights into their ways of being and thinking. This can be hugely beneficial to you in your day-to-day teaching and coaching of young people. The use of participatory methods can mean a blurring of the lines between research and pedagogy, and both enterprises can benefit. All participatory research projects, regardless of whether they are undertaken with children or adults, need the time and resources to support meaningful participation. It is not just about your choice of methods. It also takes a particular mindset to approach research this way, what we have described as a methodological sensibility. While you can gain insights into young people's thinking, you also have to be sensitive to how much you encroach into their private lives and how willing you are in turn to share some aspects of your private life with them. Managing these relations as a beginning researcher can indeed be challenging. There is a wealth of literature about undertaking research with children and young people as participants and more recently as researchers. We hope this chapter prompts you to seek out this literature and challenges you to think a little bit differently about why and how you might involve children and young people in your research.

Key terms

Authentic participation   Engaging young people in conversations that allow for their decision making, investment and participation around issues of direct interest to their lives, that is, their lived experiences.

Participatory action research   A research design and philosophy that seeks to produce knowledge and action with participants and use this knowledge to improve the life circumstances of research participants during the course of the research itself.

Participatory research methods   Participatory methods are those that facilitate participants in finding their own language to articulate what they know, and help them put words to their ideas and feelings and share understandings of their worlds, thereby giving participants more control over the research process.

New social studies of childhood   A paradigm shift in the social study of children and young people signalled by a move away from the notion of children as passive recipients and deficient adults to an understanding and recognition of children and young people as active participants, competent human beings, valid social actors, agents of their own lives and co-constructors of knowledge.

Methodological sensibility   An awareness and appreciation of the rationale for the use of certain methods and a keen intellectual and ethical perception regarding when and how particular methods may be best used to help research participants share their experiences, perspectives and feelings.

References

Alderson, P. (2000) 'Children as researchers: the effects of participation rights on research methodology', in P. Christensen and A. James, *Research with Children: Perspectives and Practice* (241–57), London: Falmer Press.

Allard, A. (1996) 'Involving young people – empowerment or exploitation?', *Children and Society*, 10: 165–7.

Barker, J. and Weller, S. (2003) ' "Is it fun?" Developing children-centred research methods', *International Journal of Sociology and Social Policy*, 23(1/2): 33–58.

Becker, H. (2002) 'Visual evidence: a seventh man, the specified generalization and the work of the reader', *Visual Studies*, 17: 3–11.

Bush, K. A. (2002) 'Listening to the voices of four African American adolescent females on physical activity', unpublished doctoral dissertation, Columbus, OH: Ohio State University.

Christensen, P. and Prout, A. (2002) 'Working with ethical symmetry in social research with children', *Childhood*, 9(4): 477–97.

Clark, A. and Moss, P. (2001) *Listening to Young Children: the Mosaic Approach*, London: National Children's Bureau for the Joseph Rowntree Foundation.

Dodman, D. R. (2003) 'Shooting in the city: an autophotographic exploration of the urban environment in Kingston, Jamaica', *Area*, 35: 293–304.

Dyson, B. P. (1995) 'Students' voices in two alternative elementary physical education programs', *Journal of Teaching in Physical Education*, 14: 394–407.

Enright, E. and O'Sullivan, M. (2010) 'Carving a new order of experience with young people in physical education: Participatory Action Research as a pedagogy of possibility', in M. O'Sullivan and A. MacPhail (eds) *Young People's Voices in Physical Education and Youth Sport*, London: Routledge.

Enright, E. and O'Sullivan, M. (in press) 'Producing different knowledge and producing knowledge differently: rethinking physical education research and practice through participatory methods', *Sport, Education and Society*.

Enright, E., Barnes, C. and Gallagher, M. B. (2010) 'Methodological attitude: Opening the door to interdisciplinary dialogue in an Irish youth research context', paper presented at the 'The doors of perception: Viewing anthropology through the eyes of children' conference, VU University, Amsterdam.

Fine, M. (2008) 'An epilogue, of sorts', in J. Cammarota and M. Fine (eds) *Revolutionizing Education: Youth Participatory Action Research in Motion* (213–35), Oxon: Routledge.

Gallacher, L. and Gallagher, M. (2008) 'Methodological immaturity in childhood research? Thinking through "participatory methods" ', *Childhood*, 15(4): 499–516.

Hill, M. (2005) 'Ethical considerations in researching children's experience', in S. Greene and D. Hogan (eds) *Researching Children's Experience: Approaches and Methods* (61–87), London: Sage.

hooks, b. (1990) 'Marginality as site of resistance', in R. Ferguson, M. Gever, T. T. Minh-ha, and C. West (eds) *Out There: Marginalization and Contemporary Cultures* (341–343), New York and Cambridge, MA: The New Museum of Contemporary Art and Massachusetts Institute of Technology.

James, A., Jenks, C. and Prout, A. (1998) *Theorizing Childhood*, Cambridge: Polity Press.

Kesby, M. (2000) 'Participatory diagramming: deploying qualitative methods through an action research epistemology', *Area*, 34(4): 423–35.

Kincheloe, J. (2007) 'Clarifying the purpose of engaging students as researchers', in D. Thiessen and A. Cook-Sather (eds) *International Handbook of Student Experience in Elementary and Secondary Education* (745–75), Dordrecht: Springer.

Kinchin, G. and O'Sullivan, M. (1999) 'Making high school physical education meaningful for students', *Journal of Physical Education, Recreation and Dance*, 70(5): 40–4.

Long, J. and Carless, D. (2010) 'Hearing, listening and acting', in M. O'Sullivan and A. MacPhail (eds) *Young People's Voices in Physical Education and Sport* (213–25), London: Routledge.

Mayall, B. (2000) 'Conversations with children: working with generational issues', in P. Christensen and A. James (eds) *Research with Children: Perspectives and Practice* (120–36), London: Falmer Press.

O'Kane, C. (2000) 'The development of participatory techniques: Facilitating children's views about decisions which affect them', in P. Christensen and A. James (eds) *Research with Children* (136–60), London: Falmer Press.

O'Sullivan, M. and MacPhail, A. (eds) (2010) *Young People's Voices in Physical Education and Sport*, London: Routledge.

Pope, C. (1998) 'Locating the stadium on the way to the school: The educative role of sport in an urban American high school', unpublished doctoral dissertation, Ohio State University. Available May 27, 2011 at http://search.proquest.com/docview/304453695/abstract/12F9 7682AF97B178ADD/1?accountid=14564.

Punch, S. (2002) 'Research with children: The same as or different from adults?', *Childhood*, 9(3): 321–41.

Rudduck, J. and McIntyre, D. (2007) *Improving Learning through Consulting Pupils*, London: Routledge.

Thomas, N. and O'Kane, C. (1998) 'The ethics of participatory research with children', *Children and Society*, 112: 336–48.

Wang, C. (2003) 'Using photovoice as a participatory assessment and issue selection tool', in M. Minkler and N. Wallerstein (eds) *Community-based Participatory Research for Health* (179–196), San Francisco: Jossey-Bass.

Part III
Selecting the most appropriate method(s)

11 Reviewing literature

Thomas J. Templin and Gemma Pearce

Introduction

'Back in the day': Turn over every stone

As a doctoral student preparing my dissertation project on the socialization of student teachers (Templin, 1978), I was certain I had reviewed all the pertinent literature in the field of education and cognate areas. The study went off without a hitch and was even recognized as 'award winning' by my alma mater. It was shortly after receiving such accolades that I discovered a study (Lacey, 1977) that ultimately became one of the seminal references in research on teacher socialization. Had I discovered this iconic work at the time, it would have transformed my dissertation theoretically and it would have altered the lenses through which I analysed my data. While my oversight was unintended and probably not all that surprising 'back in the day' when search databases were limited, it did teach me a huge lesson: try to turn over every relevant stone when searching the literature.

About us

Thomas J. Templin: Over my career, I have been involved in various projects focusing on the socialization of teachers, particularly organizational socialization, which looks at the influence of the world of work on a teacher's role. Throughout my career, my study of physical education teachers, as well as teachers from other subject areas, has been influenced by research literature in the fields of physical education and education more broadly, as well as literature from cognate areas such as anthropology, sociology, industrial–organizational psychology and social psychology. The sheer range of literature that is potentially relevant to my interests means that a clear review strategy has always been essential.

Gemma Pearce: When I first started as a student in higher education, I used to feel that writing up experiments had a clearly laid out structure, but that reviewing the literature was a more subjective process of reading articles on and around the topic and writing about it in ways that seemed relevant. However, I have since learnt that the process is usually more systematic than I realized. There are structures, methods and tools for literature reviewing to guide you and to underpin both the validity and the reliability of the whole process. The experience of conducting a systematic review was of real value to me and there are principles of systematic reviewing that are relevant to all researchers at any stage of their careers.

Traditional and systematic literature reviews

This chapter introduces two types of literature reviews. The first we refer to as a traditional review of literature, which is commonly used in dissertations, theses and research articles. The second type, referred to as a systematic review of literature, often represents a stand-alone publication and follows a replicable review process. While different, both are designed to provide a foundation for research conducted over time in order to assist the researcher in the formulation, conduct and analysis of a research project.

Traditional literature reviews

Over the past four decades, scholars have extended the state of sport pedagogy research significantly and have established an impressive literature base. Whether through scholarly articles in research journals, professional journals or books, this literature base serves as the foundation from which future research studies are designed and questions should be framed. It is critical that any researcher provides sufficient evidence to indicate that a rigorous review of literature has been conducted. That is, to lend credibility to the theoretical framework and research design of a project, the researcher must give a reader or a reviewer a solid literature foundation from which to assess a study. This chapter is designed to give the reader insight into the importance of the review of literature, the experiences of the two authors, who are at different stages in their careers, and some of the technical processes involved in conducting an appropriate review.

Since all research should be informed by existing knowledge, the literature review is a necessary process (Rowley and Slack, 2004). An exhaustive literature review will include a summary of findings related to the research question. Although the review may focus primarily on findings from a particular field, it should also be extended to include relevant information from related fields: for example, a review of literature on physical education teacher or sports coach professional development must extend into the vast general education literature. Importantly, the literature review should include a comprehensive analysis of theoretical models that are related to the area of investigation as a foundation for the model or models that will eventually provide a framework for the research. When done well, a literature review enables readers and investigators to make vital links between existing knowledge and new knowledge to be generated by research. It has been argued that the literature review can be described as an academic conversation that shapes the role of the current research in an ongoing discourse among experts in a field (Dowling and Brown, 2010).

In reviewing the literature, the researcher develops and demonstrates an understanding of the research topic area. It is likely that the researcher already has personal or 'folk' theories (Bruner, 1999) on the topic to be investigated, and these are likely to act as a guide to the early search strategy. Such theories should not, however, be allowed to dominate the whole review process. If the review is not comprehensive enough, the study could be criticized for being insufficiently grounded in previous research and/or theory. Research designs usually emanate from previous research; for example, an author may choose a data collection procedure that has proven effective in the past, or will identify a gap in the literature and use that as a basis for developing new research methods.

While the literature review is an essential part of the research process, it is not usually the stage that generates new knowledge (although systematic reviews can lead to new insights into existing findings). It is when a question cannot be answered sufficiently by a review of the existing literature that new research directions are indicated. In this way, the literature base can be seen as a library of knowledge. As in a public library, the answers to questions are not always easy to find. Therefore, a range of search strategies will be required to ensure that all relevant information is considered and this is likely to include, as a minimum, following up citations in existing research and searching appropriate databases.

An appropriate literature review is a vital step in the continuous search for new knowledge and answers to complex questions. Done well, it informs understanding on a topic and research designs, and provides the basis for analysing empirical data. Although it is common to complete the review prior to beginning an investigation, it is important to note that some proponents of grounded theory (see Chapter 21) argue against this approach in order to avoid forcing theory on the data. Instead, these researchers would argue that theories should be allowed to 'emerge' or be 'constructed' from the data during the analysis phase (Dowling and Brown, 2010), followed by a wider literature review. Either way, a thorough review of literature should accompany all research projects at some stage in the process.

Conducting a traditional literature review

Most research projects are initiated out of the researcher's curiosity about a particular concern, event or phenomenon. Even where a researcher joins an established research team, it is likely that the researcher has either personal interest in, or professional curiosity, about the research area. Curiosity and our own lived experiences tend to propel us toward certain research problems. The questions generated through curiosity are those that help to guide the researcher toward relevant literature that will help to shape the project (Thomas, Nelson and Silverman, 2005). For novice researchers, guidance from supervisors or other experienced colleagues is necessary and invaluable.

Once a research question has been developed to a satisfactory stage, it is time to begin the substantive portion of the search (Locke, Spirduso and Silverman, 2007). It is important to note that many academics argue there is no foolproof or 'right' way to sift through all of the information related to your topic (Thomas et al., 2005).

Each review will examine a different segment of the existing literature base and thus will take the reviewer in a slightly different direction. Although some authors have argued for the importance of specific and systematic review methodologies (e.g. Fink, 2005; Locke et al., 2007), in this section of the chapter, we present instead a series of 'guiding principles':

- Start with secondary sources. Systematic reviews and previous reviews of literature can help to identify primary articles related to a given topic.
- Think broad to narrow. Begin with sources more broadly related to the content area, and then move to those which are specific to the identified research question.
- Alternatively, if you have a very clear research question about which there is little published research, you might think narrow to broad. Begin with the limited published sources directly in your field and then broaden out in a range of potentially useful directions.
- Specify descriptive search terms. Keep a record of all terms used when making searches and use catalogue entry field terms such as AND, OR and NOT in order to broaden or narrow the search.
- All sources are not of equal value to the research process. Give preference to peer-refereed academic sources (e.g. journals), over those which are created for the general public (e.g. magazines).
- Read and record the literature. Read each piece of literature deemed to be relevant to the review and catalogue important information. Articles can be annotated for quick reference when beginning to write the review.
- Review references. Consult the reference sections of journal articles and books in order to identify sources that may have been omitted from the initial search.
- Maintain records of articles. Obtain copies of all sources and record citations in a database. Software programs such as EndNote (Thompson Reuters, 2010) have tended to replace manual card index systems for cataloguing references.

Search strategies

As described in the opening of this chapter, in previous decades the only way to procure sources was through a manual search of card catalogues in libraries. Computers and the internet have since revolutionized the literature review process and now most library catalogues can only be accessed electronically. Most universities have institutional subscriptions to a vast range of journals, which makes them accessible online in an electronic format. Sources not held by an individual university can usually be accessed through other means including interlibrary loan, and a search of Google Scholar provides open access to a surprising range of articles. In addition, most major universities around the world have established 'institutional repositories' in recent years and these offer open access to some of the published material authored by their own staff.

While the technological sophistication of contemporary libraries enables the user to sift through records and even obtain documents remotely, it is probable that a trip to a university or public library will eventually be required. At the time of writing, most books, especially those which are considered to be seminal works, are typically not available online.

The internet has, undoubtedly, revolutionized the process of reviewing the literature. Yet it is important for new researchers to be aware that not all – or even most – online sources are created for research purposes (Rowley and Slack, 2004). Many websites publish opinions and other non-peer-reviewed claims that are inappropriate for use in a literature review (unless, of course, the analysis of such information is *the* research question). Thus, Ballenger (2007) recommends that when using the internet the researcher prioritizes information obtained from scholarly and governmental sources and library-affiliated databases which produce results that are also available in print (e.g. SportDiscus, Google Scholar, JSTOR, Academic Search Premier). In a research context, the major strength of the internet (ease of access) is also, potentially, its greatest weakness. One of the most common mistakes novice researchers make is to assume that because material has been published on the internet it is, in some sense, authoritative.

WRITING THE REVIEW

Students often ask how much literature constitutes 'enough' for a research project. There is, however, no clear answer to this question. An undergraduate research project would necessitate a smaller review of literature than a doctoral thesis. In addition, given the differences between research topics and purposes, there is no magic number that can be given to establish when a review is complete. However, Dowling and Brown (2010) recommend that the search should continue until the literature seems to be exhausted because studies keep saying the same things; in other words, nothing new is being found. Once this happens, it is time to begin writing the review. The specific form that this takes will vary depending on the goals of the project, but Thomas, Nelson and Silverman (2005) recommend a three-pronged structure to a written review of literature. The *introduction* should explain the purpose of the review, along with how and why it has been conducted. The *body* summarizes the relevant research that was collected in the retrieval stage of the project in a clear, concise and interesting manner. Finally, the *conclusion* summarizes the review and sets up the project to be explored in the present study.

Example of a traditional literature review: An exploration of teacher burnout and emotion

Most occupations, at different times, are fraught with concerns and anxieties, but also excitement, opportunity and challenge. A worker in any occupation is faced with a variety of factors that facilitate success, failure or a level of performance somewhere in between. Those who enter teaching are no different and, dating back to Waller's (1932) classic study, *The Sociology of Teaching*, numerous studies and documents have examined the socialization experience of teachers (Lacey, 1977; Stroot and Ko, 2006). Literally thousands of studies connected to a myriad of topics related to teacher socialization have been published in education and related scholarly journals in anthropology, sociology, psychology, communication and other fields.

A project conducted at Tom Templin's institution examined teacher burnout and emotion (Carson, 2006), and this offers an example of how a vast literature base can be searched. The main purpose of the research was to develop a comprehensive understanding of the dynamics of teacher burnout through the assessment of daily emotional experiences, regulatory processes and affect-driven behaviours. Research questions included:

- How does overall burnout relate to daily burnout in teachers?
- How does emotional regulation/labour relate to teachers' overall and daily burnout?
- What is the relationship between teachers' perceptions of work-related performance and daily burnout?
- What are the daily emotional experiences of teachers with varying levels of burnout?

Beyond our initial curiosity linked to these questions, an exhaustive review of literature as described earlier in this chapter helped to develop and refine the purpose of the study, its data collection methods and the tools for analysis of the data. The review covered a wide range of topics and was divided into two foundational areas: teacher burnout literature and teacher emotion literature. Using various search bases and keywords (see examples below) linked to both burnout and emotion in teaching, nearly 700 references were cited in the final research report, which took the form of a PhD dissertation. The review of literature on teacher burnout covered four related areas:

- The teaching workforce and literature related to entry and attrition in teaching;
- The distinction between job stress and burnout;
- Burnout determinants related to demographic (e.g., gender, age, years of experience), workplace (e.g., subject area, school locale) and personal and/or psychological factors (e.g., self-esteem, efficacy, job satisfaction, commitment);
- Major consequences (e.g., coping strategies, absenteeism, job performance) of teacher burnout.

While there is a clear need for more theoretically driven, mixed-method and longitudinal research, analysis of the parameters of the literature base revealed that research on teacher burnout has exploded over the past three decades, and significant progress has been made in generating its determinants and consequences. Importantly, the review revealed that there was a relationship between teacher burnout and emotion; that is, chronic emotional responses by the teacher, on a daily basis and over time, serve as the catalyst for teacher burnout at varying levels.

This finding led to a second related review of literature on emotion in the workplace and, more specifically, emotion in teaching. Grounded primarily in research and theory from organizational and industrial psychology, the review encompassed a variety of constructs such as affect, mood, emotion regulation and various regulatory resources, and emotional labour as it related to burnout and teacher burnout. Through this process, the review revealed a dearth of research on teacher emotion at the time (Carson, 2006). Since that time, however, a number of conceptually and empirically based studies and reviews on the topic have emerged and this trend indicates that the topic is viewed as increasingly important. In particular, the research in organizational psychology and recent work undertaken in education (Schutz and Pekrun, 2007) have better informed researchers about best practice, both theoretically and methodologically, in the study of teacher burnout and emotion.

Systematic literature reviews

Traditional literature reviews use a range of strategies that vary in the degree of structure and direction that is imposed or adopted. It could be argued that in this approach, researchers sometimes follow their emerging interests in a somewhat haphazard manner. In contrast, systematic reviewing is a detailed and explicit approach to analysing existing literature. Systematic reviews are so-called because reviewers follow a standardized, logical and explicit peer-reviewed protocol. They aim to answer questions that are specified in rigorous detail, using an approach that is both transparent and repeatable. The review process is designed to ensure that the product is accountable, replicable, updateable and sustainable. The key purpose of a systematic review is to evaluate the effectiveness, meaningfulness and appropriateness of existing research, using a highly reliable process. This, in turn, highlights future needs regarding practice, policy and research (see Hemmingway and Brereton, 2009). Systematic reviews can be used in any subject and they are commonly conducted in medicine, social science, health and education. Peer-reviewed protocols for systematic reviews have been produced and developed by groups such as the Evidence for Policy and Practice Information and Co-ordinating Centre (EPPI-Centre) and the Campbell Collaboration. The EPPI-Centre is based at the University of London and predominantly focuses on reviews in education, health, social care, employment, crime and justice (http://eppi.ioe.ac.uk). The Campbell Collaboration is based in Norway and focuses on reviews in education, social welfare, crime and justice (http://www.campbellcollaboration.org/).

There are different types of systematic review depending on research purpose, the question being asked and the data being collected. The first review style is known as *a priori*, where the question and methods are set from the beginning and these are adhered to rigidly throughout the review process. The other main style is *iterative*, where the question can be reviewed and changed based on feedback from search results as they are received (i.e., the question can either be made more specific to reduce the number of articles found under that criterion, or vice versa). The search question determines whether the review focuses on quantitative, qualitative or a mixture of both types of research. As noted by Boaz et al. (2006), it is the question that should govern whether the data collected in the review will be homogeneous (same) or heterogeneous (different) in nature and what type of analysis can then be carried out.

There are two main types of analysis in systematic literature reviews: meta-analysis and meta-synthesis. Meta-analysis is appropriate where all the articles in the review are likely to be quantitative and homogeneous in key design features: for example, those concerned with randomized control trials (see Crombie and Davies, 2009). If, however, the review is focused on articles that are more heterogeneous in nature, such as qualitative or a mixture of methods, then meta-synthesis (thematic analysis of the findings) would be more appropriate. This form of narrative synthesis should also be used if quantitative findings are not homogeneous.

Although the processes involved in a systematic review are designed to reduce bias and increase repeatability, as with all research strategies these have limitations. For example:

- Article searches can be limited such that they only include published studies written in English and published in peer-reviewed journals that are viewed as relevant by the reviewer.
- Articles may be judged differently depending on the reviewer's personal research background and epistemology (see earlier chapters in this book).
- Systematic review protocols might be too demanding for some researchers, particularly at undergraduate level, where stringent quality assurance measures and reviewer triangulation are required to reduce reviewer subjectivity and error, and a 'user group' is recommended consisting of a team of 'experts' in the systematic review process, the research field, relevant policy and applied practice.

It should also be recognized that biases and subjectivity are not eradicated when using a systematic review approach, but the aim is to reduce them through the adoption of methodological protocols and transparent review reports.

Conducting a systematic review

Conducting and writing a systematic review are best structured in a manner similar to that of an empirical study. The following sections are suggested: introduction, methods, findings, and discussion.

INTRODUCTION

This section needs to include definitions of key terms (similar to a glossary) and a rationale for the review. For example: why there is a need to collate existing research on this topic; where the limitations of previous reviews in this field lie; reasons leading to this review; aims of the review; and the specific review question. The review question should summarize within it: the review objective; the type of research to be covered; the relevant population and setting; and appropriate outcomes (if relevant). The review question needs to be specific and detailed as it will guide the rest of your review:

> Example question 1: What are children's views about the meanings of obesity or body size, shape or weight (including their perceptions of their own body size), and what experiences do they describe relating to these issues?
>
> (Rees, Oliver, Woodman and Thomas, 2009)

Example question 2: What do surveys of factors associated with different physical activity patterns in children suggest are the important barriers and facilitators?
(Brunton, Harden, Rees, Kavanagh, Oliver and Oakley, 2003)

METHODS

The aim of the methods section is to detail explicitly how the review was conducted so that those reading the review can repeat it and, more importantly, conduct future reviews that extend from it. Based on the proposed review question, databases, keywords and inclusion criteria can be set. As presented above in our discussion of traditional reviews, databases and keywords are tools used to search for relevant literature from a variety of sources – both electronically and by hand at the library. In systematic reviews, it is a requirement that both the databases searched and the keywords used in your review are identified and the manner of their use explained.

Once the search for articles is complete, a process of screening is applied to the studies to assess their eligibility against inclusion criteria, in order to select those that will be included in the review. When setting the inclusion criteria, it is important to use the research question systematically to direct this process. The inclusion criteria should detail every requirement of an article that is necessary for it to be incorporated in the review. The broadest criteria are applied first, and then the most specific. Below is an example of the process of structuring the inclusion criteria.

1   The language (e.g., English only).
2   The timeline (e.g., from January 2000 to July 2010). The start date should be of relevance to the review, such as the start of a relevant policy, evidence or intervention. The end date should be when the last search was conducted.
3   The review objective (e.g., evaluation of an intervention type).
4   Research type (e.g., focusing on randomized control trials, qualitative research or a mixture of methods).
5   The population (e.g., physical education teachers).
6   The setting (e.g., extracurricular clubs).
7   Outcomes (e.g., to investigate effectiveness).
8   Any other details specific to the review question.

Screening the articles allows the reviewer to apply each of the inclusion criteria in order to judge, systematically, whether they should be included in the review. A two-stage approach to the screening process is often used where initially the abstracts of all potential publications are screened. All those papers that are not excluded from the review at the first stage are then retrieved for the second stage of screening. For example, during the first stage, the reviewer may be able to exclude a number of studies for not being in English. In some cases, papers will not be directly relevant to the topic, and in other cases it will be necessary to check the full article to find out about the population or expected outcomes of the study. This screening process allows only those articles directly relevant to the review question to be analysed.

ANALYSIS

Similar to that of an empirical study, the analysis chosen by the reviewer depends on the type(s) of data collected. In the case of systematic reviews, the 'data' are the articles themselves, rather than raw data collected in primary research. In writing up reviews, it is usual practice to begin with descriptive summary statistics of the data, such as information on the sample and setting.

In a systematic review it is of equal importance both to examine the quality of the research under review and to summarize each of the relevant findings. The reviewer needs to engage in a process of critical evaluation of the validity and reliability of the studies selected by answering a series of questions and applying answers in a systematic way. This process results in a rating of the quality of each study. Those rated as 'high quality' should be given more weighting in the review than those rated to be of a 'low quality'. It is apparent at this point that the possibility of researcher bias might influence the review and it is recommended that reviewer triangulation forms part of the process in an attempt to minimize subjectivity.

DISCUSSION

This section should: 1) summarize the main findings and provide a commentary on the quality of research used in the review; 2) discuss how this review informs the existing literature and answers the review question; 3) examine the limitations of the review and how these limitations could be overcome; and 4) conclude why the review is relevant and how it can be applied in the future to inform policy, practice and research.

A systematic review of gifted and talented students

The main stages in a standard EPPI-Centre review (see earlier in chapter) are to: 1) formulate a review question and develop a protocol; 2) define studies to be included, with clear inclusion criteria; 3) search systematically for studies using multiple sources; 4) screen studies for inclusion; and 5) review data on individual studies by giving descriptive information on each study, a summary of the findings of each study and information necessary to assess the quality of the individual studies (see EPPI-Centre for more details: http://eppi.ioe.ac.uk).

INTRODUCTION

This case is based on the first systematic review of literature on gifted and talented (G and T) education (see Bailey et al., 2008). The review question was: 'Which types of classroom-based interventions improve the educational achievement of students identified as G and T?' The review was iterative and the original question had less detail, but the initial search results were very broad and were too large to review (19,662 articles). As a result, the question was refined to specify classroom-based interventions focusing on educational achievement, and this refinement narrowed the search results down to a more appropriate level (15 articles).

METHOD

The process that led to the final 15 articles was as follows. Published literature was searched for, using online specialist journals (e.g. *High Ability Studies* and *Gifted Education International*) and online search sources (e.g., British Education Index, CERUK and ISI Social Science Citation Index). It is also important to search for 'grey literature', which, unlike peer-reviewed published articles, cannot be found easily through conventional channels. In this case, specialist agencies were contacted directly, inviting them to submit research reports and publishers' articles into the review (e.g., National Academy of Gifted and Talented Youth; Scottish Network for Able Pupils and The G&T Wise project from the Centre for Wise Education (http://www.wiseeducation.org.uk/G_%26_T_Wise.html).

Basic search keywords based on the review question were 'student', 'gifted', 'talented', 'intervention' and 'outcome'. Then, all the words that had similar meanings in the literature were brainstormed and the search regulations pertaining to each were investigated, resulting in the development of keyword strings. Examples of keywords strings from this review are those used in ASSIA and ERIC[1] databases, where * means that the term will be explored in singular, plural and other related forms (for more examples see Bailey et al., 2008, Appendix 7.3 technical report):

youth* OR student* OR pupil* OR teen* OR child* OR learner OR learners OR underachieve* OR adolescent*

AND

gift* OR talent* OR able OR genius OR intelligent* OR clever OR precocious OR capable OR potential OR accomplish

AND

intervention* OR program* OR method OR activity OR barrier* OR higher ADJ order OR creative OR classroom OR identify* OR independent OR peer OR personalize* OR pace OR provi* OR critical OR educat* OR stream* OR select* OR tutoring OR inclu*

AND

outcome* OR improve* OR result* OR measure* OR effect OR score* OR achieve* OR assess* OR attain* OR change.

When large amounts of search results came back, the review team experimented with the keywords and found that the word 'potential' was adding an extra 6,000 unnecessary (irrelevant) hits, so it was removed from the search.

The inclusion criteria for the screening process were: studies needed to be written in English; published between January 1998 (when G and T education was formally presented as an expectation for English schools) and November 2007 (review submission date to funder); focus explicitly on G and T / highly able / more able pupils; empirical;

evidence based (not conceptual or philosophical); an intervention within the parameters of the Classroom Quality Standards; include students aged from 5 to 16 years (age range of compulsory schooling in the UK); report the measure of intervention outcomes; related to the engagement of learners and learning; have a 'what works?' focus; set in a primary, middle, secondary or special needs school; relate to learners; explicitly focused on the teaching and learning process; and report on educational achievement. The specialist software program EPPI-Reviewer was used to record and code studies analysed during the review. Initially, after completing the extensive keyword search and removing duplicated articles, 19,662 abstracts were identified. After this comprehensive screening process, 15 studies remained in the review.

ANALYSIS

The review data were heterogeneous, narrative and empirical with a mixture of methodologies. The analysis consisted of two stages: 1) descriptive statistics summarizing the overall characteristics of the selected studies; and 2) an in-depth narrative synthesis that analysed the research findings systematically using a meta-empirical approach.

The quality of the 15 studies was assessed using the 'Weight of Evidence' (WoE) EPPI-Centre data-extraction framework. These WoE criteria were based on:

- WoE A: Can the study findings be trusted in answering the study question?
- WoE B: Appropriateness of research design and analysis for addressing the question, or sub-questions, of this specific systematic review.
- WoE C: Relevance of particular focus of the study (including conceptual focus, context, sample and measures) for addressing the question, or sub-questions, of this specific systematic review.
- WoE D: Overall weighting, taking into account A, B and C.

The WoE assessment was carried out by two independent blind reviewers, and included random quality assurance checks by colleagues from the EPPI-Centre. Disagreements were discussed until resolved.

DISCUSSION

The main themes of the review were discussed regarding three types of interventions: school and classroom organization; social interaction; and the development of new skills and strategies. Implications for policy, practice, and research were discussed further in the full report and this included reflections on the quality of the reviewed research.

Conclusion

The literature review is a critical part of any research process. Whether reviewing the literature prior to beginning a research project, having collected data, or as a stand-alone research activity, we encourage you to view the process in the way a prospector might view the task of mining for gold: it is hard work but when done well, the results are very rewarding.

Now that you have read about literature reviews and systematic reviews, we also encourage you to consider the following questions in relation to your own research projects:

1   What is it that you are curious to learn more about? This will guide you toward a potential topic area.
2   Where can you go to access information that relates to your curiosity?
3   Once you have immersed yourself in the literature, what specific research or review question are you attempting to address?
4   If preparing a review for a research article or thesis, how will the research question that you identify fill a gap in the existing literature base?
5   If conducting a systematic review, how will your work help to guide future practitioners, policymakers and researchers?

Key terms

Literature review   An exhaustive summary of research findings related to the research topic and questions under examination. The review focuses primarily on findings from a particular field, but it should also be extended to include relevant information from related fields.

Literature review methodology   A systematic process for collecting research findings related to the primary topic and questions under study. This may include using electronic search engines or the use of periodical indices in the identification of related literature.

Systematic review   A detailed and explicit approach to analysing existing literature. Systematic reviews are so-called because reviewers follow a standardized, logical and explicit peer-reviewed protocol.

Meta-analysis   Appropriate where all the articles in the review are likely to be quantitative and homogeneous in key design features. It is a process that employs various statistical methods to retrieve, select, and combine results from previous separate, but related studies.

Meta-synthesis   An exhaustive study that has examined and interpreted the findings of a number of qualitative research studies using qualitative methods. A meta-synthesis is focused on articles that are more heterogeneous in nature, such as qualitative or a mixture of methods.

Acknowledgements

The authors would like to acknowledge Michael A. Hemphill and K. Andrew Richards of Purdue University, USA for their contributions to this chapter.

Note

1   Both of these are web-based digital libraries. ASSIA stands for the Applied Social Sciences Index and Abstracts and ERIC is the Education Resources Information Centre.

References

Bailey, R., Pearce, G., Winstanley, C., Sutherland, M., Smith, C., Stack, N. *et al.* (2008) 'A systematic review of interventions aimed at improving the educational achievement of pupils identified as gifted and talented', London: EPPI-Centre, Social Science Research Unit, Institute of Education, University of London.

Ballenger, B. (2007) *The Curious Researcher*, 5th edn, New York: Pearson Longman.

Boaz, A., Ashby, D., Denyer, D., Egan, M., Harden, A., Jones, D. R. *et al.* (2006) 'A multitude of syntheses: A comparison of five approaches from diverse policy fields', *Evidence and Policy*, 2: 479–502.

Bruner, J. (1999) 'Folk pedagogies', in J. Leach and B. Moon (eds) *Learners and Pedagogy* (4–20), London: The Open University.

Brunton, G., Harden, A., Rees, R., Kavanagh, J., Oliver, S. and Oakley A. (2003) 'Children and physical activity: a systematic review of barriers and facilitators', London: EPPI-Centre, Social Science Research Unit, Institute of Education, University of London.

Carson, R. L. (2006) 'Exploring the espisodic nature of teachers' emotions as it relates to teacher burnout', unpublished doctoral dissertation, West Lafayette, IN: Purdue University.

Crombie, I. K. and Davies, H. T. (2009) *What Is a Meta-analysis?*, London: Hayward Medical Communications.

Dowling, P. and Brown, A. (2010) *Doing Research/Reading Research: Re-interrogating Education*, 2nd edn, New York: Routledge.

Fink, A. (2005) *Conducting Research Literature Reviews: From Internet to Paper*, 2nd edn, Thousand Oaks, CA: Sage.

Hemmingway, P. and Brereton, N. (2009) *What Is a Systematic Review?*, London: Hayward Medical Communications.

Lacey, C. (1977) *The Socialization of Teachers*, London: Methuen.

Locke, L. F., Spirduso, W. W. and Silverman, S. J. (2007) *Proposals that Work: A Guide for Planning Dissertations and Grant Proposals*, 5th edn, Thousand Oaks, CA: Sage.

Rees, R., Oliver, K., Woodman, J. and Thomas, J. (2009) 'Children's views about obesity, body size, shape and weight: a systematic review', London: EPPI Centre, Social Science Research Unit, Institute of Education, University of London.

Rowley, J. and Slack, F. (2004) 'Conducting a literature review', *Management Research News*, 27(6): 31–9.

Schutz, P. A. and Pekrun, R. (eds) (2007) *Emotion in Education*, Burlington, MA: Academic Press.

Stroot, S. A. and Ko, B. (2006) 'Induction of beginning physical education teachers into the school setting', in D. Kirk, D. Macdonald and M. O'Sullivan (eds) *The Handbook of Physical Education* (425–48), London: Sage Publications.

Templin, T. J. (1978) 'Pupil control ideology and behavior and selected socialization factors influencing the physical education student teacher', unpublished doctoral dissertation, Ann Arbor, MI: University of Michigan.

Thomas, R. J., Nelson, J. K. and Silverman, S. J. (2005) *Research Methods in Physical Activity*, Champaign, IL: Human Kinetics.

Thompson Reuters (2010) EndNote X4. Carlsbad, CA: Thompson Reuters.

Waller, W. (1932) *The Sociology of Teaching*, New York: Russell and Russell.

12 Experimental research methods in physical education and sports

Leen Haerens and Isabel Tallir

Introduction

It is not solely by satisfactory arguments that one learns how to teach or coach; it is by building up experience through continuous experimentation. In their classrooms, teachers are constantly experimenting with different ways of interacting with pupils or with methods and teaching styles that could affect student learning in a positive way. Although this type of real-life experimentation does not meet all of the criteria of a 'true' research experiment, as will be explained further in this chapter, it is by no means less valuable.

About us

Professor Dr Leen Haerens and Dr Isabel Tallir are colleagues in the Department of Movement and Sport Sciences of Ghent University. Although Leen's PhD was situated in the area of health promotion, both researchers are currently conducting research in the area of physical education (PE) and sports pedagogy.

For her PhD study, Leen designed a quasi-experimental study to evaluate the effectiveness of a two-year school-based physical activity and healthy eating intervention. The major study in Isabel's dissertation was a quasi-experimental study in which the effectiveness of a social-constructivist-oriented tactical game approach, specifically the invasion games competence model (IGCM) for teaching invasion games (in this case basketball), was compared with a traditional cognitivist and skill-oriented approach.

As beginning researchers, both were convinced that conducting research in an ecologically valid setting such as the classroom or the school would provide a more stringent and valuable test for evaluating the effectiveness of their interventions. This is because the results would then give a more realistic view of how effective the interventions would be if implemented on a larger scale. Was conducting research in an ecologically valid setting as easy and straightforward as hoped?

The purpose and main characteristics of experimental and quasi-experimental designs

In this chapter, experimental and quasi-experimental research designs, commonly configured as randomized controlled trials (RCTs), are discussed. Highly controlled, 'true' experimental designs may be considered the gold standard of scientific research in the positivist paradigm when looking from the perspective of internal validity or the ability to provide strong evidence for causal inferences.

The purpose of an experimental design is to provide a structure for evaluating the cause-and-effect relationships between a set of independent and dependent variables (Portney and Watkins, 2009: 161, 193). Experiments are, hence, considered appropriate designs for investigating the causal effects of implementing pedagogical models such as teaching games for understanding (TGfU) on pupils' or players' tactical awareness, the effects of a school-based physical activity intervention on pupils' activity levels, the protective effects of medication on cardiovascular diseases or the effects of muscle stabilization exercises on injury prevalence. In other words, an experimental design is a structure to evaluate *the effect of one variable (the independent variable)*, usually a training or intervention, *on another variable (the dependent variable)*. If your research question includes causal inferences, an experimental design might be the best choice. However, strategies employed to be able to draw causal conclusions may also limit the generalizability or external validity of the results. In consequence, experimental designs are not necessarily the best choice in every situation.

To be considered a true experiment, three characteristics have to be met: 1) experimenters manipulate the independent variable under investigation; 2) a control or comparison group is included; and 3) random assignment of participants to groups (experimental, control) takes place (Portney and Watkins, 2009: 162). When studies are conducted in an ecologically valid setting and existing groups are used (e.g., in classes and schools), quasi-experimental designs present good alternatives to true experiments.

In the following part of the chapter, we elaborate on the three main characteristics of experimental designs. Throughout, we have included boxes with examples of research designs with questions stimulating you to think critically about the characteristics of experimental research designs in a physical education or sport setting.

Manipulation

One of the main features of an experiment is that the researcher systematically manipulates the independent variable under investigation, trying to understand how this variable affects the environment or people's behaviours. In a PE or sports context, manipulation mainly refers to exposing people (athletes, trainers, teachers, pupils) to an intervention or training. The group of people that is exposed to the intervention or training condition is called the experimental group. When the independent variable cannot be manipulated by the experimenter, other types of studies such as observational studies might be more appropriate.

Control group

When designing experimental studies, researchers must find a balance between manipulating the environment and controlling for variables that could be affecting the investigated outcome.

A research team wants to investigate the effect of a new running programme on athletes' running performance. They measure running performance in 20 athletes before the training programme starts. After 20 weeks, the running performance is measured again. Running performance has improved. The researchers conclude that the athletes' performance improved as a result of the training and that the new training programme can therefore be recommended to trainers in the field. Are the researchers drawing the right conclusions? Do you consider this a good study design to assess the effects of the training programme?

In this example, the major problem is that a control group is lacking, which makes it impossible to rule out rival hypotheses as possible explanations for the observed response. A control group is a comparison group that functions in an environment similar to that of the experimental group.

In some cases, the control group is at the null level of the independent variable, hence receiving no training or intervention at all. In other cases, the control group is a group receiving a standard intervention or training. In the example above, the control group would be a group receiving their regular training programme. The inclusion of such a control group to compare with allows researchers to conclude that favourable changes in the investigated dependent variable (e.g., better running performance) in the experimental group (e.g., people exposed to the new running programme), as opposed to the control group (e.g., people exposed to their regular training programme), are likely to be due to the experimental condition as this is the only real difference between those groups. In other words, observed differences between the experimental and control groups can be ascribed with confidence to the experimental manipulation because this is the only real difference between both groups.

Random assignment

A researcher wants to investigate the effects of teachers integrating more student-centred teaching styles on pupils' motivation. One teacher, teaching in six different classes, is involved in the study. After following a training programme on how to apply more student-centred methods, the teacher applies these teaching styles in three of six of the enrolled classes. Do you consider this a good design to assess the effect of teaching styles on pupils' motivation?

One of the shortcomings in this example relates to the final feature of experiments, namely random assignment to groups. This means that each participant in the study has an equal chance of being assigned to either the experimental or the control group. This provides confidence that no systematic bias exists with respect to a group's collective characteristics that might differently affect the dependent variable (Portney and Watkins, 2009: 163). By allowing the teacher to choose in which classes the student-centred teaching style will be implemented, selection bias is very likely to occur. Teachers might feel more comfortable implementing this new way of teaching in classes with certain characteristics, such as classes that are more interested in and motivated by the topic of the lessons. Random assignment allows for participants with specific characteristics (e.g., more motivated as opposed to less motivated pupils) to have equal chances of being assigned to either the experimental or the control group. This implies that differences between experimental and control groups are totally due to chance, and cannot be ascribed to any form of selection bias. Of course, a further foundational issue here is the assumption that a teacher can change towards a 'pure' teaching style such as student centred.

The main characteristics – manipulation, control and randomization – illustrated through Isabel's PhD study

The major challenge of conducting experimental or quasi-experimental research in an ecologically valid setting such as PE or youth sport is to design studies that allow control for possible confounding variables.We have seen that a design without a control group is not likely to be justifiable. In the educational context, the control group is most likely to be a 'care as usual' group, or a group who receives their lessons as planned by the teachers, without interference of the researcher team. To illustrate, the purpose of Isabel's study was to investigate the effects of the IGCM for teaching invasion games in basketball. Two schools, each involved with two classes of fifth graders, were randomly assigned to either the experimental or the control group. Pupils in the experimental group were exposed to basketball lessons based on the IGCM (manipulation), whereas pupils in the control group received a more traditional curriculum. To control for baseline differences, the experimental and control groups' game performances were measured before the intervention. A design with only post-test measures is not a strong and desirable experimental or quasi-experimental design.

Studies in the educational context might also present some challenges related to randomization. The information above illustrates that randomization is strongly recommended and studies with a non-randomized design present serious weaknesses within this paradigm. In the example above, we could have chosen to treat one school as the experimental group and the other as a control group. This non-random assignment would result in pupils not having equal chances to be assigned to either the experimental or control group and consequently baseline differences between both groups would not be due to chance. Therefore it was an essential feature of the design that the assignment of the two schools to one of both conditions occurred at random.

Designing an experimental or quasi-experimental study

A randomized controlled trial looks different depending on the number of independent variables, the number of groups being tested, the type of randomization and the number and timing of measurements. Here, we will illustrate the design specifications of an experimental and a quasi-experimental study.

The pretest–post-test control group design as framework

The pretest–post-test control group design forms the basic structure of most randomized controlled trials. Participants are randomly assigned to either the experimental or control group. After that, a pretest measurement takes place, followed by either a training/intervention (experimental group) or no intervention (control group). After that, both groups participate in the post-test measurement and changes in the dependent variable are compared across both groups. If more favourable changes are observed in the experimental group when compared with the comparison group, the intervention/training is held responsible for inducing these changes.

The basic experimental design (see Figure 12.1) can be further modified in many ways. More than one experimental group or intervention arm can be included or more than one post-test measurement can be conducted. It is also common that the control group is replaced or complemented by a group that receives a standardized intervention or training.

Preparing the experimental study: Internal validity as the major concern

As experimental studies are designed to make inferences about causal relationships, internal validity (validity of causal inferences in scientific studies) is crucial to this type of design. Indeed, if cause-and-effect relationships are sought, internal validity should be the primary concern. The most effective strategy for ruling out threats to internal validity is through the random assignment of participants to either an experimental group or a control group.

The following part of this chapter focuses on the most significant threats to internal validity, such as selection bias, drop out, researchers' bias or confounding factors. Of course, as in any study, other types of validity, such as construct validity

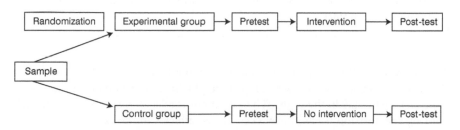

Figure 12.1 Basic structure of a randomized controlled trial (adapted from Portney and Watkins, 2009: 197)

(whether measurement tools measure what they claim to measure) or external validity (level of generalizibility to other situations), are also important to consider when preparing an experimental study. In the educational and sports context, a balance between external and internal validity is often sought when designing experimental studies because funding agencies and researchers are interested in how results can be generalized to and implemented in the real-life context.

Selection bias

Selection bias refers to the problem where, at pretest, differences between groups exist that may interact with the independent variable and thus be 'responsible' for the observed outcome. For example, the experimental group is more motivated, because coaches choose the most motivated players for treatment. Random assignment to either an intervention or control group prevents this type of selection bias.

Regression towards the mean

Children who are extremely inactive are selected to participate in a physical activity intervention. Are increases in activity levels at the end of the intervention due to the intervention's effectiveness?

Regression towards the mean occurs when subjects are selected on the basis of extreme scores. These children are in any case likely to obtain better scores. By including a pretest measurement and a control group with similar extreme values as the experimental group, it is possible to rule out the effect of regression towards the mean.

Selective drop out

Some participants dropped out from the experimental group in a study investigating the effects of the new endurance training on running performance. Let us suppose that these were individuals who were least motivated to train. Are more favourable effects on running performance still related to the new training programme?

In most studies, there are participants who drop out before the study is completed. This is a problem because those who drop out might differ on important characteristics from those who stay in the study. When drop out is related to group (experimental, control) membership (such as may occur when athletes in the experimental group who are less motivated drop out from the training programme), the effects of the intervention or training might be biased because only the most motivated athletes stay in the experimental group. One way to investigate if drop out is selective is to include measures of people's baseline characteristics in the design of the study. If drop out is not related to group membership, such that people who dropped out from the training programme were as motivated as those who dropped out from the control group, this is not likely to bias the outcomes of the study. Measuring these baseline characteristics also allows researchers to include these factors as covariates or confounding factors in further analyses.

Observational bias

Observational bias is an important concern in experimental studies. The participants' awareness of group membership or the investigators' expectations can, consciously or unconsciously, influence the outcomes. Therefore, a double-blind design is preferred where neither the participants nor the investigators are aware of the conditions until data are collected. This is often realized by different researchers delivering the training or intervention and other researchers conducting and analysing measurements. Sometimes, it is not possible to blind participants from the condition they are in; in this case, a single-blind study is carried out, where only the measurement team is blinded. The more subjective an assessment is, the more important blinding becomes.

Diffusion or contamination

In a study investigating the effects of a computer-tailored intervention on pupils' dietary fat intake, pupils of different classes within the same grade are randomly assigned to either the experimental or the control group. Can researchers rule out that information spreads over conditions?

With a single-blind study, where only the measurement team is blinded to condition, diffusion or contamination is a serious threat to internal validity. Sometimes, participants in the control group are aware of the content of the intervention or know the people who are in the experimental group.

This type of design is likely to be threatened by problems of contamination. This is because if effects spread from experimental groups to control groups, lack of differences between experimental and control groups may be observed, although the intervention was effective. However, in some cases such design, with increased risk of contamination, reduces the possible impact of confounding factors, such as the confounding influence of school environment.

Repeated measures

Repeatedly measuring the participants may lead to bias. Participants may remember the correct answers, or may be conditioned to know that they are being tested. Repeatedly taking (the same or similar) intelligence tests usually leads to score gains, but instead of concluding that the underlying skills have changed for good, the confounded effect of the repeated measures should be considered.

Maturation

In many studies, maturation should be considered. Participants change during the course of the experiment or even between measurements. For example, young children might mature and their ability to perform well on a motor skill test may change as they grow up. If maturation is measured, it is possible to control for the effect of maturation in the analyses.

Confounding factors

Many possible confounding factors that are most likely to contaminate the effect of the independent variable have been presented. When using an experimental design, it is crucial to think about possible confounding factors and decide for which factors you will standardize the protocol.

There are several ways to control for confounding factors. Let us suppose that the research question is to investigate the effects of an intervention aimed at improving the interactions between coaches and their athletes, with 20 coaches randomly assigned to either the experimental condition (coaches receiving additional training) and the control condition (coaches receiving no training). The standardized research protocol defines the characteristics of the coaches included in the study and the characteristics of the athletes they are coaching. A simple way of controlling for possible confounding factors is to eliminate them by choosing participants with homogeneous characteristics, such as including in the study only coaches with less than five years of experience. This implies, however, that the findings can only be generalized to the type of participants included in the study, which decreases external validity of the results.

Another way of controlling for possible confounding factors is to systematically manipulate these variables by building them into the experimental design. For instance, in addition to the coaches' training, participants are divided into groups based on their experience: a group with less than five years of coaching experience; a group with between five and 15 years' coaching experience; and a group with more than 15 years' coaching experience. Each of these groups is randomized into the experimental and control groups (considered as a randomized block design).

A third strategy for dealing with possible confounding factors involves matching participants on the basis of specific characteristics that are likely to influence the outcome measure. Experienced and less experienced coaches are then equally divided between the experimental and control groups.

The final method of controlling for confounding effects does not relate to the study design, but involves analysis of covariance. These types of analyses statistically rule out the effect of confounding variables by including them as covariates in the analyses.

The challenges of experimental research in real-life settings: two cases

The two case studies that follow illustrate how we designed and prepared our own experimental studies, trying to rule out the threats to internal validity discussed above. We also aim to show that conducting studies in an ecologically valid setting, such as the school or the sports club, remains a challenge, even when researchers are well prepared.

Case study 1: How effective is a middle school multi-component healthy eating and physical activity intervention? (Haerens et al., 2006)

Background to the study

The first case study concerns the evaluation of a multi-component healthy eating and physical activity intervention that was implemented in a middle school setting. A random sample of 15 schools out of the 65 Flemish schools with technical and vocational education in West Flanders (Belgium) was selected to participate. The 15 schools were randomly assigned to the intervention or control conditions: (a) intervention with parental support; (b) intervention alone; and (c) control condition. Randomization occurred twice: once when selecting the schools and a second time when allocating schools to one of the three conditions. Measures were performed at school, once at baseline (September 2003), once at the end of the first school year (June 2004) and once at the end of the second school year. Parents of 2,991 students in the seventh and eighth grades received an informed consent pro forma in which authorization was asked for their child to complete measurements. Only 151 parents (5 per cent) refused permission, resulting in a sample of 2,840 11- to 15-year-old boys and girls. Data from 2,434 and 2,287 pupils were available for analyses after the first and second school years respectively, representing the number of students who were present on the measurement days and who completed measurements accurately.

Selective drop out?

Outcome measures were BMI, physical activity levels and dietary behaviours. Analyses of those who opted out were conducted for each of these outcomes to check for selective attrition. These 'drop out' analyses were also conducted for gender and socio-economic status (SES), as both factors are known to be related to the investigated outcomes. After two years, analyses showed that boys who dropped out were older and consumed more soft drinks, but that drop out was not related to group membership (intervention versus control). Therefore, drop out was not likely to interfere with the investigated causal relationships between the independent variable (intervention) and the investigated outcomes.

The pretest–post-test control group design with randomization

The intervention started after the first measurement period in October 2003. The design of the study corresponded with the pretest–post-test control group design (see Figure 12.1), where participants are randomly assigned to either the experimental or control group. In this case, more than one intervention arm was included (intervention with parents, intervention alone) and schools (not pupils) were randomly assigned to conditions, making this study a quasi-experimental study. Thus, randomization was not complete in creating equal groups, which is often the case when randomization takes place at the group level (e.g., schools).

To illustrate, the percentage of boys and girls were unequally distributed across conditions. This is because, in Flanders, there are typical boys' schools (offering more technical courses such as mechanics) and girls' schools (offering education in nursing and cooking), and these were unequally distributed across conditions. This resulted in a higher percentage of girls in the intervention with parental support group. This unequal distribution of girls was problematic for interpreting the results. After one year of intervention, BMI increased less among girls, but only in the intervention group with parental support. Although, at first glance, the results suggested that parental support was essential to prevent increases in BMI, it was hard to draw straightforward conclusions. In the intervention group with parental support, 40 per cent of the students were girls whereas in the intervention alone group only 16 per cent were girls. Combining the fact that process evaluation measures showed that the intervention was better implemented in typical girls' schools and that the dietary intervention was only effective among girls, this may have biased the results in several ways. In this case, it was no longer clear whether the higher percentage of girls in the intervention group with parental support or the parental intervention component itself caused the differences in effectiveness for overweight prevention between the intervention with and without parental support. This example shows how ineffective randomization might interfere with the possibilities to draw straightforward conclusions about the effects of the independent variable (the intervention) on the dependent variable (e.g., BMI).

Confounding factors

The decrease of control over possible confounding factors has been mentioned several times as a limitation of conducting randomized controlled trials in an ecologically valid setting. In this study, baseline physical activity levels, eating behaviours, BMI, pupils' age, gender and SES were included as covariates in the analyses. However, including these covariates does not rule out that outcomes may have been affected by other confounding factors such as school contextual factors (e.g., sporting facilities, social support, numbers of pupils in classes, educational type) or pupil characteristics (e.g., gender, motivation to change dietary habits, SES).

Manipulation – a challenge in itself

Until now, not much has been said about the aspect of manipulation in randomized controlled trials. In clinical trials, where patients either receive a treatment (e.g., medication) or no treatment (e.g., placebo), the manipulation is rather straightforward. However, in the educational or sport context, with studies conducted in ecologically valid settings, manipulation becomes an issue in itself. In this case study, the school-based physical activity and healthy intervention designed to be implemented by the teachers and not the researchers was considered a strength of the study because results could then give a realistic view on how effective the intervention would be if implemented on a larger scale. However, implementation was also difficult to optimize for several reasons. To increase fidelity to the intervention, principals and teachers needed to be convinced of the importance of their role in promoting healthy eating and physical activity. They often felt that it was not their responsibility to devote some of their time to the implementation of the intervention. Some teachers also argued that other health-related issues such as sexuality and prevention of alcohol and drug use should receive higher priority. Although in every school a select group of teachers was enthusiastic about implementing the intervention, they were often discouraged by the limited interest from teachers and staff that were not directly involved.

Second, every school has its specific school context. Unchangeable factors within the school environment, such as the available space in the playground or the lack of flexibility in catering, limited opportunities for promoting physical activity and healthy eating. This might result in a large variability in the way the interventions were implemented in the different schools. In many studies, these problems related to standardized implementation are addressed by including process evaluation measures. Principals and teachers were therefore asked to fill out a process evaluation questionnaire, supported by interviews with teachers.

Case study 2: Do alternative instructional approaches result in different game performance learning outcomes?

The pretest–post-test control group design with randomization

The second case study concerns a randomized controlled trial, for which four fifth-grade classes (a total of 97 pupils, 10 to 11 years old) were taught basketball either through a traditional instructional approach or through a tactical game approach. All pupils had little or no experience in basketball. The experimental classes belonged to two elementary schools that are representative for the neighbourhood of the city of Ronse (Belgium). Both schools adopted the same PE curriculum.

The schools were contacted at random and asked for their willingness to participate in the study with one or more fifth-grade classes. Two classes from one school were randomly assigned to the traditional game teaching condition (TRAD) and two classes from another school received the experimental treatment based on the IGCM. Also in this case study, randomization occurred twice: once when selecting the schools, and a second time when allocating schools to one of the conditions.

The main aim of this study was to identify the differential impact of both instructional approaches on decision making and motor skill execution in authentic game situations. For assessments, each class group was divided into subgroups that played approximately 26 minutes of three-on-three and three-on-one game plays. There was a pretest, an intermediate test after four lessons, an intermediate test after eight lessons and a post-test after 12 lessons. After that, a retention test was conducted. A retention test assesses whether favourable learning effects in the experimental group remain when both groups return to their regular curriculum. The pretest–post-test control group design was elaborated by including more measurements. This is typically the case in studies assessing learning effects. One problem with multiple measurements relates to the impossibility of ruling out that pupils learn through their participation in the assessments. What and how much pupils learn through these assessments are hard to determine. One could argue that the inclusion of a control group solves this problem. However, pupils in the experimental group might learn more through the assessment in games situations than pupils in the control group because they are used to learning in these game situations.

Confounding factors

In the present study, possible confounding factors controlled for were teachers' instructional behaviours and pupils' experience levels with ball games (a homogeneous group of inexperienced pupils participated in the study).

Manipulation – a challenge in itself?

Issues related to manipulation in the second case study were the potential differences in instructor behaviour between the experimental group and the group receiving standardized treatment. Therefore, all lessons and tests were led by the same researcher to minimize factors related to the instructor (e.g., enthusiasm). A validation protocol was developed to address the issue of manipulation. During the treatment period, all lessons of both treatments were videotaped. The validation protocol included the use of an observation instrument to observe differences between the instructional approaches during the first, sixth and twelfth (final) lesson. Two observers coded these six lessons independently. These types of measures allow validation of the implementation.

Conclusion

This chapter focused on the basic designs for experimental research and illustrated this type of research design by means of examples drawn from the PE and sports contexts. Experimental designs are important because they allow researchers to draw cause-and-effect relationships between the independent and dependent variables included in the study.

Several characteristics of experimental and quasi-experimental designs have received attention in this chapter. Related to the design of the study, we recommend always including a control group, to randomize participants into conditions and to include both pre- and post-test measurements. The case studies illustrated that researchers also need to think about issues related to creating a standardized manipulation.

Randomized controlled trials in tightly controlled laboratory settings have high internal validity, but results might not be directly transferable to real-life situations. Research conducted in an ecologically valid setting has generally more advantages with regard to the external validity of the results. However, these types of designs increase the risk for threats to internal validity. Keeping a good balance between internal and external validity is a challenge when preparing your study!

Finally, with respect to the reporting of randomized controlled trials, it is important to mention CONSORT. This stands for 'consolidated standards of reporting trials' and covers initiatives to prevent inadequate reporting of randomized controlled trials. The main product of CONSORT is the CONSORT Statement, which is an evidence-based checklist with 22 items that need to be addressed in different sections of manuscripts reporting on randomized controlled trials (http://www.consort-statement.org/consort statement/overview0/). Many biomedical research journals such as *The Lancet* already require that authors submit this statement when reporting on randomized controlled designs, because research has shown that the CONSORT Statement is associated with improvements in the quality of reports.

Key terms

Cause and effect   Experimental designs are structures to evaluate the effect of one variable on another.

Manipulation   Refers to exposure of an experimental group to an intervention, treatment or training.

Control group   A comparison group that functions in an environment similar to that of the experimental group.

Randomization   Ensures that each participant in the study has an equal chance of being assigned to either the experimental or the control group.

Internal validity   The validity of causal inferences in scientific studies.

Reference

Portney, L.G. and Watkins, M. P. (2009) 'Experimental designs', in L. G. Portney and M. P. Watkins (eds) *Foundations of Clinical Research: Applications to Practice*, 3rd edn, London: Pearson Education.

Further reading

Haerens, L., Deforche, B., Maes, L., Cardon, G., Stevens, V. and De Bourdeaudhuij, I. (2006) 'Evaluation of a two-year physical activity and healthy eating intervention in middle school children', *Health Education Research*, 21: 911–21.

Portney, L.G. and Watkins, M. P. (2009) 'Validity in experimental design', in L. G. Portney and M. P. Watkins (eds) *Foundations of Clinical Research: Applications to Practice*, 3rd edn, London: Pearson Education.

_____ 'Quasi-experimental design', in L. G. Portney and M. P. Watkins (eds) *Foundations of Clinical Research: Applications to Practice*, 3rd edn, London: Pearson Education.

13 Measurement of physical activity

Stewart G. Trost and Kelly Rice

> There will always be a trade-off between practicality and accuracy when it comes to selecting a physical activity measurement tool for use among children and adolescents.
> (Trost, 2007: 15)

Introduction

With assessment of physical activity becoming more common in physical education and youth sport research, it is critically important that researchers, educators and coaches become knowledgeable about the different methods used to measure physical activity in young people. On the surface, measuring physical activity may seem straightforward. Students will obligingly wear a pedometer during a physical education lesson or complete a self-report questionnaire about their participation in organized sport. However, in reality, obtaining *valid and reliable* assessments of physical activity in children and adolescents is an extremely difficult undertaking. Unlike some other health behaviours, physical activity does not come in handy easy-to-measure packages or containers (e.g., packs per day, cans of soft drink); it cannot be placed in a test tube and assayed in the laboratory; and while cardiorespiratory fitness is modestly correlated with physical activity in youth, physical activity lacks a precise biological marker. Additionally, physical activity is a remarkably complex behaviour characterized by multiple dimensions and domains. The dimensions of physical activity are well known and include frequency, duration, intensity and type. For young people, the domains of physical activity are numerous and typically comprise in-school physical activity (including recess and physical education), out-of-school physical activity (school, club sports and dance), transportation-related physical activity (walking or biking to and from school), and physical activity in specific behavioural settings (e.g., after-school programmes, preschools). Ideally, a physical activity assessment tool would provide valid and reliable measures of all four dimensions of activity behaviour in all of the aforementioned domains. However, due to practical considerations and unresolved methodological issues, no such measurement tool currently exists. Thus, as the quote above suggests, the selection and application of a physical activity measurement tool will *always* depend heavily on the specific aims of the investigation and the resources available to the research team.

About us

Dr Stewart Trost is an Associate Professor in the Department of Nutrition and Exercise Science at Oregon State University. He has been an innovator in the use of objective monitoring devices to assess physical activity in children and adolescents. He has used accelerometers to quantify between- and within-day variability in children's physical activity and estimate the number of monitoring days required to estimate habitual physical activity in youth, validate child self-report instruments, examine physical activity differences in children with and without obesity, evaluate the efficacy of physical activity interventions, describe physical activity levels in children attending after-school programmes, and examine the psychosocial and environmental determinants of youth physical activity behaviour.

Kelly Rice is a doctoral candidate in physical and public health in the Department of Nutrition and Exercise Sciences at Oregon State University, working with Stewart. Kelly has a wide range of experience with regard to physical activity and public health. She has conducted research on the understanding and knowledge of physical activity recommendations, rate of perceived exertion in activity levels in children and physical activity interventions in children and adolescents. Kelly has also worked as a physical activity community health specialist where she was able to apply her knowledge of research to community interventions. She has used a number of different measurement systems to assess physical activity, including accelerometers, heart rate monitors, pedometers and physical activity recall surveys.

Methods used to measure physical activity

To date, a variety of methods has been used to measure physical activity in children and adolescents. These include self-report methods such as questionnaires, as well as objective measures of physical activity such as direct observation, doubly labelled water, heart rate monitoring, accelerometers and pedometers. Each of these methods will be discussed below.

Self-report measures

A number of self-report methods have been used to assess physical activity in children and adolescents. These include self-administered recalls, interview-administered recalls, diaries, and proxy reports completed by parents or teachers. Depending on the purpose of the study, self-report measures vary considerably in the specificity with which type, duration, frequency and intensity are evaluated. Recall time frames range from as little as one day to as much as one year. The most frequently cited advantages of self-report measures are ease of administration, the ability to characterize activity historically and low cost. The ability to record activity type and the context in which physical activity is performed is another advantage. As a result, self-reports are commonly used in epidemiological research and surveillance studies where objective measurement techniques are often not practical (Trost, 2007).

Although convenient, self-report methods are subject to considerable recall bias and may not be suitable for use among young children. One study demonstrated that children under 10 years of age cannot recall activities accurately and are unable to quantify the time frame of activity (Baranowski et al., 1984). In addition, younger children may not fully understand the concept of physical activity. Another study investigated the completeness of fourth-grade students' (mean age 9.8 ± 0.3 years) understanding of the concept of physical activity. Approximately 60 per cent of fourth-grade students had difficulty differentiating between sedentary activities such as playing computer games and active pursuits such as outdoor games and household chores (Trost et al., 2000). Thus, extreme caution must be exercised when attempting to use self-report instruments in children aged 10 years or under. The following are brief descriptions of two self-report measures that have been widely used in young people.

Previous-day physical activity recall (PDPAR)

The PDPAR, and its three-day recall counterpart, the 3DPAR, are self-report instruments designed specifically for children and adolescents. The instruments can be accessed from the University of South Carolina (http://www.sph.sc.edu/ USC_CPARG). To help children and adolescents recall their past behaviour more accurately, the previous day is divided into 30-minute time blocks that, in turn, are grouped into broader time periods such as morning, lunchtime, afternoon and evening. To further enhance recall accuracy, the instrument provides a numbered list of commonly performed activities grouped into the following broad categories: eating, sleeping/bathing, transportation, work/school, spare time, physical activities and sports. To help students rate the intensity of the reported physical activities, the instrument includes cartoon illustrations depicting light, moderate, hard and very hard activities.

The PDPAR and 3DPAR instruments have been used in numerous observational and intervention trials conducted in the United States, and have been shown to be valid, reliable and able to detect changes in physical activity behaviour. Importantly, the flexibility of the PDPAR and 3DPAR allows them to be used in a wide variety of research scenarios. The number of recall days can be modified to match the cognitive abilities of the study population; and depending on the aims of the study, the time segments within each recall day can be delimited to the whole day or specific segments of the day (e.g., after school until bedtime). The list of activities appearing on PDPAR and 3DPAR can be easily modified to accommodate the activity interests and cultural norms of different population groups. Recently completed studies have shown the PDPAR and 3DPAR to be reliable and valid with children and adolescents from different regions of the United States as well as with adolescents from Singapore, Brazil and Australia (Trost, 2007).

Self-administered physical activity checklist (SAPAC)

Another widely used self-report instrument for children and adolescents is the SAPAC (Sallis et al., 1996). This instrument provides a list of 21 physical activities commonly performed by young people. Respondents select the activities performed on the previous day, during each of three time blocks: before school, during school and after school. For each of the activities selected, the respondent estimates the amount of time they engaged in that activity during the specified time block. The responses can be reduced in several ways to create a number of physical activity indices. The number of activities reported for a given day can be tallied, the number of minutes of activity reported can be calculated, or total metabolic-equivalent task (MET) minutes can be determined by multiplying the number of minutes reported for a given physical activity by a MET or physical activity intensity weighting and then summing the products. The SAPAC can be completed as a series of one-day recalls of the previous day, or reports for several preceding days can be completed in one testing session. The SAPAC instruments and instructions can be downloaded from Dr Jim Sallis's website (http://www.drjamessallis.sdsu.edu/).

Direct observation

Physical activity has been assessed via direct observation in a variety of naturalistic settings. Although protocols vary from study to study, the formal observation typically involves observing a child at home or school for extended periods of time and recording an instantaneous rating of the child's activity level. Relative to other methods, direct observation has a number of important advantages. Observational procedures are flexible and permit researchers not only to quantify physical activity, but also to record factors related to physical activity behaviour such as behavioural cues, environmental conditions, the presence of significant others and availability of toys and equipment. Direct observation is not without its limitations, however. Because of the time required to train observers, the length of the observation period and the tedious data coding requirements, it is highly labour intensive and expensive. Subject reactivity to observers is also a legitimate concern; this can be minimized by performing repeat observations.

One of the most widely used direct observational systems in physical education and youth sport research is the system for observing fitness instruction time (SOFIT). This is a direct observation tool designed to measure student engagement, lesson context and teacher behaviour during physical education classes (McKenzie, Sallis and Nader, 1991) and can be downloaded from Dr Jim Sallis's website (http://www.drjamessallis.sdsu.edu/). The engagement level provides an estimate of the intensity of the student's physical activity and uses the activity codes 1 to 4 to denote lying down, sitting, standing, walking, respectively. An activity code of 5 (very active) identifies when the student is expending more energy than they would during ordinary walking. Typically, codes 4 and 5 are used to calculate time spent in moderate-to-vigorous physical activity (MVPA). While the main focus of SOFIT is the coding of student physical activity levels, selected contextual factors associated with opportunities to be physically active (lesson context and teacher behaviour) are recorded simultaneously. Lesson context time is categorized as 'management', 'knowledge', 'fitness', 'movement skills drills', 'game play' and 'free play'. Teacher behaviour is coded as 'promotes fitness', 'demonstrates fitness', 'instructs generally', 'manages', 'observes' and 'other'. SOFIT has been shown to produce valid and reliable estimates of physical activity and has been used to assess aspects of physical education instruction in multiple studies around the world.

Doubly labelled water

The doubly labelled water technique represents an unobtrusive and non-invasive means to measure total daily energy expenditure in children and adolescents in naturalistic settings. When combined with measurement of resting energy expenditure, the doubly labelled water technique can be used to estimate energy expenditure related to physical activity. The method is based on the kinetics of two stable isotopes of water, $^{2}H_{2}O$ (deuterium labelled water) and $H_{2}^{18}O$ (oxygen-18 labelled water). These stable isotopes are naturally occurring compounds without known toxicity at the low doses used. Deuterium labelled water is lost from the body through the usual routes of water loss (urine, sweat, evaporative losses). Oxygen-18 labelled water is lost from the body at a slightly faster rate since this isotope is also lost via carbon dioxide production in addition to all routes of water loss. The difference in the rate of loss between the two isotopes is therefore a function of the rate of carbon dioxide production – a reflection of the rate of energy production over time (Goran, 1994).

The doubly labelled water technique has been validated in adults and children by comparison with indirect calorimetry. These studies generally show the technique to be accurate within 5 to 10 per cent. This small amount of error has prompted several authors to view the doubly labelled water method as a potential gold standard for estimating physical activity-related energy expenditure. A major limitation associated with doubly labelled water is excessive cost. In addition, although the technique provides accurate estimates of physical activity-related energy expenditure over one- to two-week periods, it does not provide information on the pattern of physical activity behaviour – i.e., it does not provide estimates of time spent in light, moderate and heavy physical activity (Trost, 2001).

Heart rate monitoring

Relatively inexpensive heart rate monitors, with multiple-day storage capacity for minute-by-minute heart rates, have made continuous heart rate monitoring a more feasible method for assessing physical activity in children and adolescents. Heart rate monitoring remains an attractive approach to assessing physical activity because of the linear relationship between heart rate and energy expenditure during steady-state exercise. However, there are several problems associated with this method. First, it is widely recognized that factors such as age, body size, proportion of muscle mass used, emotional stress and cardiorespiratory fitness influence the heart rate–VO_2 relationship. Second, because heart rate response tends to lag momentarily behind changes in movement and tends to remain elevated after the cessation of movement, heart rate monitoring may mask the sporadic activity patterns of children. Third, because a large percentage of a child's day is spent in relatively inactive pursuits (i.e., sitting in class), heart rate monitoring may be of limited use in assessing total daily physical activity (Trost, 2001). However, it is important to note that several techniques have been devised to overcome some of the limitations of heart rate monitoring. These include the use of heart rate indices that control for individual differences in resting heart rate and calibrating heart rate and work rate on an individual basis (HR FLEX method) (Livingstone et al., 1992).

Accelerometers

Accelerometry-based motion sensors have become one of the most commonly used methods for assessing physical activity in free-living children and adolescents. Accelerometers record information related to the acceleration of the trunk, or other body segments, at user-specified time intervals. This information is processed and stored as 'counts'. Because accelerometer counts are proportional to the energy cost or intensity of movement (the higher the counts, the higher the intensity), and are stored with date-time stamps, accelerometers can be used to measure the frequency, intensity and duration of physical activity over specified time intervals such as days or weeks (Trost, 2007). To date, a large number of studies have evaluated the validity of accelerometers under both laboratory and field conditions. The most common criterion measure for laboratory-based studies is energy expenditure measured by indirect calorimetry, while energy expenditure measured by doubly labelled water or activity intensity measured by behavioural observation are typically used as validation realms in field-based studies. The vast majority of these studies report a strong positive correlation between accelerometer output and energy expenditure and/or exercise intensity (Trost, McIver and Pate, 2005).

Relative to heart rate monitors, accelerometers present fewer burdens to participants (no electrodes or chest straps) and are capable of detecting the intermittent activity patterns characteristic of small children. However, a well-recognized limitation of accelerometers is that they are not able to account for the increased energy cost associated with walking up stairs or an incline and do not accurately measure activities such as cycling, lifting or carrying objects. Nevertheless, it is assumed that the contribution of these activities to the overall physical activity is small. Because of this assumption, accelerometers may underestimate total or physical activity energy expenditure. Regardless, accelerometers are considered the most promising tool for measuring physical activity in free-living children and adolescents.

In an effort to use accelerometer output to estimate daily or weekly time spent in sedentary, light, moderate and vigorous intensity activities, a number of investigators have developed youth-specific prediction equations that allow counts to be converted to units of energy expenditure (Freedson, Pober and Janz, 2005). The most common approach thus far has been to develop a regression equation that defines the linear or non-linear relationship between counts and energy expenditure. Once a single regression equation has been developed, the activity counts obtained by an individual performing an unknown activity can be used to estimate energy expenditure. Activity-count thresholds or 'cut-points' denoting the dividing line between light-to-moderate physical activity and MVPA are typically identified. These cut-points are then used to estimate the amount of time spent in light-, moderate- and vigorous-intensity physical activity.

Although the application of cut-points to accelerometer data continues to be standard practice in the research world, there is growing recognition that the relationship between accelerometer counts and energy expenditure depends on the activity type (e.g., walking versus household chores) and that a single regression equation cannot accurately determine energy expenditure across a wide range of physical activities. Recently, machine learning or pattern recognition techniques have emerged as a viable and potentially more accurate alternative to traditional regression-based cut-point methods. In this approach to data reduction, recurring patterns or distinguishing features in the accelerometer data are 'extracted' and entered into sophisticated statistical models that predict the physical activity type and intensity. For more detailed information about pattern recognition approaches to accelerometer data reduction, the reader is referred to the paper by Staudenmayer and colleagues (2009).

Pedometers

A cost-effective alternative to accelerometry is to measure physical activity with an electronic pedometer. Pedometers have the same basic limitation as accelerometers, in that they are insensitive to some forms of movement. However, in addition to this limitation, these devices are unable to record the magnitude of the movement detected. Hence, movement above a given threshold is counted as a step, regardless of whether it occurs during walking, running or jumping. Because pedometer steps are influenced by factors such as body size and speed of locomotion, investigators should exercise caution when using pedometers in growing children or groups of children of vastly different levels of maturation. Several commercially available pedometers provide users with estimates of energy expenditure or minutes of MVPA; however, these algorithms were developed from studies of adults and are not valid for children and adolescents. To date, numerous studies have assessed the validity of electronic pedometers as measures of youth physical activity. The results of these studies show that pedometers provide accurate step counts at self-selected walking speeds and that daily step counts are moderately to strongly correlated with more accurate criterion measures of physical activity such as direct observation and energy expenditure measured by indirect calorimetry (Trost, 2007).

Case study: Physical activity levels among children attending family childcare homes

We recently used accelerometry to describe the physical activity levels of two- to five-year-olds attending home-based childcare (known in the United States as Family Child Care Homes). We wanted to know more about the physical activity levels of this population, as a significant number of US children under the age of five attend such care (~ 2 million), and there is concern among public health and education stakeholders that these children have limited opportunity to accumulate the physical activity needed for healthy growth and development. Because self-report methods and direct observation were either a waste of time or logistically impossible, physical activity was measured objectively using an Actigraph GT1M accelerometer.

Prior to visiting each family childcare home, the accelerometers were initialized in our laboratory to start collecting data at least one hour before the scheduled visit time. This ensured that the accelerometers were fully operational and collecting data the moment they were attached. To ensure we had sufficient resolution to capture the brief intermittent bursts of activity typically displayed by preschool-aged children, we initialized the accelerometer to collect data every 15 seconds.

Upon arrival at the family childcare home, a member of the research team secured the accelerometer on the right hip of each child, using a fully adjustable elastic belt. The time of monitor attachment was carefully noted so that any data recorded by the accelerometer prior to attachment could be excluded. After all the children had been fitted with an accelerometer, the research assistant and childcare provider reviewed the procedures for attaching and removing the accelerometers for the remaining days of the week. Providers were instructed to attach the accelerometer upon the child's arrival at their home and remove it just prior to their departure, noting the time of each of these events in a specially prepared log book. Midway through the week, we checked in with the provider via phone or email to confirm that the accelerometers were indeed being worn by the children and to determine if there were any problems with the monitoring protocol.

One week later, we returned to the provider's home to collect the accelerometers. We then went back to our laboratory and downloaded the accelerometer data and saved the information on a secure server for subsequent data processing and analysis. To estimate time spent in sedentary, light and moderate-to-vigorous physical activity each day, we applied physical activity intensity cut-points established for preschool-aged children (Pate et al., 2006). A total of 205 children between the ages of two and five years (mean age 3.4 ± 1.2 years) from 53 family childcare homes completed the study. Our final analyses included only those children who wore the accelerometer for at least four hours on two or more days of the week. Average daily times spent in each intensity-based physical activity category were as follows: 124.9 ± 51.2 mins/day of sedentary activity, 117.4 ± 41.2 mins/day of light-intensity physical activity, and 45.5 ± 23.3 mins/day of moderate-to-vigorous physical activity. For every hour of childcare attendance, children, on average, accumulated 25.9 ± 6.1 mins of sedentary activity, 24.5 ± 3.7 mins of light-intensity physical activity, and 9.6 ± 4.4 mins of moderate-to-vigorous physical activity. Our findings showed that children attending family childcare homes accumulate very little moderate-to-vigorous physical activity throughout the day and that policies and programmes to promote physical activity in this setting are needed.

Overall, the measurement of physical activity in this study went well. However, as with all studies using accelerometers to measure physical activity in a real-world setting, there were a number of challenges. First and foremost, a number of providers simply forgot to put the accelerometers on the child. Hence the need for a reminder phone call or email. Another problem was missing data due to absences from the childcare home. If the accelerometer was not worn during the week, the most frequent explanation was that the participant did not attend childcare due to illness. In most cases, we arranged a return to the childcare home for a second round of monitoring. Finally, a number of family childcare homes simply 'closed up shop' during the course of the study, making it impossible to complete the physical activity assessments.

Selecting a measurement tool

Table 13.1 provides a summary of how the previously discussed methods compare on key measurement attributes such as affordability, ease of administration or compliance, potential for reactivity and feasibility in large studies. Although the selection of a measurement instrument will always depend heavily on the scope and aims of a project or study, it is clear that objective measures such as accelerometry have a great deal of utility, particularly among younger children. Nevertheless, scanning across the various columns in Table 13.1, it is clear that each method has strengths and limitations that need to be carefully considered, and that no single method can be described as optimal in all situations. Indeed, as we noted at the very start of the chapter, there will always be a trade-off between practicality and accuracy when it comes to selecting a physical activity measurement tool for use among children and adolescents.

Key terms

Physical activity   Any bodily movement that results in the burning of calories.

Measurement   The act of measuring or the process of being measured.

Accelerometer   A motion sensor that records information related to the accelerations of the trunk or other body segments during physical activity.

Self-report   A report of a respondent of a survey or an interview about their internal state or perception; contrasting to measurement using a measuring device and to observations made by other people.

Pedometer   An instrument for estimating the distance travelled on foot by recording the number of steps taken.

Heart rate   The number of heart beats per unit of time, usually expressed as beats per minute.

Doubly labelled water   A method of indirectly estimating energy expenditure. The subject ingests a known volume of water labelled with two isotopes ($^2H_2{}^{18}O$). The deuterium ($^2H_2$) and oxygen (^{18}O) diffuse throughout the body's water, and their disappearance rate from the body fluid (e.g. in blood, urine, or saliva) is measured. When a subject is loaded with $^2H_2{}^{18}O$, the decrease in ^{18}O is a measure for H_2O output plus CO_2 outputs, and the decrease in $^2H_2$ is a measure of H_2O output alone. Therefore, CO_2 output can be obtained from the difference. CO_2 output is converted to energy expenditure using the energy equivalent of CO_2.

Table 13.1 Summary of key attributes for current methods to measure physical activity in children and adolescents

Method	Valid	Affordability	Objective	Ease of administration	Easy to complete, compliance	Measures patterns, modes and dimensions of physical activity	Non-reactive*	Feasible in large studies	Suitable for ages <10 yrs	Suitable for ages >10 yrs
Self-report	✓	✓✓✓	✗	✓✓✓	✓✓✓	✓✓	✓✓✓	✓✓✓	✗	✓✓
Heart rate monitoring	✓✓	✓✓	✓✓✓	✓	✓	✓✓	✓	✓	✓✓✓	✓✓✓
Accelerometer	✓✓	✓	✓✓✓	✓✓	✓✓	✓✓	✓✓	✓✓	✓✓✓	✓✓✓
Pedometer	✓✓	✓✓✓	✓✓✓	✓✓	✓✓	✗	✓	✓✓	✓✓✓	✓✓✓
Direct observation	✓✓✓	✗	✓✓	✓	✓✓✓	✓✓✓	✓	✓	✓✓✓	✓✓
Doubly labelled water	✓✓✓	✗	✓✓✓	✓✓	✓✓	✗	✓✓	✗	✓✓✓	✓✓✓

* Non-reactive: doesn't induce changes in physical activity behaviour as a result of the measurement process
✗ = poor or inappropriate
✓ = acceptable
✓✓ = good
✓✓✓ = excellent

References

Baranowski, T., Dworkin, R. J. and Cieslik, C. J. (1984) 'Reliability and validity of self-report of aerobic activity: Family health project', *Research Quarterly in Exercise and Sport*, 55: 309–17.

Freedson, P., Pober, D. and Janz, K. F. (2005) 'Calibration of accelerometer output for children', *Medicine and Science in Sports and Exercise*, 37(11 suppl): S523–30.

Goran, M. I. (1994) 'Applications of the doubly labeled water technique for studying total energy expenditure in young children: a review', *Pediatric Exercise Science*, 6: 11–30.

Livingstone, M. B., Coward, W. A., Prentice, A. M., Davies, P. S., Strain, J. J., McKenna, P. G., Mahoney, C. A., White, J. A., Stewart, C. M. and Kerr, M. J. (1992) 'Daily energy expenditure in free-living children: comparison of heart rate monitoring with the doubly labeled water ($^2H_2$$^{18}O$) method', *American Journal of Clinical Nutrition*, 56: 343–52.

McKenzie, T. L., Sallis, J. F. and Nader, P. R. (1991) 'SOFIT: System for Observing Fitness Instruction Time', *Journal of Teaching Physical Education*, 11: 195–205.

Pate, R. R., Almeida, M. J., McIver, K. L., Pfeiffer, K. A. and Dowda, M. (2006) 'Validation and calibration of an accelerometer in preschool children', *Obesity*, 14: 2000–6.

Sallis, J. F., Strikmiller, P. K., Harsha, D. W., Feldman, H. A., Ehlinger, S., Stone, E. J., Willston, J. and Woods, S. (1996) 'Validation of interviewer- and self-administered physical activity checklists for fifth-grade students' *Medicine and Science in Sports and Exercise*, 28: 840–51.

Staudenmayer, J., Pober, D., Crouter, S., Bassett, D. and Freedson, P. (2009) 'An artificial neural network to estimate physical activity energy expenditure and identify physical activity type from an accelerometer', *Journal of Applied Physiology*, 107: 1300–7.

Trost, S. G. (2001) 'Objective measurement of physical activity in youth: current issues, future directions', *Exercise and Sport Science Reviews*, 29: 32–6.

Trost, S. G. (2007) 'Measurement of physical activity in children and adolescents', *American Journal of Lifestyle Medicine*,1: 299–314.

Trost, S. G., Morgan, A. M., Saunders, R., Felton, G., Ward, D. S. and Pate, R. R. (2000) 'Children's understanding of the concept of physical activity', *Pediatric Exercise Science*, 12: 293–9.

Trost, S. G., McIver, K. L. and Pate, R. R. (2005) 'Conducting accelerometer-based activity assessments in field-based research', *Medicine and Science in Sports and Exercise*, 37(11 suppl): S531–43.

Further reading

Corder, K., Ekelund, U., Steele, R., Wareham, N. and Brage, S. (2008) 'Assessment of physical activity in youth', *Journal of Applied Physiology*, 105(1): 977–87.

Welk, G. (ed.) (2002) *Physical activity assessments for health-related research*, Champaign, IL: Human Kinetics.

14 Surveys

Hans Peter Brandl-Bredenbeck and Astrid Kämpfe

Introduction

Consider the following 'common-sense' statements about the world of sport:

- Physical education and sport promote a healthy lifestyle for young people.
- Physical education and sport support young people in their individual development.
- Physical education and sport help to keep young people off drugs and out of trouble.

These statements are examples of important claims made about the educational influence of sport and physical activity on young people's overall development. Possibly you – like many people – would support these statements; yet what do we really know about them? Is there empirical evidence to support such statements ... or are they no more than a set of myths? Lack of robust empirical evidence in the field means that there are a number of issues about which we cannot be certain whether we are dealing with realities or myths. Surveys offer one way of finding evidence about issues such as these. Generally speaking, the survey is a research technique that seeks to describe and analyse the previous, current or future behaviour, attitudes and opinions of a specified population. This chapter will introduce you to the scientific method of survey research and provide guidelines on how to conduct a survey in order to collect robust data.

About us

Hans Peter Brandl-Bredenbeck graduated with a teacher certificate in physical education and French from the Free University of Berlin. In his doctoral thesis (1999, University of Paderborn), he conducted a cross-cultural comparative survey on adolescents' sports culture in Germany and the United States. From 2006 to 2008 he was professor of movement, play and sports in childhood and adolescence at the German Sports University in Cologne. Since 2008 he has held the chair of sport pedagogy and sport didactics at the University of Paderborn.

Astrid Kämpfe graduated with a diploma in sports science from the University of Bielefeld (Germany) in 2004. In her doctoral thesis, she conducted an extensive survey to analyse the development of intrinsic and extrinsic motivation among top-level athletes (2009, University of Tuebingen). Currently, she works as a PhD research assistant at the University of Paderborn, being engaged in different (survey) research projects with a sport pedagogical perspective.

Characteristics and essentials of surveys

Conducting a survey is a complex process. To get started with the topic, we need to consider the key characteristics of surveys.

What are surveys?

Surveys are a research technique used to collect information on a certain topic. Maybe the oldest and at the same time best-known example of a survey can be found in the Bible: Joseph and Mary were on their way to take part in a survey when Jesus was born. The survey was conducted as a Roman census in order to gather information on the entire population in Palestine. Today, surveys are conducted in many different areas in order to gain knowledge about attitudes, beliefs, opinions or behaviours within a specific population. There are surveys to investigate the satisfaction or preferences of customers, to estimate the results of forthcoming political elections or simply to display a population's attitude towards a new law.

Narrowing the focus to a more scientific perspective, surveys are an important research method used for systematic data collection in the applied (social) sciences. Researchers in sport sciences and physical education (PE) employ surveys to answer research questions on complex issues, as well as to improve practical knowledge about conditions of learning and teaching.

Appropriate research questions

In order to obtain detailed information on the behaviours, attitudes and opinions of specific groups, and to compare these results with other groups, appropriate research questions have to be formulated. The fields from which these research questions may derive are manifold. To illustrate the broad scope of possible research questions, Neuman (2010) suggests some areas that could be addressed in a survey (see Table 14.1).

The relationship between theoretical considerations and the research question

Going beyond the identification of these different fields, it is of fundamental importance that the research questions and the underlying assumptions are embedded within a theoretical framework. This is important because we need to be able to determine the independent (predictor) and the dependent (criteria) variables. A very simple example illustrates the difference between the two types of variables. We know

Table 14.1 Examples of questions that can be dealt with in a survey (based on Neuman, 2010: 273, adapted to the physical education and sport context by the authors)

Behaviour	How many times per week are people performing moderate to vigorous physical activity? What kind of sports do they regularly practise?
Attitudes, beliefs, opinions	Do people think physical education should be an optional subject in school? What should be the main objectives of physical education?
Characteristics	How old is the respondent? How many people are members of a sports club? What is the educational status of the respondent?
Expectations	What should young people learn in physical education?
Self-classification	Do people consider themselves to be bad, average, good or very good at sport? Do people think that they can easily cope with new situations?
Knowledge	What do people know about the main objectives of physical education according to the curriculum?

that individuals who play basketball to the highest levels of performance tend to be taller than those who choose other sports. In this case, it is obvious that being tall is a good prerequisite (a good predictor) for playing basketball successfully and being selected by the best sports clubs. However, to assume that the correlation could be inversed – i.e., that people grow taller by playing basketball – would constitute false theorizing.

Another example can be seen when we pose the question: 'Do young people who are involved in competitive sports have a higher self-esteem than those who are physically inactive?' There are widespread theoretical (and political) assumptions that positive experiences in sports – on the motor level as well as on the emotional level – will lead children to build up a very positive view of themselves. Correlational empirical data can even support this assumption, suggesting that active children have higher self-esteem than those who are inactive. Yet caution is needed because the direction of the correlation is still ambiguous. Theoretically, for example, it could also be hypothesized that only those children who already have high self-esteem tend to remain in the competitive sports system, while those with a lower self-esteem self-select out of sport because they have difficulties in coping with the demands of competition. In this example, and more generally with regard to questions dealing with developmental issues, the explanatory power of cross-sectional data is limited. Here, only longitudinal research can tell us whether the processes at work can be classified as either selection or socialization.

Types of surveys

It is important to distinguish between two major types of survey research, both of which use questionnaires to collect self-report data from study participants as their core instrument. On the one hand, there are self-administered questionnaires which have to be completed by the individuals themselves. Paper-and-pencil questionnaires are still very much in evidence, although online questionnaires are becoming ever more popular and accessible. On the other hand, surveys may be conducted by interviewers who question the respondent in either a face-to-face or a telephone scenario. The latter method is also known as CATI (computer assisted telephone interviewing) and usually relies on a structured interview format.

Psychometric properties

The psychometric properties of the test instrument(s) are of utmost importance for the robustness of surveys. These properties refer to the criteria of standardization, reliability and validity. It is difficult to accommodate psychometric properties in surveys as they do not meet the standards of experimental research; nonetheless the process of survey development, testing and distribution must be robust. For example, with regard to standardization, the situation in which a questionnaire is administered has to be controlled for (e.g., by a cover letter; see later section). As far as reliability is concerned, the psychometrics can only be assessed post hoc by using statistical analysis. Finally, researchers in the field of physical education and sport often borrow well-known and validated instruments from social psychology, psychology or sociology in an attempt to collect data relevant to their specific problem statement.

The process of survey research

Survey research is much more complex than some novice researchers imagine. It is crucial, therefore, to plan and prepare a survey thoroughly and systematically to ensure high-quality results from a scientific and theoretical perspective, as well as from a practical point of view. As pointed out above, self-completed questionnaires and researcher-completed surveys are the two main types of survey instruments used in social sciences. Most of the steps in conducting a questionnaire survey and an interview survey are quite similar.

Figure 14.1 gives an overview of the steps to be considered in the process of survey research. The sections that follow offer some insights into each of these steps.

Step 1: Theoretical framework and objectives

Research problems are usually identified on the basis of practical experience and/or as a result of reviewing relevant literature. The identified theoretical or applied research problem is the point of origin within the survey process. As was noted earlier, in order to ensure the scientific quality of a survey research approach, it is important to embed the research problem into an appropriate theoretical context. This includes specification of the exact information required and also, from the outset, considering analytical strategies. As Thomas, Nelson and Silverman (2005: 269) argue, 'the analysis is determined in the planning phase of the study, not after the

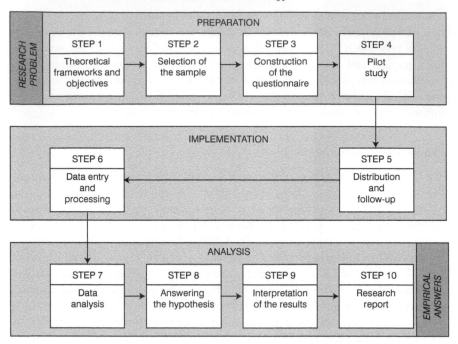

Figure 14.1 From a research problem to an empirical answer: Ten steps in survey research

data have been gathered'. Also, statistical hypotheses or at least assumptions have to be formulated which provide the frame for data processing, as well as for data analysis and interpretation to be undertaken later in the survey process.

Step 2: Selection of the sample

Since it is often impossible to question a whole population on a specific subject, surveys use different sampling techniques, which help to draw an adequate and, if possible, representative sample. There is no general rule for drawing a sample; however, there are some guiding principles that might help. The first step is to define the target population for the research question. For example, if you want to know more about activities within the PE curriculum in secondary schools in a specific country, you could ask the children or the PE teachers. In the first case, all pupils in secondary schools in that country are the target population for analysis; in the second case, the total population is all PE teachers in the same schools. In both cases, it is likely that the number of individuals is too big to distribute a survey to every individual. In these and other examples, a sample can be selected on the basis of probability or non-probability. The most common ways used in the social sciences to meet the requirements of representativeness (which is sometimes viewed as the gold standard of research) are different sampling techniques based on probability to select:

- *a random sample*, which is a totally random selection of individuals from the entire target population; or
- *a systematic sample*, which means, for example, selecting every tenth individual from a list of the entire target population; or
- *a stratified sample*, which can be characterized as choosing, for example, schools from local authorities with different facilities available, or policies for PE, and then taking a random selection of students from each of these authorities.

Whereas results based on such sampling techniques – after extensive controlling for sampling errors – can be generalized to the entire target population, the results of empirical research based on non-probabilistic samples (convenience sampling, judgement sampling, quota sampling and snowball sampling) should never be generalized in the traditional sense.

The sample size is another important aspect to be considered in order to produce valid scientific results. There are different online tools available to help with the calculation of the ideal sample size (e.g. Creative Research Systems: http://www.surveysystem.com). Despite this, it is important to remember that the representativeness of a sample is far more important than its size. For example, national polls in the United States use samples of about 1,500 participants in order to produce accurate estimates for a population of over 200 million citizens. Ferber, Sheatsley, Turner and Waksberg (1980: 3) argue that this demonstrates the value of surveys: 'They provide a speedy and economical means of determining facts about our economy and people's knowledge, attitudes, beliefs, expectations, and behaviour.'

Despite the desirability of selecting a representative sample, in practice this is often difficult and there are often compromises made in respect of time, costs and feasibility.

Step 3: Construction of the questionnaire

Neuman (2010: 277) argues that 'Question writing is more of an art than a science. It takes skill, practice, patience, and creativity.' Indeed, the 'art' of writing questions and constructing a questionnaire could easily add up to a chapter (or a whole book) in itself, and there are many detailed sources available on this topic for further reading (e.g., Babbie, 2010; Neuman, 2010). One of the key points to remember overall, however, is that in survey research, thorough planning is needed because researchers usually have only a 'one-off chance at research' (Gratton and Jones, 2010: 138): respondents cannot be re-questioned if, as a result of poor survey design, their responses are inadequate to provide data on the research problem. The following section provides an overview of the most important considerations.

An important task – although not part of the questionnaire development in a narrow sense – is to write an accompanying cover letter, which is presented to the participant with the questionnaire. This letter should include a polite appeal for support, an explanation of the purpose and intended usage of data, a phone number or email address where further information and results can be obtained, the approximate time needed to complete the questionnaire and, last but not least, the desired return date. The respondent must be informed about the confidential (and in many surveys also anonymous) treatment of data, as well as being made aware that their participation is optional. Our own research suggests that it is beneficial to inform the respondent that they are not facing a test and there are no 'correct' or 'incorrect' answers.

In terms of design, questionnaires should start with some straightforward questions that respondents can answer easily, e.g. age and sex. Complex questions requiring deeper thought, as well as sensitive or potentially threatening questions (for example, personal data concerning socio-economic status) are better presented in later sections. It is advantageous to group questions according to similar topics and to use headings when a new section starts.

For many research problems, there are numerous questions and scales available that have already been carefully tested for reliability and validity. In conducting research for a bachelor's or master's thesis, relatively inexperienced researchers would be well advised to make use of existing instruments. There are two main reasons for this. First, developing reliable and valid scales is difficult and time consuming, requiring a lot of experience. Second, using existing scales allows a comparison of your results with previous findings from other researchers. Despite these advantages, however, some research problems demand the development of new questions and scales in order to adequately match the setting, the respondents and the research question. There are precise guidelines available on how to formulate survey questions and how to avoid poor questioning. Neuman (2010: 278–81) lists ten things to avoid when writing survey questions (see Table 14.2).

In general, it is very important to give short but precise instructions on how to answer each question, especially when more than one answer can be chosen. Most surveys offer checkboxes, others ask respondents to circle corresponding answers. The following sections illustrate three different types of questions with examples from the broad field of sport.

Closed vs open questions

Closed questions provide predefined answers to which the respondent can agree or disagree, using checkboxes. The major advantages of these questions are that they are easy for respondents to answer and easy for researchers to analyse statistically and replicate. Disadvantages are that the response choice might not include respondents' preferred answers and people might be encouraged to answer even if they have no knowledge about the subject.

In contrast, open questions are used in a more explorative way: for example, when the researcher is unsure about the range of possible answers. In this case, responses can raise new points and issues, although this flexibility, of course, makes statistical analysis and comparison between subjects increasingly difficult. Neuman (2010: 286–8) also highlights the possibility of using partially open questions, i.e., by offering a number of answers in combination with a category specified as 'other' (see Table 14.3).

Table 14.2 Things to avoid in survey questions (based on Neuman, 2010: 278–81; adapted to the physical education and sport context by the authors)

Avoid	*Examples of poor questioning*
Jargon, slang and abbreviations	'Do you like the way your PE teacher pulls off classes?'
Ambiguity, confusion and vagueness	'Do you exercise regularly?' (i.e., what is meant by 'regularly'?)
Emotional language and prestige bias	'What do you think about the despicable, merciless achievement ideal in modern sports?' 'Most doctors recommend physical activity to enhance a healthy lifestyle. Do you agree?'
Leading questions	'You exercise on a regular basis, correct?' 'Should elite athletes earn even more money?'
Double-barrelled questions	'Do you agree that boxing provokes aggression and that it should be banned from TV?'
Questions beyond respondent's capabilities	Asking a young pupil: 'Do you think physical achievement should be the main criterion of grading in physical education?'
Assumptions about people's beliefs	'Physical education is under-represented among school subjects. Do you think we should cut down the hours of other subjects or should the overall amount of school hours be increased?'
Asking about distant future intentions	'Will you enjoy physical education classes in the next school year?'
Double negatives	'Do you agree or disagree with the following: "Students should not be forced to participate in physical education class"?'
Overlapping response categories	'How often do you work out per week?' Not at all ☐ 1–2 times ☐ 2–3 times ☐ 3–5 times ☐

Contingency questions

Sometimes, questions are not relevant to all respondents of the sample; in these cases contingency or filter questions can be inserted. For example, when measuring levels of physical activity engagement, there will probably be a question such as 'Are you engaged in any physical activities?' People who answer 'No' can then skip the questions asking for the frequency, duration and intensity of the sports engagement and should be guided to the next relevant question.

Table 14.3 Examples of closed, open and partially open questions regarding motives in sports

'What are your reasons for engaging in sport?'		
Closed question	*Open question*	*Partially open question*
☐ fun		☐ fun
☐ health & fitness		☐ health & fitness
☐ social interaction	_____	☐ social interaction
☐ competition	_____	☐ competition
	_____	☐ other: _____

Table 14.4 Matrix question to measure physical activity in transportation

	Never	*Sometimes*	*Often*	*Always*
Travelling to and from places, I walk.	☐	☐	☐	☐
Travelling to and from places, I use a bike.	☐	☐	☐	☐
Travelling to and from places, I go by car or bus.	☐	☐	☐	☐

Matrix questions

Matrix or grid questions contain a set of questions that are based on the same answering scale. They are convenient to use because they save space and can be answered quickly (see Table 14.4).

It is important to note that once respondents reach the end of any questionnaire they should, if at all possible, have the opportunity to comment on the questionnaire and to express topic-related, personal thoughts that have not been covered. It is also important to remember that the layout of a questionnaire should have a motivational character. Squeezing questions onto a single page in order to save space (or printing costs) will result in confusion or misinterpretation, and so should be avoided. Depending on the target group, pictures (visual aids) can be used to loosen up the appearance of the questionnaire or to emphasize certain aspects. When questioning young children, elderly people or populations requiring special consideration, both font size and colour can be important aspects to consider. In summary, a questionnaire is more likely to attract a respondent's interest if it is clear and easy to read and follow.

Step 4: Pilot study

After constructing a questionnaire, a pretest is mandatory in order to detect errors and weaknesses, which are very likely to exist, no matter how carefully the tool has been designed. The necessity of proofreading by the researcher is self-evident but, on its own, this will never be sufficient. Therefore, a three-step routine is required to eliminate or at least to minimize errors: First, colleagues should be consulted – for example, experts in the specific field of the research. After adjusting the questionnaire according to their comments, the second step is to distribute it as a pilot study to test practicability with regards to content, clarity and methodological issues. The sample for this study does not necessarily have to be representative, but it should certainly be drawn from the same target group as that to which the questionnaire is addressed. At this stage of testing, the pilot has at least three core functions:

- The instructions, and especially the wording of each item, can be checked for comprehensibility. Some researchers use a technique called cognitive interviewing to detect weaknesses in phrasing. Respondents are asked to 'think out loud' while completing the questionnaire (Beatty and Willis, 2007).
- Items can be analysed with respect to their consistency (reliability of scales).
- The time needed to complete the questionnaire should be documented and considered.

In the third step of the pilot routine, the questionnaire has to be revised and then a process of re-piloting will be necessary until the researcher is completely satisfied with the survey tool developed.

For further information on pretesting strategies, Neuman's compilation (2010: 312) and the work of Presser and Blair (1994) are very helpful.

Step 5: Distribution and follow-up

Once the questionnaire is ready, a distribution strategy has to be developed. Depending on the target group, it may be necessary to take account of unfavourable times such as vacations, holidays or notably busy periods in the year. Paper-and-pencil questionnaires may be distributed personally or sent via mail, accompanied by the covering letter and a stamped and self-addressed return envelope. To reduce costs, an online questionnaire may be a sound alternative. However, this approach is limited to respondents who have access to appropriate technology – which may mean that the sample becomes biased and unrepresentative.

To ensure as high a response rate as possible, a follow-up process for non-respondents is needed. If the inquiry is anonymous, all prospective participants have to be contacted again using a follow-up letter. As well as thanking respondents for their support, the letter should encourage non-respondents to participate by emphasizing the importance of the study and the valuable contribution of every individual person. It is difficult to determine a common satisfactory response rate for surveys because rates vary dramatically. For example, an assessment of physical activity levels of schoolchildren in which they complete survey questions at school during class, can easily produce a response rate of nearly 100 per cent. On the other hand, the response rate can drop down to 20 per cent if questionnaires have to be sent back by mail. Anonymous online surveys may result in a return rate even lower than this. Besides the follow-up letter, there are further methods that can be used to increase response rates including (monetary) inducements or sending a preceding letter of information (Babbie, 2010: 272–3; Gratton and Jones, 2010: 146–7; Neuman, 2010: 295–9).

Step 6: Data entry and processing

Once the follow-up process is completed and a sufficient number of returned questionnaires achieved, the data have to be coded numerically and then entered into a statistical program for further processing. The Statistical Package for the Social Sciences (SPSS; version 19) is commonly used in this context. However, for some less complex surveys, which rely on basic descriptive analysis, Microsoft Excel might be effective and adequate. Depending on technological capability, approaches to data entry range from typing in all data manually or scanning the questionnaires, to simply exporting all data from online software directly into the chosen statistical program.

After all data have been entered into a computer program, a comprehensive data cleaning process should be conducted. This includes checking the data set for errors from the entry process and following strict guidelines about handling missing values. Respondents might fail to answer a certain question by mistake or on purpose. If, for example, a respondent had to specify their age and failed to do so, their other data can still be used for analysis. If a respondent of a survey addressed to university students indicates that they are 99 years old, it can be assumed that the questionnaire has not been treated seriously. Therefore, the case should be removed. Further information on how to handle missing values can be found in Chapter 24 of this book.

Step 7: Data analysis

Statistical analysis ranges from very basic to quite complex methods and has to be carried out taking account of the hypotheses or assumptions established in step 1. Basic methods cover descriptive statistics such as frequency counts, means and dispersion. In most research projects, descriptive analysis is used as a first step to recheck the data for errors from the entry process, as well as to organize and summarize the data for a general overview and first indications of results. The graphic presentation of descriptive data is usually quite helpful in moving towards the next step of analysing the data using complex methods known as inferential statistics (e.g., correlations, regression analysis and analysis of variance). These methods aim at generalizing results from the sample to the population and focus on correlations and differences between two or more variables.

In order to decide whether a result is significant or not, inferential methods provide a level of significance (p-value). In most studies from the field of sport sciences, a p-value lower than or equal to 0.05 is generally accepted as the level of significance. For example, if descriptive data show that children attending sports clubs have a more favourable self-concept compared with children not attending sports clubs, $p = 0.03$ indicates that the difference is statistically significant. In order to evaluate findings properly, an effect size (e.g., eta-squared) has to be computed and classified for each significant result. There are plenty of books available on how to analyse survey data; for an overview see Chapter 24 in this book.

Step 8: Answering the hypothesis

Having analysed the data, all hypotheses established – and only those – have to be evaluated and, depending on the result, either formally adopted or declined. This decision is based on the significance of the results. If the result is not significant ($p > 0.05$), the null hypothesis, stating that there is no difference between the compared groups, has to be accepted. If a result turns out to be significant, the alternative hypothesis, which suggests a difference between the groups, may be adopted. In the earlier example ($p = 0.03$), the alternative hypothesis, stating that there is a difference in self-concept between children attending and not attending sports clubs, would be appropriate.

Step 9: Interpretation of results

Once the selection of a hypothesis has been made, the interpretation of the findings with special interest to the effect sizes of the significant results may be started. Using eta-squared in this context, a value of $\eta^2 = 0.06$ represents a medium effect, whereas $\eta^2 = 0.14$ can be interpreted as a large effect. Using again the example above, a hypothetical effect size of $\eta^2 = 0.04$ implies that the finding – although significant – has only a small practical relevance. Additionally, it is necessary to embed the findings into the context of the theoretical framework and the results should be related to previous empirical findings on the topic.

Step 10: The research report

Writing a research report, for example a thesis, is the key to communicating the results of a survey effectively to the required audiences. As with all other stages in the research process, this activity needs much attention and effort because the report displays and documents the approach of the researcher step by step. It provides the basis for a critical evaluation and discussion by colleagues, other researchers and, of course, research supervisors. Depending on the complexity of surveys, the structure of reports might differ considerably. Certainly, each report should include an attention-grabbing introduction; a chapter dealing with theoretical input, the scientific state of the art and a concrete problem statement including statistical hypotheses or assumptions; a section documenting the method; presentation of results according to the established hypotheses; and, finally, an extensive interpretation and discussion of the results. In addition to these contents, the use of clear language and an appealing layout as well as a proper handling of the sources consulted (e.g., to avoid plagiarism) are self-evident requirements.

With the final research report, the process of survey research comes to a preliminary end – at least until the next survey based on the results is planned, implemented and analysed. Research is, of course, an ongoing process.

Examples from a recent research project

In order to pick up some relevant aspects mentioned above, this section delivers insights into a research project in which the authors are engaged. The project focuses on university students and uses a survey to identify problematic health-related issues by analysing students' lifestyles. Based upon the results, arrangements of support and health promotion within the university setting will be developed for the student population. The section discusses two aspects that turned out to be of special interest during the project: the development of the questionnaire (including the pilot study) and the length of the online survey with special regard to the response rate.

Astrid's experiences

With respect to the specific target group of university students, an online survey was developed. After determining relevant contents of the questionnaire by literature review, existing scales were used where available (e.g., health status, physical activity, self-concept). Due to a lack of scales suitable for the target group, however, self-developed instruments were also chosen (e.g., pressures resulting from the course of studies, changes of health-related aspects during the course of studies, presence of the topic 'health promotion' in everyday life). The entire survey development stage lasted almost six months and finally came to an end after piloting the instrument, as well as adapting it according to the problems identified. The piloting process turned out to be extremely important and, with the help of a small sample from the target group (N = 53) as well as experts in this field (university staff), the instrument was improved by eradicating minor errors and enhancing comprehensibility, accuracy and completeness. Some of the scales had to be replaced completely, while others were revised in some areas. Also, a selective calculation of results proved to be helpful in detecting whether the research questions could be answered adequately by the methodology applied. Last, but not least, the layout was improved significantly according to the feedback of pretest participants. Although bachelor's and master's theses usually require relatively small surveys, it is still advisable to allocate a sufficient amount of time to these preparatory stages. In other words: *Do not rush through the process of designing your survey!*

Another important issue, which has only been covered briefly so far, is the length of a survey. This issue seems to be very important with regard to the response rate, which is certainly affected by the time needed to complete the questionnaire. In the current study, approximately 15,000 students of the University of Paderborn were asked to participate, using multiple strategies such as email information, posters and personal approaches. Also, several inducements sponsored by the university, as well as by local businesses, were offered in a lottery (e.g., win a bicycle, games console, weekend trip). A total of 3,264 students opened the link to the online questionnaire, of whom 1,884 completed the survey – a number that was easily sufficient for statistical analysis. However, considering the response rate in the context of the total number of students (12.8 per cent), the situation appears less satisfactory which, in this case, can be attributed to the length of the questionnaire. On average, participants needed 30 minutes to answer all questions, and 22 per cent of those who quit did so after reading the first page, which indicated estimated time requirements. Therefore, it is strongly recommended that you consider carefully whether every single item is required and contributes significantly to answering the research questions. Quite often, researchers have to find compromises between the essential content of a questionnaire and its length. In other words: *Keep your survey as concise as possible!*

Hans Peter's comment

You have learned by now that to conduct a sound survey is complex in nature and needs quite a lot of experience. Most enthusiastic young researchers start out with a survey that aims to answer a lot of questions in a single project. However, there are no such things as a 'theory of everything' or all-embracing methodological tools. Therefore, it is important to ruthlessly narrow down the research question and to think about how it can be operationalized by adequate, reliable and valid instruments. I strongly recommend that you keep in mind the two suggestions offered above by Astrid. In the case of surveys, less can easily be more and can lead to more satisfying and relevant results.

Finally, a last but important comment: consult regularly with your supervisor if you have any doubts on how to proceed.

Conclusion

To conclude this chapter, the strengths and weaknesses of survey research are summarized as follows. First, when choosing a survey to answer a research question, it is crucial to understand the advantages and – equally important – the disadvantages of this method (see Table 14.5).

Second, a solid database created by thoroughly planned, carefully carried out and accurately interpreted surveys serves as a starting point for changes and interventions in the field of physical education and sport and can be used to convince policy and decision makers where required.

Table 14.5 Strengths and weaknesses of surveys

Strengths	Weaknesses
Information on large populations	No in-depth analysis of an individual's understanding
Information on different topics	Not contextualized in the respondent's everyday life (artificial character)
Economic way to gather information	Not flexible enough to react to changes during the research process
Allows for testing assumptions and hypotheses	Social desirability of some answers
Reliability and comparability between studies	Validity of the instruments and concepts

Key terms

Research problem   Research problems or research questions constitute the initial point of any survey research. They are usually identified on the basis of practical experience, or as a result of reviewing relevant literature.

Questionnaire   A prevalent tool in the social sciences to gather self-report data from individuals within a specific target population.

Sampling   Since it is often impossible to question a whole population, surveys use sampling techniques to choose a certain number of individuals in order to draw an adequate and, if possible, representative sample.

Pilot study   A small study which is conducted before the main investigation in order to pretest the instruments and strategies of analysis concerning errors and weaknesses.

Empirical evidence   What the data tell us. With the help of empirical evidence, assumptions are confirmed or disproved.

References

Babbie, E. (2010) *The Practice of Social Research*, Belmont: Wadsworth.

Beatty, P. C. and Willis, G. B. (2007) 'Research synthesis: The practice of cognitive interviewing', *Public Opinion Quarterly*, 71(2): 287–311.

Ferber, R., Sheatsley, P., Turner, A. and Waksberg, J. (1980) 'What is a survey?', edited by the Subcommittee of the Section on Survey Research Methods, American Statistical Association. Retrieved from <http://client.norc.org/whatisasurvey/downloads/pamphlet_1980.pdf>

Gratton, C. and Jones, I. (2010) *Research Methods for Sports Studies*, New York: Routledge.

Neuman, L. W. (2010) *Social Research Methods: Qualitative and Quantitative Approaches*, 6th edn, Boston: Pearson Education.

Presser, S. and Blair, J. (1994) 'Survey pretesting: Do different methods produce different results?', in P. Marsden (ed.) *Sociological Methodology* (73–104), San Francisco: Jossey-Bass.

Thomas, J. R., Nelson, J. K. and Silverman, S. J. (2005) *Research Methods in Physical Activity*, 5th edn, Champaign, IL: Human Kinetics.

15 Observational studies

Marie Öhman and Mikael Quennerstedt

Introduction

Imagine a physical education (PE) lesson where a game of 'dodge ball' is on the agenda and the teacher starts the lesson in the following way:

Teacher: Today we are going to cooperate in different ball games; that is to say, we will do some cooperation activities in conjunction with playing ball games. We'll form two teams and the players in one team have to throw the ball and try to hit the players in the other team. If the ball hits someone's head, it doesn't count. One team has to try to beat the other team by throwing the ball at somebody – dodge ball. In short, the aim of the game is to cooperate.

Some of the pupils are very active during the game. They pass and throw the ball, run around and cooperate. However, four girls remain quite motionless beside the wall.

Teacher: Come on! Don't get stuck to the floor. Move around a little bit more, catch the ball and try to hit somebody from the other team.

At the end of the lesson the teacher assembles the class:

Teacher: A lot of you have cooperated well, but the same people can't throw the ball all the time. Time's up. Do your stretching in the shower.

There are a lot of analytical questions to explore here. How do students cooperate? What does 'cooperated well' mean? To what extent do students participate in the ball game? How many times do different students touch the ball? What is meant by 'Don't get stuck to the floor'? Why is it important to do stretching in the shower?

About us

In this chapter, Marie Öhman and Mikael Quennerstedt guide you through the use of observation as a research method, and in particular, how video-recorded observations can be used as a helpful tool in research. Their main area of research is teaching and learning in physical education in terms of 'what is going on in the gym'. In Marie's research, questions of health, body, subjectivity, power relations and governing processes within physical education have been prominent. She is also involved in research in the field of education for sustainable development.

Mikael's research is related to physical and health education, with a specific focus on health, body, artefacts, subject content, learning processes and privileging within educational practices, using both written texts and observational data.

Observational studies

Observational studies can be carried out in many different ways, and have been used in many disciplines – for example, social anthropology, sociology and education (Bryman, 2008). Observational studies can be quantitative in nature, investigating questions such as how many times girls and boys respectively touch the ball during basketball in school PE, or how many times and for how long a coach interacts with each individual in a girls' hockey team. They can also be more qualitatively oriented, for example in terms of observing aspects of children's motor development or addressing how coaches and teachers support young people in specific situations. The choice between qualitative and quantitative, or participatory and non-participatory observations, or the use of video recordings, observation schedules or field notes thus depends on the research question(s) to be investigated and the theoretical position from which the study is executed (e.g. see Chapters 1 and 5 in this book).

Within sociology and education, ethnographic (Gobo, 2008; Pink, 2007), ethnomethodological (Heath and Hindmarch, 2002) and socioculturally (Wertsch et al., 1995) inspired studies have frequently been used as theoretical frameworks for observational studies. In this chapter we will not go into the details of these perspectives, but will instead concentrate on more comprehensive presentations of non-participant qualitative, theoretically driven and purpose-related studies using video-recorded data. We also illustrate this with a study of PE in Sweden and contrast it with a systematic observation of the same study.

In observational studies, the use of new technologies and video-recorded data has grown in several fields, especially in studies of human interaction.[1] This is certainly reasonable within a field such as physical education and youth sport, where linguistic methods that focus solely on verbal communication are inadequate due to the large proportion of non-verbal bodily actions and communications involved.

One main advantage of many observational studies is that the research gets close to social practices and everyday situations, or what Potter (2002: 12) refers to as passing the 'dead scientists test'. This means that the investigated situation, in contrast to, for example, interviews, would have occurred even if the researcher had been taken ill or the car had broken down on the way to the observation or recording. In this way, observational studies often offer authentic first-hand impressions of ongoing practices that cannot be covered by other methods, where second-hand reports of the same practices are available. Of course, video-recorded or other observational data are not closer to 'reality' than data that are affected by the researcher in interviews or questionnaires. Different kinds of data answer different questions. However, getting close to the situation makes it possible to document, view, re-view and analyse what occurs when people act in context. It is also possible to focus on the actual context where material aspects like equipment, locality or discourses 'surrounding' the specific situation can be involved in the study (Quennerstedt, Almqvist and Öhman, in press).

Another advantage is that observations, and especially video-recorded observations, facilitate our understanding of what is said and done when language use is put in context. Utterances like 'Come on' or 'Go, go, go' acquire meaning through the possibility of observing what is happening in the event as it occurs. As Wittgenstein (1953) argues, a specific word acquires meaning by how it is used in certain situations. Utterances like 'Don't get stuck to the floor', as in the introductory illustration, acquire specific meaning when we hear how they are said and link this with what is happening contextually, in this case in the gym. But we can also take embodied actions into account and explore how certain actions acquire meaning in the investigated practices. In our own studies, a focus on embodied actions helps us to explore what is said and done, as well as how it is said and done. We can consequently investigate the functions that a specific act or activity has in a certain event, where individuals' actions and utterances constitute the focal point of the analysis.

With other kinds of data, such as texts, we can examine the content of the specific practice, e.g., what type of knowledge is offered. This can include techniques in sport or biophysical knowledge about the body. With observational data, on the other hand, we can explore the question of *what* and also investigate the different processes – such as learning processes, governing processes, or how gender orders are upheld and created – through the question of *how*. In relation to the question of *what* type of knowledge above, for example, *how* specific knowledge about techniques in sport is formed through instruction, correction or experimentally through trial and error. Another example can be how biophysical knowledge about the body is formed through the activities the teacher or the coach chooses.

Our own experience of conducting in-depth analyses of video-recorded data is that the social interplay in a movement context such as physical education or sport is too complex and comprehensive to capture through observations alone (see Table 15.1). Through repeated viewing, details and events that initially seem insignificant and not really relevant to the study later stand out as highly critical and relevant. In observational studies using field notes, it is also difficult to make detailed analyses of bodily movements and gestures in ongoing activities. Here, the use of a video camera is advantageous.

However, working empirically with observational data, and especially video data, has its disadvantages, in that it involves time-consuming transcriptions and ethical approvals for the filming of young people doing physical activities. Another shortcoming with in situ studies is that we can only investigate what is distinctly

Table 15.1 An overview of different observational methods

	Participant observation	Non-participant observation
What is explored?	Uncovering phenomena (e.g., behaviour) that is not directly observable	Phenomena that are possible to capture and observe from the outside
How is that captured?	The researcher experiences the setting and the experiences provide the data capture	Distanced observation using schedules or video recordings
The role of the researcher	The researcher takes active part in the investigated practice, interacting with participants and learning the 'code'	The researcher is often passive and tries to affect the situation as little as possible
Data gathering	Descriptive and reflective field notes or summaries	Quantitative or qualitative observation schedules or video recording
Analysis	Seeks explanation of social and/or cultural behavioural patterns	See below under systematic observation and video-recorded data
The role of theory	Theory, if used, is often added after the analysis to explain the investigated phenomena (e.g., ethnographic studies)	See below under systematic observation and video-recorded data
Strengths and weaknesses	+ Closeness to the situation	+ Closeness to the situation
	+ Possible to capture subtleties in the setting through researcher's own experiences and active involvement	+ Observation of naturally occurring activities in everyday settings
	– The effect of the active researcher	– The effect of the observer
	– The possibility to write the field notes and not rely too much on what is recalled	
	Non-participant systematic observation	*Non-participant video-recorded data*
What is explored?	Quantitative questions such as 'How much?' or 'For how long?'	Qualitative questions such as how people act and interact in context
How is that captured?	Through observation schedules and instruments with pre-given clearly identified variables	Through video recordings of ongoing practices

	Non-participant systematic observation	Non-participant video-recorded data
The role of the researcher	Passive observer	Passive recorder; however, becoming familiar with the setting
Analysis	Quantitative analysis and description	Qualitative, often theoretically driven and purpose-related analysis
The role of theory	Theory is often used to create reasonable variables for the observation schedule	Theory is used throughout the study: for example, to pose the research question, do the analysis and discuss the results (for example, conversational analysis, ethnomethodology, sociocultural theory, discourse analysis, pragmatic approaches)
Strengths and weaknesses	+ Quantitative observation of actual behaviour in natural settings	+ The possibility to capture phenomena not possible to capture with other data (e.g., ongoing processes)
	+ The possibility to use easily managed checklists	+ To be able to document, view, and re-view data of human interaction and non-verbal bodily actions
	– The effect of the observer	+ The explored phenomena are explored in context
	– The limitation of the number of variables possible to observe	– The effect of the video camera and the observer
		– Time-consuming transcription and analysis
		– Ethical issues in video filming

observable in a particular PE lesson or specific training session. We cannot determine, for example, the meaning or the learning. Further, in contrast to using interviews in which particular questions can be posed about specific issues, questions relating to, for example, moral issues in sport or conflict management might not necessarily appear in the recorded practices.

Even if the intention is to capture the whole or parts of the content of a certain practice with the video camera, a fully adequate account of what is happening is unattainable. In the myriad of actions and episodes, conversations and actions, important details can escape the researcher. The video camera simply cannot register everything, and even if plenty of material is captured, it can only represent a limited picture of the practice or event on which the researcher has chosen to focus. Video recordings accordingly produce a selective data set that provides a partial view of the observed practice.

Doing observational studies

In quantitative observational studies, the methodological steps include creating observation schedules or using ready-made instruments such as, for example, direct instruction behaviour analysis (cf. Zeng, Leung and Hipscher, 2010). These studies often claim 'objectively' measured results that indicate what is happening in a certain practice as explanation of the reality of the situation. On the other hand, qualitative observational studies are about finding ways of seeing and understanding and do not in the same way involve a clear set of methodological steps and procedures. However, while they often share features of how to explore naturally occurring and everyday settings (see Heath and Hindmarch, 2002; Pink, 2007), other parts of the study need to be designed innovatively within the research project's purpose and theoretical position.

What appears in people's actions?

In our own studies, we start from the premise that different phenomena are constituted in certain situations and that practices take shape in the relations between people. It is thus about exploring what stands out, what can be observed, the obvious, i.e. what is said and done, how it is said and done and what can be said and done in the investigated practice. Analytical interest can then be directed towards how individuals shape, describe or constitute the content in a certain practice, such as how knowledge about cooperation is produced and reproduced, or how gendered identities are constituted in a specific event.

Events explored with a specific purpose

In a PE lesson or training session in youth sport, a multitude of actions and interactions take place at the same time. We can all imagine the great variety of actions, activities and events in progress. All these actions can be regarded as an assemblage of actions – actions upon actions – without any beginning or end. Potter (2002: 7) argues that 'actions do not hang in space, but are responses to other actions, and they in turn set the environment for new actions'. The different actions that take place in a sports context can consequently be regarded and explored as interlaced and part of the same process. Hence, it is important to selectively explore the observed practice from the point of view of a certain purpose and a certain perspective. This includes selecting a purpose-related sample of events and looking at the observational data in a specific way. By focusing on the purpose and the perspective of the study, a coherent context can be both created and analysed. For example, if you are interested in how the body is constituted in PE or youth sport, there is little point in concentrating on why or whether a child is participating, asking if he can go to the toilet or why she couldn't be in the same team as Ibrahim. Instead the focus is directed towards how the participants talk about the body and the activities, and how they act in relation to embodiment. For a researcher, it is about creating a coherent story about how the body is constituted by exploring what is said and done – what appears in action – and which patterns of action are constituted or sustained as a result.

Factors to take into account when doing observational studies

In the initial stages of the study, it is important to think about the selection of sporting practices. Questions that the researcher needs to consider are the number of practices, whether a random sample or a purposeful selection of practices is required, the geographical spread, rural and/or urban, gender mix or single-gendered groups etc. The answers to these questions depend on the purpose of the study and the accompanying research questions. In other words, what is it that we want to know something about?

Access to the investigated practice is crucial, i.e., informed consent needs to be obtained for the video recording. In the case of exploring school PE, the principal or the school's management board and the teachers involved should be contacted. When consent has been given, it is appropriate to visit the school to discuss the particulars of the study with the teachers and the students. Our recommendation would be to write a brief letter for distribution that details the purpose of the study and the ethical considerations involved, with regard to things like anonymity, access, informed consent from students and/or parents and how the results of the study will be used. You will have university-specific ethical guidelines to follow in these matters.

This draws attention to specific ethical issues and ethical approvals for videoing young people in physical activity. Potter (2002) addresses these issues in general, and argues that video recording as data collection constitutes a greater interference in people's private lives than, for example, questionnaires. In our studies, we have videoed ongoing educational situations, which are everyday situations students are familiar with. This in turn reduces the possible risk of discomfort or harm. Considerable effort has also been put into obtaining the informed consent of both students and parents. However, the use of video-recorded data means that as individual students can be identified in the analytical phase of the study, anonymity cannot be guaranteed. However, confidentiality can be achieved by not using real names in the transcripts, and by focusing on the actions performed in certain events rather than on individual students.

A common question in relation to video recording as data collection is the effect of the researcher, i.e., whether the researcher and the camera affect the actions and activities in the gym or in the sport being practised. Some scholars argue that the presence of the observer almost always affects the behaviour of the participants (Thomas et al., 2005: 297). While we agree with that, we would also like to draw attention to the difficulty of determining the extent to which video filming actually affects the situation. This particular question is thus not easy to answer, since we don't know whether the teacher or the coach does things differently when the researcher isn't present, or whether the students act in a different way from usual. Our experience is, however, that neither the teachers nor the students seem to take much notice of the camera, or of us as researchers, because they are busy concentrating on the activities at hand.

Transcription and analytical procedures

Doing the recordings and transcribing the data can be regarded as the first steps of the analytical process of the study. In short, the analytical process begins at the site of the study and with the data collection. How, then, do we transform what we see into a paper or a thesis? When starting to work with the data, the analytical process includes getting to know the data, looking at the films, transcribing what is said and done, looking at the films again and again, and in this way trying to capture the investigated practice by using the theories and assumptions that are relevant to the study (see Table 15.1).

In the next step, what is relevant to transcribe has to be related to the purpose and the theoretical perspective of the study. It is not possible to transcribe everything, and we don't see the need for the transcription of all the collected video data. In more linguistically oriented studies, symbols and signs are often used in the transcription in order to depict the nuances in and of the language, including pauses for breath etc. (Bryman, 2008). In other studies, like our own, the focus is on transcribing the central segments of the data, which means that the transcription is more 'direct', and where the context as well as the spoken and embodied actions of the participants is taken into consideration (Quennerstedt, Öhman and Öhman, 2011; Spiers, 2002). The selected transcribed segments can then be regarded as narratives to be analysed, in that they say something about the purpose of the study. In the transcribed data, or in the computer program used to manage the data, it is advisable to first of all make field notes in order to comprehensively highlight important parts of the data. This method is used to draw attention to those events that are particularly significant for the study. In a second step, applying preliminary labels is appropriate, such as: interaction student–teacher; interaction student–student; content; activities; privileged knowledge; norms; how the participants talk about the body etc. This way of preliminarily organizing the data can be modified, abandoned or confirmed in the subsequent analytical work. This procedure should not be understood as unbiased, or as some sort of 'open coding', where the researcher approaches the data without pre-formulated questions and theories. Instead, the data are approached by using the concepts, perspectives and purposes that have guided the study from the beginning.

Engaging in analytical work is a creative process. When the above steps have been completed, the researcher then has to transform the data into a scientifically acceptable text. Regardless of the amount of data the video has produced, and their unstable and disparate nature and the challenges of managing and working with them, they have to be organized into some kind of systematic order. Foucault (1971) argues that this third part of the analytical process is about identifying the coordinated ways of speaking, acting and thinking in a specific context. Burr (1995) further argues that the analysis has to focus on that which constitutes a certain version of something: a distinct way of talking about and understanding the world. Through processes of inclusion and exclusion, the so-called discursive order of a certain practice can be identified. In this in-depth part of the analysis, regularities and recurrent patterns about what is said, done, stated, indicated and established in the practice are identified through the functions that these actions constitute in a certain situation. This important part of the coding process implies categorizing how actions, in the constant flow of actions, contribute to other actions being oriented in a specific direction in a certain event.

An illustration

We now illustrate an observational study using events from one of the lessons included in a larger empirical material of 15 video-recorded PE lessons in Sweden. In an investigation based on rich empirical material, consideration is given to the material as a whole. However, in this chapter, events from only one lesson have been selected as an illustration. Of course, this brief illustration of the practice of the method cannot fully exemplify the complexity, richness and analytical depth of this kind of study. Our hope is, however, that it will indicate the possibilities. Our specific interest in the illustration is directed towards how the body is constructed in the practice of PE. In the following, we present four steps of the analysis: (i) a general picture, (ii) the primary purpose, (iii) the construction of knowledge, and (iv) bodily messages in PE.

A general picture

In any analytical work it is important to provide a general picture of the entire setting in which the observation takes place. Patton (2002: 262) also emphasizes the importance of describing the location in which the observations are made. The purpose of this description is to situate the reader in the investigated setting in order to bring the studied environment to life. Describing and setting the scene helps the reader to follow the formation of the study and understand its design. However, it is important to be aware that the description is not an analysis but a necessary and relevant start for the subsequent analytical work. This kind of description can of course be presented in different ways, and below we provide an example from the study in question.

> The gym is small and quite worn out, with painted lines on the wooden floor. The students are 18 girls in school year seven, some of whom are wearing veils and are not Swedish speakers. The female teacher gives a brief introduction, pointing out that the students are familiar with the activities and asking them to prepare the various kinds of fitness training equipment. She asks the students to explain how to perform the exercises, what the different activities are good for in training purposes, and to say which muscles they are exercising at each station. The teacher explains why it is good to develop muscles and how to avoid muscle soreness by stretching. Students are divided into pairs and kick off at the various stations that include: running between two cones, hanging on the high beam and pulling up to 90 degrees, sit-ups, push-ups, skating with a hula hoop, skipping, leg bends with a medicine ball, back lifts, and arm bending on a low beam. All the students work on their exercises for a minute and then move to the next station during the short break. The teacher walks around and talks to the students, touches their backs, corrects certain body positions, encourages, cheers and shows enthusiasm. The students do not say very much, there is no hesitation and everything runs its course. At the end of the lesson everyone helps to remove the equipment and then assembles. The teacher

explains that these activities will help to strengthen the body and emphasizes that it is important to do physical activity because inactivity is so widespread both in school and in leisure time. Students are praised highly by the teacher, who says that they have been really good and that she is proud of the students having worked so well.

Primary purpose

As a second step in the analysis, it is advisable to investigate the main content and purpose of the teaching practice in order to explore how these purposes appear in the activities. Institutionalized practices like PE or youth sport can be said to focus on something: they have a primary purpose. Out of everything that is said and done in the teaching of school subjects or activities in a sports club, certain things are more important than others – they have a certain subject focus. Here it is important to identify that which emerges as being the most essential in the investigated practice. By examining the regularities (verbal and non-verbal) that appear in the data as a whole, the primary purposes of the institutionalized practice are crystallized. This can be done by, for example, looking at the main concepts and dominant activities that are both typical and prominent.

The results of the illustrated study show that one of the primary purposes of PE is *physical exertion*. Physical exertion and the desire for physical activity are also threads that run through the analysed material as a whole. Within this frame, PE is about stimulating physiological training effects so that oxygen uptake and muscle strength increase. In our study, the main concepts and activities in the illustrated lesson include hard work, tired, sweaty, training sessions and fitness training. The importance of physical exertion is also apparent in the teacher's statements, e.g. 'Keep going', 'Come on' and 'Don't stop'. Inactivity appears as something that must be checked, and passivity becomes the object of correction. Being slow, standing still or pausing during the activities does not appear to be acceptable.

The construction of knowledge: what and how

As mentioned previously in this chapter, observational data can be used to explore the question of *what* and the question of *how*. In a third step, we draw attention to the specific knowledge that is acquired and how certain types of knowledge about the body are constructed. The analysis is directed towards knowledge that guides students towards a particular way of viewing the body, which means focusing on how the body is portrayed, i.e., actions that include certain ways of regarding and understanding the body. The questions used in this part of the study are: What kind of descriptions, explanations and statements are made about the body? Which bodily messages result from the application of this specific knowledge? How is certain knowledge about the body constructed?

In the event illustrated, the following dialogue takes place at the beginning of the lesson:

Teacher: Girls, today we will work with fitness training with the aid of some equipment. What is the aim of these physical activities?

Student: Strength training.

Teacher: Yes, that is good for you and very important.

They all start to construct the different stations, and repeat the various kinds of activities in terms of which muscles are working.

Teacher: Which muscle works here?

Student: The upper arm.

Teacher: Yes, but what is it called?

Student: Biceps.

Teacher (pointing to her arm): Yes, and triceps. (They move on to the next station where sit-ups are to be performed.) When you work with this you will not get out of breath, but you will feel tension in the stomach. To avoid the build-up of lactic acid you can stretch after the lesson.

At the station where students are expected to run between two cones:

Teacher: What happens to the body here? It is oxygen capacity training and how do you find out?

Student: You breathe faster.

Teacher: Yes, you get out of breath. While you experience shortness of breath you also work with the leg muscles.

They move on to jump skipping.

Teacher: Skipping is a very good warm-up exercise; you get out of breath and work with the arm and leg muscles. Let's start, work hard from beginning to end. We'll work for one minute, then rest for 30 seconds. It is important that we keep going for the whole minute. Come on, work for it! On your marks, get set, go!

During the performances, the teacher notices that a student is doing push-ups incorrectly. The teacher calls for the attention of the class and starts to demonstrate a push-up.

Teacher (demonstrates): Here we go for the usual, but you can keep your knees on the floor if you want. Straight arms, straight backs, not like this (showing with the bottom towards the ceiling), then bend your arms, down and touch (shows with her chest and nose to the floor).

Student: Can you do push-ups in different ways?

Teacher: Yes, the narrower the space between the arms, the more you feel it in the muscles. The wider it is, the more the chest works (pointing to chest).

Let us now go back to the first of our questions: What kind of descriptions, explanations and statements are made about the body? The concepts mentioned in the event include strength, muscles, oxygen capacity, lactic acid, biceps and triceps. Here scientific knowledge about the body is mainly referred to in the teaching practice. This is displayed through the use of scientifically inspired language when talking about the body, where effects on the muscles and the degree of oxygen intake are considered in connection with the physical activities. It appears to be important that students understand the body from an anatomical and physiological perspective, and the insights to be internalized are based on knowledge about how the body functions.

In the event, we can also see *how* the students are guided towards this specific knowledge. By constructing facts about the body, physical activities are turned into experimental situations where the objective is to discover facts about how the body works. Constructing facts about the body means that reality is constituted through a specific use of language. By using words like 'is/are' and 'one' – 'This is physical fitness' and 'One gets out of breath' – facts are constructed about how things *are* and what *one* ought to feel. This general body has to be experienced in the same way by everybody. The teacher often poses questions such as 'What happens in the muscles when you do that particular activity?' We can also see how the teacher corrects bodily movements. Through bodily corrections, and through a demonstration of both desirable and undesirable examples of bodily movements, correct performance norms can be identified.

Bodily messages in PE

We also considered the question of which bodily messages result from the application of this specific knowledge. In a fourth step, we conclude that scientific knowledge creates the prerequisites for how students should perceive themselves as physical beings and plays a significant role in the formation of the individual's bodily understanding within PE. This knowledge facilitates an understanding of the body as something that should, through physical exertion, be developed into something that is strong, full of stamina and well trained; i.e., a way of understanding how a healthy, well-trained and fit body can be created. This creates an understanding of the body as a 'natural' biological organism. It also conveys that the body is understood in terms of cause and effect: an object to be controlled in a particular way. The implication of this type of knowledge is that the body becomes generalized, objectified and materialized – the body is something one has and that one can and ought to control. In this privileged knowledge, the body becomes demystified and objectified, and an individual's unique bodily experiences and 'spontaneous' bodily actions are rationally reshaped. The experiencing, feeling and expressive body is given little scope in the utilitarian way of rational thinking. It is not the individual's unique experience that is being examined here, but the biological functions that can be discovered by means of a number of different activities.

Systematic observation as a comparison

In order to acquire a different kind of understanding of the body, it can be fruitful to study how often and in which ways body movements are performed in PE and youth sport. This could be done by systematic observation using an observation schedule. This means that during the observations the researcher can count how often and for how long an activity or a certain type of bodily movement occurs. This constitutes an attempt to explore the frequency of content and different body movements. In our recorded material consisting of 15 physical education lessons, ball games occurred in eight, strength and endurance training in seven, other games in three and gymnastics in two of the lessons. Specific body movements like push-ups, sit-ups and high jump occurred in 14 of the recorded lessons. By systematically observing the types of activity and the body movements that dominate in the lessons, it is possible to clarify the content and identify which patterns of bodily actions are constituted or sustained.

Another possibility would be to calculate the number of specific body movements during a single lesson in terms of how many and for how long one pupil does different movements: for example, push-ups, sit-ups, jumping, jogging, standing still, queuing, sitting. By measuring how many times and for how long a pupil does different movements, it is possible to say something about the content and participation in a PE lesson from a physiological point of view. Importantly, as should be clear, different types of observational research allow us to answer different research questions.

Conclusions

In this chapter we have shown how observational studies can be used in research to get close to social practices and to document and explore what happens when people act in context. Observational studies also make it possible to investigate the processes that are taking place in sporting practices and to take embodied as well as spoken actions into account. We would thus argue that it is possible to explore what expressions like 'Don't get stuck to the floor' and 'cooperating well' mean in the specific practice in which these actions take place. In this way, observational studies can be used not as a way to explain what the reality of a certain practice is, but as ways of exploring and understanding different aspects of that practice from a certain perspective.

In our research, the objective is not to assess which kind of bodily constitutions are better or worse, or which perspectives should be privileged over another. The results of our analyses can instead be seen as a tool with which to critically examine and discuss what is included and excluded, how this is done and what the consequences are.

Key terms

Video recording   One way to do observational data collection.

Embodied actions   Non-verbal actions explored in order to analyse what is said and done, as well as how it is said and done.

Event   A series of actions in a certain context demarcated in order to investigate the functions that a specific act or activity has in that certain situation.

Context   Different aspects of the studied event including material aspects like equipment, locality or discourses 'surrounding' the specific situation.

Process   When exploring different processes in observational data the focus lies on the question of how.

Note

1   For physical education and youth sport see e.g. Clarke and Quill, 2003; James, Griffin, and Dodds, 2008; MacPhail, Kirk, and Griffin, 2008; Rønholt, 2002; Rovegno, Chen and Todorovich, 2003; Wright, 2000.

References

Bryman, A. (2008) *Social Research Methods*, Oxford: Oxford University Press.

Burr, V. (1995) *An Introduction to Social Constructionism*, London: Routledge.

Clarke, G. and Quill, M. (2003) 'Researching sport education in action: a case study', *European Physical Education Review*, 9(3): 253–66.

Foucault, M. (1971) 'Orders of discourse', *Social Sciences Information*, 10(2): 7–30.

Gobo, G. (2008) *Doing Ethnography*, London: Sage.

Heath, C. and Hindmarch, J. (2002) 'Analysing interaction: Video, ethnography and situated conduct', in T. May (ed.) *Qualitative Research in Action* (99–121), London: Sage.

James, A. R., Griffin, L. L. and Dodds, P. (2008) 'The relationship between instructional alignment and the ecology of physical education', *Journal of Teaching in Physical Education*, 27, 308–26.

MacPhail, A., Kirk, D. and Griffin, L. (2008) 'Throwing and catching as relational skills in game play: Situated learning in a modified game unit', *Journal of Teaching in Physical Education*, 27, 100–15.

Patton, M. Q. (2002) *Qualitative Research & Evaluation Methods*. 3rd edition, London: Sage.

Pink, S. (2007) *Doing Visual Ethnography*, London: Sage.

Potter, J. (2002) 'Two kinds of natural', *Discourse Studies*, 4(4): 539–42.

Quennerstedt, M., Öhman, J. and Öhman, M. (2011) 'Investigating learning in physical education – a transactional approach', *Sport, Education and Society*, 16(2): 157–75.

Quennerstedt, M., Almqvist, J. and Öhman, M. (in press) 'Keep your eye on the ball – investigating artefacts in use in physical education', *Interchange: A Quarterly Review of Education*.

Rønholt, H. (2002) ' "It's only the sissies … ": Analysis of teaching and learning processes in physical education: A contribution to the hidden curriculum', *Sport, Education and Society*, 7, 25–36.

Rovegno, I., Chen, W. and Todorovich, J. (2003) 'Accomplished teachers' pedagogical content knowledge of teaching dribbling to third-grade children', *Journal of Teaching in Physical Education*, 22, 426–49.

Spiers, J. A. (2002) 'Tech tips: Using video management/analysis technology in qualitative research', *International Journal of Qualitative methods*, 57–61.

Thomas, J. R., Nelson, J. K. and Silverman, S. J. (2005) *Research Methods in Physical Activity*, Leeds: Human Kinetics.

Wertsch, J. V., Del Rio, P. and Alvarez, A. (eds) (1995) *Sociocultural Studies of Mind*, New York: Cambridge University Press.

Wittgenstein, L. (1953) *Philosophical Investigations*, Oxford: Blackwell.

Wright, J. (2000) 'Bodies, meanings and movement: A comparison of the language of a physical education lesson and a Feldenkrais movement class', *Sport, Education and Society*, 5(1): 35–49.

Zeng, H. Z., Leung, R. W. and Hipscher, M. (2010) 'An examination of teaching behaviours and learning activities in physical education class settings taught by three different levels of teachers', *Journal of Social Sciences*, 6(1): 18–28.

16 Case study research

Kathleen Armour and Mark Griffiths

At its best, case study provides the most vivid, the most inspirational, analysis that inquiry can offer. Einstein did it; Newton did it. Sociologists do it; psychologists do it. Doctors do it; teachers do it; lawyers do it; nurses do it. It is done across the disciplinary and methodological spectrum ... Case study provides a form of inquiry that elevates a view of life in its complexity ... It's the realization that complexity in social affairs is frequently indivisible that has led to case study's status as one of the most popular and most fertile design frames open to the researcher.

(Thomas, 2011, preface)

Introduction

Case studies are used extensively by researchers in numerous disciplines. Their appeal lies in offering contextually grounded, holistic and detailed accounts of phenomena. Case reports have the potential to be interesting and informative for research users who can draw comparisons with other cases or with their personal experiences. Yet, despite their intuitive appeal, there are numerous challenges to be faced when undertaking case study research; not least the belief by some researchers that case studies are, in some sense, 'unscientific'. As Thomas (2011) points out above, however, case study is also a very popular research method, which suggests that it has something of value to offer. The task, therefore, is to ensure that case study method is used to address appropriate research questions in appropriate ways. In this chapter, we consider some of the key issues to be taken into account when embarking upon case study research, and we provide illustrative data from the second author's PhD research.

About us

Kathleen Armour, co-editor of this book, is Professor of Education and Sport and Head of the Department of Sport Pedagogy at the University of Birmingham in the UK. Throughout her research career, Kathy has been interested in qualitative research and has used case study methods extensively. In recent years, she has been involved in multidisciplinary research teams engaged in large-scale evaluations of social programmes in physical education and sport. In each of these evaluations, case studies have formed an important part of the research design. Although, initially, the research funders were sometimes sceptical about the value of case studies, they were convinced once they realized that case studies were invaluable in illustrating the pathways to programme impact for different participants.

Mark Griffiths is a lecturer in the Department of Sport Pedagogy at the University of Birmingham in the UK. Mark undertook case study research as part of his PhD. He writes:

> Much of my research adopts a case study approach. That is, I'm particularly interested in examining peoples' experiences of sport in the context of real sporting situations. As in any field of human interaction, the experiences of teachers, coaches, pupils and athletes is characterized by different levels of complexity, and a case study approach can help to elevate these complexities, allowing the researcher to gain rich insights into a particular issue. In so doing, case study research seeks to examine a unique issue by viewing the 'wholeness' of it, as opposed to positivist research methods that might break the issue into digestible chunks. As Thomas (2011: viii) noted, 'we all like easily digestible food, but it's often not the most nutritious'. For me, case study research offers a 'healthy' way of trying to understand a particular area of interest in sport, and by so doing, offers another view from which to examine sport experiences.

What is case study research?

Yin (1994: 13) defined the case study as 'an empirical inquiry that investigates a contemporary phenomenon, the "case", within its real-life context'. This definition summarizes the key features of case study research: a very specific focus of inquiry investigated in a specific context. Thomas (2011) further elaborates that case study researchers are interested in 'that thing in itself, as a whole' and, moreover, that they are not setting out to generalize from it. Taken together, these comments begin to reveal both the strength and also the perceived weaknesses of case study research, i.e., What is the point of knowing about one 'thing' in detail, when surely the whole purpose of research is to find out information that can be generalized to large populations? Perhaps it is helpful to address this issue now because it is one of the first questions that new researchers tend to ask: How can a case study constitute worthwhile research? Following this, some of the classic typologies of case studies will be reviewed before providing some examples of these issues as they were considered in the design of one PhD study.

The validity question

Other chapters in this book have considered, in some depth, issues of validity and generalizability in qualitative and quantitative research, so we will not repeat them all here. In the case of case study research, however, the issue is a little more complex because 'case study' is both a method in itself and a framework within which other research methods sit. So, whereas the overall approach taken to address a research question might be a case study, perhaps selecting one particular 'case' to study in depth, a range of methods will be employed to investigate the research questions. For example, a research question might ask: 'How do pupils learn to work collaboratively in physical education lessons?' The question is complex, and there are numerous contextual details to take into account. For this reason, the decision could be taken to select a lesson – or a series of lessons (depending on the level of depth required for each case) – as case studies in order to investigate the issue in depth and in context.

Having selected a case study approach, the next task is to decide which research methods are needed, within the case study, to investigate the question. In this hypothetical study, it could be speculated that the following methods might be appropriate: document analysis (to investigate the lesson planning process); interviews (pupils and teachers); and observations of lessons. In the observations, we could choose to take an open field notes approach, or we might decide to video the lesson and count (or code) what is observed in order to provide quantitative data. In other words, selecting case study as method requires the selection of a range of other, more specific research methods in order to gather data. In that sense, it can be argued that every chapter in this book is relevant to anyone considering case study research because questions about research quality must be addressed in each method used. Taking the case as a whole, however, questions about validity can be answered by reference to appropriate case selection, detail provided on context, accuracy and appropriateness of the individual methods used, accurate and authentic reporting, and the extent to which the conclusions drawn are warranted by the data (see later section in this chapter).

The generalizability question

Generalizability at the level of the case is, of course, a different matter. Stake (2000) cautioned against focusing on generalizability to such an extent that the core purpose of case study research is lost – which is defined by Thomas (2011) as the 'thing' itself. Concrete examples are helpful when considering this issue, for example by using the research question used earlier: How do pupils learn to work collaboratively in physical education (PE) lessons? Let's assume that three different PE classes, from different schools, were selected as cases. It becomes immediately apparent that if the methods used to investigate the question within these three cases are robust, then the findings should be valid for those three cases. It should also be apparent, however, that to claim the findings can be generalized to *all* PE classes would constitute gross over-claiming. On the other hand, to claim that the findings have no application at all for anyone outside the three classes would constitute gross simplification.

In other fields, such as medicine and law, practitioners learn as a matter of routine from case studies, although it is vital to ensure that the salient details of the case are provided and that no simple transfer is attempted from one patient or client to another. What seems clear, however, is that traditional notions of generalization from quantitative research are difficult to apply in case study research. What is also clear is that case studies offer valuable opportunities to shed light on research questions.

Lincoln and Guba (2000) argued for alternative concepts to describe the kind of generalization that is possible from case study research – for example, transferability, fittingness, trustworthiness and authenticity. These terms, and others like them, can be helpful in alerting the novice researcher of the need to exercise caution in making generalized claims while, at the same time, signalling the potential value of case study research.

'Types' of case study

A review of the case study literature can be confusing because different authors have categorized case studies in different ways, although the meanings behind the terms used can be quite similar. In some cases, the labels used refer to the purposes of case studies, while other typologies refer to the number of cases selected. For Yin (1994: 5) case studies can be exploratory, descriptive or explanatory:

> An exploratory case study ... is aimed at defining the questions and hypotheses of a subsequent (not necessarily case) study ... A descriptive case study presents a complete description of a phenomenon within its context. An explanatory case study presents data bearing on cause–effect relationships – explaining which causes produced which effects.

Stake (2000) also identified three types of case studies that he labelled intrinsic, instrumental and collective. An *intrinsic* case study describes a case study that is undertaken in order to seek a better understanding of a particular or unique 'case'. *Instrumental* case studies are those where one case is examined with the aim of providing insights into something else, i.e., the phenomenon under investigation. In this type of research, although the case itself is of secondary interest, 'it is examined in depth, its context is scrutinized, and its ordinary activities are detailed to help the researcher to pursue the external interest' (p. 437). Multiple or *collective* case studies are instrumental studies that are extended to several cases in order to learn from these cases about a phenomenon, population or general condition (Stake, 2005). Yin (1994) also categorized case studies according to the number of cases studied: single or multiple. Perhaps the key point to be made is that case studies can do different things; as ever, the choice of 'type' or number of cases depends on the research question. This, too, underpins another key question: 'What is the case?' This question is considered by Mark in the next section, and again in the section that follows.

Comment by Mark Griffiths on undertaking case study research as part of a PhD

In this section, I talk about my experiences with using case study research to examine the impact of formalized mentoring with a group of volunteer sports coaches in one region of England. The coaches operated in a county sports partnership (CSP), which was a network established to organize and promote sport and sport coaching in the region. Initially, and perhaps like many new researchers, I approached case studies from a rather naive perspective. That is to say, in choosing to look at the impact of mentoring with this specific group, I naturally assumed that my research was a case study; namely, it was about something *distinctive* (formalized mentoring), *specific* (mentoring as a learning strategy) and *situated or bounded* (a particular community of coaches). A review of the case study literature and my own experiences of using case studies have made clear that the method is somewhat more complex. Indeed, a number of issues need to be addressed before engaging with this type of research. For example, 'What is a case study?' 'Is a case study a process or a product?' 'What is the purpose of a case study?'

In the first instance, I needed to be clear about what constitutes case study research. As a starting point, I understood that case study is a generic term concerning the broad investigation of an individual, group or issue. A case study is more than this. As Thomas (2011) has described, a case is something that is interesting, possibly remarkable, but certainly unusual in some sense. My PhD is a case in point. Mentoring as a learning strategy used to support volunteer sport coaches is an under-researched area. From my starting point of understanding a case as something interesting and situated or bounded, I found Stake's (2005: xi) definition of a case study to be helpful: 'the study of the particularity and complexity of a single case, coming to understand its activity within important circumstances'. This definition encouraged me to view the coach mentoring programme from a multidimensional perspective, i.e., taking into account the mentors' views, the coaches' views and also the impact of the particular 'circumstance' (the CSP structure) on how mentoring was received by participants. Accordingly, I used a case study approach to shape my inquiry.

The second issue I needed to be clear about was the precise purpose of the case study. Of course, all research is characterized by choice, and PhD researchers are drawn to a particular approach for a number of reasons (e.g., background, interest, or even the culture of the university department in which they are situated). I found Bassey's (1999) conceptual reconstruction of types of case studies to be particularly useful because it seemed to 'fit' my aim of examining a specific learning strategy in action. Bassey identified three types of case study:

- theory-seeking and theory-testing case studies (focusing on a specific issue);
- storytelling and picture-drawing case studies (narrative/descriptive accounts of events/programmes/systems);
- evaluative case studies (enquiries into events/programmes/systems to determine their worthwhileness).

While there are dangers of simplistic categorization and although there is much overlap between them, these categories make statements about the *purpose* of a case study. The case study, from which I report extracts later in this chapter, is consistent with Bassey's evaluative case study approach. Its focus was on understanding the concept and value of mentoring as a learning strategy with volunteer sports coaches.

In adopting a case study approach for my PhD, I was ever mindful of issues of generalizability and trustworthiness, particularly given my background in different – more quantitative – research traditions in sport science. Reflecting the practical challenges that present themselves in any research project, case studies are often selected because of direct accessibility, convenience and the straightforwardness with which data that are pertinent to the research question can be collected (Silverman, 2005). Certainly, this was a contributing factor in my study where contacts with local coach education stakeholders facilitated introductions to a readily available community of volunteer coaches. However, the selection of such case studies is also characterized by purposive sampling (also synonymous with theoretical sampling; Charmaz, 2006), in which the researcher selects cases because they illustrate features which are of interest. As Patton (2002) has suggested, the power and logic of purposive sampling is that this strategy seeks out 'information-rich' cases for study, such that the researcher is making a theoretical choice around the issue of sampling.

In addressing the issue of generalizability, one line of argument that I found helpful is that it is important to make explicit the features of the case so that other cases with similar features might be compared (Silverman, 2005). An example of this can be illustrated through the work of Tripp (1985), who has argued for a process of bringing cases together in what he calls 'qualitative generalization'. In order to do this, the researcher must be sensitive about reporting the salient features of the case. These features can be divided into what Tripp (1985) called comparable features (e.g., sex of the participants, socio-economic status and age) and comprehensive features (particular circumstances of the case). By doing so, 'localized narratives', in this case around the CSP mentoring programme, offer possibilities to connect with 'grand narratives' (Hargreaves, 1999), where participants' individual social constructions can be understood in relation to the wider coach learning discourse. This, to me, appeared to be a compelling argument.

Doing case study research

In explaining the early thinking in his PhD study, Mark has already introduced this section. It is also important to remember that 'doing' case study research requires the employment of any number of specific research methods; however, as these are covered elsewhere in this book, only issues unique to case study research will be addressed here.

What is your case?

Defining the case to be studied, and the boundaries to that case, are essential first steps in the research process. A 'case' in the field of physical education and sport can be almost anything: an individual teacher, pupil, administrator, inspector or academic; a small – or large – group of individuals; a school, classroom or friendship group; a sports club or wider sports organization; a particular programme, innovation or event; a concept; or a general phenomenon. Yet, taken on its own, none of these examples would necessarily constitute a case for research. Instead, as Thomas (2011) argues, they would need to be a case *of* something that we need to investigate. It is also possible to identify one umbrella case study, within which there are several other case studies. An example would be the identification of a sports club as an umbrella case, and particular coach–athlete dyads as cases within the case. In each of these examples, it is essential that the key contextual features of the case are described in order to make sense of any findings. This necessity explains the rationale for ensuing that the boundaries of the case are established at the outset.

Case selection

The points made earlier in this chapter about generalizability offer clues about issues to be considered in case selection. For most case study research, the intention is not to generalize to a wider population, but to provide detailed insights into the phenomena under investigation. As Thomas (2011) reminds us, therefore, sampling procedures used in other forms of research simply don't apply in case study research. On the other hand, questions about which cases to select, how many and why, are often challenging for new researchers to address. Stake (2005: 451) has suggested that case selection should be based on 'opportunities to learn', which is similar to the notion of purposive sampling:

> My choice would be to choose that case from which we feel we can learn the most. That may mean taking the one most accessible or the one we can spend the most time with. Potential for learning is a different and sometimes superior criterion to representativeness.

The key point, as has already been noted, is the imperative to provide enough information on the context to ensure that the findings are properly grounded. Indeed, Stake (2005) argued that one of the greatest strengths of case studies is that they offer opportunities for readers to experience vicariously aspects of the lives of others, enabling them to draw comparisons with themselves and contexts with which they are familiar. Stake linked this to the 'epistemology of the particular' developed by Hamilton (1980) among others. For example, Flyvbjerg (2004) explained that case studies produce the type of context-dependent knowledge that, from a phenomenological perspective, is vital to the process of learning. Flyvbjerg further argued that intimate knowledge of concrete cases can help to move a learner from beginner to expert, in a process known as 'naturalistic generalization'.

Designing a case study protocol

As with all research, the questions in case study research should determine both the initial selection of a case study approach and the specific methods used to investigate the case. Although it is possible to investigate a case using just one research method, the complexity of the issues to be studied often necessitates multiple methods. It is advisable, therefore, particularly where more than one case is selected, or where different cases within a case are to be studied, to design a research protocol. Of course, the nature of some of the research methods will necessitate flexibility (for example, qualitative, interpretive methods) and a protocol is not intended to act as a form of restrictive straitjacket. Nonetheless, cases can become complex and it is, therefore, helpful to have an overall design for each of the different levels of case. A case study protocol might include the following:

- ethical clearance procedures;
- details of key contact points in the setting;
- a plan for contacting respondents;
- a plan of the visits to be made (if conducting fieldwork);
- an outline of each method to be used and the detail of its use.

Analysing and reporting findings

Given the range of possible methods used within case study research, it is clear that data analysis and reporting can also take many formats. Nonetheless, there are four points to bear in mind in any analysis/reporting of case study data:

- You are likely to need strong writing skills to draw all your data together and to report them in analytical ways; the essence of case studies is that they are *interesting* to the reader.
- You can analyse findings horizontally across case studies, or vertically within cases; either way, it is important to contextualize the data at some point, which means that some grounded theory coding processes that lose context may be inappropriate for case study analysis.
- As with all forms of research analysis and reporting, it is important to make your processes as transparent as possible.
- The nature of case study research means that respondents could be more easily identified than in some other forms of research; if you have promised anonymity, you will need to identify all possible threats to it and take active steps to protect participants.

Case study research in action: Volunteer sport coaches learning through mentoring

The example presented below illustrates the suggestion that case study research can offer important insights into phenomena; in this case why a mentoring scheme that was developed to support volunteer sport coaches in their learning had variable impacts. Although it was recognized that coaches mentor each other informally, the goal of the scheme under investigation was to formalize mentoring to ensure it was as effective as possible. The CSP reported in this study mirrored the functions and structures of the other CSPs in England; essentially they were organizations established to organize sport and coaching across specific regions of the country in order to enhance participation and performance. The following are extracts from a 'nested' case study. Thomas (2011) defines a nested case study as a subunit that fits within a larger unit; so the following is an illustration of a mentor–coach case, which was situated within the broader unit of the CSP case. The nested case was made up of David (the mentor), and Nick and Paul (two volunteer coach mentees).

David (mentor)

The coach mentor, David, was a dominant and commanding figure, not only within the boundaries of this case, but also within the extended coaching community that participated in this study (CSP). Such a presence was a result of his professional role as a coaching development officer for a national sports organization, a role that allowed for extensive contact and influence with a multitude of coaches, sports and sports clubs. However, alongside this professional role, David's biographical experiences had blended to fuel his interest and enthusiasm for examining and developing 'quality' coaching practice through mentoring. For example, he had been a Royal Air Force (RAF) engineer for 15 years; his partner was a head teacher at a local primary school and had stimulated his interest in coaching as a pedagogical act; and he had over 20 years' coaching and playing experience in the region. The following quote provides an example of the way in which biography and perceptions of mentoring were linked:

> as an electronics engineer [in the RAF] I would go into mechanical engineering, and ask fundamental questions about practice, and challenge practice which has been going on for years. I think I know obviously a lot about the how to coach and the methodology, and impart knowledge, and I can question. But you think how much experience and knowledge you really need to mentor effectively and ask the right questions.
>
> (David: interview 1)

From the start, David was concerned that any professional development activities needed to have immediate and contextual impact. As a result, he believed that formalized mentoring initiatives should be about 'providing the right learning opportunity for the coach at the right time'. Formalized mentoring for volunteer coaches, therefore, had a temporal dimension that should be recognized:

> I mean what is happening in the field at Level 1 is that coaches don't want to be sat down and said, well how do you think you could have done that better? They want telling what the bloody hell to do and want to do it. They want content knowledge delivered to them on a plate which impacts. Tell them the bloody answer. They just want to know how to teach this girl how to hit the ball.
>
> (David: interview 1)

David's reflections on formalized mentoring centred on identifying and developing dedicated mentoring time. The voluntary nature of the domain was a key consideration, because it meant that for both coaches and mentors, time was a premium commodity. Even so, David argued that mentoring required mentors whose time was dedicated to facilitating the mentoring process.

Nick (coach)

Nick was 23 years old and a newly qualified PE teacher in a local school who wanted to enhance his coaching skills. Prior to engaging in the formalized mentoring programme,

David (the mentor) and Nick had an existing informal coaching relationship through their involvement in a local hockey club. This existing relationship had the potential, therefore, to offer an ideal opportunity for David and Nick to meet, and for David to mentor Nick. Both usually attended the hockey club on Wednesday evenings, resulting in informal co-coaching activities, with each taking different parts of the session with the men's teams (1st XI and 2nd XI). However, because of (salaried) work commitments, David found it increasingly difficult to be available for these Wednesday night sessions and hence contact between David and Nick became irregular. Following the establishment of the formalized mentoring programme, David and Nick proceeded to arrange a series of meetings. During the first six months of the programme, they met four times: an initial, one-to-one meeting to explore goal setting and profiling, followed by three meetings at the club to discuss progress. In the following account, Nick described how he found these interactions useful, but he also lamented the lack of practical opportunities, which he felt were much more valuable:

> I think that the actual coaching sessions are more useful than sitting down and talking. It is nice to sit down and see where I have progressed, and what I want to focus on next in a nice quiet environment. I think that the majority of me developing as a coach is through me doing it at a coaching session or watching him [David] doing it at a coaching session.
>
> (Nick: interview 1)

Throughout early conversations with Nick, it was interesting to note how he perceived his involvement in the mentoring programme. He expected coach mentoring to address two distinct areas of his development: coaching styles and coaching content. Nick had clearly identified David's most valuable input to be around content knowledge, i.e., David represented an accessible resource from which Nick could retrieve 'ready-to-go' drills and practices. Yet Nick felt uncomfortable with David's coaching 'personality', revealing, perhaps, Nick's confidence, derived from his teaching background, in his ability to evaluate the strengths and weaknesses of his matched mentor:

> Mostly just his kind of knowledge really because he has done it for so many years and he has some really good ideas. I split it myself into the coaching styles and the content. His coaching style I really dislike, so I'm not getting much from that at all. The way he talks to players and the way he comes across, his communication. So I'm more with him because of his knowledge, and content, and the details of skills and drills.
>
> (Nick: interview 2)

At the end of our first research meeting, Nick expressed concern that David wasn't going to be coaching at his club (because of his salaried work commitments). For Nick, mentoring had potential only where it was local and accessible. It was unsurprising to find, therefore, that after six months, Nick and David's mentoring relationship dissolved. As David explained in a post-programme interview:

Accessibility and time are barriers. We need to look at the structures where the mentor's time is more of a barrier than the coach's time. Say we take Nick, who came to me for the best part of a year (2004), because he stayed after school, he was a teacher and he assisted me with coaching, so he was operating in my environment and as a mentor, that was very, very easy.

(David: interview 3)

Paul (coach)

From the outset, Paul was an enthusiastic and engaged participant in the formalized mentoring programme. Paul was 42, married, had two children, and was an experienced volunteer coach who had previously coached a range of teams and at a variety of standards. During his first interview, Paul discussed his commitment to mentoring and other forms of professional development. In the following extract, Paul described the limitations of the Level 1 (entry level) coach qualification but also recognized the catalytic effect it had in moving his interest in coach development forward:

You come away from a Level 1 course thinking I enjoyed that but all it really taught me was that I know nothing. That's all it does. It gives you the confidence of actually standing in the right place but if I'm honest about what I achieved from Level 1 is where to stand, and to project my voice and get attention. That's it. You don't use anything else. But it gave me the appetite to go learn more, I think.

(Paul: interview 1)

This 'appetite' for learning led Paul to sign up for the Level 2 qualification, during which he first experienced formalized mentoring as a form of learning support. A noticeable attribute of Paul's relationship with David was the compatibility of their personalities. The rapport between the two allowed for clear and effective communication, as Paul explained:

I get on well with David. We both tell each other when to get off. We did the Belbin profile and those sorts of things, and I'd seen them before, and I knew what the results were and I gave it to him, I done them at work, and I said 'So what does this say, David?', and he said 'It means I can tell you to piss off and you tell me to piss off first.' He is straight-talking and I think I'm straight-talking. There's no misunderstanding.

(Paul: interview 3)

During another interview, Paul was asked to consider his experiences of the formalized programme and how it had, or had not, impacted upon his coaching. Although recognizing that his continuing coaching development was also an outcome of existing informal relationships, he identified an increasing level of confidence as a consequence of his interactions with David:

A lot of people said, like, they could see I had stepped up. I just came back full of, like confidence, of what I was delivering and why I was delivering it. Because I think I was mentored effectively by David.

(Paul: interview 3)

What did the case study method offer to this research?

Although the coaches in this nested case acknowledged the potential of mentoring as a means of constructing and supporting coach development, mentoring interactions were tempered by conditions of context and intervening barriers. Thus, for these volunteer coaches, coach learning through formalized mentoring had boundaries. Importantly, coaches and mentors in this case approached the mentoring relationship from a personal biography that guided, focused and engaged their professional learning actions. Although it is not possible to provide all the important contextual information on this case that can be found in the original study (Griffiths, 2010), it is difficult to imagine how the depth and complexity of the data could have been accessed or reported without doing case studies.

Conclusion

Case study research has been criticized for lacking 'validity' and 'objectivity'. It has been argued that the freedom to select cases based on convenience and desire to learn might lead researchers to choose cases and interpret findings in ways that support and confirm existing assumptions and preconceptions, i.e., the bias of verification. Thomas (2011), however, points out that it is mainly in the social sciences that such critiques are found, because in other fields case studies are used routinely. Moreover, as Yin (1994) reminds us, questions about subjectivity and bias apply to all research methods. Perhaps, some of the critiques of case study research are the result of a fundamental misunderstanding of its main purpose. Indeed, Stake (2005: 443) argued that 'Case study is not a methodological choice but a choice of what is to be studied' and this goes some way towards clarifying the purpose and potential value of this form of research. As was noted earlier, it can also be helpful to consider the ways in which cases and case studies are used in other fields, for example law and medicine, to understand their value – as well as their limitations – in our own field.

Key terms

Case study   The precise unit of study. This should always be specified clearly; for example, a pupil, group of pupils, school, class, sports club, sports team, sports person, policy, aspect of practice etc.

Cases within a case   Within a case study, such as a school or sports club, there are likely to be other potential cases, such as individuals or specific practices.

Case study typologies   A range of different 'types' of case study that address different purposes.

Case study protocol   The design of the fieldwork to be used in researching the case study, including details of which methods are to be used and when.

Case reports   Reports of the research findings on the case study.

References

Bassey, M. (1999) *Case Study Research in Educational Settings. Doing Qualitative Research in Educational Settings,* Florence: Taylor & Francis.

Charmaz, K. (2006) *Constructing Grounded Theory: A practical guide through qualitative analysis,* Thousand Oaks, CA: Sage.

Flyvbjerg, B. (2004) 'Five misunderstandings about case study research,' in C. Seale, G. Gobo, J.F. Gubrium and D. Silverman (eds) *Qualitative Research Practice,* London and Thousand Oaks, CA: Sage pp. 420-434.

Griffiths, M. (2010) 'Formalised mentoring as a learning strategy with volunteer sports coaches', unpublished PhD thesis, Loughborough: Loughborough University.

Hamilton, D. (1980) 'Some contrasting assumptions about case study research and survey analysis', in H. Simons (ed.) *Towards a Science of the Singular* (76–92), Norwich: University of East Anglia, Centre for Applied Research in Education.

Hargreaves, A. (1999) 'Schooling in the new millennium: educational research for the post-modern age', *Discourse: Studies in the Cultural Politics of Education,* 20(3): 333–55.

Lincoln, Y. S. and Guba, E. G. (2000) 'The only generalisation is: there is no generalisation', in R. Gomm, M. Hammersley and P. Foster (eds) *Case Study Method,* London: Sage.

Patton, M. Q. (2002) *Qualitative Research and Evaluation Methods,* Thousand Oaks, CA: Sage.

Silverman, D. (2005) *Doing Qualitative Research,* London: Sage.

Stake, R. E. (2000) 'Case studies', in N. K. Denzin and Y. S. Lincoln (eds) *Handbook of Qualitative Research,* 2nd edn (435–54), London: Sage.

Stake, R. E. (2005) 'Qualitative case studies', in N. K. Denzin and Y. S. Lincoln (eds) *The Sage Handbook of Qualitative Research* (443–66), Thousand Oaks, CA: Sage.

Thomas, G. (2011) *How to do Your Case Study: A Guide for Students and Researchers,* London: Sage.

Tripp, D. (1985) 'Case study generalisation: An agenda for action', *British Education Research Journal,* 11(1): 33–43.

Yin, R. K. (1994) *Case Study Research: Design and Methods,* 2nd edn, Thousand Oaks, CA: Sage.

17 Interviews and focus groups

Catherine D. Ennis and Senlin Chen

Introduction

> Ya gotta be in there fighting for the ball or the other guys won't want you. If you don't, they be saying stuff like, 'You be sorry ... you play like a mother ...' I try to drive around the girls and not hit or hurt them, but sometimes they're in my way. I can't be backing down to no girl ... no matter what. I would never be allowed to play on Sean's team again. And you know that's real important to me.
>
> (Ennis, 1999)

This is a quote from a very anxious African-American high school boy who was involved in Cathy's research examining the Sport for Peace curriculum in six urban high schools. He was reflecting on the dilemma that was unfolding on his three-versus-three basketball team. He wanted to work cooperatively with the girls on his team, yet he could not afford to lose face in front of Sean, his player-coach. In the meantime, Sean also was trying to decide how to encourage girls on his team to participate without losing face to the other boys on his team.

Qualitative interviews can open researchers' eyes to the thoughts, concerns, anxieties and jubilations experienced by their participants as they unfold within a research study. As Kvale and Brinkman (2009: 2) point out, 'An interview is literally an inter view, an interchange of views between two persons.' Before discussing different types of interviewing and focus group research, let us introduce ourselves.

About us

Professor Catherine Ennis is a curriculum specialist and ethnographer in physical education (PE), who has been interviewing teachers and children since she was a doctoral student in the early 1980s. Since then, Cathy has used a number of interviewing formats to talk with kindergarten – 12 grade (students ages 5–18) PE teachers and students, to examine issues and opportunities that promote or constrain curriculum. She teaches graduate classes in qualitative research design and has just created a new field-based graduate course entitled 'Conducting qualitative research' in which students move fluidly between their research sites and the classroom to gain a more dynamic understanding of the interview process. Currently, she is directing a large mixed-method research study examining students' conceptual change and knowledge growth associated with the 'Science, PE and me!' curriculum.

Senlin Chen is an advanced doctoral candidate in pedagogical kinesiology where his specialization is achievement motivation for learning. He is currently the project director for Cathy's large mixed-method research study, in which 10 data collectors are gathering instructional, observational and interview data from 13 classes of elementary (ages 8–11) students. Although Senlin is completing a minor in educational measurement and statistics, he has found that qualitative perspectives add background and meaning to his statistical data. Further, his statistical findings have given him new ideas for qualitative research studies that he hopes will lead to deeper understandings of students' motivation to learn in physical education.

Cathy: Senlin, I have learned so much about curriculum design and teaching just from talking with teachers about the opportunities and challenges they face in schools today. Although many of the articles we read and write make it sound like quality physical education is easy to achieve, interviews with teachers really make it clear that planning and teaching quality physical education require teacher skill, sensitivity and some fancy dancing to increase student learning.

Senlin: I understand what you are saying. I was talking with third- to fifth-grade children during our team research study, last week, to understand what they were learning in the 'Dr Love's healthy heart' unit in the 'Science, PE and me!' curriculum. It was clear that they were beginning to gain a coherent understanding of the cardiovascular fitness concepts taught in the curriculum. Rarely did they construct concepts in an isolated or fragmented fashion like they did during the pre-instruction interview. What I learned from these interviewing experiences is that without asking a series of key questions face-to-face, it would be difficult to deeply understand student cognition and learning.

Interview as a methodology in physical education and youth sport research can take many forms, from informal, mobile conversations to highly structured, formal interviews. The researcher may have only a few moments to ask one critical question or a year to develop rapport with key informants in a series of life history interviews. The nature of the research interview and focus group varies based on the research purpose and the role participant perspectives play in understanding the investigated phenomenon. We begin this chapter with a brief discussion of the purpose of research interviews and focus groups, emphasizing a continuum of structured to less-structured formats. In the second section, we describe research-based examples of individual and focus group interviews within physical education and youth sport contexts, emphasizing interviews with children as one unique participant group that requires special consideration. We provide brief discussions of several research interview contexts, including ethnographic, phenomenological, life history and narrative. We conclude the chapter with a description of different parts of the interview and warnings about interviewing traps that can threaten the trustworthiness of your data.

The purpose of qualitative interviewing is to gain a deeper understanding of your interviewees' perspectives. Researchers use interviews to structure conversations with participants, to gather their insights, probe their understandings, and, sometimes in critical ethnographies, help them become more aware and reflective about issues that impact their lives. In each interview, the interviewer must convey to participants that their views are valuable and useful. The quality of the interview depends directly on the rapport developed between the interviewer and the participants and the extent to which participants feel the interviewer genuinely wants to understand their perspectives.

Types of interviews

Interviews reflect the purpose and assumptions of the research design and are informed by the research questions that motivate and focus your research. Prior to deciding the type of interview, researchers should consider the social and contextual circumstances surrounding the research and the amount of time available to interview participants within the comprehensive design. In this section, we will briefly discuss two frequently used interview types, one-on-one and focus groups.

The one-on-one interview

The purpose of one-on-one interviews is to gain in-depth information about participants' and key informants' culture, world view and beliefs about the research topic. A secondary purpose is to verify the trustworthiness of data collected from observations, artefacts and previous interviews. The researcher conducts each interview with one interviewee, sometimes called the participant or respondent. The one-on-one interview focuses primarily on examining the participant's *emic,* or insider perspective. Therefore, it is essential to develop questions that provide participants with a structure in which to explain and elaborate their culturally-based understandings on the topics. When one-on-one interviews are used as the primary data source, questions should be adequately detailed to permit the researcher to understand the interview topics from the participant's standpoint. Topical questions can be followed by 'probes' or 'probing questions' to encourage respondents to think carefully and reflectively about one or more aspects of the topic. When one-on-one interviews are the primary data source, the researcher should structure questions carefully so that data from other informants can be used to verify trustworthiness.

Focus groups

Ethnographic interview formats provide the basic framework for other types of interviews. A focus group, for example, is an interview with from four to ten participants, conducted for the purpose of elaborating participants' perspectives on a given topic. Originating in market research, focus groups are now widely used in social science and applied research. Rather than a single, one-on-one format,

Box 17.1 Example of focus group

In research examining gender issues, Oliver, Hamzeh and McCaughtry (2009) conducted two focus groups of four and six fifth-grade girls whom their physical education teachers described as resistant to participate in physical education. Students described their resistance as reflecting a 'girly-girl' perspective on physical activity. The researchers explained:

> These girls were often strategic in performing girly girl when it served their mood or physical activity opportunities. Sunshine explained, 'Sometimes if I don't like the sport they are playing in PE, then I'm a girly girl.' Kim [researcher] asked, 'So on PE days, most of the time you are not a girly girl, right? Unless you don't like an activity … so girly girl becomes your excuse for not doing the sport. Is that how it works?' Sunshine replied, 'Yeah.' Kim responded, 'That is a really interesting strategy for getting out of being active.'
>
> (Oliver, Hamzeh and McCaughtry, 2009: 101)

focus groups bring together a group of individuals in a supportive environment. Participants are selected to represent common perspectives or a range of different philosophies or viewpoints associated with the research questions. Box 17.1 provides an example of a focus group interview with adolescent girls.

In focus group interviews, the interviewer structures a series of topical and probing questions to encourage participants to talk with each other, drawing out common group understandings. In some instances, respondents express the group consensus confirmed by nods and smiles, adding additional information or elaborating explanations. When focus group members are selected to reflect a range or dichotomous perspectives, group members may disagree, resulting in debates framed by the interviewer's carefully guided questions (Robertson, 2006).

Some focus groups are conducted electronically on a dedicated internet blog. These 'virtual' focus groups bring diverse individuals together from around the world in an asynchronous environment. Real-time, face-to-face, and virtual focus groups assume that, because individuals' attitudes and beliefs are socially constructed, participants' viewpoints are being shaped and even changed *within* the focus group itself. Focus groups are often more cost effective than one-on-one interviews, permitting the researcher to hear from many individuals almost simultaneously, increasing sample size and breadth of perspective. Focus groups may also introduce the researcher to new informants and facilitate access to cultures or groups that the researcher has heretofore not known to exist or been unable to gain access to. Focus group interviews usually follow semi-structured, guided, open-ended formats, allowing the researcher to probe and follow up on new topics of interest, while continuing to add, clarify and validate information within the focus group experience (Marshall and Rossman, 2011).

Interviewing children

In physical education and sport pedagogy, children and youth are central to our quest to better understand the lived experiences of the PE classroom or coaching context. Most programme and teacher/coach decisions impact children, as they participate in educational experiences in a very public domain in which their motor competence is visible to all. Each age group holds unique opportunities and challenges for the interviewer. Young children, for example, may not understand the interview topic or may not find it interesting (Moore, McArthur and Noble-Carr, 2008). Catching and holding children's attention while not distracting them from the interview topic can require careful planning and practice. At other times, adolescents and youth may be reticent to talk with the interviewer regarding sensitive topics. In this situation, focus groups can provide the supportive peer structures that contribute to openness and willingness to answer the researcher's questions.

Researchers need to analyse carefully the nature of the power relationships between adult researchers and child interviewees. The researcher should take special care to avoid coercion and to create a pleasant atmosphere and rapport in which children *want* to become involved in the conversation. Conducting interviews in a different location, such as in the school lunchroom instead of the gymnasium, can help children feel more comfortable. Power relationships can be neutralized, somewhat, when the researcher has known the children for an extended time, or has interacted with them outside the research setting. These settings provide ideal environments to take advantage of previously developed trusting relationships, often leading to in-depth, honest conversations. Nevertheless, age and power differences between adults and children are always present and may impact data trustworthiness.

In physical education, many children like to talk about lessons or activities they enjoy. These interviews often start with students' physical activity likes and dislikes, gradually moving toward more substantive topics. One way to introduce and engage students in interviews is to begin with a story or activity scenario that catches children's attention and immerses them in a story context that is familiar and comfortable. Although researchers use scenarios frequently when examining children's social environments, they also are effective when assessing children's content understandings. Griffin, Dodds, Placek and Tremino (2001), for example, used a soccer game board with player pieces and encouraged students to manipulate the players in response to questions about invasion game tactics. They recorded students' responses, using videos of their verbal explanations and player-piece movements on the game board. Senlin and our research team are using an activity scenario interview focus to assess children's knowledge gains. This research examines how students come to understand cognitive fitness-related concepts, described as conceptual change.

Senlin's comment: Interviewing children can be an enjoyable and smooth research process when students are engaged in the conversation. The above paragraphs pinpoint several guidelines and caveats that need deliberate attention when conducting interviews with children. I concur on all these points, and would like to reiterate and contextualize them a bit based on my interviewing experiences in our 'Science, PE and me!' research project.

First, children are sensitive to even subtle changes in the context. It is important for adult interviewers to become familiar with their interviewees *before* the interview whenever possible. In our research project, some data collectors found it beneficial to have positive interactions with their child interviewees a few days or weeks prior to the interview. They joined the physical education lessons they were observing and chatted with the children about the activities. Through our positive interactions, children relaxed and were more willing to speak openly. This also taps into the power relationship, where children's perceptions of the adult interviewer change gradually from an authoritative stranger to a non-threatening friend.

Second, interview warm-up activities or questions are crucial to facilitate more open conversations with children. Either planned or improvised activities or questions can be effective. For example, in the semi-structured interview guide used in our research project, we planned to tell them a PE activity scenario in which the child and their best friend are performing an enjoyable physical activity together. We found the scenario really helpful in making the subsequent questions tangible and relevant. Further, the child interviewees were ushered into the topics quickly and engaged in a contextualized interview.

In addition to the planned warm-up scenario and semi-structured questions, interviewers had flexibility to ask additional questions each thought might be interesting to the children in physical education classes they had observed. For example, right before my interview with eight-year-old Devon, he spotted a large activity ball located in the corner of the interview room. His eyes lit up and he said, 'That's a really big beach ball!' I reacted by asking him a series of questions relevant to his personal interest in this ball. He quickly became one of the most engaged interviewees in the project and I returned to the interview questions having established a better rapport.

I learned some techniques from both textbooks and my experiences that can facilitate the interviewing process. For example, be sure to memorize the topics and sequence of the interview questions to avoid constantly looking at your interview guide. This allows you to maintain eye contact with the interviewee. When discussing pleasant topics, keep a smile on your face throughout the interview. Help children understand your questions and feel relaxed and comfortable during the interview by using child-friendly language and avoiding abstract, professional terminology. Finally, react frequently to students' answers with encouragement and positive feedback. Make your interview a pleasant experience and children will look forward to talking with you again. Interviewing skills develop with experience. Although during my doctoral training programme, I first learned to conduct research using the quantitative research paradigm, I now have evolved from a 'disbeliever' of qualitative research methodology into a researcher who has reconciled these methodologies, and I will need both to answer my research questions in my dissertation study.

Structured to unstructured formats

Interview structure is usually dependent on the purpose of the interview, the familiarity of the interviewer with the participants, and the number of different individuals who will be conducting the interviews. Interview formats can range from tightly structured to flexible, fast-paced mobile interviewing, depending on the research purpose and context.

Tightly structured

When the interview purpose is to gain the *same* information from different individuals, interviewers use a tightly structured format in which carefully worded questions are asked in the same order to every participant. If several interviewers are working as a research team at different sites, it is critical that they ask similar questions to all participants within particular groups (e.g., students, teachers, administrators). When the questions are informational (as opposed to reflective or elaborative), researchers can often save time and travel expenses by asking participants to complete an open-ended questionnaire or survey instead of a face-to-face interview. However, when personal contact is essential, interviewers can gain more information using uniform, tightly structured interviews. In these formats, interviewers pose specific, carefully worded questions to elicit details or context-relevant examples to develop a richer understanding of phenomena than they might elicit with a questionnaire. In these relatively rigid formats, many different interviewers ask the same questions in the same sequence to many different participants at multiple sites. The pre-planned structure does not permit probing or follow-up questions because of the requirement to collect uniform data from multiple individuals. This type of format or design can be quite expensive and is often limited to funded, large-team research or programme evaluation studies.

Semi-structured or guided

In semi-structured interviews, also called focused or guided interviews, researchers present the same topics to all participants, but do not need to ask the questions in a specific order or use the same wording in each interview. Similar to the interview format Senlin described above, these interviews are carefully planned, using interchangeable topic and question sequence, depending on the role of the participant or their access to information. Many interviews consist of both structured and semi-structured components, depending on the sensitivity of the information requested and the importance of verifying critical facts or opinions across individual participants.

Conversational

Frequently, the most informative interviews are structured as conversations between the researcher and the participant. In these instances, researchers have developed rapport with the participants prior to the interview by observing in the setting, serving as interns or working in some other capacity in which they have had regular interactions with participants. Conversational interviews are actually partnerships between the interviewer who wants to understand and the interview partner who possesses that information.

The conversational interview or focus group may be scheduled well in advance, or be the result of 'spontaneous' questions, such as those asked of a teacher between classes or a group of children standing at the water fountain. Planning for conversational interviews entails identifying primary topics and nesting specific questions within topics. Topics can be arranged in any order and the question wording can vary to fit the conversational flow. Often in conversational interviews and focus groups, interviewees might provide information early in the interview that the researcher planned to ask later. Because the question order and wording *emerge* from the conversation, it is best to go with the flow of the conversation, asking follow-up questions on topics as they arise in the conversation. In a conversational interview, Senlin's advice to memorize the questions is critical to creating a relaxed conversational atmosphere that encourages participants to speak freely.

Mobile interviews are a special case of conversational interviews conducted as the researcher and participant are on the move. Brown and Durrheim (2009) advocate this interviewing format as a means to disrupt the fixed nature of one-on-one interviews, breaking down barriers through situated talking while walking or driving. These are loosely structured interviews conducted opportunistically in informal sites, where the conversation can occur as the researcher and interviewer are walking down the hall or out to the athletic field. They can also be conducted in a car or a bus and represent an effort to gain increased insights as a result of the more spontaneous situations that arise during these interactions with key informants.

The dialogic interview is a form of conversational interview co-constructed by the researcher and the participant. Tanggaard (2009) explains that they can take place anywhere individuals congregate and often arise spontaneously and serendipitously. There is no interview guide, topical structure or set of pre-planned probes. After the researcher has been in the situation for a period of days or weeks, it is likely that questions are already formed and waiting for the right time, place and participants in order to gain critical insights into participants' spontaneous thoughts and cultural beliefs.

Tightly structured and dialogic interviews represent opposite ends of the interview structure continuum. Interviewers should be creative in using interview guides, when appropriate to structure topics, order questions and pre-plan wording to meet the unique situation surrounding each interview. If the research purpose is to gather answers on a specific topic from many participants, then a questionnaire or tightly structured interview can provide reliable data. Conversely, if the research purpose is to collect in-depth reflections from a few purposefully selected interview partners, a conversational interview might be the best option within a phenomenological or life history interview. In the next section, we will discuss several of these interview types that have evolved to address specific research purposes and designs.

Placing interviews within a methodological context

Ethnographic

The origin of the term 'ethnography' is Greek and means 'to write people'. Thus the purpose of ethnographic interviews is to describe people and focus attention

---

Box 17.2 Example of ethnographic interview

Chepyator-Thomson and Ennis (1997) interviewed 36 high school students, using a one-on-one, semi-structured, open-ended format. The research suggested that students reproduced and resisted gender-patterned life configurations in physical education such as European American, middle class, heterosexual, traditionally dominant forms of masculinity and femininity. They found cultural reproduction of, and resistance to, gender-patterned behaviour in aerobics, weight training and team sports classes. One female student explained her perspective on the gender appropriateness of different physical activities:

> A lot of jock-type people go for team sports, and girls don't. I think a lot of people in this class [aerobics] are probably on the lower end of the spectrum physically and they don't want the team sports ... the guys who are here are training for their particular sport.
>
> (Chepyator-Thomson and Ennis, 1997: 93)

This one-on-one interview was used to elaborate the perspective of low-skilled girls who rejected the dominant team sport discourse in high school physical education.

---

on the events, situations and life experiences of people of interest to the researcher. The researcher may seek to convey and interpret participants' perspectives, or ask a respondent or interview partner to explain an inside perspective or insights about a group, institution or community to the researcher, who is an outsider. Although the researcher structures the questions and focuses the topics, the emphasis of the interview is on the participants' lived experiences. Ethnographies are often efforts to explain the participants' school or workplace or some event through the eyes of this individual. Key informants are sought who can provide this insider perspective. Researchers, in turn, attempt to report this perspective with as little distortion as possible. A brief exerpt from a one-on-one ethnographic interview is presented in Box 17.2.

Phenomenological

Most of us develop our viewpoints, perspectives and beliefs based on our histories of experience in which we have lived in situ, or in the situation. In these instances, the situation can become 'part of who we are' and may be based on events that we are eager to discuss, or those we have hidden deep inside. Phenomenological researchers seek to understand participants' lived experiences; the events or experiences that 'turned' them to the phenomenon of interest and the ways they interpret those experiences; and how they have impacted participants' lives. Further, phenomenological interviews assume that researchers and participants share many common experiences, although they may have constructed unique meanings from these events. These in-depth interviews paint the structure and essence of lived experiences that participants and interviewers share in vivid life colours, providing important insights into shared meanings, concepts and phenomena. Xin Li (2005) used a phenomenological design to weave her stories of school experiences in China with those of her multicultural students in a teacher-education programme in California. An example of her phenomenological reflection is provided in Box 17.3.

Box 17.3 Example of phenomenological self-reflective 'interview'

Xin Li's (2005: 342) account of her school experiences in China were told in response to student writings in her inquiry-based multicultural teacher education classes:

> As a punishment, I was sent to the principal's office at the end of the day, where I met my elder brother. I was told to face the corner of the room to think, which meant to confess in a progressive school like that. I insisted that the teacher was wrong using 'Peking Duck Stuffing Method.' After my brother left the room, I admitted to the principal that I was not being considerate of a new teacher, and was let go. This was my first rebellion against 'Peking Duck Stuffers'.

> I got home after my brother and missed his story for being sent to the principal's office. I was ready for some severe punishment from my parents, such as switching my seat at the dinner table so that I would stop talking 'too much'. However, after hearing my story, they smiled at each other and went on with the meal as if nothing had happened. My parents were the people from whom I, at that young age, learned the idea about the Peking Duck Stuffing Method. They used to tell stories at the dinner table about teaching, because my father was a teacher educator and my mother taught biology and entomology in an agricultural university. One of their traditional stories is the Peking Duck Stuffing Teaching Method.

> Peking duck is a famous delicacy in Mandarin cuisine. It attracts many gourmets, professional and amateur. But if one knows how people feed the ducks, they might not want to eat it. The Peking ducks are given the maximum amount of food while confined in the smallest possible space so that they grow very fat in [the] shortest possible time. The meat of a duck raised in this way is very tender and delicate, but the poor duck has no time in its short life to swim in the pond, dive in water to catch fish, or even the right to refuse being stuffed. A traditional teacher in China is called a Peking Duck Stuffer, implementing 'Peking Duck Stuffing Teaching Method', and her or his students are Peking Ducks.

Life history

Similar to phenomenological research, life history researchers endeavour to understand individuals' perspectives based on the retelling of their histories. Life histories involve in-depth examinations of how an individual's subjective experiences, known as a history, has influenced their socially constructed interpretation of life. These in-depth interviews provide understandings of culture or cultural events through the eyes of an individual intricately immersed in the experience or phenomenon. Life histories, for example, may reflect how the person became part of the group, their interactions within the group, and the events, practices and beliefs that eventually led to the individual's socialization within the group. Researchers who examine group socialization processes, such as becoming a teacher, often use life history interviews as a method to trace acculturation and socializations within institutions and professions. The focus is on how individuals create meaning and contribute to the meaning of others or the society. Needless to say, eliciting and documenting life histories is a complex process that can require a number of lengthy interviews to understand and interpret life events. Box 17.4 reflects an example of an interview conducted with a 35-year veteran physical education teacher. Cathy conducted this life history study to examine retrospectively how federal policies, such as Title IX, the 1972 US law legislating gender equity, affected physical education curricula in the United States between 1970 and 1997.

Narrative

Marshall and Rossman (2011: 53) explain that narrative inquiry 'assumes that people construct their realities through narrating their stories'. The participant or narrator and the interviewer tell the story collaboratively, reliving personal experiences that inform their shared narrative. Because it is collaborative, both the narrator and the researcher contribute to the voices or the data heard in this research. Although there is an individual focus to each story, the storytellers elaborate the sociocultural context in which the story is lived as the story is (re)created. Narratives are in-depth interviews that blend both researcher's and interview partner's selective, salient memories as the story impacted their lives. Narratives are not considered objective, factual accountings, but rather convey the participants' impressions and meanings as they reflect on lived experience. Robertson's (2006) narrative research was conducted with a focus group that she labels a narrative 'panel discussion'. She guided a group of near-peers (undergraduate, high, middle and upper elementary school) in an in-depth discussion of their experiences with 'favourite' teachers. Excerpts of the panel discussion that build and blend student perspectives on effective teaching are presented in Box 17.5.

Narrative inquiries may require a number of extended interviews with each participant. The stories are developed and elaborated as they are told or retold, evoking new understandings and reflections. The narrators (both researcher and interviewee) develop reciprocal caring relationships that are built on trust and extend over time as the story is constructed. Each interview plays on the information from previous interviews, weaving the story thread over time and between the narrators.

Digital storytelling has evolved from narrative inquiry as a means to provide opportunities to integrate writing, audio and video to build and enhance the story.

Box 17.4 Example of life history interview

Ennis (1998) conducted life history interviews to examine the professional careers of 12 middle school physical education teachers who had been teaching in the same large urban school district for more than 25 years (range = 26–35 years). She conducted three narrative interviews, returning each interview transcript to the teacher for review prior to conducting the next interview. During the first interview, teachers described the teaching environments when they were first hired in the district in the 1960s, tracing how their careers had evolved to the present (in 1997). During the second interview, teachers commented on the accuracy of the transcript from the first interview and responded to follow-up questions requesting clarification of comments during the first interview and elaboration of particular events and how these had impacted their planning and teaching. The third interview asked teachers to elaborate any part of the second interview and encouraged reflection about the significance or impact of these social events on their physical education curriculum, changes in students' opportunities for learning and the teachers' current level of job satisfaction (Ennis, 1998: 752).

One female teacher provided insights into girls' physical education in her programme prior to the advent of Title IX, mandating equal educational and sport opportunities for girls and boys in the United States that resulted in co-educational classes in most schools:

> We had a varied programme in girls' physical education prior to Title IX. We had gymnastics, dance and individual sports as well as team sports. But girls rarely played as competitively as the boys. Most games were relaxed, half-speed games that focused on enjoyment, not competition. Girls who wanted to be athletic easily dominated the games. When we went to co-ed classes, even these girls had trouble. Most of the time we taught team sports because that's what the men [physical educators] were used to teaching and it was very difficult to get the boys to do anything else. Male teachers were not interested and unwilling to teach traditional girls' activities. We found that the boys' games were so much faster and more intense. The girls who had hung back before [in single-gender physical education] were absolutely lost and intimidated by the power and speed of the boys. It was like they really gave up then. They hung back, avoided the ball and just tried to get out of the way.
>
> (Ennis, 1998: 753)

Digital stories are often built first on a written script that is then enhanced with others' audio stories and video clips of relevant events. This multi-method technique takes advantage of rapidly evolving technology within a traditional approach to research-oriented storytelling (Marshall and Rossman, 2011).

Box 17.5 Example of focus group narrative

Robertson (to audience): Think back to your favourite teacher. You probably can create a vivid image of that person in your mind. Today, students will share their thoughts about the teachers who make a difference in their lives. Distinguished educators Brian Cambourne, Alfie Kohn and Donald Graves, as well as Bigelow Brother of the Department of Misinformation, will join today's panel. The undergraduates will begin the discussion.

Undergraduate #1: Professors should not always show off what they know. We understand that you're more intelligent, but we want to learn.

High school student: Teachers shouldn't take advantage of their authority and have that whole 'I have a master's, so I don't make mistakes' attitude.

Undergraduate #2: Right, anyone can know the information, but not anyone can actually teach it in a way that students feel as though the professor cares whether or not they understand it.

Fifth grader: A teacher should have good people skills.

Seventh grader: And respect students' opinions.

Robertson: So, what we're talking about is respect and expectations?

Cambourne: Engagement is increased when teachers and learners have high expectations for one another.

Undergraduate #1 (to Cambourne): And, if you know our names it helps! Seriously, the best professors go that extra mile.

Robertson (turning toward elementary students): What about your favourite teacher?

Fifth grader: I like teachers that make time for you – no matter what.

Kindergartner: They care for you.

Fourth grader: Not ignore you.

Sixth grader: They help you with work and the conflicts you go through.

Undergraduate #1: Teachers should remember, though, that they're not a peer and not a friend. Most of us see a clear line.

High school student: Just listen to both sides of a story.

Seventh grader: And, don't assume we're good or bad just by looking.

Sixth grader: Don't say one student is better than another.

Undergraduate #2: We want to do well for professors we respect. We want them to be proud of us.

Fifth grader: The best teachers are hopeful that we will succeed. They believe in us.

Second grader: They love us as we love them.

Sixth grader: We can talk to them seriously.

Undergraduate #1: You know, just as professors classify what a good student is, students do the same for professors.

Stages of an interview

Unlike randomly developing informal conversations, interviews are carefully constructed to gather information on specific topics and assist the respondent to clarify, explain, discuss and sometimes analyse participants' perspectives, experiences and interpretations. Planning is critical to eliciting useful and focused data and involves question wording and question and topic order, groupings and placement within the interview structure. Interviews are often most effective when they evolve through several distinct and carefully planned stages. Rubin and Rubin (2005) argue that interviews evolve through seven stages. Although each stage may not appear in every interview, stages can merge or several stages may be integrated into a single stage or interview section. The stages presented below should not be used as an outline, but more like choreographical elements that are used to deepen and enrich the interactions between the researcher and the interviewee.

Building rapport

Often even the most structured interviews begin with an informal conversation that focuses the participant on the topic to be discussed. If the topic is serious or investigates legal or integrity issues, the interviewer might express sincere concern and ask how the participant is handling the stress of the situation. Conversely, if interviewers want to signal that the interviewee should relax and enjoy the conversation, they might begin with an amusing anecdote or other pleasantry. Early conversations at this stage should convey interest in the participant, a supportive and caring attitude when appropriate and, perhaps, refer to something the interviewer has in common with the participant. Senlin provided an example of rapport building in his conversation with the third grader about the big ball. He expressed sincere interest in something the child valued, creating an increased sense of comfort and trust.

Reassuring nervous or anxious interviewees

At times, interviewees might be unsure of their ability to answer the questions and might feel a good deal of stress associated with the interview process. When interviewing children about their content knowledge understanding, the reassurance stage is very important to encourage students to try to answer the question, rather than responding with an ubiquitous 'I don't know.' The researcher might indicate that others, such as their teachers, have recommended them for the interview because of their expertise, or make reference to adult interviewees' current or former positions or specific accomplishments, reassuring participants of their competence to answer the questions.

Showing understanding

Throughout the interview, the interviewer works to develop a rapport with the participant to increase trust and to provide reassurances that their information is valuable. The interviewer does this by using non-verbal nods and smiles and verbal comments such as 'Yes' and 'Hmm'. In more formal or structured interview formats, the interviewer works to ask the questions succinctly and clearly and then minimize further comment, permitting the participant to talk with little interruption. In semi-structured or guided interviews, once the interviewee has provided their initial response, it is appropriate to show that you have understood the response by summarizing briefly, asking a follow-up or probing question that demonstrates that you have understood and would like more information, perhaps, about one aspect of their response. To show emotional understanding, the researcher can express pleasure with the success of a project, for instance, or concern when the teacher explains the impact of increasing class size or diminishing instructional time on student learning. It is important, however, that these expressions be sincere and authentic. Interviewees quickly lose interest when they realize that the interviewer is not focused on the topic or is simply collecting 'data'.

Gathering facts and basic descriptions

Once the desired tone of the interview has been established, the interviewer next asks informational questions to permit the participant to explain what they know about the topics of interest. These questions usually begin with a very broad focus, so that the interviewee can tell the researcher their perceptions of the most relevant information. Typically, interviewees first provide information that is most salient to them. Their responses might elaborate their perspective on the needs of students in their school or classes, the opportunities they have to increase students' learning, or limitations in facilities or equipment that may constrain their physical education programme. It is important to listen carefully during each response. The conversational flow will be enhanced when the researcher can construct specific follow-up questions from comments the participant has just provided, rather than simply stating the next question (regardless of topic) on the interviewer's question list. Semi-structured, guided or conversational interviews provide exceptional opportunities to acknowledge the participant's answer with a focused follow-up. The focus of this interview stage is informational or descriptive. You should delay asking difficult or emotional questions until you have established a connection or created rapport with the respondent.

Asking difficult questions

At times, verbal questions about content knowledge can seem to student interviewees like an oral examination. These topics can present difficult and occasionally uncomfortable situations for the respondent. When asking students questions about their content understanding, begin with relatively easy questions that you expect all children to know and then gradually increase the difficulty until the questions become more demanding. The use of stories, scenarios and player-piece manipulations can increase the quality of information children can provide beyond written test formats, permitting them to elaborate and explain in ways not otherwise possible. Although many children are not hesitant to say that they do not know the answer, others become concerned, worried or anxious that they cannot answer the questions. It is helpful to begin these interviews by explaining that some questions will be too easy, while others may be too hard, reassuring students that they are not expected to answer all of the questions. Likewise, giving students opportunities to guess if that is appropriate within the research design or following up with a pre-planned easier question is often helpful in distracting anxious children and assisting them to refocus on the next easier topic that they can answer successfully. Many children enjoy the opportunity to show what they know and readily talk with the interviewer, explaining their solutions to tactical and other problem-based learning scenarios.

Asking emotional or controversial questions

Typically emotional questions involve participants' perceptions of barriers, limitations or injustices. Interviews with children who are bullied in the locker room, selected last for teams or simply do not like physical education can cause hesitancy and discomfort. Think carefully about probing or following up with emotionally sensitive topics unless they are central to your research questions. Plan probes carefully and be ready to abandon the topic if the interviewee appears anxious, angry or reluctant to discuss the issue, or if they become uncomfortable and unhappy. You may decide to schedule a separate interview later to discuss this topic.

There are times when your interviewees may be hesitant or afraid to talk with you. They might be worried their answer is incorrect or that you will not agree or support their perspective or that you cannot maintain confidentiality. Conversely, there are other times when interviewees want to talk to you and give information that might reveal anxiety, abuse, harassment, illegal behaviour or other very sensitive matters. Sometimes, they may use the interview as an opportunity to ask for your assistance. These are times when the interviewing situation becomes a conversation. In these situations, you want to convey your concern and care for your participant, and offer assistance when you can. Understand the laws in your area. In the United States, teachers and adults working with minors are required to reveal information about child abuse to authorities that may violate confidentiality arrangements. Be realistic and honest in limiting promises of confidentiality to participants in these situations.

In the United States, Institutional Review Board (IRB) policy requires the interviewer to break off the interview and destroy all interview data at the participants' request. Additionally, unless these sensitive topics have been screened and approved by the IRB and the researcher has parental permission (for children and adolescents) to discuss the topic prior to the interview, it is often necessary to abandon the topic for this interview. Failure to do so might force you to drop the research participant, abandon the data collection site, or halt the research altogether. This does not mean that you will abandon the interviewee. Instead, seek help from authorities who are trained to address the situation or gain permission through appropriate individuals and channels to continue the interview, if appropriate. Your sensitivity is important whether you report the data in the future, or use the data to enhance an individual's life.

As you begin to move the interview focus away from difficult or sensitive topics, it is important that the interviewer continues to ask questions that are engaging for the participant. Questions might redirect the focus back to earlier more pleasant or less controversial topics, plans for the future, or a request for additional comments or information that the participant wants to share. You might let the interviewee ask you a question about your experiences, study completion timeline or your intentions to use or publicize the findings.

Closing while maintaining contact

As the interview is closing, you want to signal to the participant that the interview is ending. It is important to express your thanks to the participant and acknowledge the importance of their information in your study. You may want to let the interviewee know that you might have additional questions, or that you would like them to review the interview transcript in the future to increase accuracy, to clarify or elaborate topics, or as part of member-checking procedures. You also may want to return to a more informal conversational style similar to that used in the beginning interview stages.

The interview stages do not constitute a lockstep approach to structuring, but instead serve as a reminder not to dash into the middle of the interview or end the interview abruptly. Similar to the importance of a physical warm-up and cool-down, the interview warm-up and cool-down help to focus the participant's attention and build toward a higher degree of trust before asking difficult or emotional questions. The cool-down decreases the intensity of the questions and the experience and prepares the participant to return to their day, while still maintaining contact with the interviewer for future conversations or member checks.

Avoiding common interviewing traps

There is no substitute for experience and practice when it comes to successful interviewing. Plan opportunities to practise your interview questions, first with a critical friend, then with individuals who fit the same demographics as your interviewees. For example, if you are planning to interview 13-year-old students, arrange an interview with a few young teens to be sure you are communicating clearly and feel comfortable and confident with your interview topics and questions. The following are a few interviewing traps to avoid that can jeopardize the trustworthiness of your interview.

The bumbled interview

This occurs when *you* are not familiar with the order or sequence of your interview questions and the question wording. As Senlin pointed out earlier in the chapter, it may result from a failure to practise your structured interview. It is embarrassing to stumble on the wording, read the conversational interview questions, or ask a question that your respondent has just answered! Be sure the wording is targeted appropriately to your audience, and that the questions actually result in answers to your research questions. Practise speaking your questions aloud; look at your expression in the mirror. Do you appear too serious or too stern? Rehearse interviews; planning and preparation prior to the interview can contribute substantially to data quality and trustworthiness, saving immeasurable time over the course of the study.

Interviewing yourself

The chatty trap occurs when interviewers talk too much, monopolizing the conversation with their personal perspectives and often leading respondents to a particular desired response. When possible, try to make your questions brief and precise. State your question and then be quiet. Let your respondent think quietly; avoid talking to fill the silence. Of course, clarify the question when asked, but hopefully your efforts at piloting your questions will lead to a clear understanding. Typically, we structure initial topical questions to encourage participants to respond with information that is most relevant to them; then follow up with a more focused probe to encourage reflection. Avoid giving clues about the nature of the response you are hoping for, or the response needed to answer your research question. Let respondents answer in their own voices. Check your interview transcripts later to be sure you are not dominating the interview – avoid interviewing yourself!

Who's in charge?

Be aware that some interviewees have an agenda when they agree to be interviewed. They may have a particular message they hope to convey, or want to gain your support of their perspective in situations where others might disagree. Provide opportunities early in the interview for interviewees to tell you their side of the story. Try to engage with their topic by asking a few follow-up questions or probes. Then, gently encourage them to answer your questions that may be on a different topic entirely. In programme evaluation interviews, it is likely that some respondents may want to directly influence your perceptions and findings. Additional efforts to triangulate data from these interviews with other more objective data sources can present a more balanced recommendation based on a range of participant perspectives.

Power up!

Famous last words: Be sure your equipment is working properly. Regardless of whether you are using a voice-activated digital transcription computer program, or your grandmother's tape recorder, be sure you have a reliable power source and that your equipment is recording properly – *before* you arrive at the interview site. Do not be surprised to find that your interviews will be conducted on the playing field or in the equipment room. Be prepared with extra batteries in case a power source is unavailable. Do you have extra tapes or memory for extended interviews with key informants, or for the times students return twice as many signed consent forms and you can interview more students than you had planned?

Conclusion

As you consider the uses of interviewing in light of your draft research questions, remember that interviews can be the primary data collection method, or one of many methods in a comprehensive, mixed-method research design. Asking different interviewees to comment on the same topics builds data confidence, strengthening the trustworthiness of your research. As new participants are identified, interview formats and questions may need to grow and change to explore new topics while asking interviewees to comment on factual and interpretive information gained in previous interviews. Regardless of the interview format or type, interview data that reflect participants' emic perspectives and deeply held cultural beliefs enrich your findings and lead to new insights into the research topics.

Key terms

Critical friends Typically, colleagues who review interview questions and transcripts to assist the researcher to clarify question wording or intent, offer advice about question order and pose alternative interpretations.

Dialogic interviews Often described as mutual conversations between interview partners. This form of conversational interview is used to bring new meaning to responses as they are co-constructed, often within phenomenological, narrative and life history research studies.

Follow-up or probing questions These ask the respondent to clarify, elaborate or focus a previous response, to provide more specific information on a particular topic of interest to the interviewer.

In-depth interviewing Qualitative, often dialogic, interviews where the interviewer and interviewee together construct their understanding of events, experiences or phenomena. Typically, these interview topics are of mutual interest and occur more as conversations that follow a loosely structured interview guide.

Interview guides Composed of question lists often arranged topically. The interviewer may begin all interviews with the same introductory question for all respondents and then skip around on the topical question list to ask questions that follow from the respondent's previous response. Thus, the interviewer is careful to ask all interviewees to respond to a similar set of questions, but the interview structure appears more free flowing and authentic.

Rapport Feelings of comfort, closeness and engagement that reflect the give and take of conversational interviews. This relationship that develops between the researcher and the interviewee can assist both to see new and deeper meanings as they discuss the topic of mutual interest. It takes extended periods of time, shared experiences and common interests to develop rich rapport.

Standardized, open-ended interviews Carefully worded or scripted series of specific questions that are followed in the same order for all interviews. This structure is frequently used when multiple researchers are instructed to ask the same questions to a larger number of participants at many different research sites.

References

Brown, L. and Durrheim, K. (2009) 'Different kinds of knowing: generating qualitative data through mobile interviewing', *Qualitative Inquiry,* 15: 911–30.

Chepyator-Thomson, J. R. and Ennis, C. D. (1997) 'Reproduction and resistance to the culture of femininity and masculinity in secondary school physical education', *Research Quarterly for Exercise and Sport,* 68: 89–90.

Ennis, C. D. (1998) 'The context of a culturally unresponsive curriculum: constructing ethnicity and gender within a contested terrain', *Teaching and Teacher Education,* 14: 749–60.

Ennis, C. D. (1999) 'Creating a culturally relevant curriculum for disengaged girls', *Sport, Education, and Society,* 4: 31–49.

Griffin, L. L., Dodds, P., Placek, J. H. and Tremino, F. (2001) 'Middle school students' conceptions of soccer: their solutions to tactical problems', *Journal of Teaching in Physical Education,* 20: 324–40.

Kvale, S. and Brinkman, S. (2009) *InterViews: Learning the Craft of Qualitative Research Interviewing,* 2nd edn, Thousand Oaks, CA: Sage.

Li, X. (2005) 'A Tao of narrative dynamic splicing of teachers' stories', *Curriculum Inquiry,* 35: 339–65.

Marshall, C. and Rossman, G. (2011) *Designing Qualitative Research,* 5th edn, London: Sage.

Moore, T., McArthur, M. and Noble-Carr, D. (2008) 'Little voices and big ideas: Lessons learned from children about research', *International Institute for Qualitative Methodology,* 7: 77–91.

Oliver, K. L., Hamzeh, M. and McCaughtry, N. (2009) 'Girly girls *can* play games: *las niñas pueden jugar tambien*: co-creating a curriculum of possibilities with fifth-grade girls', *Journal of Teaching in Physical Education,* 28: 90–110.

Robertson, J. (2006) ' "If you know our names it helps!": students' perspectives about "good" teaching', *Qualitative Inquiry,* 12: 756–68.

Rubin, H. J. and Rubin, I. S. (2005) *Qualitative Interviewing: the Art of Hearing Data,* London: Sage.

Tanggaard, L. (2009) 'The research interview as a dialogical context for the production of social life and personal narratives', *Qualitative Inquiry,* 15: 1495–1515.

Further reading

Patton, M. Q. (2002) *Qualitative Interviewing: Qualitative Research and Evaluation Methods,* Thousand Oaks, CA: Sage.

Seidman, I. (2006) *Interviewing as Qualitative Research: a Guide for Researchers in Education and the Social Sciences,* New York: Teachers College Press.

18 Narrative research methods

Where the art of storytelling meets the science of research

Kathleen Armour and Hsin-heng Chen

Introduction

We may say that biographical research has both *general* and *specific* purposes. The *general* purpose is to provide greater insight than hitherto into the nature and meaning of individual lives or groups of lives. Given that individual lives are part of a cultural network, information gained through biographical research will relate to an understanding of the wider society. The *specific* purpose of the research will be the analysis of a particular life or lives for some designated reason (Erben, 1998: 4).

Stories and storying are central to our lives and to learning. From the stories parents use to teach children, to the blizzard of daily reportage, to intergenerational storytelling as a way of remembering history and preserving culture, stories touch our lives in numerous ways. We can also use stories in research. Captured by a researcher, biographical – or autobiographical – stories can illustrate the ways in which individual lives map against social, cultural and historical phenomena, offering both unique and shared insights into those phenomena and the lives themselves. This chapter explains how the art of storytelling meets the science of research. It includes an overview of different genres in narrative research, including life history, life story and fictional representation, and considers the data collection methods most commonly used and the key methodological challenges. Examples are drawn from the PhD study of the second author. The main purpose of this chapter is to introduce narrative research in enough detail to inspire you to read further about the research possibilities it offers.

About us

Kathleen Armour, co-editor of this book, is Professor of Education and Sport and Head of the Department of Sport Pedagogy at the University of Birmingham in the UK. Throughout her research career, Kathy has been interested in qualitative research methods and, in particular, narrative methods. In her own PhD, she undertook ethnographic research with a physical education (PE) department in a secondary school in order to build a detailed narrative of its daily professional practice. One of the key attractions of narrative research is the potential it seems to have to 'touch' readers, i.e., teachers and coaches. It is a form of research that many practitioners seem to find both accessible and compelling. The challenges of undertaking robust narrative research should not, however, be underestimated.

Hsin-heng Chen is a PhD student under the supervision of Kathy Armour. Formerly, Hsin-heng was a young elite sportsperson, teacher education student and physical education teacher in Taiwan, where he had already developed a research interest in the content and development of practical knowledge of experienced physical education teachers (at master's degree level). He has continued this interest through PhD study, focusing specifically on understanding Taiwanese teachers' professional development through researching their life histories. Hsin-heng was particularly curious to analyse teachers' professional learning in the wider socio-historical context of a major curriculum reform in Taiwan. He decided to use a life history approach in order to map and contextualize teachers' learning. During this process, he encountered numerous methodological challenges, such as researcher positionality, data analysis, validity and the presentation of life history data. These issues are considered in this chapter and illustrated through three extracts from his research.

What is narrative research?

At its simplest, narrative research is about collecting data in the form of stories, and 'storying' the lives, events, experiences, perspectives and actions of individuals or groups. It is a form of research that tends to be undertaken using mainly qualitative methods, and it usually involves spending considerable amounts of time with respondents in order to represent their lives in credible ways in the context of the research question. The main categories of narrative research are biography and autoethnography, life history and life story. Biographical forms of narrative research are those undertaken by a researcher on another person. Autobiographical narrative research – or autoethnography – is where the researcher takes the dual role of both researcher and researched (possibly guided by an external researcher). There is also an important distinction to be made between life 'story' and life 'history' methods. Life stories are very selective, and can be constructed using a range of data about a life. Life histories, on the other hand, have the key task of locating life story data in relevant historical contexts. As Goodson (1988: 80) argued: 'The life historian must constantly broaden the concern with personal truth to take account of the wider socio-historical concerns *even if these are not part of the consciousness of the individual*' (our emphasis).

In addition to these types of narrative research, there is a smaller narrative tradition in the use of fiction as a research tool. For example, Sparkes (1996) used ethnographic fiction to create a story about Alexander, a gay, male PE teacher. Sparkes argued that the story was written to 'present a view of schooling from a particular standpoint that for the most part has been repressed' (p. 167) and he justified the use of fiction on the grounds that, at the time, he had 'never met a gay male PE teacher who was explicitly out' (p. 174). In response to questions about the validity of the use of fiction, Sparkes suggested that we should, instead, consider whether we can learn from it and whether it is plausible. Another example of a fictional account is Tinning's (1997) monograph written specifically to support teachers' learning as they undertook a master's degree at Deakin University in Australia. A further example is that by Oliver (1998), who used fictional writing techniques, arguing that such research is helpful for 'accessing and framing' (p. 246) the stories people tell.

In their work on teaching, Clandinin and Connelly (1996) added another element to the narrative mix. They drew an important distinction between stories *of* teachers and schools, and teacher/school stories. In other words, stories constructed by researchers (for example, life stories) are important, but we also need to recognize the research potential in stories that are central to the 'professional knowledge landscape' (Clandinin and Connelly, 1995) of a profession or occupation. This argument extends beyond teaching to any social setting where stories are likely to be defining and defined by the daily context. It is widely recognized, for example, that both teaching and coaching are storied professions; thus the stories that abound and the ways they are used can be fascinating topics for research.

Oliver (1998) argued that narrative analysis in research must move beyond telling a story; it must offer insight and explanation using the three key components of setting, character and plot. In this regard, Oliver concludes that physical education scholarship 'needs narratives that touch the hearts and minds of readers' (p. 257). As was noted earlier, research conducted and written in narrative traditions has immediate appeal for many practitioners. This has long been recognized in teaching; as Clandinin (2001: viii) put it: 'When teachers told their stories and responded to others' stories in sustained conversation groups, they came to understand their own practices in new ways.' Similarly, in the study of sports coaching, Jones and colleagues have argued that traditionally research has been quantitative or positivistic in nature, and that it has missed the 'details and nuances on which much of coaching actually rests' (Jones, Bowes and Kingston, 2010: 15). Sport coaching, these authors argue, is a dynamic, unfolding social activity requiring in-depth research methods. Indeed, in their earlier work, Jones, Armour and Potrac (2004: 98) took a narrative, case study approach to their study of eight top-level sport coaches:

> The key to analysing and understanding coaching pedagogy resides precisely in exploring the articulations … between all the elements of the human encounter that is coaching. Coaches' lives and careers are central to their coaching philosophies that are, in turn, central to coaching pedagogy.

What seems clear is that in the hands of a skilful researcher, narrative research has the potential to be a powerful and dynamic research tool. The potential dynamism of narrative research is, perhaps, something that is often overlooked by novice researchers. For example, Clandinin and Murphy (2009: 601) suggested that through narrative analysis 'we can, perhaps, change how we imagine and live out the storied structures … that shape our lives'. Similarly, Barone (2001: 150) argued that narrative research strives to offer 'a degree of interpretive space', by using stories as a way of learning. In particular, Barone (2009: 592) uses the concept 'doxa' to describe 'a network of values and opinions that are learned but self-evident, taken for granted' and argues that narrative analysis can enable participants to 'rethink doxic structures'. What we can conclude from all this is that far from being a passive form of storytelling, narrative research has the potential to be transformative. Indeed, as Carlisle Duncan (1998: 106–7) argued, 'This is the point of storytelling: We express others' voices, yet in so doing we recognize them as our own … This is the truth of the narrative turn.' A good example of this can be found in the work of Duckworth (1997), who compiled a book of American teachers' learning experiences on a professional development programme. The purpose of the programme was described as to help the participants 'to develop their own views of what it means to learn and what it means to know something, and to develop ways of teaching that are consistent with these views' (p. 2). One of the teachers used a narrative to write about his struggles over a school year to reach a difficult pupil. He concluded:

> This roller coaster ride tires both of us. I'm afraid we'll get to a point where neither of us wants to try anymore. I am left wondering if he will ever experience the joy of learning. It doesn't feel as if the things I did made a difference in his life this year. I wish I knew.
>
> (Whitbeck, 1997: 53)

Such accounts, written in the voice of experience, can surely 'reach' teachers. Nonetheless, the challenges facing a relatively inexperienced researcher in embarking upon narrative research can be considerable. One reason for this is that narrative forms of research seem to lack the structure that is common in other forms of research, and also their claims to certainty and objectivity. Indeed, some researchers may wonder whether 'mere' stories can be counted as research at all.

Comment by Hsin-heng Chen on undertaking life history research for a PhD

I chose to undertake life history research with nine PE teachers in Taiwan to find out how teachers learned – and why – in response to a new curriculum reform in physical education. The curriculum reform was a key event in education in Taiwan and it was introduced into a traditional and largely conservative schooling context. Understanding how teachers coped with the reform in this context, based on their previous experiences, was a key aim of the study; hence the decision to use life history research. Despite having read much about life history research, and following available guidelines, I still encountered several methodological challenges while conducting my study. For example, when I started considering interviewing and writing, I realized that different styles of presenting life history data could change the way in which the reader might interpret the findings. I could present holistic life histories – allowing readers to discover links that made sense to them – or I could be more selective in the life histories in order to highlight certain issues. In the end, I decided that my findings should be selective, particularly given the word limit of a PhD thesis.

Doing narrative research

Writing

It is important to recognize at the outset that narrative research techniques place a strong emphasis on the skill of writing. At one level, this seems counter-intuitive. How, for example, can literary skills be such a prominent feature of 'scientific' research? Richardson (2000) considers the historical divide between 'literary' and 'scientific' writing, and the belief that literary forms of writing are fictional and, therefore, subjective and untrue. This seems to be the antithesis of objective and 'true' research. Yet it is important to recognize that different kinds of research have different purposes. Wolcott (1990: 133), for example, argued that in presenting narrative accounts, 'objectivity is not my criterion as much as what might be termed rigorous subjectivity'. What is clear is that through storytelling skills, the narrative researcher has the task of making apparent an issue, question or event as seen through the eyes of research participants and experienced by them. This is not, therefore, a research method to be undertaken by a researcher who prefers numbers to words.

Methods

As might be anticipated, narrative researchers tend to use qualitative, interpretive or ethnographic research traditions. Interviews, observation and document analysis are all methods that are commonly used – with individual interviews being the predominant approach. These individual methods are covered in greater detail elsewhere in this volume. As with all forms of research, qualitative research methods are subject to potential criticisms (e.g. see Chapters 7 and 9). A key weakness of some qualitative research is highlighted by Ritchie and Spencer (2004: 2) who comment: 'It was often hard to know how people dealt with the rich, voluminous and often tangled data they had collected.' This is a fair critique. If data are collected – then reported selectively – it is incumbent on the researcher to make transparent the process of data selection. On the other hand, in narrative forms of qualitative research, data tend to be presented in rich and detailed 'stories' and so, to some extent, data selection issues can be overcome. The work of Ivor Goodson is seminal in this field and, in the 1980s, Goodson argued strongly for the use of life history methods of research into teachers' lives and careers (see Goodson, 2005). At the same time, physical education researchers began to use narrative forms of research, and there is a comprehensive overview of this emerging research, including the very influential work of Andrew Sparkes, in Armour (2006). These early papers are helpful starting points for any researchers coming to narrative research for the first time in the field of physical education and sport.

Life story/history and autoethnography

As was noted earlier, there are two main traditions in narrative research: life story/history and autoethnography. Of the two, life story/history research has a stronger tradition. In a chapter written for the *Handbook of Physical Education* in 2006, I (Kathy) defined life story/history research as follows: 'biographical research where a researcher constructs, or co-constructs, a story about a life, or part of a life. The purpose is to better understand that life, to shed light on similar or contrasting lives, and/or to inform an analysis of a particular issue or event' (Armour, 2006: 472). Importantly in life history and, to some extent, life story research, the researcher triangulates data on the life under investigation with other evidence. Autoethnography, on the other hand, can be defined by drawing on the work of Ellis and Bochner (2000: 739) who noted that:

> Autoethnography is an autobiographical genre of writing and research that displays multiple layers of consciousness, connecting the personal to the cultural … Usually written in first-person voice, autoethnographic texts appear in a variety of forms – short stories, poetry, fiction … etc.

In terms of method in autoethnography, Ellis and Bochner (2000: 737) suggest the following:

> I start with my personal life. I pay attention to my physical feelings, thoughts and emotions. I use what I call systematic sociological introspection and emotional recall to try to understand an experience I've lived through. Then I write my experience as a story.

It is important to note that this is not simply a process of writing personal memoirs. The autoethnographer draws on evidence from a series of sources to provide a wider structural and temporal framework for the story. Sparkes (2004) provides a good example of this genre in his story about his own transition from being an elite sports person to an injured one. He reminds us that such stories are not about 'facts', but are essentially about '*retelling* of the past from the experience of the present' (p. 158; our emphasis). What this means is that although Sparkes was able to draw on medical records and other documentary evidence to underpin his story, essentially his autoethnography gives us insights into the process from the vantage point of the storyteller as he looks back on the experience *from the present time*.

How many respondents are 'enough'?

Sparkes's (2004) research raises another issue that is often a concern for researchers in narrative research: How many stories are 'enough'? In the case of autoethnography the answer is, of course, one. To see an example of the depth of data collection and analysis that can be undertaken through autoethnography, you might find the work of Karl Attard to be illuminating. For his PhD, Attard undertook an autoethnographic study of himself as a new teacher, charting his personal and professional learning over the course of almost three years (Attard, 2006). He kept detailed reflective journals, and ended up focusing extensively on the *process* of critical reflection as a professional learning tool. He characterizes this process as a 'reflective odyssey' and has described the links between personal life and professional learning in detailed ways (see also Attard and Armour, 2006).

For life story/history research, the decision about the number of participants required is less straightforward. The answer tends to be 'It depends.' Erben (1998: 5) offered the following advice about collecting biographical forms of data: be open to a range of methodologies, search a wide variety of documentary evidence if the 'life' under study requires it; and select a sample size that reflects the key purpose of the study:

> The exact size of any sample in qualitative research cannot be ascertained through quantitative methods. It is for this reason that the conspicuously chosen sample must correspond to the overall aims of the study.

In some sense, this advice on number of cases is, of course, unsatisfactory. Another way to look at the question is to consider how much *depth* is required for each case in order to answer the research question (see also Chapter 16 on case study research by Armour and Griffiths in this volume). Researchers rarely have limitless time and budgets, so consideration of the amount of time that is needed in order to collect sufficient data on each respondent can be a helpful guide to both the feasibility of the research question and the appropriateness of the method to answer it.

Data analysis and reporting

Finally – what to do with all the data? Decisions must be taken about whether to present data wholly within single case studies, to present segmented data under core themes, or to develop a grounded theory from data within or across cases. It is certainly necessary, in most narrative research, to give readers a sense of the holism of the respondents at some point in the reporting process.

Beyond writing holistic, individual stories, it is common where multiple stories have been collected for researchers to segment the data into categories that fit the research purposes. For example, in her earlier research on the lives and careers of four PE teachers (Armour, 1997), Kathy reported the research not as four teacher case studies, but under headings relating to family influence, school experiences and employment. There are, however, dangers in this approach, especially if the individual stories are not analysed and reported holistically at some point in the process. As Erben (1998) points out, segmenting life stories can result in a loss of the very insights that are central to narrative research. In addition, Usher (1998) suggests we might need to 'deconstruct the dominant self of the story' (p. 30) in order to see the lives under investigation as lives 'in process' (p. 27). It is possible, therefore, to be creative in analysing and reporting narrative research as long as the approach taken offers insights that are warranted by the data.

Excerpts from the life history of one PE teacher in Taiwan

Hsin-heng Chen writes: I have selected three examples from my life history research on one of the Taiwanese teachers in my PhD study. In this way, I can offer insights into the research question in three areas: the impact of governmental policy; the link between culture and school policy; and links between teachers' past experiences and current actions. I do this by using excerpts from one of the teacher's life histories (Cheir, a pseudonym) in order to highlight the connections between them in the context of one teacher's life.

In data analysis, I used a constructivist revision of grounded theory (Charmaz, 2006) to ensure data were systematically analysed in the context of the research question and located in the individual's life story (Goodson and Sikes, 2001). However, this analysis process raised another critical question: what personal experience is counted as 'too personal' and what is 'significant' to the study? I had many experiences in common with participants, and so at first every minute detail seemed meaningful to me. The solution was to keep referring back to the research questions and to draw continuous links between past and present, the different cases, and also key personal and societal incidents. For example, I found that when tracing the development of PE teachers' personal philosophies, pre-service teacher training had an important impact on both their current teaching practice and their engagement in further training through continuing professional development. This approach also helped me to critically review their – and my – taken-for-granted assumptions.

I acknowledge that different researchers could have interpreted these data in different ways. I have, however, used respondent validation to ensure that I am representing the teachers in ways that they recognize. Additionally, in trying to offer some practical/substantial examples of life history research for novice researchers/ readers such as I was, I feel a need to stress that the following examples are one – but not the only – possible approach to presenting the findings.

Life history research example 1

The text below reveals an educational problem that arose as a result of a governmental policy that encouraged young talented players to engage in elite sport, but did not provide adequate support for, or regulation about retaining engagement in academic study at school at the same time. This means that these young people struggled to accommodate both sport training and academic learning, and this affected their lives.

As a comparative beginner in sports, Cheir had to work very hard to catch up with the other players. After only one year, Cheir, along with her team mates, won championships and received scholarship offers from several senior high schools. Although Cheir was very keen to continue with her sports career, her mother strongly opposed it because of the frequent injuries she sustained. With her father's help, however, Cheir left home to continue her football life in another county. Like the other young players, she put all of her energy into training and therefore rarely focused on academic study.

At the time, Cheir's position as an elite sportswoman enabled her to enter the Normal University and additionally guaranteed her work as a teacher after graduation. In her father's view, being a teacher was a fine career for a girl.

Meanwhile, Cheir's long period of concentration on sports training appeared to give her a positive outlook, which influenced her life and career development profoundly.

> Being a player, there are lots of tough and unreasonable trainings you must tolerate ... The only way of your thinking was to win, win, win ... and to be the best ... You should never think about giving up ... Even you fell down, you'd then try to get up again, and again ... The training was to ... make you to have the persistence to face anything in your life.
>
> (ICh-1-14)

However, Cheir's lack of academic study at high school caused some difficulties in her first year study at university. Cheir stated: 'Sport training helped me to get to university and get a job smoothly ... However, at that time, I started to realize that I'd missed many opportunities in learning' (ICh-1-14). This feeling seemed to influence Cheir's involvement in learning and work afterwards.

Life history research example 2

The text below illustrates the difficulty Cheir experienced in teaching PE in the academic learning-dominated school policy climate.

In 1986, Cheir graduated from university and began teaching at a junior high school in Taipei County. She described the early years as a difficult period. In the first year, she was assigned to be a tutor, to teach PE, health education, citizen education and association education. Apart from PE teaching, none of these was taught in her pre-service training. In the following years, she continued to undertake different types of work. Although the preparation work exhausted her, Cheir just took it without any argument. It could be argued that this compliant attitude might be as a result of her early sports training. In addition, Cheir seemed to consider the process as essential training, and carried on involving herself in additional work even when she moved to the next school.

> A few years after that ... I found myself more competent than others ... At that time, maybe you just did. But the more you did, the more you learnt.
>
> (ICh-1-28)

Additionally, in learning to overcome challenges when working as a teacher, Cheir suggested that 'learning should be you actively asking' (ICh-1-34), although in her school, teachers tended to be reserved in their professional communication and support: 'We usually worked independently from others' (Chi-2-29). When Cheir taught PE, she was shocked by how other teachers presented PE lessons on the playground. What she saw could be identified as a PE lesson, but without teaching behaviour; instead the pupils seemed to be engaged in just free play. Cheir then came to understand that this was due to problems of *teacher distribution* as a result of the academic performance-dominated school policy at the time.

> They were not PE teachers, but teachers of other 'main subjects' … Except holding exams of their own subject in the classroom, it would be a favour that they let the kids get out of the classroom and play.
>
> (ICh-1-25)

Life history research example 3

The text below illustrates the links between Cheir's past and current experiences in relation to PE teaching, revealing some of the ways in which her philosophy about PE was shaped by her experience.

For Cheir, skill and performance were the foundation of PE. This idea was built through her pre-service teacher training, although Cheir has since developed different approaches to implementation. This is due to the discovery that students seem to have changed over the years.

> The pupils' physical ability nowadays is not as competitive as they used to be. If you still simply emphasize skill learning … it will be a frustration for both teacher and pupil.
>
> (ICh-3-08)

Thus, Cheir believed that teachers should use alternative methods to meet the core goals of PE. The use of alternate skill learning and modified games would be an approach she suggested. Besides the changes in students, Cheir was also influenced by a governmental programme – 'Fun PE teaching' – launched in the 1990s.

> I know that some skill-oriented people really disagree with it. It's like … if PE is only fun, then why would you need a PE teacher? But I think it really depends how you use it!
>
> (ICh-3-08)

In addition, Cheir seemed to be increasingly concerned with students' attitudes while teaching. This appeared to connect with her consistent focus on moral education and the importance of trying hard. Despite this adjustment, developing high levels of skill and performance in PE remained a priority for Cheir, even when it became apparent that they were unlikely to be achieved.

> To compare with my friend who worked at university, now I felt like … you couldn't have much opportunity to really teach PE … in junior high school.
>
> (ICh-3-20)

Conclusion

Boler (1999: xvii) argued that education is 'by no means merely "instruction" and transmission of information. Education shapes our values, beliefs, and who and what we become.' If we accept this view, we might argue that narrative research has much to offer in enhancing our understandings of teachers, coaches and learners in physical education and sport. Narrative research is, however, demanding at many levels. If biographical forms of research are undertaken, they require good interpersonal skills in order to develop productive research relationships with respondents over time. In all forms of narrative research, a unique form of researcher discipline is required in order to simultaneously 'see' the perspective of the researched while maintaining the critical faculties of a researcher. Moreover, the researcher's writing skills must be of a level that will allow the text to represent the lives under study. Narrative research is, therefore, no easy option. On the other hand, if you have the required skills, narrative research offers insights that can add much to our knowledge of physical education and sport. Done well, narrative research is indeed the place where the art of storytelling meets the science of research.

Key terms

Narrative research   Research that uses different forms of storying in data collection or analysis.

Life history   Life story located in historical context.

Life story   Data collected on an aspect of an individual's life history that may not be potted specifically in historical context.

Autoethnography   Narrative of self.

Writing   Not only used to report data, it can also form part of the data collection and analysis process.

References

Armour, K. M. (1997) 'Developing a personal philosophy on the nature and purpose of physical education: Life history reflections', *European Physical Education Review*, 3(1): 68–82.

Armour, K. M. (2006) 'Narrative research in physical education: The way to a teacher's heart', in Kirk, D., Macdonald, D. and O'Sullivan, M. (eds) *Handbook of Research in Physical Education* (467–87), London: Sage.

Attard, K. (2006) 'Reflecting on reflection: A case study of one teacher's early-career professional learning', unpublished PhD thesis, Loughborough: Loughborough University.

Attard, K. and Armour, K. M. (2006) 'Reflecting on reflection: a case study of one teacher's early-career professional learning', *Physical Education and Sport Pedagogy*, 11, 3, 209–30.

Barone, T. (2001) *Touching Eternity: The Enduring Outcomes of Teaching*, New York: Teachers College.

Barone, T. (2009) 'Narrative researchers as witnesses of injustice and agents of social change?', *Educational Researcher*, 38, 8, November, 591–7.

Boler, M. (1999) *Feeling Power. Emotions and Education*, London: Routledge.

Carlisle Duncan, M. (1998) 'Stories we tell about ourselves', *Sociology of Sport Journal*, 15: 95–108.

Charmaz, K. (2006) *Constructing Grounded Theory: A Practical Guide Through Qualitative Analysis*, London: Sage.

Clandinin, D. J. (2001) 'Foreword', in C. M. Clark (ed.) *Talking Shop* (viii), New York: Teachers College.

Clandinin, D. J. and Connelly, F. M. (1995) *Teachers' Professional Knowledge Landscapes*, New York: Teachers College.

Clandinin, D. J. and Connelly, F. M. (1996) 'Teachers' professional knowledge landscapes: Teacher stories – stories of teachers – school stories – stories of schools', *Educational Researcher*, 25(3): 24–30.

Clandinin, D. J. and Murphy, M. S. (2009) 'Relational ontological commitments in narrative research', *Educational Researcher*, 38, 8, November, 598–602.

Duckworth, E. (and the experienced teachers group) (1997) *Teacher to Teacher. Learning from Each Other*, New York: Teachers College Press.

Ellis, C. and Bochner, A. P. (2000) 'Autoethnography, personal narrative, reflexivity. Researcher as subject', in N. K. Denzin and Y. S. Lincoln (eds) *Handbook of Qualitative Research*, 2nd edn (733–68), London: Sage.

Erben, M. (ed.) (1998) *Biography and Education: A Reader*, London: Falmer Press.

Goodson, I. (1988) *The Making of Curriculum: Collected Essays*, Lewes: Falmer Press.

Goodson, I. (2005) *Learning, Curriculum and Life Politics: The selected works of Ivor F. Goodson*, Abingdon: Routledge.

Goodson, I. and Sikes, P. (2001) *Life History Research in Educational Settings: Learning from Life*, Buckingham: Open University Press.

Jones, R. L., Armour, K. M. and Potrac, P. (2004) *Sports Coaching Cultures: from Practice to Theory*, London: Routledge.

Jones, R. L., Bowes, I. and Kingston, K. (2010) 'Complex practice in coaching: studying the chaotic nature of coach–athlete interactions', in J. Lyle and C. Cushion (eds) *Sports Coaching: Professionalisation and Practice* (15–25), London: Elsevier.

Oliver, K. L. (1998) 'A journey into narrative analysis: A methodology for discovering meanings', *Journal of Teaching in Physical Education*, 17(2): 244–59.

Richardson, L. (2000) 'Writing. A method of inquiry', in N. K. Denzin and Y. S. Lincoln (eds) *Handbook of Qualitative Research*, 2nd edn (923–48), London: Sage.

Ritchie, J. and Spencer, L. (2004) 'Qualitative data analysis: The call for transparency', *Building Research Capacity* (issue 7), Cardiff: Cardiff University School of Social Sciences.

Sparkes, A. C. (1996) 'Physical education teachers and the search for self: Two cases of structured denial', in N. Armstrong (ed.) *New Directions in Physical Education. Change and Innovation* (157–78) London: Cassell.

Sparkes, A. C. (2004) 'From performance to impairment: A patchwork of embodied memories', in J. Evans, B. Davies and J. Wright (eds) *Body Knowledge and Control. Studies in the Sociology of Physical Education and Health* (157–72), London: Routledge.

Tinning, R. (1997) *Pedagogies for Physical Education: Pauline's Story*, Victoria 3217, Australia: Deakin University.

Usher, R. (1998) 'The story of self: Education, experience and autobiography', in M. Erben (ed.) *Biography and Education: A Reader* (18–31), London: Falmer Press.

Whitbeck, C. (1997) 'Against all odds: Creating possibilities for children to invent and discover', in E. Duckworth (and the experienced teachers group) *Teacher to Teacher. Learning from Each Other* (48–53), New York: Teachers College Press.

Wolcott, H. F. (1990) 'On seeing – and rejecting – validity in qualitative research', in E. W. Eisner and A. Peshkin (eds) *Qualitative Inquiry in Education. The Continuing Debate* (121–52), New York: Columbia University.

Further resource

The Centre for Narrative Research offers some useful research papers: <http://www.uel.ac.uk/cnr/>

19 Action research in physical education

Cycles, not circles!

Anthony Rossi and Wah Kiat Tan

Is action research really *research* or is it something else? ... [R]esearch is no place for the amateur.

(Hodgkinson, 1957)

I suppose some might describe action research as an exercise in going round in circles!
(Tony Rossi in conversation with Wah Kiat Tan as they wrote this chapter)

Introduction

Action research can be summarized as research undertaken or led by practitioners, most commonly in their own practice settings. When we began to write this chapter, and in subsequent conversations, we considered what action research 'can do' and 'ought to do' given its long and mostly distinguished 'social mission' history. Seeking to lighten the mood, one of us (Tony) made the tongue-in-cheek suggestion about action research going round in circles. We were aware of Hodgkinson's (1957) critique of action research as being something less than 'real' research. Although his comment was written well over 50 years ago, Hodgkinson believed that teachers were not suited to the demands of research. He also questioned whether action research could be classified as research at all. Action research has had to counter such charges for most of its existence.

In this chapter, Tony will cover some of the historical background and original intentions of action research, to ground it as a democratic form of social practice. This is important because sometimes this aspect of action research is lost and action research as a way of bringing about change functions at only a technical level. In other words, change has no social meaning; instead functional change is about how practice (e.g., instruction, curriculum implementation, sports coaching) is 'done'. This was *not*, however, a limitation in the original idea of action research. The historical overview that follows includes literature from the field of physical education (PE), although there is relatively little available. Tony will continue by describing some of the common techniques and methods used in action research and that might be employed in studies within, for example, physical education, sport or even personal training.

In the second half of the chapter, Kiat describes how he undertook a comprehensive doctoral study in Singapore, using an action research approach as one of his methods.

It was a detailed study undertaken initially in an unsympathetic context. Kiat provides an extensive explanation of what is required to enter a research context, gain trust from the participants, and then conduct a study that entails engaging the participants in a process of scrutinizing their own practice in order to find ways to improve it. By providing real case material in addition to the historical and the methodological discussions, we believe we are able to demonstrate that action research is far from 'lightweight' research and, secondly, not only provide detail about the procedures one might use in action research, but also describe some of the challenges it presents.

About us

Dr Anthony Rossi is a senior lecturer in the School of Human Movement Studies, University of Queensland. He writes: I met Kiat in 2003 in Singapore, when he was a master's student in a class I taught. I already had interest and experience in critical action research and took the principles with me to Singapore and embedded them into the class. I was unsure how this form of critique of the practices of physical education might be received as course content. For some students, it was a challenge; but for others it was a turning point. Kiat joined us at the University of Queensland in 2007 to undertake action-oriented doctoral research based in Singapore. It was a courageous decision.

Wah Kiat Tan is a doctoral student in the school of Human Movement Studies. He writes: Prior to my doctoral study, I was an experienced physical education teacher in a Singaporean secondary school. I was first introduced to action research during my master's research course with Tony as one of my lecturers. Convinced that action research could bring about genuine change and authentic improvements, I used this method to undertake research into ways to challenge gendered practices in physical education. However, my critical approach differed from the dominant trend of action research practice in Singapore that seeks to prove the effectiveness of interventions rather than to improve, challenge or critically question current practices (Tan, Macdonald and Rossi, 2009).

A very modest (and incomplete) overview of action research

Kurt Lewin is usually credited with coining the term 'action research'. In 1933, Lewin, a social psychologist, fled to America to escape the tyranny of the Third Reich in Germany. He came to prominence in the 1940s for his work that attempted to bring together 'the experimental approach of social science with programmes of social action in response to major social issues of the day' (Kemmis and McTaggart, 1988: 29). In particular, Lewin saw action research as having great potential to improve the position and well-being of minority groups in post-war America, and his work on 'race relations' (a term that appears rather awkward now) across the country is a testament to his commitment to social betterment (Lewin, 1946).

Lewin (1946) was one of the first social researchers to use an action research process that was characterized by deep levels of consultation through each of the key steps and the spiralling, progressive actions. He was well recognized for work with groups where, through a 'planning – fact-finding – execution' sequence of actions, behaviour changes could result that would advantage the group. Examples of such changes included food consumption practices or group solidarity and factory worker rights in an increasingly industrialized and urbanized America. Subsequently, the versatility of action research has been demonstrated in a wide range of contexts:

- institutional and organizational research and workplace change (see Jolley, 2008 as an example);
- in third-world contexts as a form of liberation politics (for example, see Fals Borda, 1979; Friere, 1982);
- in education, where perhaps action research has had its greatest impact.

Lewin worked with teachers and teacher educators in the United States from the mid-1940s. At the Horace Mann Lincoln Institute of Teachers' College (at Columbia University in New York), action research was well recognized in the early 1950s under the leadership of Stephen Corey. However, by 1957, action research had declined in importance and visibility. Hodgkinson's (1957) stinging criticism was that action research was a form of 'common' sense, drawing on lightweight data gathered by amateurs (i.e., teachers with no formal training in research), which failed to measure up to the standards of 'real' scientific inquiry.

Interest in action research was maintained in the UK through the late 1960s and into the early 1970s, mainly through the Humanities Curriculum Project, under the leadership of Lawrence Stenhouse (Stenhouse, 1975). In this context, action research was an experimental form of curriculum development that placed teachers at the centre of curriculum change and development. There were also other developments at the time in the UK, notably the Ford Teaching Project, that drew upon Stenhouse's early work to build teacher-driven innovation into pedagogy and curriculum design (see Elliot and Adelman, 1973).

Action research in physical education

There has been relatively little action research undertaken in physical education. Richard Tinning has been one of the most ardent advocates for action research in the field, as evidenced by his chapter in an earlier research methods text edited by Andrew Sparkes (Tinning, 1992). Other influences within physical education are harder to trace. Len Almond in the UK was an advocate of action research but his approach lacked the political edge proposed by Tinning (see Almond, 1976). In the United States, a paper published in 1988 by Martinek and Butt detailed an action research project aimed at changing pedagogical practices. This project, while drawing on the cyclical procedures of information gathering, reflection and action, took a technical rather than a social mission approach to the method.

A recent example of a critical action research project is Ken Cliff's (2007) work in Australia on the PE curriculum. Cliff used action research in order to introduce a sociocultural perspective on curriculum change in health and physical education (HPE). In the study, Cliff used a critical action research model in order to 'conceptualize the research as practical and collaborative, based in the practices of the classroom and with the cooperation and contribution of practising teachers' (p. 58).

More recently still, Ashley Casey's use of action research (see Casey and Dyson, 2009) to investigate his teaching and learning provides an example of a teacher-researcher taking a personally and socially critical approach to the research process. These authors explore the use of action research as a framework to investigate the effectiveness of cooperative learning, and teaching games for understanding as instructional models in physical education. In this research, Casey provided an insider's view of the action research process with the aid of an outsider who acted as a critical peer 'debriefer' to suggest ways in which a perceived gap between theory and practice could be bridged.

Having discussed, albeit briefly, some of the contexts within which action research has been used, it is prudent to explain how one goes about 'doing' action research. At this stage, it may still seem like a mystery; however, as Wadsworth (1998) suggests, the emphasis is very much on 'action'.

Doing action research

As critical researchers, we start from a philosophical position that educational action research should be underpinned by emancipatory goals. Such goals include emancipation from injustice, alienation and suffering, and from the domestication of education such that it becomes a matter of convention, procedure or routinized practice. To achieve these goals, there are some well-established steps that form the core of action research in practice.

Going round in circles!

In action research, a key design feature is that the research is conducted in *cycles*. Tony's opening comment about action research 'going round in circles' had a serious edge. Cycles in action research build progressively on each other through the research process. Action research that fails to progress in this manner could, indeed, be described as going round in circles and would be poor research as it would achieve very little. The cycles of action research can be described by the use of a diagram, and the one devised by Stephen Kemmis and Robin McTaggart (1988) (see Figure 19.1) is simple but effective.

It is evident from this diagram that action research involves four basic steps within each cycle. These steps are:

- planning;
- action;
- observing;
- reflecting.

This provides a deceptively simple summary of the action research process.

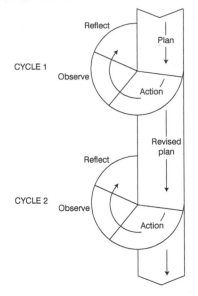

Figure 19.1 Kemmis and McTaggart's (1988) model of action research cycles

What do the terms mean?

Perhaps the first question to be posed about the action research steps is 'Steps towards what?' First of all, imagine a problem, any problem connected with professional practice in teaching or coaching. It could be the research question you identified in Chapter 1, or it might be about the introduction of a new curriculum initiative or behaviour modification programme within a youth sport context (particularly those emphasizing collaboration, fair play, honesty, etc.). Having identified a question or problem, it is important to develop a plan to address it. The planning phase is about the planning for, and design of, the first cycle of action to be taken to address the previously identified problem.

The next step is the enactment of the plan (the 'doing' bit or the 'action'). This is where the detailed plans that have been drawn up are put into action, with the intention of bringing about different (better!) outcomes, usually for the learners or players. The action should mirror the plan as closely as possible, and for good reason. In the third step, the information gathering phase or observation (i.e., data gathering about what happened when the plan was implemented), you will need to gather information about the plan as it was designed. This will enable genuine modifications (rather than contextual tinkering) to be made at the most appropriate points. Therefore, during the observation phase (step three), information needs to be gathered that is accurate and pertinent to the questions asked, which is an expectation of all research. The final step is where the data gathered are reflected upon in order to revise the plan accordingly; this leads back to the beginning, but with progression to the second cycle of the operation. This cyclical process continues until, ideally, the professional practice under scrutiny has improved to a point where only very minor modifications need to be made, mainly for maintenance purposes.

The language used to describe the phases and cycles of action research varies from researcher to researcher. For example, Lewin used the word 'reconnaissance' as a way of 'learning' from the action to bring about a change in what he called the 'general plan'. However, the underlying principles are the same and the intention is to effect change in order to improve some aspect of 'action' (or practice). Arguing, as we have, that action research should be guided by an emancipatory agenda, it is apparent that the problem or question driving the research should have, at its core, a social mission of improvement. This type of action research is often referred to as participatory action research (PAR). As Wadsworth (1998:2) suggests, participatory action research is 'more *conscious* of its underlying assumptions, and collectivist nature, its action consequences and its driving values' (emphasis in original). Wadsworth (1998) goes on to suggest that PAR is characterized by being critically aware of the intended intervention within the social context in which it is operating (see Kiat's 'intervention' to understand his intention). PAR is about a consciously applied effect: the intention is to bring about change through collaborative inquiry. Thus, the distinction between researcher and participant is intentionally blurred and the collaborative effort involved is the search for new possibilities. In short, its purpose is to enable action, leading to change (Baum, MacDougall and Smith, 2006).

The case study example that follows illustrates precisely the points made above. Kiat was interested in changing the gendered dispositions of PE teachers in a Singaporean school; he had already determined that such a change was both necessary and desirable. In particular, Kiat's case study describes some of the critical incidents in the study that serve as an illustration of, first, the intention of the phases and cycles, and second, how they were used during the research process. What this example illustrates is that action research is, more often than not, a 'messy' process. This leads Kiat to further reflect on some of the ethical dilemmas and challenges he faced and which are often present in this type of research.

A Singaporean case study

This section describes the action research process as planned and conducted by Kiat in Singapore. The narrative is only an overview, but it is detailed enough to illustrate the nuances of each phase and cycle of an action research. It must be noted, however, that like all case studies, this account serves only as a preliminary guide, because action research (by definition) is contextual and hence unique in its implementation. The four basic steps of planning, action, observing and reflecting within the first cycle of the action research project will be described. We should point out, however, that in reality, the action research process is rarely as neat as this structure implies, meaning that it is important to be flexible, without losing the research focus.

The focus of this case study was a year-long action research project undertaken as part of Kiat's doctoral study. The purpose of the project was to use critical participatory action research to disrupt the gendered practices and dispositions of the members of a department of physical education in a Singaporean high school. The rationale for this study was to use action research as an active tool to empower the teachers to reflect upon their possible gendered practices and dispositions based on collaborative and systematic data collection and analysis.

A comment from Tony: It is important to note that this is a slight departure from the more common action research format, where the participants conduct the research on themselves. In such cases, the participants are both subject and object of the research. In the example reported here, however, it would be more accurate to say that this project was a case study of action research in use. This means that Kiat had a very specific role both as the director of the project (it was his PhD), but also as someone that is often referred to as a 'critical friend' (Kember et al., 1997) in this type of research. Critical friends are important in action research as they provide both an insider and an outsider view of the action as it takes place. We talk more about this later. Before we detail the technical phases of the research, we describe some preparatory steps that Kiat considered to be essential in the context and which he was determined to follow with care and sensitivity.

Gaining access

To embark upon this research, Kiat had to recruit participants. An important reason for the purposeful selection in this case was that Kiat is a friend of Yong (his pseudonym), the head of department of the intended research site. This friendship facilitated easy negotiation and subsequent permission to enter the school. At the same time, the implications of this relationship had to be made transparent and fully accounted for during the research process. Yong was not therefore involved in the early phases of action research until the rest of the teacher-participants were certain that he would not be assessing their teaching performance based on the findings of the project. However, Yong's eventual participation as a middle manager was pivotal to the action research process because he became a catalyst for influence and change to certain practices in the school.

Participation

At the beginning of the research, Yong asked his principal (head teacher) for permission to engage in the research, and also asked his department for their consent to participation. While they were generally agreeable to the idea, it is important to recognize that the teacher-participants may have had the sense that they were being 'volunteered' for participation by Yong. Nonetheless, and consistent with ethical procedures, the participants were given detailed information about the project, so they were able to give informed consent to participation. They were also aware that they could leave the project at any time without giving reasons. While it is an ideal for the participants in any action research process to have a common goal, in reality each participant has unique dispositional viewpoints (Cohen, Manion and Morrison, 2007). Kiat also acknowledged, and accepted, that the teacher-participants may not have fully understood the purpose of the action research based on the initial information given to them during the informed consent process.

A comment from Tony: In his dual role as critical friend and PhD student, it took considerable time and effort for Kiat to build rapport and understanding with the participants.

Building rapport

Building rapport in action research is important in order to establish the trust and understanding required. As noted earlier, a role that is often central to action research is that of *critical* friend. A critical friend is often someone located outside the immediate action but who is also connected to it. Kiat's role as a facilitator and critical friend meant that he was placed in a position where sometimes his emerging findings were challenging for the participants; however, he adopted a policy of openness, having decided that this was the key to building good rapport.

Kiat built and sustained mutual understanding by talking, but more importantly by listening, to the teacher-participants. For Kiat it was crucial to communicate and share his ideas and perspectives with the teacher-participants, both on a group and individual basis, in order that they could comprehend the underlying intentions of the action research tasks they undertook. In turn, he listened sensitively and non-judgementally to their contributions and feedback, offering encouragement and, at times, critical advice.

Holier than thou?

It is vital to remember that Kiat's role was neither to impose his ideology, nor dictate the action research process. Although Kiat had a gender equity agenda at heart, he had to reflexively remind himself that the purpose of the action research was for the teacher-participants to reflect and become more critically aware of their own practices. Kiat's position, then, was not as a person standing on some predetermined moral high ground, 'correcting' the oppositional viewpoints of the teacher-participants. An example of this was when one teacher-participant, in his bid to motivate girls to participate in football, suggested a double points scoring system for girls. Rather than asking the teacher to change this practice, Kiat simply asked the teacher-participant to consider whether or not the rule should apply to *all* girls. In the end, the teacher conceded that there were a few girls for whom the extra points were not required as a form of motivation and he came up with a plan to create more goal scoring opportunities for everyone instead.

Conducting the study

Planning

The general plan for the conduct of the study was, first, to build sufficient intellectual resources by reading summarized readings and short excerpts of journal articles such as Wright's (1999) work on changing gendered practices in PE. Following this, appropriate action research tasks were designed for the teacher-participants in order to investigate potential gendered practices and dispositions. Group discussions on action research and gender were planned and carried out with Kiat as the facilitator. For example, positivistic forms of research are the norm in Singapore, meaning that mechanical questions are asked, or hypotheses tested and interventions measured. However, Kiat juxtaposed traditional forms of research with the critical, emancipatory intentions of this project. Similarly, issues on gender in physical education were discussed at the outset, with most teacher-participants claiming that they had 'no problems with gender equity in their practices'. Following these initial stages, action research tasks were planned collaboratively such that the teachers could investigate their own practices.

Action

The planned action revolved around the idea of modified teacher behaviours related to gendered practices. Examples include: how the teachers would use language to ensure it was gender neutral; how particular tasks could be set without differentiated expectations; and even ensuring that certain activities were not made unavailable to girls simply because they were regarded as 'boys' sports'. In addition to the changes in practice (action) taking place, it is necessary to try to record observations and reflections on or about such changes. In this study, one approach taken was the use of a personal digital assistant (PDA) as a data collection tool. Some teacher-participants used the voice-recording function to record their instructions during coaching sessions, while others simply used the note-taking function of the PDA to record critical incidents and moments in real time. Of course, there were some who resisted, preferring to rely on pen and paper to record their thoughts, or to simply relate their thoughts to Kiat verbally. Although this implementation was inherently messy in terms of data collection, the flexibility allowed for customization of the process to individual teacher-participants, enabling greater autonomy in their participation.

In the early action cycle, teachers concentrated on taking note of their gendered language as it occurred and making conscious comments about any observations that might be deemed as gendered. In addition, Kiat also observed their lessons and made comparative field notes for future reflexive discussions with the teacher-participants.

Observing

Action research, like most social research, is unpredictable and does not always go according to plan. Originally, the action research tasks were to take place during normal lesson time to capture possible gendered practices. However, because of the pressure to do well in the National Physical Fitness Award (NAPFA),[1] many of the scheduled lessons were converted to training and testing sessions instead. Undeterred, Kiat and his teacher-participants took this opportunity and investigated possible gendered practices within the fitness testing sessions. For instance, Knight (a pseudonym) noted in his PDA that he was asked by a female student why 'girls usually get worse NAPFA results' (Knight, PDA journal, 26 August 2008). In our discussion over this reflexive input, Knight recalled that his response to the female student was 'so my explanation was it (the body of a girl or boy) was biologically built different. A lot of the stations that we do, NAPFA, the boys have the physique to excel better than the girls. I mean from what we learn from anatomy' (Knight, interview transcript, 26 August 2008). Other observations by teachers included Yong's acknowledgement that he 'looked at improving girls in certain stations because they were the easiest group to make an impact on' (Yong, conference script, 1 June 2009). This brought up further discussion on the different standards of fitness test criteria based simply on biological sex.

Reflecting

Taking the example of Knight above, we can see there was an attempt by a female student to question why girls were perceived as inferior to boys in fitness testing. This question represents a potential site of contestation for both the student and Knight. In his response, Knight reinforced gender-stereotypical assumptions by using a scientific justification. It was also interesting to note the language Knight used to motivate his students. For example, his justification for sit-ups and the motivation to do them was framed thus: 'Sit-ups help: girls cut tummy fat; boys build six-packs.' In the run component of the test, Knight noted to himself through a PDA entry that he had used gender in a negative mode to motivate boys. He noted: 'Comments for some slower boys in 2.4 km test: You run slower than the slowest girl' (Knight, PDA journal, 26 August 2008).

It could be argued that Knight's identification of these critical incidents of gendered teaching and learning in his reflexive journalling is an indication of the small success we had in the action research project. When these reflections were further shared and discussed with the rest of the teacher-participants, the communicative action process heightened awareness of the possible negative consequences that such gendered remarks could have on the students. In turn, this awareness allowed for deeper negotiations and some consensus on subsequent actions. For example, in this case, the action research team agreed to be more critically aware of their comments to students.

The cycle repeats ... but not quite as neat?

It might be expected that, in taking a standard approach to action research, the next stage in the process would have been to establish research tasks to support the teacher-participants to become critically aware of their comments to students. In reality, however, it must be emphasized that action research cycles are not necessarily linear in sequence and cycles are often repeated or overlapping. This, in part, is due to the different rates of pickup, progress and productivity of each teacher-participant, and including Kiat. For instance, enthusiastic and reflexive teacher-participants, like Yong and Knight, proceeded to write narratives to make sense of their changing identities. Others, who were perhaps more reticent in their written reflections during their first cycle, were encouraged instead to provide more examples of possible gendered practices in their next cycle. What became apparent was that although the project had begun as a group project, it soon became a series of individual cycles, with the teacher-participants each working at a pace and intensity appropriate to them. Hence, group meetings become an important means to update and synergize the different viewpoints and maintain group integrity.

Reflections on the action research process

Reflections on the action research process led to plenty of learning points for Kiat. Below are just some of the essential learning questions that may be helpful to those contemplating doing action research:

Time

Action research requires a lot of time that is, in some cases, difficult to predict and schedule into a neat research plan. Examples include: time to build rapport with your participants; time to collaborate and plan with them; time for your participants to implement strategies, and to collect data; time to reflect and analyse the data; time to plan for the next cycle; and so it goes on. There is much negotiation with the teacher-participants on what needs to be done and what they can actually complete. The bottom line is, do the teachers see the point of the research in what is generally accepted as their time-poor context?

Telling unwelcome truths

There are times when the findings of action research might be uncomfortable for the participants and/or the school/organization. Though there is a necessity for the researcher to speak candidly in action research, it may be prudent not to be antagonistic to the point that it impedes progress. Importantly, this does not suggest evading unwelcome truths or giving up foundational principles. Rather, it is important to be a tactful protagonist who can engage the participants in a learning journey. In this case, it is also important to remember that the head of department, Yong, provided a much-needed link, who could relay some of the suggestions from the research findings to the school's senior management.

Ethical dilemmas

Ethical dilemmas are present in all research, and action research is no exception. Cohen et al. (2007) raise questions about action research reports that show areas of improvement through the project but that are, in effect, revealing instances of poor practice/planning undertaken before the project. For example, would an action research report made public tarnish the image of the school? Would the principal even allow the report to be published? Is it ethical not to report? Is it ethical to report when anonymity may be compromised? In this case study, Kiat and the teacher-participants chose to present some of their action research findings at a local educational conference, thereby surrendering anonymity and confidentiality. At the same time, this was regarded as an empowering process, whereby the presenters had the opportunity to share and learn from the process.

Conclusion

We have demonstrated an unmistakable, socially critical intention in action research. The basic cyclical framework of action research has been discussed and illustrated through a project undertaken in Singapore. The account raises questions about both the challenges and the emancipatory potential of action research. Since the challenges inherent in action research are contextual and so would vary from case to case, there are no simple, easy-fix solutions. However, we argue that this is what makes critical action research unique, because it can 'change poison into medicine', as every problem and obstacle becomes an opportunity to be the next stepping stone for progression.

Tony: So, Kiat, in your experience, is action research just an exercise in going round in circles, as I said at the beginning?

Kiat: I would argue that it is not. However, I do acknowledge that it can be daunting. That said, I consider the rewards of authentic improvement and the struggle against social injustice and oppression to be sufficient motivation to forge ahead.

Key terms

Action research A reflective process involving progressive problem solving to address (generally) social issues through improved social and/or professional practices.

Participatory Action research is participatory in that it is inclusive and invites all involved to contribute to the design and implementation of the research. All participants bring their own perspectives to the analytical aspects of the research process.

Critical friend Someone who may sit outside the research but looks 'in' as an observer to advise the research group members about 'what is going on'.

Research cycles As action research is an ongoing iterative process, the research is conducted cyclically, allowing for reflection, change and adaptation, and then new action where the cycle begins again.

Acknowledgement

Kiat: I acknowledge the commitment of Yong and Knight and the other teacher-participants not mentioned who are co-researchers in the study. Although their names cannot be mentioned because of ethical reasons, their contributions have been invaluable.

Note

1 NAPFA: Singapore's mandatory fitness testing in school with sex- and age-based standards. The passing percentage for the school is used as part of the scoring system for a national school ranking exercise.

References

Almond, L. (1976) 'Teacher involvement in curriculum planning', in J. Kane (ed.) *Curriculum Planning in Physical Education* (96–121), London: Crosby, Lockwood and Staples.

Baum, F., MacDougall, C. and Smith, D. (2006) 'Participatory action research', *Journal of Epidemiology and Community Health*, 60(10): 854–7.

Casey, A. and Dyson, B. (2009) 'The implementation of models-based practice in physical education through action research', *European Physical Education Review*, 15(2): 175–99.

Cliff, K. (2007) 'A sociocultural perspective as a curriculum change in health and physical education', PhD thesis, Wollongong: University of Wollongong.

Cohen, L., Manion, L. and Morrison, K. (2007) *Research Methods in Education*, 6th edn, New York: Routledge.

Elliot, J. and Adelman, C. (1973) 'Reflecting on where the action is: The design of the Ford Teaching Project', *Education for Teaching*, 92: 8–20.

Fals Borda, O. (1979) 'Investigating reality in order to transform it: The Columbian experience', *Dialectical Anthropology*, 4: 33–55.

Friere, P. (1982) 'Creating alternative research methods: Learning to do it by doing it', in B. Hall, A. Gilette and R. Tandon (eds) *Creating Knowledge: A Monopoly?* (29–37), New Delhi: Society for Participatory Research in Asia.

Hodgkinson, H. (1957) 'Action research – a critique', *Journal of Educational Sociology*, 31: 137–53.

Jolley, G. M. (2008) 'Evaluation of an action research project in workforce development and organizational change: Healthy ageing – nutrition', *Evaluation Journal of Australasia*, 8(1): 11–19.

Kember, D., Ha, T.-S., Lam, B.-H., Lee, A., Ng, S., Yan, L. *et al.* (1997) 'The diverse role of the critical friend in supporting educational action research projects', *Educational Action Research*, 5(3): 463–81.

Kemmis, S. and McTaggart, R. (1988) (eds) *The Action Research Reader*, 3rd edn, Geelong: Deakin University Press.

Lewin, K. (1946) 'Action research and minority problems', *Journal of Social Issues*, 2(4): 34–46.

Martinek, T. J. and Butt, K. (1988) 'Chapter 8: An Application of an Action Research Model for Changing Instructional Practice', *Journal of Teaching Physical Education,* Special Monograph, 7(3), 214–20.

Stenhouse, L. (1975) *Introduction to Curriculum Research and Development*, London: Heinemann Education.

Tan, W. K., Macdonald, D. and Rossi, T. (2009) 'Educational action research in Singapore: to prove or improve?', *Asia Pacific Journal of Education*, 29(3): 357–71.

Tinning, R. (1992) 'Action research as epistemology and practice: Towards transformative educational practice in physical education', in A. C. Sparkes (ed.), *Research in Physical Education and Sport: Exploring alternative visions* (188–209), London: Falmer Press.

Wadsworth, Y. (1998) 'What is participatory action research?', *Action Research International*, paper 2. Available online at: <http://www.scu.edu.au/schools/gcm/ar/ari/p-ywadsworth98.html> (accessed 27 January 2011).

Wright, J. (1999) 'Changing gendered practices in physical education: Working with teachers', *European Physical Education Review*, 5(3): 181–97.

20 Visual methods in coaching research

Capturing everyday lives

Robyn Jones, Sofia Santos, Isabel Mesquita and David Gilbourne

Figure 20.1 What are we seeing?

Introduction

The aim of this chapter is two-fold: first, to make the case for visual research methods as means of investigation (as opposed to presentation, although in many ways they are synonymous); and second, to present some preliminary findings from a visual project, where the everyday actions of coaches are portrayed as examples of practice. In terms of structure, following this introduction we start by addressing the questions of 'What are visual methods?' and 'Why might they be useful?' This is followed by an examination of more respondent-centred as opposed to research-centred methods; specifically, those of photo-elicitation and photo-voice. We then discuss a principal issue within the field of visual research methods: that of the (quasi-)constructivist nature of the subsequent data. This is because the line between capturing something 'real' and constructing portrayals through such means as photography is quite elusive. Finally, to include an examination of the ethical implications of such work, an example is given of the method in practice from Sofia's PhD project. Here, data (i.e., photographs of coaching) are framed by Sofia's reflections on the dilemmas she faced in coming to terms with the images she produced.

About us

Professor Robyn L. Jones: I am a Professor of Sport and Social Theory at the University of Wales Institute, Cardiff (UWIC), Wales. For some years, I have followed a qualitative research path, which has led me to become increasingly attracted to the field of critical ethnography. My research agenda has also been guided by issues of the everyday in sports coaching: how coaches, athletes and other contextual actors (e.g., assistant coaches, managers and various support staff) generally get on with each other, and the power dynamics inherent within these interactions. Engaging with visual research methods marks a further attempt to explore such relationships and the related social nuances of coaching.

Sofia Santos: I am a PhD student at the Cardiff School of Sport, UWIC. As a researcher, I began by looking at coaches' interventions and related skills in order to inform professional preparation programmes. However, being a coach myself, I recognized that many gaps remained in relation to what we know about the essence of coaching before we could be prescriptive about practice. Consequently, I felt the need to go back and attend to the everyday issues that coaches face; that is, what they actually think, feel and do. Hence, my doctoral work centres on how coaches manage, cope and generally orchestrate others and context towards desired ends. I use critical ethnography as a methodology, of which photography is one aspect.

Dr Isabel Mesquita: I am an Associate Professor at the Faculty of Sport, University of Porto, Portugal. My research interests focus on pedagogical issues related to the coaching process, coach education and coach development. Although much of my work to date has involved the use of quantitative means, I have increasingly used qualitative methods to better engage with the social complexity of coaching. For me, as for Robyn, visual methods mark another step along that road.

Professor David Gilbourne: I am a Professor of Qualitative Research in Sport at UWIC and have specialized in self-narratives in the forms of auto-ethnography, poetic monologues and drama. My interest in representation through theatre and film has led to an associated interest in visual methods as a means of conveying the perceptions of both researcher and participant. In following the above lines of inquiry, I also work alongside specialists from the arts in an attempt to use skills and techniques that relate to the acts of writing, communicating and performing. In that regard, representing qualitative data can become a collaborative venture that draws upon the skills and practices of creative writing, drama and the visual arts. To an extent, and in different ways, these themes relate to issues discussed in the present chapter.

Context

Before we begin in earnest, some brief context is required. As highlighted in our biographies, on first reading it appears that, as authors, we come from quite different investigative roots: from ethnography, from creative writing and even from quantitative means. What unites us, however, is a fascination about sport, and in particular the human interactions to which it gives rise. This led us to jointly conceive of Sofia's PhD project: a critical ethnography of coaching practice, which has a definitive phenomenological bent. This chapter reflects an aspect of this doctoral work, with the other three authors, Robyn, Isabel and Dave, overseeing its progress. What motivated us in conceptualizing the project was a desire for a greater understanding of the essence of coaching; to move away from existing structures and methodologies, towards alternative means of examining the nuances and complexities of how coach, athlete and context all interact to create coaching: a desire that led to the adoption of visual methods.

What are visual methods and why might they be useful?

Recent years have witnessed a growth in visual methods of research inquiry in a number of fields (Stanczak, 2007): for example, sociology, education, cultural studies, anthropology, American studies, communications, gender studies and political science, to name but a few. For many, such methods hold considerable promise for elucidating, clarifying and even redefining established concepts from epistemological, methodological and representational standpoints. It is a movement which Jipson and Paley (1997: 3) claim to have 'pushed beyond conventional formulations', creating an animated experimental and analytical research climate.

Despite this enthusiastic expansion and the rather longer history of the genre (the journal *Visual Studies* celebrated its 25th anniversary in 2010), and notwithstanding the recent special issue of *Qualitative Research in Sport and Exercise* (2010), the impact of visual methods within and on the field of physical education and sport remains meagre. Indeed, according to Grady (2008), visual methods are at something of a crossroads, in that although the field is flourishing in many ways, we still need to convince the established social (and sport) sciences that such methods can benefit their traditional fields of study. This chapter marks an attempt to contribute to that justification and debate. Before we go further, however, it is worth addressing some fundamental questions often posed by those new to the area of visual research methods. These include: What precisely are visual methods? What are they supposed to do? (Becker, 1995) And why might they be useful? (Phoenix, 2010).

Visual methods are, according to Harrison (2004), any research design that uses visual evidence. The general purpose is to further develop our understanding of the social world through studying images produced as part of a culture. It is an approach which engages with visual media through the processes of research and representation. Most often, this involves photography, but can also include maps, videos, sketches, posters, and signs and symbols (Phoenix, 2010). For the sake of expediency, we will concentrate on the use of photographs within this chapter, although much of what we say will have relevance for the other means mentioned.

An often-mooted value of visual methods is that they can offer a different way of knowing our social world, while possessing the ability 'to amass complexly layered meanings in a format which is both easily accessible and retrievable' (Phoenix, 2010: 94). The material is commonly considered rich enough to bear continual reanalysis in different ways. Visual methods are also deemed well situated to explore the mechanisms and context that lie on the fringes of well-visited areas of inquiry, while holding the potential to better understand the complex narratives that participants construct about how they experience life events (Keats, 2009). It has been similarly argued that the resulting images can 'do things': they can make arguments more vivid and lucid, evoking engagement at a number of levels (Grady, 2004). In this respect, pictures are able to 'provide insight and knowledge about the human condition, and lead to a richer understanding of social, cultural, and contextual factors' (Keller et al., 2008: 429).

Although such urgings are persuasive, they have yet to convince all. Critics of visual research methods alternatively contest that the purpose seems merely to 'celebrate what we see', as opposed to carrying out a 'dispassionate examination of relationships' (Grady, 2008). Meanwhile, other criticisms centre on the inadequacy of such methods to record non-visual sensory perceptions (Marks, 2000). Our intention here, however, is not to specifically address these (and other) perceived shortcomings (others have done so in much greater depth and detail, e.g., Pink, 2009) but to acknowledge that visual research methods remain a contested area.

In challenging this dissenting view, advocates of visual methods believe that a particular value lies in their ability to 'open up zones of possibility for intellect and imagination', to journey into 'unexplored space' (Jipson and Paley, 1997: 5). This notion of exploration is important and is certainly worth emphasizing as we build the case for significance. This is because the worth of visual methods is often posited in terms of not reproducing existing narratives, of decentring and even of re-thinking fundamental issues of research practice, such as construction, representation and meaning. Such a journey, however, demands the company and commitment of 'readers' as well as 'authors'. This is because the analytical frame or scaffold found in other forms of research, such as the null hypothesis, the rigid interview schedule or systematic data analyses, is generally absent from visual methodologies.

At a more practical level, the wider point of using visual methods is to draw attention to both the banality and the spontaneity of existence; the largely taken-for-granted clandestine world which nevertheless forms the connective tissue of human activities (Gardiner, 2000; Lefebvre, 1987). For example, the intensity of gaze, the distance between colleagues, a gentle moment between friends. The use of such methods, then, suggests a quest for particularity, not sequence, aligning them with the practical and the everyday, as opposed to the foundational and eternal (Deleuze and Guattari, 1983). In the words of Robert Frank, who became one of the main visual artists of the mid-20th century, as he went about developing his seminal reality-documentary project *The Americans*:

> I speak of the things that are there, anywhere and everywhere – easily found, not easily selected and interpreted. A small catalogue comes to the mind's eye: a

town at night, the man who owns three cars and the man who owns none, the farmer and his children, the dictation of taste, the dream of grandeur, the faces of the leaders and the faces of the followers.

(Tucker and Brookman, 1986: 20)

Visual researchers can categorize and analyse such images, or can study the social settings in which they are produced and absorbed. Rather than the obvious foreground, then, visual methods are often capable of generating considerable detailed information about background context. Indeed, such images are surrounded by a sociological text: the seating or standing arrangements evident on public transport, the proximity or distance between the people when socializing, the facial emotions and the sideways glances. An examination of such components holds the potential to bring the unconscious to the surface by engaging the self in reflexive conversations about the other and context (Jones, 2008; 2009): that is, to 'turn the internally *somatic* into the externally *semantic*' (Spry, 2001: 721). The images produced, through our examination of their creation, consumption and meaning, hold the promise of communicating sociological understandings.

The differing faces of visual methods

What we have discussed so far in this chapter can be loosely termed *researcher-created data*: that is, empirical researchers typically looking and perceiving, and recording or documenting their observations. Another principal means of visual research, however, results in *respondent-centred data*, which frequently involves collaboratively producing visual materials with research participants. This latter method is often said to be an empowering one (although such claims appear a little ambitious at times) since it gives participants a creative opportunity to explore and examine issues from their viewpoint. Such methods include photo-elicitation (Prosser, 1998), and photo-voice (Lopez, Eng, Randall-David and Robinson, 2005; Wang and Pies, 2004). Although gaining credibility as their usage increases, they remain rather under-used methods, which nevertheless hold the potential to 'uncover "edge" or frontier elements that enhance self-report measures' to better capture the framing cultural and social context (Keller et al., 2008: 429).

Photo-elicitation is based on the simple idea of inserting a photograph into a research interview. It consequently involves a 'select number of photographs assembled by the investigator, or produced by the participant and used to stimulate interview dialogue' (Keller et al., 2008: 429). Photographs are selected for this purpose based on their significance to the interviewee, with this meaning being discussed with an interviewer (i.e., the researcher) (Collier and Collier, 1986). By prompting the interviewee to 'tell me about this photograph', the focus is shifted from the empirical objective (of the image) to what it means for those being questioned. In this respect, photographs are used as a 'can opener' for deeper reflection and discussion within the interview process (Collier and Collier, 1986). Using images in this way holds the potential to relocate research participants more as collaborators rather than mere passive subjects. It is a means capable of capturing contextual social and cultural knowledge, while also allowing space for participants to take photographs of themes important to them (Pink, 2001). The method, of course, is based on the assumption of the utility of photographs in prompting reflections that words alone cannot.

An insightful example of photo-elicitation in practice was provided by Clark-Ibáñez (2007) in her study of inner-city Los Angeles children. The author explains not only her rationale for using the method, but also some of the problematic logistics associated with it. These included issues of access and institutional support (magnified when working with children) and the development of further levels of intimacy with the participants (as compared with regular face-to-face interviews). In doing so, Clark-Ibáñez (2007) injects a degree of realism into the method that is sometimes overlooked. Nevertheless, hearing the children talk about the(ir) photographs through greatly extended personal narratives about what was important to them in their lives and why, alerted Clark-Ibáñez (2007) to details she might have otherwise considered 'background': a development which considerably enriched her 'findings'.

Photo-voice, developed primarily by Caroline Wang and Mary Ann Burris, is another participatory research method which differs from photo-elicitation in that it definitively involves giving cameras to participants whose agency in deeply engaging with, and representing their own, social contexts has been limited (Wang and Burris, 1997; Wang, Wu, Zhan and Carovano, 1998). Like photo-elicitation, however, it uses a combination of photography and discussion of the resulting images to articulate participants' experiences and views on a certain topic. The intention is to gain insight into how social actors conceptualize their circumstances and contexts, thus bringing the perspectives of those being studied into the heart of the unfolding investigative and policy-making process. The subsequent goal, which again highlights a divergence from photo-elicitation, is to assess community needs and to act on that assessment. In this respect, it is a practical (action research-orientated) investigative means, with a mission to bring positive social change to generally marginalized communities.

An issue to consider: The quasi-constructivist nature of visual research methods

The line between capturing something 'real' and constructing portrayals through photography is elusive. Indeed, images tend to ask us to hold both positions simultaneously (Stanczak, 2007). They demand that 'this has been' (as captured in the photograph), while also eliciting various subjectivities which can and should be further scrutinized (as related to the role of the photographer in being responsible for the photograph). Recent analyses, in line with a post-modernist turn, have tended towards this latter view, claiming that because such images, like other texts, are constructed, they may be deconstructed in a variety of ways. Hence, reality is not simply captured in the photograph, but chosen, interpreted and framed by the photographer. Such a view adheres to Urry's (1990) 'social construction of gaze' (a construct based on the earlier writings of Foucault [e.g., 1975]), where the eye is never considered 'naked'. Of course, this is a notion that applies equally to the viewers of the images taken. Here, what is perhaps missing from the image for some is not missing for others, who have looked for and found something totally different in the pictures presented: the interpretation dependent on the assumptions, positions and experiences each reader brings to the text (Stanczak, 2007).

The constructivist nature of the process of visual work was well argued by Goldstein (2007) in his chapter provocatively titled 'All photos lie'. Goldstein claimed that every image is manipulated, with the content dependent on a large number of (technical and aesthetic) choices made by the photographer based on intent. Any photograph then, represents 'a choice by the photographer to depict one among an infinite number of moments' (p. 72). The intent can be further buttressed or realized through selective editing, sequencing and/or cropping (i.e., opting for one portion of an image over others) (an example of this is provided later in the case study section). Hence, for Goldstein, the *decisive* moment is really the *decided* moment. As researchers with post-modern tendencies, we can easily relate to such sentiments. However, despite this subjective or interpretive turn, we would like to re-emphasize that realist assumptions are also present within visual research methods. In this respect, although 'the camera is susceptible to the selectivity of the operator, it is not selective once the shutter is opened' (Stanczak, 2007: 7). This was a point also made by Grady (2008), who believed that pictures provide us with two different kinds of information: a *personal* record of affective engagement with a particular scene which, in turn, produces an *impersonal* record of actuality. Such duality suggests that images should not be confined to one discipline, epistemology or reading. This, of course, is a question which stretches from epistemology to methodology. That is, visual methods range from empirical documentation (echoing a realist stance) to that of narrative storytelling (an interpretive or critical position). The point to remember here perhaps is that images (to various degrees) are both *decided* and *decisive* (Stanczak, 2007). It is a debate that is both ongoing and challenging, and one with which visual researchers certainly need to engage.

A case study in practice

The case study on which we draw is an aspect of Sofia's ongoing PhD work at UWIC. The aim of the study lies in exploring the complexities in terms of the contested and negotiated nature of (trampoline) coaches' practice. More precisely, the principal objectives relate to examining such issues as why do coaches think what they do works? How do coaches ensure athlete (and other stakeholder) compliance? What social power structures are at work? And what types of social interactions and exchanges do coaches engage in to realize desired ends (and why)? Taking account of its interpretive epistemology, we decided to employ an ethnographic methodology that included visual means, together with interview and observational methods.

Although certainly important within ethnographic research in general, the use of visual images within the project brought issues of ethics sharply to the fore: particularly, and rather unsurprisingly, those related to participant (non-)anonymity. Being guided by the British Sociological Association's (BSA) (2006) code of ethics as related to visual methods, all respondents at the beginning of the research were fully informed about the purpose of the work (i.e., its non-evaluative, exploratory nature), who would be undertaking it, why it was being undertaken, and how the resultant findings were to be disseminated and used. Written informed consent was obtained from the participants, with care being taken not to give unrealistic guarantees of confidentiality (BSA, 2006). Although it wasn't invoked, as initial agreement did not pose a problem, we developed the caveat here that if informed consent was not totally forthcoming from a particular individual, the level of confidentiality agreed with that particpant would dictate the use of the visual data collected about them. Consent was not assumed as a once-and-for-all event, but as a process subject to constant renegotiation as the project unfolded. Here, pictures taken were presented to those who featured prominently in them to ascertain agreement for use, which occasionally required a further explanation of their purpose. The participants were also reassured that they retained the right to withdraw at any time. Although following such guidelines was certainly not totally unproblematic, they nevertheless served as a useful framework in remembering, although the project was committed to the advancement of knowledge, that, in itself, 'was not an entitlement to override the rights of others' (BSA, 2006). Here, then, we hand over to Sofia and her reflections on using visual methods, before presenting some images from her unfolding work to conclude the chapter.

Sofia's reflections

I felt my preparation for the photographic data-gathering component of the project was pretty comprehensive. I had attended the required research methods component which is built into the PhD programme at UWIC, in addition to more critical qualitative research sessions run by one of my supervisors, Dave Gilbourne. I was also engaged in a continuous dialogue about the methodology with my other supervisors, Robyn and Isabel, while I had earlier attended a photographic course at home in Portugal before starting the PhD. Like many ethnographers (and in particular, phenomenologists), however, entering 'the field' with my trusty camera was far from being an unproblematic process. Decisions about what to observe, what to look for and what to record required much time, consideration and thought. Right from the start, I was constantly reflecting (with my supervisors) about why I took the pictures I did. What were my intentions? What did they really reflect? And how did they complement or conflict with the textual narrative?

To begin with, I tended to use the camera to qualify or justify my preceding field notes: to record 'stuff' I'd already seen. I just found it hard to wander outside those parameters. The objectives (although loosely intentioned) were a comforting yet rather restrictive safety net. However, once I started to really reflect on the pictures, I began to see other things in them: small things that I hadn't really noticed (or intended) when I took the shot. These included a particular look or glance, the general messiness of the context, and how interaction in the foreground (the principal reason for taking the picture) impacted on what was happening in the background. A particular example of this was when I compared photos from training sessions and those from competitions. On reflection, the training images highlighted a certain detached observation by the coaches: a focus on precision, instruction and feedback.

Conversely, the photographs taken within competitions increasingly reflected the coaches' ethic of care and support.

I consequently became a little more relaxed in terms of not looking for definitive, decisive moments, and being more satisfied with capturing the mundane, which had a particular richness of its own. No doubt, with hindsight, this was a part of my evolution and maturity as a researcher of the 'everyday'. On further reading, however, I became somewhat aware that I was perhaps experiencing a greater personal engagement with what Sarah Pink (2009) recently termed 'sensory ethnography'. This was where (as a former and still occasionally practising coach) I used my own sensorial experiences of the context to apprehend and comprehend the experiences, ways of knowing and practices of those I was studying. I suppose, in Pink's words, I was developing a better feel for accessing the coaches' 'embodied, emplaced knowing' (2009: 47) as a basis to understand their culturally located perceptions, actions and meanings. However, I feel I'm drifting into another area of ethnography here, which probably deserves a chapter of its own. Suffice to say that this personal evolution was far from being a linear process; it took (and continues to take) much reflection, reflexivity and critical conversations on a personal and social (with the supervisory team) level.

The issue of 'creating' the pictures (or not) also played on my mind. That is, although I take full responsibility for the photographs taken in terms of constructing them, I can't help thinking that pictures hold the capacity to show the accuracy of context 'as is' much more than written text. They are certainly able to depict in much greater clarity than my written descriptions, however carefully crafted. In that respect, I like their immediacy. On the other hand, though, I'm fully aware that others will see them differently, as my interpretations, and they will be read accordingly. It is a debate that I've not yet fully resolved, but then again maybe that's the way it's meant to be, in that there are no clean or clear-cut answers.

Finally then, I present the pictures overleaf as some early results from my visual ethnographic project. As a group, we debated if they needed some theoretical framing; some 'telling' as opposed to 'showing'. Being aware of the benefits of the latter in guiding discovery, we nevertheless concluded that the pointers already given within the text in relation to exploring coaches' everyday feelings and actions were probably enough. This was because the last thing I wanted to do was to encourage a single reading of this multilayered, dynamic, complex text (Jones, 2009). I hope you find the pictures both interesting and stimulating.

Key terms

Visual research methods   Any research design that uses visual evidence (Harrison, 2004). The general purpose is to further develop our understanding of the social world through studying images produced as part of a culture.

The 'everyday'   A sociology of the everyday relates to the value of examining the subterranean social bonds that make human relationships work.

Sports coaching/pedagogy   The activity of educating, developing or improving others; within coaching, in the context of sport.

Figure 20.2 Data from Sofia's visual ethnographic project

References

Becker, H. (1995) 'Backup of visual sociology, documentary photography, and photojournalism: It's (almost) all a matter of context', *Visual Sociology*, 10(1–2): 5–14.

BSA (2006) 'Statement of Ethical Practice for the British Sociological Association – Visual Sociology Group.' Available: http://www.visualsociology.org.uk/about/ethical_statement.php.

Clark-Ibáñez, M. (2007) 'Inner-city children in sharper focus; Sociology of childhood and photo elicitation interviews', in G. C. Stanczak (ed.) *Visual Research Methods; Image, Society and Representation* (167–96), Thousand Oaks, CA: Sage.

Collier, J. and Collier, M. (1986) *Visual Anthropology: Photography as a Research Method*, Albuquerque: University of New Mexico Press.

Deleuze, G. and Guattari, F. (1983) *Rhizome. On the line* (trans. J. Johnson), New York: Semi(o)texte.

Foucault, M. (1975) *Birth of the Clinic: An Archaeology of Medical Perception*, New York: Vintage Books.

Gardiner, M.E. (2000) *Critiques of everyday life*, London: Routledge.

Goldstein, B. (2007) 'All photos lie', in G. C. Stanczak (ed.) *Visual Research Methods: Image, Society and Representation* (61–81), Thousand Oaks, CA: Sage.

Grady, J. (2004) 'Working with visible evidence: An invitation and some practical advice', in C. Knowles and P. Sweetman (eds) *Picturing the Social Landscape: Visual Methods and the Sociological Imagination* (18–32), London: Routledge.

Grady, J. (2008) 'Visual research at the crossroads', *Forum Qualitative Sozialforschung/Forum: Qualitative Social Research*, 9(3), Art, 38, <http://nbn-resolving.de/urn:nbn:de0114-fqs0803384>

Harrison, B. (2004) 'Photographic visions and narrative inquiry', in M. Bamburg and M. Andrews (eds) *Considering Counter-narratives, Narrating, Resisting, Making Sense* (113–36), Philadelphia: John Benjamins.

Jipson, J. and Paley, N. (1997) 'Daredevil research: Re-creating analytic practice; An introduction', in L. Jipson and N. Paley (eds) *Daredevil Research: Re-creating Analytic Practice* (1–24), New York: Peter Lang.

Jones, R. L. (2008) 'Representing coaching through the visual arts: Stories through photography', presentation given at the Narrative Research in Sport and Exercise: Exploring the Themes of Story Analysts and Story Tellers conference, Wales Millennium Centre, Cardiff, 24–25 June.

Jones, R. L. (2009) 'Coaching as caring ("The smiling gallery"): Accessing hidden knowledge', *Physical Education and Sport Pedagogy*, 14(4): 377–90.

Keats, P. A. (2009) 'Multiple text analysis in narrative research: visual, written, and spoken stories of experience', *Qualitative Research*, 9(2): 181–95.

Keller, C., Fleury, J., Perez, A., Ainsworth, B. and Vaughan, L. (2008) 'Using visual methods to uncover context', *Qualitative Health Research*, 18: 428–36.

Lefebvre, H. (1987) 'The everday and everdayness', *Yale French Studies*, 73, 7–11.

Lopez, E. D., Eng, E., Randall-David, E. and Robinson, N. (2005) 'Quality-of-life concerns of African American breast cancer survivors within rural North Carolina: Blending the techniques of photovoice and grounded theory', *Qualitative Health Research*, 15(1): 99–115.

Marks. L. (2000) *The Skin of the Film*, Durham, NC: Duke University Press.

Phoenix, C. (2010) 'Seeing the world of physical culture: The potential of visual methods for qualitative research in sport and exercise', *Qualitative Research in Sport and Exercise*, 2(2): 93–108.

Pink, S. (2001) *Doing Visual Anthropology*, London: Sage.

Pink, S. (2009) *Doing Sensory Ethnography*, London: Sage.

Prosser, J. (1998) *Image-based Research: A Sourcebook for Qualitative Researchers*, London: Falmer Press.

Qualitative Research in Sport and Exercise (special edition) (2010) 2(2).

Spry, T. (2001) 'Performing autoethnography', *Qualitative Inquiry*, 7(6): 706–32.

Stanczak, G. C. (2007) 'Introduction: Images, methodologies and generating social knowledge', in G. C. Stanczak (ed.) *Visual Research Methods: Image, Society and Representation* (1–22), Thousand Oaks, CA: Sage.

Tucker, A. W. and Brookman, P. (1986) *Robert Frank: New York to Nova Scotia*, Boston: Little Brown.

Urry, J. (1990) *The Tourist Gaze*, London: Sage.

Wang, C. and Burris, M. A. (1997) 'Photovoice: concept, methodology and use for participatory needs assessment', *Health and Behaviour*, 24, 3: 369–87.

Wang, C. C. and Pies, C. A. (2004) 'Family, maternal, and child health through photovoice', *Maternal and Child Health Journal*, 8(2): 95–102.

Wang, C. C., Wu, K. Y., Zhan, W. T. and Carovano, K. (1998) 'Photovoice as a participatory health promotion strategy', *Health Promotion International*, 13: 75–86.

21 Grounded theory

*Nicholas L. Holt, Camilla J. Knight and
Katherine A. Tamminen*

Grounded theory methodology is by far the most widely used research method across a wide range of disciplines and subject areas, including social sciences, nursing and healthcare, medical sociology, information systems, psychology, and anthropology.

(Grounded Theory Research Group on Facebook)

Introduction

Grounded theory emerged in the discipline of sociology in the 1960s. At that time, the prevailing approach to conducting research was that researchers developed theories in their labs or offices and then went out to collect data in order to prove or disprove their hypotheses. Grounded theory turns this process on its head. Instead of testing preconceived theories, a grounded theory researcher would go out into the field and collect data in certain settings, or with a certain population, in order to develop a theory based on and relevant to the participants' experiences. Such theories can be tested later, of course, but the strength of using grounded theory is that the theories created are 'grounded' in data that reflect people's experiences in the social world.

About us

Dr Nicholas Holt conducts research examining psychosocial aspects of youth sport. He has used grounded theory methodology to study talent development in professional soccer and parental behaviours during youth sport competitions. He studied and published with Dr Juliet Corbin, who contributed to the development of one of the best-known versions of grounded theory. He has recently been involved in a 'debate' published in the journal *Psychology of Sport and Exercise* regarding the strengths and weaknesses of grounded theory studies. He is particularly interested in helping to improve the use of grounded theory methodology and how to move data analysis beyond 'description' and into the realms of theory development.

Camilla Knight is a PhD candidate who is working with Nicholas Holt and using grounded theory to develop a framework of parenting in youth tennis. Her research has an applied focus and the grounded theory she produces should provide guidelines that can be used by sport organizations to optimize parental involvement in sport.

Dr Katherine Tamminen is a post-doctoral fellow who used grounded theory for her PhD work, which she completed at the University of Alberta under the supervision of Nicholas Holt. She created a grounded theory of how adolescent athletes learn to cope with stressors in sport. Her research will help advance conceptual understanding of socialization processes as well as provide practical guidelines for helping to teach athletes how to cope with stress.

What is grounded theory?

There is not just one version of grounded theory. Rather, the term 'grounded theory' refers to a 'family' of methodologies that share the same basic principle of creating explanatory theories based on data collected 'in the field'. Grounded theory is based on the premise that theory is indispensable if the aim is to gain deep knowledge of social phenomena (Glaser and Strauss, 1967). Thus, the purpose of using grounded theory is to create theories that explain some kind of social phenomena. The production of a theory, rather than a hierarchical list of themes or ideas, is the distinguishing feature of this qualitative methodology.

Theories can take many forms, varying in terms of their sophistication, structure and modes of derivation (Morse, 1997). Some theories are highly conceptual, with broad applicability and scope, whereas other theories are more parsimonious. From a grounded theory perspective, Strauss and Corbin (1998: 22) suggested:

> Theory denotes a set of well-developed categories (e.g. themes, concepts) that are systematically interrelated through statements of relationship to form a theoretical framework that explains some relevant social, psychological, educational, nursing, or other phenomenon. These statements of relationship explain who, what, when, where, why, how, and with what consequences an event occurs.

Glaser and Strauss (1967) differentiated between formal (concept-focused) theories, and substantive (topic-focused) theories. Substantive theories are more specific to group and place, whereas formal theories are less specific, and can be applied to a wider range of disciplinary concerns and problems. Most grounded theories are process bound, not extending beyond the scope of the phenomenon under study and are only generalizable to other contexts and other participants experiencing similar phenomena (Morse, 1997).

Why do researchers use grounded theory?

The selection of any method is based on the research question posed. The research question is the specific query 'that sets the parameters of the project and suggests the methods to be used for data gathering and analysis' (Strauss and Corbin, 1998: 35). Strauss and Corbin suggested that grounded theorists are not solely interested in individual experience. Rather, grounded theorists are more concerned with discovering participants' patterns of action/interaction with changes in conditions, either internal or external, to the process itself. Indeed, 'grounded theory is a transactional system, that is, it allows you to study the interactive nature of events' (Strauss and Corbin, 1990: 159).

The focus on processes of change and interactions between individual experiences within a larger structure (e.g., a sport context) makes grounded theory an appealing methodology for a range of research questions. Some of the research questions we have answered using grounded theory include: 'What does it take to make it as a professional soccer player?' 'How can parental involvement in tennis be optimized?' 'What are the roles of parents and coaches in helping adolescent athletes learn to cope with stressors?' Each of these questions requires an understanding of a process involving interactions between participants and their social context.

Grounded theory methodology is particularly useful when there is no pre-existing theory available to explain a certain social process, where theories are under-developed for particular populations, or if existing theories are incomplete. Good grounded theories also have practical applications. The methodology is less useful in areas that have numerous well-tested, existing theories. After all, there is little value in creating new theories if there are already extensive pre-existing theories (although most theories are contestable and hotly contested!). Grounded theory, like many other qualitative approaches, is not particularly well suited to *testing* existing theories, although it has clear value in *explaining* or *illustrating* such theories.

Distinguishing between different versions of grounded theory

Grounded theory was originally introduced by Barney Glaser and Anselm Strauss (Glaser and Strauss, 1967). Their fundamental concern was that concepts and the overall theory must emerge from the data, rather than researchers forcing data into pre-defined categories. Upon completion of their joint work, Glaser and Strauss continued to develop their individual conceptualizations of grounded theory (Glaser, 1992; 1978; Strauss and Corbin, 1990; 1998). Although both remained true to the basic features of grounded theory, it became apparent that Glaser and Strauss held different opinions regarding certain aspects of the methodology. As such, the originators of the methodology 'split' and developed their own versions of grounded theory. Since then, each has shifted his position on certain points and added others, while a 'second generation' of grounded theorists with their own unique perspectives has emerged.

Expanding Glaser and Strauss's original work, several different perspectives on grounded theory methodology now exist. For example, Bryant and Charmaz's (2007) edited work titled *The Sage Handbook of Grounded Theory* has 27 chapters from 34 contributors who have all 'studied, applied, taught, and/or written about' grounded theory (p. 11). Arguably, there are three distinct versions of grounded theory, namely the Glaserian approach, the Straussian approach and Charmaz's constructivist approach. Although there are many common features in the different versions of grounded theory, there are also several subtle differences. For example, Glaser defined grounded theory as a method of discovery and treated categories as emergent from the data. Researchers using this approach often attempt to maintain distance from the data and limit the extent to which their own experiences or knowledge are integrated within the theory. Strauss, while agreeing that theories should be traceable to the data, argued that researchers' interaction with data leads to the construction of a grounded theory, rather than a theory emerging from the data. Similarly, Charmaz's approach is situated within this type of constructivist perspective. That is, researchers construct a theory through their interactions with the data and, while the theory will be grounded in the participants' experiences, Charmaz argued that it is impossible to create a theory entirely separate from the researcher.

For the purposes of comparison, we provide three examples upon which versions of grounded theory differ. These examples by no means do justice to the history and development of grounded theory, and there are important philosophical and epistemological issues that we do not address. Indeed, it would be almost impossible to capture the variations in grounded theory in a single chapter because each version and other derivatives have evolved and changed from their original conceptions (for further information on the history of, and variations in, grounded theory see Bryant and Charmaz, 2007; Morse, Noerager Stern, Corbin, Bowers, Charmaz and Clarke, 2009).

Coding

Coding (most simply explained as the allocation of labels to data) is fundamental to the process of data analysis and the production of a grounded theory. Ultimately, by coding data using various techniques, researchers move from interview transcripts (and other raw data) into interpretation of data and the production of a grounded theory. In this sense, coding serves the same purpose in each version of grounded theory. However, there are slight differences in the processes of coding between the versions of grounded theory – most obviously in terms of the language used to describe coding procedures. Table 21.1 provides brief descriptions of the coding process used in Glaserian, Straussian and constructivist grounded theory. Although the table clearly shows differences in some of the terms used, we would argue that the basic underlying functions of coding do not vary hugely across the different versions of grounded theory. There are, however, differences in the ways in which different grounded theorists think that coding procedures should be applied.

Forcing versus emergence

Glaser (1992) argued that Strauss's analytical tools could be criticized for 'forcing' the data into preconceived concepts rather than allowing concepts to 'emerge' from the data (i.e., pre-existing ideas may be placed on the data rather than the data guiding the generation of the theory). However, the notion of 'emergence' has also been criticized because it implies that 'a theory is embedded in the data and it is the task of the analyst to discover what the theory is' (Corbin and Holt, 2005: 49). In other words, emergence implies that there is one 'true' or 'real' theory that exists in the data and the researcher is responsible for 'finding' it. Constructivist grounded theory also rejects this idea of emergence (i.e., finding the theory in the data) and

Table 21.1 Comparison of coding across different versions of grounded theory

Glaserian (Glaser 1978, 1992)	Straussian (Corbin and Strauss, 2008; Strauss and Corbin, 1998)	Constructivist (Charmaz, 2006)
Two stages of coding to move from substantive codes to a grounded theory:	Three stages of coding to move from description to theory:	At least two stages of coding, followed by theoretical integration:
1. Substantive coding; Through a process of open coding (examination of all the pieces of data), researchers develop substantive codes, which specify the substance or meaning of each segment of data. Substantive codes are developed by comparing data and incidents through constant comparative analysis.	1. Open coding; Described as a brainstorming approach, in which researchers fracture the data into their smallest units. Microanalysis, which is the detailed coding of each identified concept, is an important form of open coding.	1. Initial coding; Detailed examination of each fragment of data to identify actions. Words/labels are allocated to data to reflect the actions identified. It is critical that the researcher stays close to the data during this process. Coding may occur through word-by-word, line-by-line or incident-to-incident coding.
2. Theoretical coding; Following substantive coding, theoretical codes are applied to the data to allow researchers to integrate substantive codes into a theory. Theoretical codes are always available to researchers and are based on concepts inherent in sociology and philosophy. Theoretical codes provide researchers with a means of ordering substantive codes within the social world. Glaser established a list of 18 coding families (groups of theoretical codes) that researchers may use to identify relationships between substantive codes, leading to the development of fully integrated theories.	2. Axial coding; Through this process concepts identified during open coding are related to each other. In their original texts, Strauss and Corbin (1990; 1998) placed greater emphasis upon axial coding, encouraging researchers to consider their data in terms of conditions, actions and consequences to identify relationships.	2. Focused coding; The process of selecting the most useful codes developed during initial coding and then testing them against further data. Coding of larger segments of data occurs. Through this process, codes become more directed and selective. Researchers also begin to think more conceptually, leading towards theoretical integration.
	3. Theoretical integration: Originally termed selective coding, theoretical integration is the process of linking all the categories together and refining ideas. Categories are eventually integrated within the core category, leading to the generation of the grounded theory.	3. Theoretical integration: This is the process by which categories identified in focused coding are integrated. Specific relationships between categories are identified. Charmaz encourages the use of Glaser's 18 coding families at this point, if they fit the data and the previous analysis.

rather suggests that theory is constructed through the interaction of the researcher and the data collection and analysis process (Charmaz, 2006). Different researchers may develop slightly different theories when presented with the same data. Therefore, it is important that researchers are transparent and document the way in which they develop their theory.

Use of theory

Glaser (1992) argued against conducting a review of literature (and using pre-existing theory) early in the research process, because he believed it could lead to researchers applying preconceived ideas to the data, rather than letting the data speak for themselves. As grounded theory methodology is designed to create new theories grounded in data collected in the field, it is inappropriate for existing theory to be identified a priori and then data simply matched with that theory. Similarly, though, researchers seldom commence a study with a tabula rasa (blank slate), entering the field with no knowledge of the research areas (Weed, 2009). Previous research and theory may inform the conceptual context and research questions, may be used at some point during the analysis, or even as late as the discussion/interpretation of the results (Sandelowski, 1993). A literature review is a valuable and necessary tool to develop research questions, identify whether pre-existing theories exist and provide justifications for a study (Corbin and Strauss, 2008). Charmaz (2006) agrees with Glaser that researchers should avoid imposing pre-existing theory onto data, but recognizes that it is impossible to approach research without pre-existing ideas. Thus, it has been argued more recently that grounded theory researchers should approach their studies with an open mind but not an empty mind (Dey, 1999).

As the three points discussed above should indicate, the differences between versions of grounded theory are often subtle and nuanced, further complicated by the fact that these versions of grounded theory have all evolved over time. Perhaps the most important issue to emphasize is that researchers new to grounded theory need to grasp the history of the methodology and all its versions. Researchers should then clearly specify which version of grounded theory they are using and avoid 'mixing and matching' techniques from different versions of the methodology (Weed, 2009). In other words, pick the most appropriate approach for your study (and your philosophical perspective) and stick with it!

How to use grounded theory

Having established some of the differences between the three main versions of grounded theory, in this section we list some of the common features (also see Holt and Tamminen, 2010a; 2010b; Weed, 2009). Again, this list is by no means definitive. Furthermore, it is heavily influenced by our own background in the Straussian approach. But it does provide a fair representation of the key techniques usually associated with a grounded theory methodology. Of course, to reiterate, researchers must also read the original methodological guidelines associated with the particular version of grounded theory they are going to use.

Iterative process of simultaneous data collection and analysis

A classic feature of grounded theory studies is that they follow an iterative and cyclical process of data collection and analysis. That is, data analysis begins as soon as the first data are collected, and there is an interaction between data collection and analysis throughout the study. In other words, data collection and analysis occur *simultaneously*. Importantly, this early engagement in data analysis allows researchers to redirect the focus of data collection *during* a study, which may result in the revision of interview guides and, often more importantly, the need to sample additional participants or settings beyond those originally identified in a research proposal. Hence, the principle of simultaneous data collection and analysis requires researchers to have a flexible study plan.

Theoretical sampling

The interplay between data collection and analysis is facilitated via theoretical sampling, another crucial feature of the methodology. Theoretical sampling is 'sampling on the basis of emerging concepts' (Strauss and Corbin, 1998: 73). As data collection and analysis interact they influence the ongoing sampling process. Theoretical sampling drives the iterative process and is associated with sampling new people and settings to advance the research process. There are several different ways to design studies that embrace the concept of simultaneous data collection and analysis and theoretical sampling. But, whereas a great deal has been written about how to conduct analysis in grounded theory, far less attention has been devoted to explaining how theoretical sampling may actually occur. (The case studies at the end of this chapter detail two different ways to approach theoretical sampling.)

One exception is the work of Bruce (2007), who described two ways in which theoretical sampling may progress: the funnel and the hourglass approaches. The terms 'funnel' and 'hourglass' refer to the shape of the sampling strategies, were they to be presented in a visual way. The funnel strategy involves initially obtaining a very broad selection of participants' experiences and then slowly focusing in on key participants, events and concepts. The hourglass strategy, while also starting broad to gain a range of participants' experiences, becomes more focused earlier in the study. Then, through the iterative process of data collection and analysis, researchers may realize the need to broaden their sampling in the latter stages of the research to ensure an adequate level of data saturation (also see Holt and Tamminen, 2010a).

Coding techniques

As previously mentioned, specific coding techniques differ depending on the version of grounded theory adopted. However, the fundamental principle of analysis is the same – researchers move from basic description to theory development by analysing the data at increasingly abstract levels. To do this, researchers attach codes (labels) to segments of data. Coding then moves to more abstract levels as relationships are identified between segments of data. The higher, more abstract level of coding continues until a core category (i.e., the idea that represents the main focus of the research) is identified.

Strauss and Corbin's (1990; 1998; Corbin and Strauss, 2008) approach to grounded theory is often selected by new grounded theorists because it has a clearly described data analysis process. In this approach, data analysis occurs through three basic coding stages: open coding (including microanalysis), axial coding, and theoretical integration (Corbin and Strauss, 2008). Microanalysis is word-by-word, or line-by-line coding, during which the researcher identifies individual segments of data and uncovers the range of potential meanings contained within the participants' words. Microanalysis underpins open coding, which is the process of breaking data apart and separating data into distinct concepts, while also defining concepts in terms of their properties and dimensions. Axial coding then allows the researcher to reconstruct the data as relationships between concepts are identified. The final stage of coding is theoretical integration (Corbin and Strauss, 2008), or selective coding (Strauss and Corbin, 1998). This is the process through which concepts are integrated within the core category to develop and refine the theory. In this stage, the researcher outlines the theoretical scheme and explains relationships between the concepts as they relate to the core category.

For example, in a recent study (Knight and Holt, 2011) examining parental involvement in junior tennis conducted by two of the co-authors (from Camilla's PhD work), initial codes relating to tournament goals, long-term goals and reasons for involvement in tennis were identified. As coding progressed, it became apparent that these codes were related and a broader category labelled 'goals' was developed. Further analysis indicated that parents, players and coaches should share such goals, and communication of goals was fundamental to parental involvement in tennis. In developing this category, and moving to more abstract levels of thinking, it was apparent that these shared goals required understanding from parents and were specific to the individual player. Thus, this category of 'shared and communicated goals' was integrated within a core category labelled 'understanding and enhancing your child's tennis experience', which captured all the properties of the initial, more descriptive, codes. Table 21.2 contains three excerpts from interviews to illustrate the coding process as it was conducted for this study.

At the risk of oversimplifying the process, in broad terms it would be fair to say that the coding process first deconstructs the raw data (i.e., interview quotes) into meaning units via open coding. Data are then reconstructed in meaningful ways through axial coding, and then the researcher seeks to 'bring it all together' during theoretical integration. But this process is complicated by the fact that analysis is a free-flowing (rather than linear) process repeated from the moment the first data are collected, until a final grounded theory is created. Therefore, skilled grounded theorists are able to move between applying different coding techniques at different stages in the research process, while always being mindful that the ultimate goal is to produce a grounded theory explanation (see Corbin and Holt, 2005; 2011).

Table 21.2 Examples of coding

Interview excerpt	Open coding	Axial coding	Theoretical integration
Coach 7: Well, I think the bottom line is that the kid has to make those goals and the self-belief is a massive issue in the sport, I think the sport's becoming more mental. So I think first of all that kid needs to believe that whatever goals they're setting are achievable. It can't be a goal that is set by the coach or the parent. I think communication is also key, whether they agree the goal, ultimately that kid has to agree that goal, otherwise it's going to be difficult to do.	Child goals Self-belief Mental side Set goals Realistic Communicate Accept goals	Long-term goals Shared and realistic Discussed	Individual goals Understand tennis context
Player 39: Well, my goals would have to be, probably, to be a professional, umm, and to really, I just want to enjoy how I play and just enjoy the competition as well. But my parents, I think they would like me to get out of tennis as much enjoyment as I can and umm, only do it if I really really want to, but umm, I think for them, it's also a way to keep me occupied, sometimes, hmmm, yeah, I'd just say that.	Reasons for involvement Changing goals Parents' goals Support child Child's choice	Long-term goals Shared goals	Changing goals Understand child
Parent 9: Well, we have been working together on a general set of goals for my son particularly, we've also done it for my daughter, it's less far reaching but it's something the LTA require you to do anyway, ummm, and so we've been sort of, that's sort of provided a decent amount of information, so whether it's myself and Robert sit down and work out what we think he should be aiming for for the next few months and it sort of puts some structure on it, so again I think it's important that it's all sort of linked together and the coach isn't setting one set of goals for the player and the player isn't setting another set of goals and the parent has a different set of ideas, you know.	Shared goals Standards NGB required Given focus Current goals Focus Consistent Shared goals Same target	Shared goals Direction Shared goals Current goals Shared goals	Understand standards Enhance experience Understand child

Analytic tools

In addition to the principal coding techniques described above, a number of other analytic tools can be used to advance the coding process and help researchers to interact with their data as they move to increasingly abstract levels of thinking (Corbin and Strauss, 2008). There are many different analytic tools (e.g., considering meanings of a word, diagramming, the flip-flop technique, questioning data, and thinking in terms of metaphors and similes); however, one of the most important analytic tools is writing memos. Writing memos is necessary to record immediate illustrations of an idea (Glaser and Strauss, 1967). Memos can aid the exploration of all data, stimulate the development of properties and dimensions of concepts, encourage the researcher to question the data, aid comparison of relationships between concepts, and produce the story to link concepts together. After every coding session, researchers should take the time to write memos in order to track how their analytic thinking is progressing. Memos may take varying forms; below is an example of memos that were written during data collection for the study examining parental involvement in tennis (Knight and Holt, 2011). In keeping with the previous example, these extracts from memos all relate to tennis goals.

15 April 2010: transitions and changes in goals

It seems that it is very important for parents to understand the transitions that tennis players go through regarding competition experiences and reasons for playing tennis. I feel this is particularly important as children get older and their goals change to become more realistic. Additionally, it seems that whether parents or players initiated tennis involvement and the subsequent development of goals is extremely important. It seems that those parents who were initially more involved in tennis might be more likely to become too involved in tennis. It also seems that those parents might be less likely to alter their goals as their children experience transitions. Understanding changes in players' goals and reasons for involvement is important so parents know they have to change their behaviours.

24 April 2010: varying goals for different matches

It seems players develop different goals for different matches – these goals might be developed with coaches or independent of coaches. They might be related to the anticipated outcome of the match, how they perceive their opponent's abilities, how they feel their training is going, what they hope to get out of the tournament etc. The goals may be in relation to specific training goals and progress goals. However, they may also be related to whether players have any expectations (own or parent related) for the outcome of the match. It seems that these various goals are related to the social process of outcome, performance and expectation.

Constant comparison is another technique used within the process of data collection (and further embedded in the simultaneous approach to data collection and analysis). Constant comparison involves 'comparing incident with incident ... in order to classify data. As the researcher moves along with analysis, each incident in the data is compared with other incidents for similarities and differences' (Corbin and Strauss, 2008: 73). In addition to comparing data with data, data can also be compared with concepts, comparisons can be made between concepts, and with the developing theory. This process allows researchers to identify relationships between concepts, develop the properties and dimensions of categories and see what new information they are gaining from the data. Thus, constant comparison aids theory development and helps researchers to recognize when they have reached the point of theoretical saturation.

Qualitative data analysis software packages are often used in grounded theory (in particular, the program NVivo, which was developed specifically for grounded theory). Researchers should view such software packages more like *data management* packages rather than *data analysis* programs. Although programs offer a range of ways of organizing and coding data, we should not lose sight of the fact that the researcher (not the software program) is the analyst in grounded theory. We have found that the premature use of software programs can create a 'code and retrieve' mentality in which researchers seek data (i.e., words, phrases) without engaging in the cognitive process of analysis. That said, these programs are exceptionally useful for organizing and managing large data sets and therefore can help the analyst greatly. But there is no requirement to use data management software when conducting grounded theory studies. In our lab, we tend to have students engage in manual coding first until they demonstrate their understanding of the cognitive components of analysis. They are then free to choose whether or not they need/wish to use particular software programs.

Theoretical saturation

Ultimately, the researcher is working towards obtaining an adequate level of theoretical saturation. Theoretical saturation is 'a matter of reaching the point in the research where collecting new data seems counterproductive; the "new" data that is uncovered does not add that much more to the explanation at this time' (Strauss and Corbin, 1998: 136). Morse (1995) proposed principles that can be used to plan for and make judgements about data saturation. For example, if one selects a 'tight' and cohesive sample, this will provide faster saturation but less generalizability. She suggested that saturation will be achieved faster if theoretical sampling is used, but cautioned researchers to sample all variations in the data. Ultimately, saturated data are full and complete and the theory does not have gaps – the more complete the theoretical saturation, the easier it is to develop a comprehensive theoretical model.

Final product

In terms of producing a final grounded theory, Glaser and Strauss (1967) suggested that the concepts of fit, work, relevance and modifiability can be used to judge the theory. Strauss and Corbin (1998) made suggestions for evaluating the data, theory, research process and empirical grounding of the research. Similarly, Charmaz (2006) recommends judging grounded theory studies in relation to credibility, originality, resonance and usefulness. Again, we encourage investigators to become familiar with their chosen version of grounded theory and the associated criteria for evaluating their research. It is also important to remember that theories can be produced at different levels. For example, substantive theories are relatively specific to a group and/or a place, and therefore apply most readily to issues within a particular discipline (Strauss and Corbin, 1998). On the other hand, it is possible to use grounded theory to create more abstract and formal theories, which are less specific to a group and place and apply to a wider range of issues across disciplines. Generally speaking, most single studies using grounded theory will produce substantive-level theories, which may become more formal theories through additional follow-up research.

Case studies

Two examples from the co-authors' PhD work are provided to bring some of the key concepts reported above to life. Specifically, we focus on the mechanics of theoretical sampling, because although this process is central to grounded theory methodology, it has not been described in much detail in the literature (Bruce, 2007). Theoretical sampling is constrained by the logistical demands of a study, especially for graduate theses or dissertations when students are working on relatively short timelines and tight budgets. These two examples show different ways to adhere to the principle of theoretical sampling within the logistical demands of the research.

A traditional approach

One of the co-authors (Katherine) used a traditional approach to theoretical sampling. Katherine's research involved creating a grounded theory of adolescent athletes' process of learning to cope with stressors in sport, and the way parents and coaches influence that process (Tamminen and Holt, in press). Her research was conducted over the course of several months with athletes, parents and coaches from the same Canadian city in which she resides and studies. The context and logistics allowed her to conduct interviews, transcribe and analyse the interviews, and then redirect her sampling according to the concepts revealed in the analysis, thus adhering closely to the traditional concept of theoretical sampling. In total, she interviewed 17 athletes (8 females, 9 males, mean age = 15.6 years), 10 parents (6 mothers, 4 fathers), and 7 coaches.

In the first phase of data collection (see Figure 21.1), Katherine sampled youth sport participants (aged 11–14 years) and their parents, as well as coaches of adolescent athletes to discover their views about athletes' stress and coping strategies. Once these interviews were analysed, it was apparent that older athletes, who could reflect on their experiences and describe in detail how they learned to cope with stressors, should be sampled. Hence, the analysis redirected the sampling process such that athletes aged 15–18 years were interviewed, as well as their parents and

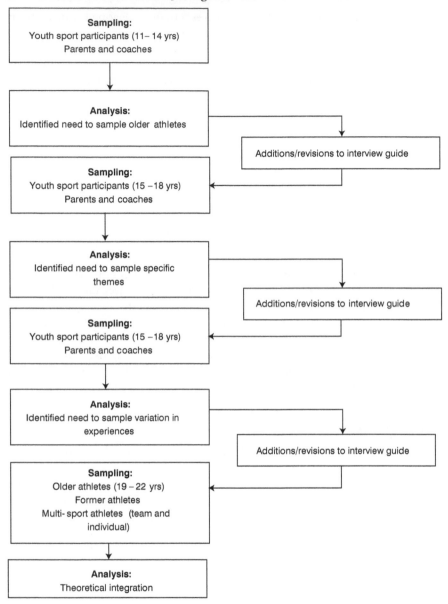

Figure 21.1 A traditional approach to theoretical sampling

coaches. Following the analysis of these interviews, the theoretical sampling changed from sampling *different people* to sampling *different concepts* in the interviews. Thus, more athletes (aged 16–18 years), their parents and coaches were interviewed, but the structure of the interview guide was changed to ask questions about themes that arose from prior analyses. Then, variation sampling was used to interview older athletes

(19–22 years old), athletes who were no longer involved in sports, as well as multi-sport athletes who participated in individual and team sports. This added breadth to the sample and further informed (and helped saturate) the grounded theory Katherine was creating. Participants interviewed in the latter phases of data collection were presented with a model of the emerging theory and were asked to comment on it in order to refine the results. Because Katherine's research was not constrained by time or location, her sampling first examined athletes of different ages and their experiences of learning to cope, and then her sampling focused on specific concepts arising from the analyses undertaken later in the research.

An innovative feature of Katherine's study was that after each interview she recorded memos using an audio recorder. She would record her thoughts/memos in order to capture details that might otherwise be lost and difficult to remember. Later, these audio memos were transcribed and expanded upon in writing, and details were added which helped to contextualize the interview data and document Katherine's thinking about the research process and the analysis. She also engaged in the process of writing memos after every coding session.

A creative approach

In contrast to the traditional approach used by Katherine, the other graduate student co-author (Camilla) used a creative strategy in order to adhere to the principle of theoretical sampling within the strict logistical demands of her study. Camilla developed a grounded theory of optimal parental involvement in junior tennis. Although she is based in Canada, she decided to collect data in the UK because she has extensive knowledge of the British tennis system, having grown up and played tennis there. Her fieldwork was conducted over the course of a 10-week trip to the UK. During this time, she conducted three focus groups (two with tennis players and one with tennis coaches) and 72 individual interviews (17 with tennis parents, 14 with tennis coaches, and 41 with current or ex- junior tennis players).

As mentioned previously, a key feature of grounded theory is the interaction between data collection and analysis. However, the logistical aspects of Camilla's study meant that it was unrealistic for her to follow the traditional route – of conducting an interview, transcribing it, analysing it for concepts and relationships, making the appropriate changes to the interview guide, and selecting participants – that might verify, expand upon or explain emerging ideas. Instead, she engaged in a more immediate process of data analysis and theoretical sampling to enable her to make a judgement that she had achieved an adequate level of theoretical saturation while she was on her fieldwork trip (see Figure 21.2).

Camilla adopted the following strategy. Following every interview or focus group, she engaged in what she called 'audio analysis'. After every interview – and prior to the next interview – she listened to the recording of the interview and wrote notes identifying ideas, possible concepts and relationships. In other words, she did microanalysis of the audio files, rather than of the written transcripts (because she simply did not have the time to transcribe each interview during the fieldwork trip). Based on this initial audio analysis, she often made changes to the

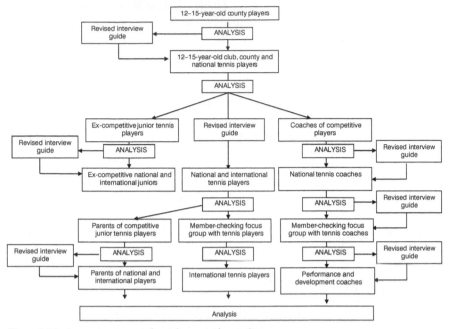

Figure 21.2 A creative approach to theoretical sampling

interview guide in preparation for the next interview. She also sought new settings (locations) to sample as a result of the concepts identified during early stages of analysis. In this case, Camilla had to 'cram' the multiple techniques of grounded theory into a 10-week period. This highlights not only that there is a need for flexibility when conducting grounded theory studies, but also that researchers should enter a research setting fully familiar with and trained in the guiding principles of grounded theory. To reiterate, the goal is to create a grounded theory and the researcher should not lose sight of this when involved in the minutiae of data collection and analysis. For some of the challenges new grounded theorists face, see Corbin and Holt (2005; 2011).

Conclusions

Grounded theory is a challenging methodology and although there are few certainties in the process, there are clear guidelines. Working with grounded theory can be both rewarding and valuable by producing studies that offer new insights into seemingly intractable research problems and issues in the field. Drawing on a number of well-constructed and implemented grounded theory studies across a range of topics in sport psychology (the field in which the authors work), our understanding of social influences on athletes' sporting experiences and talent development has been greatly enhanced. For example, Holt and Dunn (2004) conducted a grounded theory study examining the psychosocial and environmental influences associated with success in Canadian and English soccer players. Adhering closely to the principles of grounded theory, Holt and Dunn collected and analysed data simultaneously across three fieldwork trips in Canada and England. Specific settings were theoretically sampled and players and coaches were interviewed in these settings. Data analysis proceeded following the steps outlined by Strauss and Corbin (1998), moving from a descriptive to more theoretical level. Through this process, Holt and Dunn identified four core categories (discipline, commitment, social support and resilience) that were fundamental to the development of soccer success. Inherent within these categories were the roles and requirements of parents in aiding talent development.

In another example of grounded theory, Sabiston, McDonough, and Crocker (2007) conducted a study examining the psychosocial experiences of breast cancer survivors involved in a dragon boat programme. In contrast to Holt and Dunn's study, Sabiston and colleagues elected to use Charmaz's (2006) constructivist approach to grounded theory. The researchers recognized their role in co-creating the knowledge presented in their grounded theory and acknowledged the multiple subjective realities of the participants. As with the creative data collection and analysis approach described earlier, Sabiston and colleagues also had to adapt their analysis process due to logistical constraints. Given the time constraints between their interviews, the researchers only had time to review interview notes and analyse major themes based on these, rather than the full interview transcript. Once they were engaged in complete data analysis, Sabiston et al. used sensitizing concepts to help them identify relationships between concepts. Analysis revealed that involvement in dragon boat racing facilitated social support and led to participants regaining personal control, developing new identities and overcoming physical challenges.

Although the two grounded theory studies (Holt and Dunn, 2004 and Sabiston et al., 2007) examined entirely different topics, both indicated the role of social support within the physical activity and sport context. However, the theories developed were also substantially different, illustrating the influence that the topic and population sampled, the researcher and the adoption of different grounded theory approaches can have on the grounded theory that is produced.

We have provided a brief overview of grounded theory that should give the reader a taste of the methodology and its variants. Following Bruce (2007) and Holt and Tamminen (2010a, b), we conclude this chapter by making some practical suggestions, which may help to create optimal conditions for planning grounded theory studies. These are not fixed prescriptive criteria, but a flexible list offered as tips that may be useful for planning research.

1   Researchers should consider the variants of grounded theory and select the approach that is most relevant to the study in question. At this point, it may be useful to consider which variant of grounded theory methodology best matches personal philosophical orientations, because different versions of grounded theory have been associated with different philosophical underpinnings (see Weed, 2010).

2   Having selected a version of grounded theory and in continuing to design a study, it is important to remember that participants should be identified via theoretical sampling. The researcher anticipates the settings to study and the people to speak with in order to get the 'best' (i.e., the most detailed) answers to the research question. Researchers should prepare for theoretical sampling from the start of a study by having a flexible plan for data collection. Researchers should plan to engage in data analysis as soon as the first data are collected; this should be an iterative (i.e., repeated) process throughout the study, until an adequate level of data saturation is attained.

3   Sample size is difficult to establish a priori because it is based on the principle of data saturation. The amount of data required to saturate a narrowly defined issue will be less than the amount of data required to saturate a much broader topic (Morse, 1995). From a practical perspective, sample sizes can be proposed based on the samples used in previously published grounded theories.

4   Finally, researchers must 'think theoretically' from the start of a study. This is a problem the first author faced when conducting his first grounded theory study for a PhD (described in Corbin and Holt, 2005). The lesson learned was to encourage students to realize that the point of using grounded theory methodology is to create a theory. In other words, grounded theorists should strive to produce theoretical models rather than merely a hierarchical list of descriptive themes and sub-themes.

Acknowledgements

During the preparation of this manuscript, Camilla Knight was supported by an Izaak Walter Killam Memorial Scholarship from the University of Alberta and Katherine Tamminen by a Doctoral Fellowship from the Social Sciences and Humanities Research Council of Canada Sport Participation Research Initiative.

Key terms

Grounded theory   A collection of qualitative methodological approaches that enable researchers to develop theoretical explanations that are 'grounded' in data collected in the field.

Theoretical sampling   Sampling on the basis of emerging concepts – as new data are collected and analysed, additional participants/settings are theoretically sampled to further develop the emerging theory.

Iterative process   A repeated cyclical process of data collection and analysis – data analysis begins as soon as the first data are collected, and data collection and analysis continue simultaneously throughout the study.

Theoretical saturation   A matter of reaching the point in the research where collecting new data does not add extensive new information and explanation to the findings.

Constant comparison   An analytic technique that involves comparing data, incidents, and concepts for similarities and differences.

References

Bruce, C. (2007) 'Questions arising about emergence, data collection and its interaction with analysis in a grounded theory study', *International Journal of Qualitative Methods*, 6: 1–12.

Bryant, A. and Charmaz, K. (eds) (2007) *The Sage Handbook of Grounded Theory*, Thousand Oaks, CA: Sage.

Charmaz, K. (2006) *Constructing Grounded Theory: A Practical Guide through Qualitative Analysis*, Thousand Oaks, CA: Sage.

Corbin, J. and Holt, N. L. (2005) 'Grounded theory', in B. Somekh and C. Lewin (eds) *Research Methods in the Social Sciences* (49–55), Thousand Oaks, CA: Sage.

Corbin, J. C. and Holt, N. L. (2011) 'Grounded theory', in B. Somekh and K. Lewin (eds) *Theory and Methods in Social Science Research*, 2nd edn (113–120), London: Sage.

Corbin, J. and Strauss, A. L. (2008) *Basics of Qualitative Research: Techniques and Procedures for Developing Grounded Theory*, 3rd edn, Newbury Park, CA: Sage.

Dey, I. (1999) *Grounding Grounded Theory*, San Diego: Academic Press.

Glaser, B. (1978) *Theoretical Sensitivity*, Mill Valley, CA: Sociology Press.

Glaser, B. (1992) *Basics of Grounded Theory Analysis: Emerging vs. Forcing*, Mill Valley, CA: Sociology Press.

Glaser, B. G. and Strauss, A. L. (1967) *The Discovery of Grounded Theory: Strategies for Qualitative Research*, New York: Aldine de Gruyter.

Holt, N. L. and Dunn, J. G. H. (2004) 'Toward a grounded theory of the psychosocial competencies and environmental conditions associated with soccer success', *Journal of Applied Sport Psychology*, 16: 199–219.

Holt, N. L. and Tamminen, K. A. (2010a) 'Improving grounded theory research in sport and exercise psychology: Further reflections as a response to Mike Weed', *Psychology of Sport and Exercise*, 11: 405–13.

Holt, N. L. and Tamminen, K. A. (2010b) 'Moving forward with grounded theory in sport and exercise psychology', *Psychology of Sport and Exercise*, 11: 419–22.

Knight, C. J. and Holt, N. L. (2011) 'Parenting in competitive tennis: Understanding and enhancing children's experiences', manuscript submitted to journal.

Morse, J. (ed) (1997) *Completing a Qualitative Project: Details and Dialogue*, Thousand Oaks, CA: Sage.

Morse, J., Noerager Stern, P., Corbin, J., Bowers, B., Charmaz, K. and Clarke, A. (2009) *Developing Grounded Theory: The Second Generation*, Walnut Creek, CA: Left Coast Press.

Morse, J. M. (1995) 'The significance of saturation', *Qualitative Health Research*, 5: 147–9.

Sabiston, C. M., McDonough, M. H. and Crocker, P. R. E. (2007) 'Psychosocial experiences of breast cancer survivors involved in a dragon boat program: Exploring links to positive psychological growth', *Journal of Sport and Exercise Psychology*, 29: 419–38.

Sandelowski, M. (1993) 'Theory unmasked: The uses and guises of theory in qualitative research', *Research in Nursing and Health*, 16: 213–18.

Strauss, A. and Corbin, J. (1990) *Basics of Qualitative Research: Grounded Theory Procedures and Techniques*, London: Sage.

Strauss, A. and Corbin, J. (1998) *Basics of Qualitative Research: Techniques and Procedures for Developing Grounded Theory*, 2nd edn, Newbury Park, CA: Sage.

Tamminen, K. A. and Holt, N. L. (in press) 'Adolescent athletes' learning about coping and the roles of parents and coaches', *Psychology of Sport and Excercise*.

Weed, M. (2009) 'Research quality considerations for grounded theory research in sport and exercise psychology', *Psychology of Sport and Exercise*, 10: 502–10.

Weed, M. (2010) 'A quality debate on grounded theory in sport and exercise psychology? A commentary on potential areas for future debate', *Psychology of Sport and Exercise*, 11: 414–18.

Further Resource

<http://www.groundedtheory.com/>

22 Discourse analysis and the beginner researcher

Kathy Hall and Fiona C. Chambers

All words have the 'taste' of a profession, a genre, a tendency, a party, a particular work, a particular person, an age group, the day and hour. Each word tastes of the context and contexts in which it has lived its socially charged life.

(Bakhtin, 1981: 293)

Introduction

The term to 'spin a yarn' was coined in the early 19th century and was first described in James Hardy Vaux's *A New and Comprehensive Vocabulary of the Flash Language*, in 1812 (Hardy Vaux, 2008): 'Yarning or spinning a yarn, signifying to relate their various adventures, exploits, and escapes to each other'. And so, 'spin' became linked with telling a story. More recently, the term 'spin' has been associated with political and governmental campaigns. Every story being told has a plot or spin, which is planned by the storyteller. Every person is a spin doctor of their own lives – and the lives of others – weaving a plot into their respective stories whether spoken or written. The accounts are woven in two parts:

A story (histoire) and a discourse (discourse). The story is the content or chain of events. The story is the 'what' in a narrative and the discourse is the 'how'. The discourse is rather like a plot, how the reader becomes aware of what happened [and] the order of appearance of the events.

(Sarup, 1996: 17)

And so, simple questions – such as 'Where were you last night?' 'What did you do yesterday?' – may trigger a number of possible responses (or stories). Much depends on the context, who is asking the question and the nature of the relationship you happen to have with that person. Your mother, your best friend, your partner, your boss may each get different responses. It is not necessarily the case that you intend to deceive, but you will interpret the situation and decide how best to respond.

About us

Professor Kathy Hall is head of the School of Education in University College, Cork (UCC). She is interested in sociocultural perspectives on learning, inclusion and pedagogy. She has a particular interest in language and literacy as situated practice, coming to discourse studies via this route.

Dr Fiona C. Chambers is a lecturer in pedagogy of sport and physical education at UCC. Her main research interest is in initial and career-long professional learning for teachers (particularly mentor education) and its impact on young people's learning in physical education and sport.

Discourse analysis

Discourse analysis (DA) is the study of texts. Texts are what people say and what people write. Texts can include multimodal texts incorporating a combination of visual, print, image and audio texts. They can, for example, include all of the following: policy documents, school texts/books, advertisements, film, posters, research field notes, interviews. In this chapter, we introduce you to an approach to the study of texts – DA. As several authors on this topic have pointed out (Janks, 1997; Rogers et al., 2005; Gill, 2000), DA is the term given to a whole range of approaches to the analysis of texts. There is no single way to define or do DA. In this chapter, we will address some key aspects of DA that we think will be useful to you. We have structured this section as follows:

- What is discourse analysis?
- Assumptions underlying discourse analysis;
- Discourse analysis and other kinds of analysis;
- Doing discourse analysis.

We will then illustrate aspects of the process by briefly considering some of the rhetorial devices used in a significant international policy text – the European Union's White Paper on Sport (2007). This policy document offers a strategy for sport across Europe, seeking to enhance the visibility of sport and sport-related activities in the public sphere over the next several years. The policy has generated considerable debate, it spans cultural contexts, and is referred to in other chapters in this volume. As a policy, political and contentious document, it offers interesting raw material for discourse analysis. However, a separate extended chapter would be required to offer a serious and in-depth analysis of the discourse of this elaborate text. Rather, our intention is to help you consider how you might begin 'to read against the grain' of such a text and begin to notice some of the rhetorical devices used by its authors.

What is discourse analysis?

DA does two things simultaneously: it draws attention to the language used and it draws attention to the social dimension of its use. Discourse analysts identify the preferred or intended meaning a text seeks to convey and, crucially, they also identify the linguistic devices used to construct that preferred meaning. They seek to establish the dominant version of reality that is brought into life via the text. By showing how a text achieves its desired effects, i.e., how we are persuaded to read it as the author intends us to read it, the discourse analyst renders something of the process visible. Thus, the text is opened up for deeper scrutiny and review and, in the process, alternative readings to the preferred or intended reading can be offered.

Education researchers, especially those in the area of language and literacy, have a long history of work in discourse analysis. Indeed, elaborate coding frames have been developed to capture and examine the moment-by-moment interactions in classrooms, as well as in more non-formal educational settings. From around the late 1970s, such micro-level analyses were extended and enriched with macro-level analyses that sought to understand how social structures are reproduced through interaction and other practices and traditions of institutions (especially schools). Ideas from the fields of sociology, cultural studies and anthropology were highly influential in this regard. One classic example is Paul Willis's (1977) account of how working-class boys become working-class men through the interactions, rituals and practices of the school. Schools were shown to be implicated in the reproduction of social structures. In the fields of physical education and sport, Ronholt (2002) used DA to expose the hidden curriculum of physical education, showing how discourses of physical education and discourses of gender relations are connected, and how these construct and are constructed by the social structures of the physical education lesson, and ultimately influence student learning.

The main points we wish you to note here are that contemporary approaches to DA involve the use of micro and macro analyses and that the researchers who do DA investigate the relationship between texts and social practices. They bring together micro and macro analyses to describe, interpret and explain social events. The explanatory side of the analysis is key as the assumption of DA is that language constructs versions of reality. How this construction occurs is what the analyst seeks to understand and make visible. Also of note is that theoretically DA is interdisciplinary, drawing on various fields of study, especially linguistic, sociocultural, sociological and psychological perspectives.

You can think of discourse as the words uttered or written, but discourses are also ways of being and acting in the world. They are like mental scripts that you take for granted as you go around acting in different situations, being a member of different groups and communities, and participating in different activities. You can think of discourses as taken-for-granted ways of behaving, doing and being. People who are 'in the know', i.e., who are on the inside of a discourse, view the world through their own discursive lens and so they take certain behaviours and ways of thinking for granted. We are all 'in the know' in the case of some discourses – think of the discourses of rugby, trainspotting, schoolteaching, parenting, hockey coaching, cooking, shopping. Think also, for example, of deficit discourses, e.g., lifestyle diseases (the obesity epidemic and the increase in diabetes), which are related to physical inactivity and sedentary behaviours and disengagement in schools. In DA, one attends to ways of interacting, being, doing and representing, recognizing that these are ever in a dynamic set of relationships such that one has to be attentive to changes, contradictions and shifts within and across discourses, contexts and time (see Rogers, 2002 for an example).

Frequently, those on the inside of a practice see their own position and practices as matters of common sense, rather than as a particular version of reality. Those outside a discourse, those wholly unfamiliar with a practice and thus lacking the insider's lens through which to look and act, tend to be mystified and may even consider the insider 'strange'. The discourse analyst does not consider that the insider speakers and writers, be they children, teachers, carers, athletes, parents, researchers, are acting in a totally autonomous way, unconstrained by their versions or their perspectives of how to be a teacher, runner, researcher etc. Rather, analysts are interested in what the taken-for-granted, insider scripts and discourses are, and how they might enable and constrain what is doable, sayable and thinkable.

Posing these questions means you are interested in the constructedness of a discourse and that you hold it up for scrutiny and critique. By so doing, DA makes it easier to examine and challenge the constructions the author is persuading us to adopt in the text.

It is worth bearing in mind that those discourses that are most taken for granted and assumed to have the status of common sense result in the strongest forms of domination and influence. Because they are so deeply embedded and tacit, they prove to be the most resilient and the most difficult to notice and, therefore, challenge. For example, it is perhaps unthinkable to challenge a pervasive discourse such as the obesity epidemic. DA helps with this noticing and challenging and is often referred to as critical discourse analysis (CDA) – critical because it recognizes how discourses are about power and influence. In a fundamental sense, therefore, discourses speak through us and we become unaware of the discourse we are drawing on or speaking/writing from, so enmeshed are they in our doing and in our living. Discourses are at their most powerful when they are invisible. The kind of deconstruction of text that is needed to render the discourse visible is very challenging for the analyst.

Assumptions underlying discourse analysis

The single most important assumption underlying DA is that language is never innocent or neutral. It is always partial, always from a position. This means that language is shaped by social life and language shapes social life. It is simultaneously determined and determining, constructed and constructing. In describing the world, language also creates it. Put another way, this means that language is not merely a communicative tool; it is also a rhetorical tool that produces effects. As a social practice, it is deeply implicated in the production of the social and cultural world. In the case of the EU White Paper (2007), therefore, we would argue that it doesn't simply describe the practice of and thinking about sport in European countries. As a text, it writes and draws a certain version of sport into life, into being. Understood in this way, language is not transparent, it doesn't ever describe an objective reality 'out there'.

DA, or CDA more specifically, adopts a critical stance towards knowledge and how we come to know the world (Fairclough, 1995). Rejected is the idea that you can observe some aspect of social life and thereby come to know its true nature. Knowledge of the world is socially constructed, which means that the way you look, the tools you use – the conceptual frameworks or lens through which you observe – matter, since they determine, in huge measure, what you decide is noteworthy and significant.

It is worth bearing in mind that while texts are always from a position and while texts use a range of representational/rhetorical devices to accomplish their persuasive and authoritative effects, we do not see this as in any way dishonest or duplicitous. We all use rhetorical devices in our speech and in our writing. The concept of intertextuality is important for the discourse analyst. It refers to ways in which texts are related to other texts by virtue of the discourses embedded in them (MacLure, 2003). As one analyses a text, one's intertextual knowledge is recruited through the connections with other texts, although these connections are usually implicit. By making some of the intertextuality explicit, one can begin to explain how a text is organized to achieve its effects. You might reread the quotation from Bakhtin at the beginning of this chapter, which captures how language, expressions, words and ideas always have a history.

Discourse analysis and other kinds of analysis

As should be clear from the discussion so far, DA starts from a different position from more conventional research approaches in relation to how we come to know and study the world. A statistical survey analysis, for instance, uses statistical tools and established processes in the discipline of statistics to explain, perhaps, people's attitudes, beliefs and practices on the basis of responses to a questionnaire. Frequently, the assumption of attitude scales and inventories is that some underlying set of ideas and dispositions on the part of the respondents can be ascertained. The discourse analyst does not expect that what an individual says will be consistent and coherent; rather the focus is on the discourse itself – how it is organized and what work it is doing in making itself persuasive. DA involves a radical epistemological shift in that it requires one to exercise considerable scepticism, to suspend belief in the taken for granted, to challenge one's own assumptions, and to render the familiar strange (Gill, 2000).

Doing discourse analysis

We start this section with a caveat taken from Rosalind Gill's work (2000: 117) where she warns:

> It is much easier to discuss the key themes of discourse analysis than it is to explain how actually to go about analysing texts. Pleasant as it would be to be able to offer a cookbook recipe for readers to follow methodologically, this is just not possible. Somewhere between 'transcription' and 'writing up', the essence of discourse analysis seems to slip away, ever elusive, it is never quite captured by descriptions of coding schemes, hypotheses and analytic schemata.

Having flagged the slipperiness of the process, we suggest some strategies here, drawing on the work of several discourse theorists. Fairclough (1995), for instance, talks about three interrelated levels of analysis – description, interpretation and explanation – and he identifies three domains of discourse abstraction: local/textual, institutional and societal/sociocultural. Analysis at the local or textual domain directs attention to such textual features as vocabulary, grammar and interactional properties of texts. For example, the use of third person pronouns would indicate a distancing and a separation of the author or reader from the thinking or activity in question.

Similarly, the verbs used, the passive as opposed to the active voice (transitivity) might similarly distance and objectify. This dimension might also look at the mood of an interaction or document by checking sentence constructions: statements, questions or declarations. Modality, i.e., the degree of assertiveness in the exchanges, gives clues as to the nature of the relationships between people in an interaction.

A recent analysis of the Reggio Emilia approach (Hall et al., 2010), an educational philosophy focused on preschool and primary education, showed how the approach is sweeping the world and providing a substantial income to the Reggio Emilia international organization. During the course of this analysis, we noted how all of the following rhetorical devices were used to persuade readers of the authority and credibility of various Reggio texts: oppositional positioning or negative comparing (where authors positioned the Reggio approach in opposition to poor practices that were assumed to be typical in some Western countries, in order to claim the superiority of Reggio); enhancing claims of credibility through references to international, well-known scholars ('Trust me, I'm a world famous author!') as opposed to a serious analysis of evidence; a journalistic/realist style that spoke to the reader in a concrete fashion. In another study using DA, learners' lack of agency could be shown through their use of noun clauses and their non-use of verb clauses or first person pronouns. In contrast, their teacher's language was peppered with these same linguistic devices signalling her agency and power (Hall, 2002).

Fairclough's second domain of abstraction refers to how people interpret, reproduce or transform texts. Most texts are hybrids, which means they draw on more than one discourse. In the case of the Reggio texts, old discourses around progressive education were found to be woven in with newer discourses of neuroscience but, the connections were mostly implicit and tacit. The effect is an implicit appeal to other times and other, pioneering thinkers, but this resulted in frequent contradiction. This is so because discourses conflict and contradict.

Within the third domain of abstraction, the analyst may identify larger systems of meaning-making that function at a sociocultural level. Fairclough thinks of these as larger discourse systems, e.g., discourses of poverty, discourses of disability.

Discourses do not have discrete boundaries, so in the course of conducting an analysis you are likely to move across and within the different domains in describing, interpreting and explaining. As we have already highlighted, DA involves a close reading that moves between text and context to study content, organization and how a text functions.

Rosalind Gill outlines several other rhetorical devices that are frequently used to make claims and justify one's stance in a text. One device is the statement about what the argument is not – e.g., 'It is not an argument for … ' – a move designed to protect the forthcoming argument from a counter argument and offer a preferred reading. Another is the notion of balance, calling for a 'balanced' approach. Gill (2000) notes how the concept of 'balance' has no negative connotations, but conjures up notions of health, naturalness and harmony. Yet another is inexplicitness and vagueness: where there is no clear referent the speaker or writer is provided protection against critique; and in any case, if a criticism is made, the person can claim other interpretations and deny the original presumed meaning.

As you might expect, it is much easier to read against the grain, to read against the preferred reading when you disagree with a text. This might occur when you read texts which highlight a deficit discourse, e.g., the obesity epidemic. If you are dealing with a highly polemical text, it's probably easier to expose ambiguities and conflicting discourses. However, we would agree with others (e.g., Janks, 1997) that it is sensible when getting started, to *read with the grain first*. Go with the author's intended meaning before you read against the text. Locate the text, note its genre and try to establish what, if any, point of view or stance it is speaking/writing from. Make notes about what is missing, where the silences are. Who, what groups perhaps, are privileged, powerless, passive and agentic. Note the tone of the text: is it polemical, tentative or definite in orientation? Remember too you are looking for patterns in the text you are working with, patterns that surface across linguistic functions, and these may endorse or conflict one with another. Janks also recommends that you work from text to discourse, so it makes more sense to start with a textual analysis. However, inevitably you are likely to move within and between levels of analysis throughout.

Case study: The European Union White Paper on Sport (2007)

Reading with the text

At the time when the White Paper was devised in 2007, the European Union (EU) had no 'competence for sport' (or sport remit) under the European Treaties. Prior to the White Paper, the EU engaged with sport primarily through Declarations adopted when signing the Treaties of Amsterdam in 1997 and of Nice in 2000. The Treaty signed in Lisbon on 13 December 2007, however, includes a provision stating that:

> The Union shall contribute to the promotion of European sporting issues, while taking account of the specific nature of sport, its structures based on voluntary activity and its social and educational function.
>
> (Article 2 (124), Lisbon Treaty)

And that the action shall be aimed at:

> Developing the European dimension in sport, by promoting fairness and openness in sporting competitions and co-operation between bodies responsible for sports, and by protecting the physical and moral integrity of sportsmen and sportswomen, especially the youngest sportsmen and sportswomen.
>
> (Article 165, Lisbon Treaty)

The effect of this Article is to introduce a 'soft competence' (a skill related to personal development) for sport, enabling the EU institutions to support Member State activity by adopting 'incentive measures' and 'recommendations', but not to regulate or harmonize it. The Treaty has, in some ways, overtaken the White Paper. Indeed, at the conference on the White Paper organized by the Commission in October 2007, the Commission said that the White Paper and the 'structured dialogue' should now be viewed largely as the preparatory work and structure for the implementation of the Treaty Article on sport.

The White Paper consists of three policy areas: (a) the societal role of sport; (b) the economic dimension of sport; and (c) the organization of sport. Various action points are listed within each of the three policy areas and together these form the 'Action Plan Pierre de Coubertin', named after the founder of the modern Olympic movement (for more details see http://ec.europa.eu/sport/white-paper/doc/sec934_en.pdf).

Reading against the text

As a European policy document (see http://ec.europa.eu/sport/white-paper/doc/wp_on_sport_en.pdf), the text adheres to the conventions of the policy genre, written in numbered paragraphs, without named authors, thus immediately demonstrating a remove from an actual person or persons. As a European Commission text, we can assume that the people who crafted it are on the inside of EU ideals, language, values and goals. Also important, it is a European Commission document, not regional or not national; it is an international production. The European Commission presents itself as a neutral agency (at once a strength and a weakness in different spheres: it can't legislate just yet, it is a discussion document). As such, some of its power to convince stems from its location: it is everywhere and nowhere in particular, it is overarching and all-encompassing.

According to the House of Commons Culture Media and Sport Committee Report (Parliament of Great Britain, 2008: 4), the White Paper was influenced by the Independent European Sport Review. The Review was funded by the Union of European Football Associations (UEFA). The report can be accessed through www.independentfootballreview.com, which may point to the influence of soccer on the Review and ultimately on the White Paper itself. Some groups who represent specific sports question this affiliation and note the importance of recognizing the specificity of all sports and not just sport in general.

In terms of text organization, it has a summary at the beginning and appendices full of extensive accounts of surveys, consultations and sources of evidence geared to enhance the claims made in the main text.

At the textual level, we would suggest that it is a tentative and conservative document in the main. It does not, for instance, evoke earlier controversies about inclusion/exclusion, or glorify elite athletes as may have occurred in earlier national level texts (e.g., pyramid in sport). However, it can afford to be tentative – it has power by virtue of its international/EU status.

From the perspective of the discourse analyst, a key question is: What are its dominant discourses?

Sport as fixer and protector

We would argue that a dominant discourse in the document is that of sport as instrument and fixer. This is evident in the references and claims in the text to all of the following:

- that sport appears to be uniquely placed to promote physical, mental, moral qualities;
- that sport can address the twin (often conflicting) imperatives of social cohesion and economic advancement;
- that sport can foster a wide range of skills and lifelong learning;
- that sport fosters tolerance, personal development and fulfilment;
- that sport can prevent crime and delinquency;
- that sport is good for democracy and social participation;
- that sport has the capacity to enable citizens to belong and be included in valuable activities;
- that sport teaches.

The dominant, celebratory discourse of 'sport as fixer' conceptualizes sport as being of outstanding significance to society and to the economy. The text seeks to justify sport as a natural, taken-for-granted enterprise that all citizens should endorse and embrace. The instrumentalist stance on sport is evident via the value attributed to it for what it can do for society. Backgrounded or missing, we think, is the intrinsic value of sport as a fun, leisure and cultural activity. In some respects, one might argue that the White Paper adopts a narrow definition, where sport is only about organized activities – other aspects of physical activity are not incorporated. Sport as instrumental misses this intrinsic dimension and by the same token is probably unrealistic in its claims that sport can do so much for society. Also, the whole emphasis on governance, commercial/economic, media and the competitive side of sport denies any possible intrinsic dimension.

The valorization of Europe

Early on in the text we see the recruitment of 'the Olympic ideal' and a link is made between sport and peace. A rhetorical device here is the binary opposites – the old and the new are being evoked; the heritage and the contemporary. In the process, one glimpses a certain, superior kind of Europe. This is a golden age narrative that valorizes Europe.

A prescriptive text

There are indications of prescription, of assumptions about how best to conduct one's life – at least physically. We are told that we should take exercise for 30 minutes per day, albeit recruiting the WHO to justify this. In this sense, European citizens are encouraged to take responsibility and monitor themselves.

A neo-liberal discourse

Language or discourse is pivotal to the spread and acceptance of a set of ideas. While the negative aspects of the world of organized sport are listed in the policy, arguably these are all the same things that one would associate with capitalism: commercial pressure, exploitation (of young players), doping/drugs, racism, violence, corruption and money laundering.

Sometimes the text is explicitly neo-liberal, i.e., it is oriented toward the building of capital, the importance of a market economy, and the role of competition and efficiency, e.g., 'through its role in formal and non formal education sport reinforces Europe's human capital' (2.3). You can see the linguistic 'fingerprints' of this human capital discourse in many other EU texts. Other examples of a neo-liberal discourse in the White Paper include the following:

> The Commission, in close co-operation with Member States, will seek to develop a European statistical method for measuring economic impact of sport …
>
> (3.1)

> Sustainable economic growth, competitiveness and employment …
>
> (3.1)

Yet there are fear and anxiety around the tendency to practise sport individually as opposed to collectively, thus reducing the potential for promoting social solidarity.

Conclusion

We didn't set out to do a discourse analysis of the White Paper text; rather our intention was to make a start at orienting you towards some of the strategies you might apply. DA involves considerable time, coding and analyses to identify and confirm patterns in a text. While we have flagged some possible themes and what we think are dominant discourses here, we have not presented a detailed evidential tracing of these discourses that would allow the confirmation and validation of our claims. However, we hope we have whetted your appetite for discourse analysis and introduced you to its key dimensions.

We leave you to ponder on this poem where the shadow represents the meaning of language, the meaning of texts:

> Between the idea
> And the reality
> Between the motion
> And the act
> Falls the Shadow
> …
> Between the conception
> And the creation
> Between the emotion
> And the response
> Falls the Shadow

(The Hollow Men, T. S. Eliot, 1961)

Key terms

Texts What people say and write, and can include multimodal texts e.g., visual, print, image and audio texts. They are also ways of being and acting in the world.
Discourses Texts.
Discourse analysis The study of texts.
Intertextuality The process of relating texts to each other during discourse analysis.

References

Bakhtin, M. M. (1981) *The Dialogic Imagination: Four Essays*, Austin: University of Texas Press.
Eliot, T. S. (1961) *Selected Poems*, London: Faber & Faber.
Fairclough, N. (1995) *Critical Discourse Analysis: The Critical Study of Language*, New York: Longman.
Gill, R. (2000) 'Discourse analysis', in M. Bauer and G. Gaskell (eds) *Qualitative Researching with Text, Image and Sound* (172–190), London: Sage.
Hall, K. (2002) 'Co-constructing subjectivities and knowledge in literacy class: an ethnographic–sociocultural perspective', *Language and Education*, 16, 3: 178–94.
Hall, K., Horgan, M., Ridgway, A., Murphy, R., Cunneen, M. and Cunningham, D. (2010) *The Reggio Emilia Experience and Loris Malaguzzi*, London: Continuum.
Hardy Vaux, J. (2008) *A New and Comprehensive Vocabulary of the Flash Language*, Gloucestershire: Dodo Press.
Janks, H. (1997) 'Critical discourse analysis as a research tool', *Discourse: Studies in the Cultural Politics of Education*, 18, 3: 329–42.
MacLure, M. (2003) *Discourse in Educational and Social Research*, Buckingham: Open University Press.
Parliament of Great Britain (2008) *Report on European Commission White Paper on Sport: Seventh Report of Session 2007–8*, in House of Commons Culture Media and Sport Committee (ed.), London: The Stationery Office.
Rogers, R. (2002) 'Through the eyes of the institution: a critical discourse analysis of decision making in two special education meetings', *Anthropology and Education Quarterly*, 33, 2: 213–37.
Rogers, R., Malancharuvil-Berkes, E., Mosley, M., Hui, D. and O'Garro J. (2005) 'Critical discourse analysis in education: a review of the literature', *Review of Educational Research*, 75, 3: 365–416.
Ronholt, H. (2002) ' "It's only the sissies … ": analysis of teaching and learning processes in physical education: A contribution to the hidden curriculum', *Sport Education and Society*, 7: 25–36.
Sarup, M. (1996) *Identity, Culture and the Post-Modern World*, Athens: University of Georgia Press
Willis, P. (1977) *Learning to Labour*, Aldershot: Ashgate.

Further reading

As well as reading about DA, we would advise beginner researchers to become acquainted with a wide range of approaches to DA and their application. Good places to start, in our view, would be Janks (1997), Gill (2000) and Rogers (2002).

Part IV
Data analysis – consider it early!

23 Analysing qualitative data

Peter Hastie and Olga Glotova

Introduction

You know you are doing qualitative research analysis when ... 'you can't see the kitchen table because it's completely covered with paper'. As both authors of this chapter can attest, 'there are times when you have *so* much data, it can get quite overwhelming deciding how to start making sense of everything'. Of course, the key here is to be diligent in turning all those concrete bits of data into abstract concepts; helping you to do that is the purpose of this chapter.

About us

Peter Hastie is a professor in the Department of Kinesiology at Auburn University. His research focuses on two lines of inquiry that are particularly amenable to qualitative research methods. In sport education research, qualitative methods have been used extensively to reveal the responses of both teachers and students to participation in sport seasons. In his research on classroom ecologies, field notes and interviews were used to understand the processes through which teachers and students negotiate the work that gets accomplished during physical education. In both these fields, the challenge has been to look for innovative ways in which to present a compelling story to the reader, while remaining true to the data at hand.

Olga Glotova has just completed her doctoral studies in kinesiology at Auburn University, having graduated in 1988 from the State Pedagogical University in Ulyanovsk, Russia, and receiving a master's degree at the University of Connecticut in 2007. Olga's early research focused on the motivation of mothers with respect to their children's participation in youth sport. More recently, she has been using action research techniques to investigate how pre-service Russian physical education teachers learn about – and learn to teach – sport education. Like her co-author, the key questions for Olga as a qualitative researcher are those such as 'How do you take all the data and make sense out of it?' and, in particular, 'How do you know what to keep and what to leave out?'

Qualitative research analysis: What is it, what can it do, what can't it do, and when could I use it?

In Chapter 7, a definition of qualitative research was provided as follows: qualitative research is a process of inquiry that seeks to understand phenomena in real-world settings, where the researcher does not attempt to manipulate the phenomenon of interest. Creswell (2009) explains that qualitative research is exploratory and is useful 'when the researcher does not know the important variable to examine' (p. 18), while quantitative research is best used to 'test a theory by specifying narrow hypotheses and the collection of data to support or refute the hypotheses' (p. 16). What this means is that qualitative research is, by definition, exploratory, and it is used when the aim is to delve deep into issues of interest and explore nuances related to the problem at hand. Quantitative research, on the other hand, is essentially conclusive because its purpose is to try to quantify a problem and understand how prevalent it is by looking for results that can be generalized to a larger population. This is not to suggest, however, that quantitative and qualitative research can't be used together to investigate an issue or problem from different perspectives. Indeed, in Chapter 9, Gorard and Makopoulou make a strong case for the value of mixed-methods research.

Let us quickly review the parameters of qualitative research for the purposes of informing its analysis. First, qualitative research is often *inductive*, which affects the degree to which the research design and analysis can be specified at the beginning of the project. Second, qualitative research designs are often *emergent* and *flexible* and, as a consequence, analysis of data in the early stages of the research may have a significant effect on subsequent stages of the research process. Third, the qualitative research process is often *non-linear* and *non-sequential*, meaning data collection and analysis tend to proceed simultaneously (Frankel and Devers, 2000). In light of early findings, it is acceptable – even desirable – to modify subsequent data collection and analysis procedures in order to gather more specific information or explore new and unanticipated areas of interest. In rare cases, early findings may suggest that the original research question itself should be changed because the underlying premise is not supported, or the initial question was not salient in the context studied. It is important to note, however, that even though initial research designs have a degree of flexibility and researchers can be responsive to emerging findings, qualitative research is no different from other forms of research in that a clear research design is required at the outset and data analysis should be pre-planned. Indeed, while the changing of methods and hypotheses during a study has been criticized as 'continually moving the goalposts', of more concern is that such flexibility can slide into sloppiness as researchers cease to be clear about what they are investigating. Qualitative researchers, then, should allocate time away from their data collection in order to reflect, plan and share their current understandings with others (Britten, Jones, Murphy, and Stacy, 1995).

By its very nature, qualitative research generates a plethora of messy data. The problem facing a researcher is how to take all these data and make sense of them in ways in which a reader can trust, and to which they can relate. Unlike quantitative data, where the challenge is to select the most appropriate methods of statistical analysis, and where there are set conventions for the reporting of results, qualitative research involves extensive use of deductive and inductive techniques. In this chapter, we take the reader through a series of 'steps to consider' when engaging in this complex process of analysing qualitative data. The steps are:

1 getting your data into a usable form;
2 beginning the sorting process;
3 deciding on the type of analysis;
4 developing initial categories or structures;
5 checking category validity; and
6 writing – or constructing – themes, cases or narratives.

Within each of these topics, we discuss the key elements that represent good scholarship, but we also provide lessons learned from experience that help researchers to avoid some of the pitfalls commonly encountered in this less-than-exact science.

Comment/analysis from Olga: Learning to analyse qualitative data is an ongoing process. Recently, I came across a quote that helped me to clarify my thoughts about qualitative research analysis. Creswell (1998: 24) states:

> Qualitative research is complex, involving fieldwork for prolonged periods of time, collecting words and pictures, analysing this information inductively while focusing on participants' views, and writing about the process using expressive and persuasive language.

The main message from the quote was that qualitative research is not so much about individual data; it is about the process. It is not only a result that makes your qualitative analysis and later your study look interesting, naturalistic and credible. It is a process of data analysis that makes your findings attractive to the readers, and/or intriguing for your dissertation committee members, and/or even impressive for your colleagues. No matter how much data you have, you should go through the process of analysis using certain methods or steps that would help narrow the data first and only then make the decision of what to use for the research project.

Methods of analysing qualitative research data

When describing the nature of qualitative data, Miles and Huberman (1994) reflected Berg's (1998) work by implying that 'in some senses, all data are qualitative; they refer to essences of people, objects, and situations' (p. 9). In this section, we will focus on data in the form of words, i.e., language in the form of extended text. The words are usually the result of observation or interview research methods, and they are not usually immediately accessible for analysis. Instead, some form of processing is required; this is represented in our series of 'steps to consider'. Before beginning, however, it is worth reminding ourselves of a particular maxim about qualitative research that reads: 'Do not try to analyse badly gathered data. It takes too much time for too little knowledge gained. If the data are bad enough, you may reach erroneous conclusions' (Stevens, n.d.) The other side of the coin is that if data have been gathered in painstaking and credible ways, the researcher has a duty to ensure they are analysed appropriately. As Chenail (1995) puts it: 'I believe that the data, which have been painfully collected, should "be the star" in the relationship.'

Getting your data into a usable form

When you use observation methods, data in the form of handwritten field notes must be corrected, edited and typed up. It is always better to do these tasks as soon as possible while your memory of events – and your own reactions, feelings or comments – are still fresh. Sometimes, it is important to recall exactly who said what and the nature of non-verbal communications, tone of voice and other relevant details. Here is an example of how to organize field notes that have been recorded in written form:

1 *Preliminaries*: a detailed description of the setting, participants, any diagrams/ tables of the settings and any movements that may have occurred among participants.
2 *Event*: a detailed description of what happened.
3 *Comments*: a record of your participants' comments, suggestions, emotional reactions, doubts and concerns.
4 *Memos*: a record of your own reflections on what you have observed.

If the method of data collection was interview, recordings (video or audio) need to be transcribed and corrected. In order to remain true to the data – and to avoid over-sanitizing transcripts – it is recommended that a verbatim transcription is done that includes all the 'ums' and 'ahs' of normal speech as well as sentence fillers such as 'like', 'so', 'you know'. Also, keep a record of the number of seconds any pauses last. The reason for this is that such details can provide important clues about your participants' feelings, positions or states of mind – and even your own (Oliver, Serovich and Mason, 2005).

Beginning the sorting process

During the process of conducting interviews or field observations, you will already be engaged in some form of data analysis. It is inevitable that you will be considering what you see or hear, and you will be processing the information in informal ways based on your personal background and general knowledge. The key thing for any researcher at this stage of analysis is to be critically alert to this analytical process, to keep notes on it as evidence, and to be critically reflexive about its influence both on the direction of the research and its emerging focus.

Once your data have been typed up (if required) and filed, the main sorting process can begin. The precise conduct of the next stage of analysis depends on the particular form of qualitative research in which you are engaged. There will be slight differences, of course, between the analysis of case studies, narratives, discourse analysis or grounded theory. Nonetheless, the process described below is an outline of a generic interpretive research process that is seeking to find – or construct – key 'themes' from interview or filed observation notes:

1   Highlight all quotes that you can later identify as interesting or significant or unexpected.
2   Affix codes to a set of field notes drawn from observation or interviews.
3   Make reflections or other remarks in the margins.
4   Sort and sift through your materials and identify similar phrases, patterns, themes or relationships between variables and common sequences.

Perhaps you can already see that in qualitative research, data analysis involves a high level of researcher subjectivity. This explains why researcher reflexivity is so important, and why it is essential to explain the nature of key decisions taken in order to ensure the analysis process is as transparent as possible for any reader. As Creswell and Miller (2000) note, 'researchers might use several options for incorporating this reflexivity into a narrative account. They may create a separate section on the "role of the researcher", provide an epilogue, use interpretive commentary throughout the discussion of the findings, or bracket themselves out by describing personal experiences as used in phenomenological methods' (p. 127).

Deciding on the type of analysis

Once the data are sorted, you have to decide on the type of analysis. There are two basic approaches for this. First, analyse data by using pre-established categories. These can be generated from interview questions or research questions. For instance, you may have asked a physical education teacher about his experience using a new curriculum model. Obviously, you would then have 'general experience' or 'personal experience' as your pre-established categories for analysis and you would have developed interview questions to gather information for those categories.

In other cases, where you do not have pre-established categories, you analyse your data by 'themes'. This type of analysis is highly inductive; that is, the themes are *generated* from the data and are a construction of the researcher. When reading papers that use qualitative methods, you will often see statements such as 'Four main themes *emerged* from the analysis … '. It is important to understand that themes don't magically appear or emerge; rather they are creations of the researcher and their interpretations of the available data. Indeed, two different researchers reading the same data set may well generate different themes, or at least different labels for those themes.

In thematic analysis, the data collection and analysis take place simultaneously. Even background reading can form part of the analysis process, especially if it can help to explain a theme. Closely connected to thematic analysis is comparative analysis. Using this method, data from different people are compared and contrasted and the process continues until the researcher is satisfied that no new issues are arising. Comparative and thematic analyses are often used in the same project, with the researcher moving backwards and forwards between transcripts, memos, notes and the research literature. Content analysis is based on principles similar to grounded theory (see Chapter 21). Data are analysed systematically as the researcher works through each transcript, assigning codes at different levels. This process is much more systematic than thematic or comparative approaches, and analysis only begins once all the relevant data have been collected. Nevertheless, even in this arguably more systematic or 'objective' approach, it is likely that the researcher enters into the process with tentative categories and themes already apparent. This point reinforces the claim made earlier about the importance of researcher reflexivity.

Developing initial categories or structures

Whether pre-planned, thematic or a more systematic content analysis is used, a key part of the process is reconsidering all materials you have highlighted or coded to find patterns, commonalities or differences. At this stage, data management may be manual, but it is more likely to be done electronically, either in the form of word documents or using specific qualitative data analysis software (see below). When initial category development begins, the researcher is engaged in a process of asking questions of specific pieces of the data. Categories tend to be developed as the answers to those questions are converted into a word or short phrase that can best describe a particular category. In the early stages of this process, there are often many codes and categories, but these can be reduced as the analysis is refined (for an overview of a five-stage analysis process see Harry, Sturges, and Klingner, 2005).

After completing initial category development, and identifying major categories for further analysis, the validity of the newly developed categories should be checked. Remember, no matter how the findings are organized, it is important to describe any general patterns in the data and the exceptions to the patterns.

Checking category validity

Checking the validity of the categories developed is a key step in data analysis because it is linked to the trustworthiness of the findings. A number of issues should be considered:

1   For pre-planned categories, check whether they correlate with the conceptual framework around which the project is designed.
2   For themes, confirm whether there is support from existing research.
3   From your own general knowledge as a researcher, support the selection with professional and personal experience and values.
4   Gradually elaborate a small set of generalizations that cover the consistencies determined in the database.
5   Check these generalizations with the existing knowledge from previous research and locate this knowledge in the various theories relating to the topic.

Writing – or constructing – themes, cases or narratives

A few tips can be identified to help in writing themes for data analysis:

1   You can't classify something as a theme unless it cuts across a preponderance of the data.

2   A theme can be selected directly from the research question(s), from pre-established category development, or based on findings. Also, when a new theme is organized, it should relate to other apparent themes. This will make the whole writing part much easier when the association among themes is obvious.

3   When writing an excerpt, commentary is essential. The researcher must examine closely the strategies and check whether idea or description reinforce each other.

4   It is a job of the researcher to convince the reader that the themes are properly interpreted and justified. Bazeley (2009: 19) provides the following advice:

> Reliance on presenting brief quoted segments of text as 'evidence' encourages superficial reporting of themes, whereas building an argument requires that conclusions are drawn from across the full range of available texts.

5   Editing is the last necessary step of writing themes. When editing, the researcher should consider the length and relevance of the theme to the research questions and the existing literature in which those questions were based.

6   Keep in mind the importance of relevance. Are these themes related to the research project?

A note on qualitative software

There are many software programs that are available for use in data coding, management and analysis. Current examples include Atlas.ti 4.2, The Ethnograph 5.03, QSR Nud*ist 4, and winMAX 97 professional (see http://www.quarc.de/body_overview.html for program characteristics such as data entry, coding and other features). These should be regarded as tools to assist you as the researcher. It is critical to note that you are the central agent in any interpretive process of data analysis. In summary, there are two types of qualitative data management software programs available. One is a coding and retrieval program that facilitates a more complex coding schema than the researcher may be able to perform manually. These programs allow you to retrieve text segments throughout the data set. The second is a theory-generating program that facilitates the exploration of relationships between coded categories in one file and theoretical explanations in another file. When exploring software options, it is important to remember that learning how to use any program efficiently and effectively will require an investment of time and money. In addition, identifying a readily available mentor who is familiar with the software is important for troubleshooting during data entry and manipulation.

Some examples of qualitative data analysis in practice

'Undoubtedly, no consensus exists for the analysis of the forms of qualitative data. But, at the outset, it might be useful to explore common features espoused by other authors' (Creswell, 1998: 140). In this section, we would like to illustrate the data analysis process by sharing experiences from projects in which we are engaged. To make this easy to follow, we will use the same steps for qualitative analysis that have been explained above.

Getting your data into a usable form

This part of your data analysis should be straightforward – get your data, organize and type it. The only inconvenience here is time. Some people underestimate the time that should be spent on typing and editing. For example, Olga's first qualitative research project involved 10 individual interviews for 30 minutes each. The interviews were with mothers who had children in a local soccer club and the topic of discussion was mothers' motivation for their children's sport participation. In reflecting on this first experience, Olga recalls she significantly underestimated the time it takes to organize all these data. She comments:

> My guess was, if I spent 30 minutes on an interview, I would type it within the same time. Wrong! It turned out that the ratio for me was 1 to 5. For one minute of the interview I spent five minutes listening to it and typing, then listening again and checking the clarity of the words I just typed. I don't want to scare anyone away, but my point here is it can take more time than you plan initially.

Beginning the sorting process

When researchers begin to sort data, they use different methods. Some use index cards; some just do copying and pasting of quotes. Some put everything on a wall to see the whole picture. Others prefer computer-based programs such as NVivo or ATLAS.ti. Again, from Olga's personal experience, she found one simple technique for sorting interviews from her study with pre-service teachers about their learning of a new curriculum model:

> When you type an interview, the order is question–answer. That is your horizontal order. When you have all of the interviews in front of you, it can be very hard to go through each interview to find how your participants responded to questions 1, 2, 3 etc. Instead, take a question and have responses to it across all of your participants. That would be your vertical order of the data. In that case, you can simply open a question and have all responses right below this question.

There is also another point to remember in sorting data. We have already mentioned in this chapter the importance of counting the number of seconds the pauses last. For example, after a question or a statement, one of the participants was silent for 15 seconds. That is quite a long time for the interview. If you begin to wonder why that happened, check the same question or statement for your other participants and see if it also happened with them. If the answer is yes, this can be significant and the reasons may be worth investigating.

Developing initial categories or structures

Developing preliminary categories is a process of turning large amounts of data, sometimes hundreds of pages, into smaller groups or clusters of information on a particular subject or query. It might be helpful if during the development of a category, a researcher asks questions such as: 'What specific information can I get from this?' 'What am I trying to accomplish?' 'What assumptions can I make here?' These questions give priority to the process rather than seeking causes or psychological motives.

Once you have grouped your data, it is time to choose a name for your categories. There are three ways in which names can be selected:

1   words from research and theory;
2   words from your participants that best described the category;
3   words from your own knowledge and experience as a researcher.

After you have selected categories and have identified participants' responses or field notes for each of these categories, re-read them using the new classification you have created. It may be that you had 20 different categories for your interview, but only five or six relate to your research question(s). These are your five or six categories that you use throughout the rest of the analysis. As Olga notes:

> For example, you study parents' motivation on their children's sport participation. During the initial analysis, you discovered that participants mentioned factors such as health, skill development, extra curriculum activity, socialization, team affiliation, recognition as their primary motivators. However, they also talked about how they encouraged children to participate and what barriers they encountered for sport participation. You, as a researcher, agreed that encouragement from the parents' side is important and barriers exist for many families in term of kids' sport participation but how is all of this relevant to your research question? You are looking for motivation factors and not for factors that prevent families from sport participation.

Alternatively, you might find the data are better represented as subcategories within individual themes, a situation that occurred in one of Peter's papers with Terry Carlson (see Carlson and Hastie, 1997). Here, while examining the student social system in a sport education season, the data from field notes, interviews and videotapes led to the generation of four major themes. However, within each of these themes, a number of related categories were developed. For example, in the major theme of 'Student roles and decision making', key words included 'coaching', 'disputes', 'selection', 'responsibility' and 'refereeing'. Each of these key words was explained and supported from the various data sources.

Checking category validity

One of the most helpful ways to check category validity is to go back to your research question and see how the categories you developed from data analysis are relevant to the goal of your project. Remember, category validity concerns the degree to which a finding is judged to have been interpreted in a correct way that correlates with the research question(s). For example, when Olga studied parental motivation on children's sport participation and found that health was mentioned as an important factor by all of the participants, it was concluded that health was indeed a valid category for this project. For another category – for example 'recognition' – only a few parents briefly talked about it and did not explain this factor in terms of where (within a team or outside the team) and to what extent it featured. In this case, Olga decided that the validity of this category was questionable. You may also want to ask questions that identify what was occurring at the time, in what order, and 'why'. These questions focus on particular concerns, which means you pay attention to patterns or commonalities that emerged from the category development.

Another step to consider in validating your categories is peer debriefing. This involves discussing data analysis with colleagues, i.e., those who are experts in the field of study and those who are not, in order to see if your thoughts on the data can be challenged. If there are discrepancies, you may be prompted to ask why and to what extent. You can ask peers to code a few transcripts to see if you would analyse them similarly or differently. Alternatively, you could ask peers simply to listen to the analysis you are in the process of developing and provide feedback.

Writing – or constructing – themes, cases or narratives

When writing themes, consider the following suggestions:

1   Decide if you have one solid independent theme or whether it has sub-themes within it.
2   Make sure that you have the best quotes from your participants to support the theme.
3   Quotes should be interesting, meaningful and, most importantly, easy to follow. It is your job to hold the reader's attention for as long as possible.
4   Begin each theme or sub-theme with a brief introduction followed by quotes from participants, and end each excerpt with a conclusion.
5   Any big theme should include a summary, but should not end with a participant's quote.

Conclusions

As Seidel (1998) notes, analysing qualitative data is essentially a simple process. It consists of three parts: noticing, collecting, and thinking about interesting things. More importantly however, these parts are *inter*dependent and not linear. That is, the process is iterative and progressive, because it is a cycle that keeps repeating. For example, when you are thinking about things, you also start noticing new things in the data. Additionally, the process is recursive because one part can call you back to a previous part. Finally, the process is holographic in that each step in the process contains the entire process.

Nearly all qualitative research projects will result in large amounts of textual data, whether from interviews, field notes or other sources. Moreover, the systematic and laborious preparation and analysis of these data are time consuming and labour intensive. In contrast to quantitative research, data analysis in qualitative studies often takes place alongside data collection to allow questions to be refined and new avenues of inquiry to develop. Inductive strategies are used to generate categories and explanations. Perhaps the key point to remember, however, is that during this intensive data coding, disassembly, sorting and sifting, you run the risk of finding the codes but losing the phenomena (Seidel, 1998). It is critical to remember that your codes are simply heuristic tools for the development of themes and narratives; they should not be seen as objective facts.

Finally, in any qualitative project, it is important to remember three critical features:

1   You are not a neutral/mechanical tool.
2   You are not doing an experiment in which you set the agenda.
3   The people you talk to are not inanimate objects; they also have agency and together you 'co-produce' social encounters, and hence data.

As a consequence, it is vital that you reflect and think critically, carefully, honestly and openly about the research experience and process, during both the analysis and reporting phases.

Key terms

Coding   The process of categorizing qualitative data, initially in 'open' form, where the data are considered in minute detail, and later in 'selective' form, where one systematically codes with respect to a central concept.

Inductive analysis   A deep examination of the details and specifics of the data to discover important patterns, themes and interrelationships.

Reflexivity   Refers to the idea that a person's thoughts and ideas tend to be inherently biased. In other words, the values and thoughts of a person will be represented in their work.

Thematic analysis   The process of identifying, coding and categorizing patterns found in the data. Theme identification is one of the most fundamental tasks in qualitative research.

Validation   Also known as credibility and/or dependability. Achieved through member checks, interviewer corroboration, peer debriefing, prolonged engagement, negative case analysis, auditability, confirmability, bracketing and balance.

References

Bazeley, P. (2009) 'Analysing qualitative data: More than "identifying themes" ', *Malaysian Journal of Qualitative Research*, 2: 6–22.

Berg, B. L. (1998) *Qualitative Research Methods for the Social Sciences*, 3rd edn, Boston: Allyn and Bacon.

Britten, N., Jones, R., Murphy, E. and Stacy, R. (1995) 'Qualitative research methods in general practice and primary care', *Family Practice*, 12: 104–14.

Carlson, T. B. and Hastie, P. A. (1997) 'The student social system within sport education', *Journal of Teaching in Physical Education*, 16: 176–95.

Chenail, R. J. (1995) 'Presenting qualitative data', *The Qualitative Report*, 2(3): <http://www.nova.edu/ssss/QR/QR2-3/presenting.html>

Creswell, J.W. (1998) *Qualitative Inquiry and Research Design: Choosing among Five Traditions*, Thousand Oaks, CA: Sage.

Creswell, J. W. (2009) *Research Design: Qualitative, Quantitative, and Mixed Methods Approaches*, Thousand Oaks, CA: Sage.

Creswell, J. W. and Miller, D. L. (2000) 'Determining validity in qualitative inquiry', *Theory into Practice*, 39: 124–30.

Frankel, R. M. and Devers, K. J. (2000) 'Study design in qualitative research 1: Developing questions and assessing resource needs', *Education for Health*, 13: 251–61.

Harry, B., Sturges, K. M. and Klingner, J. K. (2005) 'Mapping the process: An exemplar of process and challenge in grounded theory analysis', *Educational Researcher*, 34(2): 3–13.

Miles, M. B. and Huberman, A. M. (1994) *Qualitative data analysis*, Thousand Oaks, CA: Sage.

Oliver, D. G., Serovich, J. M. and Mason, T. L. (2005) 'Constraints and opportunities with interview transcription: Towards reflection in qualitative research', *Social Forces*, 84: 1273–89.

Seidel, J. V. (1998) *Qualitative Data Analysis*: <ftp://ftp.qualisresearch.com/pub/qda.pdf>

Stevens, M. M. (n.d.) 'Selected qualitative methods', in, M. B. Max and J. Lynn (eds) *Interactive Textbook on Clinical Symptom Research*: <http://symptomresearch.nih.gov/chapter_7/index.htm>

Further reading

Taylor-Powell, E. and Renner, M. (2003) *Analysing Qualitative Data*: <http://learningstore.uwex.edu/assets/pdfs/g3658-12.pdf>

Gibbs, G. (2007) *Analysing Qualitative Data (Qualitative Research Kit)*, London: Sage.

24 Analysing quantitative data

Beverley Hale and Alison Wakefield

> Oh, I know I need to know about research methods to pick up good grades at university, but when would I really need [this knowledge] as a physical education teacher?

Introduction

A feeling that research methods and statistics are peripheral to your university course in physical education (PE) is common among undergraduates. It is likely that you will begin to see the relevance after the units or modules of study have been completed. The realization of the importance of statistics usually occurs as you try to analyse quantitative data for a dissertation, or when you find it necessary to make meaning from information generated by the PE and youth sport contexts in which you work.

About us

Beverley Hale has been teaching statistics to university students following sport-related degree courses for many years. New students often think that they will not be able to do statistics because they have never been any good at mathematics. Beverley is convinced that statistics is *not* mathematics. Analysis of numeric data does not require you to be good at mathematics, although it does require a logical approach. Beverley's contribution to this chapter does not assume mathematical prowess and aims to demonstrate that anyone can do it!

Alison Wakefield is a trained secondary PE teacher who has been working in higher education for over 10 years. Her research interests have focused on physiological factors affecting performance within team sports and the factors affecting physical activity levels of children within school and beyond. Alison's view is that research projects should celebrate the achievement of students and showcase the research skills they have learned. Achievement is often overshadowed by students' lack of confidence in those skills. The assumed difficulties and complexities of data collection and analysis can consume the energies of undergraduate and postgraduate students, engulf their research questions and prevent the formation of pedagogical ideals and philosophies that should shape future professional practice.

Why use quantitative techniques?

Statistical procedures are used for three main purposes:

- *Data description* – Numerical summaries and graphs are used to describe large sets of numbers so that the key characteristics of the data can be appreciated. For example, reducing the actual ages of the members of a community gym to the mean and standard deviation, so that a reader can see the mid-point of the ages and how the members' actual ages spread away from that average.
- *To test for differences* – Data from more than one group are subjected to specific statistical tests to see whether there are group differences that might occur again in the same population.
- *To assess relationships* – Correlations and regression models (these look like mathematical equations) can be produced to see how two or more variables interrelate.

For example, if data were collected about young people's motivation for exercise participation, and the hours on average that they spend exercising in a week, it is possible to find out whether different types of motivation can predict participation levels.

Data description forms a part of every quantitative research project, but either an evaluation of group differences or an assessment of relationships usually follows the descriptive stage. The precise choice of statistical procedure is governed by the research question and the 'level' (or type) of data collected to investigate the research question.

This chapter does not tell you how to compute statistics and graphs, either by hand or with computer software, because there are many other texts that fulfil these functions. The 'References' section of this chapter suggests some texts that our students find helpful. The chapter is designed to help you make decisions about your choice of statistical procedures. It aims to address *why* a particular technique is applicable to specific contexts, and what the resultant values *mean*. We include some of the tricks of the trade that have helped our students to make informed decisions about the choice of statistical procedures for their own research, and to prepare them to critique the methods documented in published papers.

It is vital to appreciate what quantitative analysis can achieve, and where its limitations lie. The most important thing to realize is that quantitative data can rarely explain *why* an observed phenomenon occurs or how to deal with it. Qualitative data are usually needed to augment quantitative findings if you are looking for solutions.

Common approaches used to formulate research questions in PE and youth sport, within undergraduate and postgraduate courses and professional practice, have been outlined in Chapters 1 and 8 of this book. Research questions at undergraduate level may aim to investigate topics such as physical activity levels of children, the effect of music on training intensity, or the relationship between reaction time from the start gun and finish time in competitive swimming events. All such questions generate quantitative data that can be described and summarized. In some circumstances, these summaries can be augmented with statistical tests that aim to generalize the findings for the particular sample to other groups of similar people. Much is made of 'significant differences' or 'significant relationships', but these results must be interpreted in the context of the research. For example, if a particular running shoe shows a 'significant improvement' in run times, the magnitude of the difference and its consistency over the sample of runners caused the statistics to produce a significant result. However, the size of the improvement (as represented by the mean) must be considered in the context of race distance. A one-second improvement could be important for 400 m success, but of little consequence to marathon runners.

Statistical findings will never 'prove' anything; the best they can accomplish is to disprove, or falsify, something. Statistical tests are based on probability, measured on a scale from 0 (zero – impossible) to 1 (dead certain). If a particular sample of people participates in a piece of research, it is impossible to know whether selection of one further or one different person might have altered the findings. If we test only five or six people, it could be quite likely that other people would behave differently. If we test five or six hundred people, that likelihood diminishes, but it does not ever go away completely; hence, the inability to 'prove' anything with statistics. Disproof is easier because one participant who behaves contrary to a belief is sufficient to show that the belief is not always true.

One of the biggest limitations of quantitative analysis is imposed by the data collected. The assumption that all numbers have the same integrity can cause misapplication of statistical procedures, which generates meaningless results. Computer software will conduct an analysis if there are sufficient numbers to fit into the formula for the generation of results. The problem is that some of the data we can collect and recognize as numbers are not suitable for the calculations included in those formulae. A consideration of the types (or levels) of numerical data that can be collected forms the initial part of the next section of this chapter.

Things to consider when choosing a statistical procedure

Quantitative texts often focus on statistical processes to the detriment of the link between the research question and analysis procedures. Crucial issues for selection of an appropriate analysis are:

- The overarching research question;
- The research design and its influence on data collection – i.e., data from questionnaire research are different from data measured in a laboratory;
- The interrelationship of data – have many variables been collected from a sample? Are there repeated measurements on the same group of people (within-groups design), or is a comparison of two different groups required (between-groups design)?
- The level and potential variability of the data – numeric data do not have uniform meaning. Sometimes they are simple codes; at other times they represent a measurement on either a discrete scale (fragmented, such as the number of PE

lessons in a week where half or quarter lessons are not possible), or a continuous scale, such as age, where each year can be split into months, weeks etc.

- The structure of the data – do they follow a recognized distribution?

Levels of data

Numeric data must have equal intervals between each value if most statistical procedures are to provide a meaningful result. Some data do not meet these criteria. Table 24.1 describes the four levels of quantitative data, providing examples of each.

Table 24.1 reveals that each level has the properties of the one before, but with additional refinement. Only interval and ratio data are strong enough for the application of most statistical formulae, so the level of data exerts a very strong influence on the choice of analysis. A limited range of statistical procedures can be applied to ordinal and nominal data, since the numbers lack sensitivity. To appreciate what we mean by sensitivity, consider the child who comes second in a race. 'Second' is an ordinal-level numeric description. The child finished behind one person, but in front of everybody else in the race. Any situation in Figure 24.1 could apply, among several other possibilities. However, knowledge of the race times (ratio-level data) is necessary to evaluate the child's performance.

What shape is the distribution of the data?

The pattern of data distribution is important for interval- and ratio-level data, since more rigorous summaries and tests can be applied if it conforms to one of a family of recognized distributions. The distribution most relevant to PE and youth sport is the

Table 24.1 Characteristics of each level of quantitative data

Data level	Characteristics	Examples
Nominal	Numbers do not have any numerical meaning. The values are used as codes, for example to differentiate between groups. No hierarchy is implied.	Coding school subjects: Maths = 1, English = 2, Science = 3, PE = 4 etc.
Ordinal	Numbers still describe categories, but there is a hierarchy implied by the values.	Coding of Olympic medals to produce a medals point score for each nation: Gold = 3 points, Silver = 2 points, Bronze = 1 point.
Interval	The gaps (intervals) between the values are equal, but the scale does not start from zero. This means that comparisons such as half or double are not meaningful.	Temperature on the Celsius or Fahrenheit scales.
Ratio	Numbers on a measurement scale that has equal intervals and starts from a meaningful zero. This means that comparisons such as half or three times as big are meaningful.	Height. Time – when the clock starts at the beginning of an event. Relative time is interval level.

Finish line			Race
1st	2nd, 3rd, 4th, 5th		A
1st, 2nd, 3rd, 4th		5th	B
1st	2nd	3rd, 4th, 5th	C

Figure 24.1 Situations that could arise from ordinal-level reporting of race finish positions. Spaces are indicative of time lapses.

normal distribution. There are many normal distributions, but they all conform to a 'bell-shaped' pattern: most data values should be close to the mean and there should be fewer data points as values move further from the mean. The mean of the data should be situated such that 50 per cent of the data are one side of the mean value and 50 per cent on the other.

Histograms are a good method of visually representing the shape of data distribution. They are rather like bar charts, but have a continuous scale on the x-axis, where bar charts have discrete group labels. As a consequence, there are no gaps between the bars. The histograms in Figure 24.2 show the distributions of finish times in 4 × 400 m relay races over two seasons. In season one, the mean (marked by a vertical line on the graph) is not in the middle of the data. A few slower finish times raised the mean. The graph lacks symmetry and is said to be 'positively skewed'. The race times in the second season are more evenly balanced, with a more obvious bell shape to the distribution. Season two is likely to be normally distributed.

Other frequently used checks for normal distribution are the standardized skewness and kurtosis values. Skewness indicates lack of symmetry and kurtosis evaluates distortion in the vertical plane (the curvature). To calculate skewness and kurtosis it is best to use computer software because the calculations are very complex and time consuming. Software usually provides what is known as a standardized

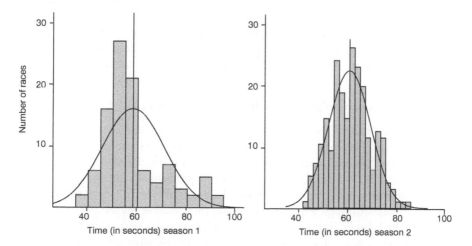

Figure 24.2 Finish times for 4 × 400 m relay races over two different seasons

or Z-skewness and Z-kurtosis. Values between ±2 are said to indicate data that are near normal. We suggest that if most groups give values between ±2 but there are a few between ±3, then statistical tests that require normally distributed data can be employed.

The purpose of the mean, median and mode is to provide a measure of central tendency – the middle of the data. They are all different forms of average. In general, the mean is appropriate for interval and ratio data, the median for ordinal data and the mode for nominal data. However, it is important that summaries represent the data in a way that reflects the set of values. Interval or ratio data that do not follow a normal distribution are often better represented by a median. The median is the middle value when all data are put into order and is therefore not sensitive to unusually high or low values. For example, a sample of athletes from a youth basketball squad will generate skewed performance data if one athlete is of international standard. In this circumstance, the median of the data may be more representative of the sample. The mode is the most common value in a data set and is the best summary to use with nominal data, which assigns people to categories. Always use the standard deviation with the mean and the range with the median as a measure of data variation or spread. There is no measure of variation to accompany the mode, because it summarizes data that have arbitrary numerical codes with no true value.

Normally distributed data allows the use of procedures known as *parametric tests*. Parametric tests are able to identify smaller differences than their *non-parametric* equivalents. Parametric tests transform data and then compare the extent to which the groups differ from a standardized normal distribution through knowledge of the distribution boundaries or parameters. Non-parametric tests rely on ranking the data values in each of the groups and then examining the extent of overlap. Ordinal-level data are sufficient for non-parametric tests. Fallowfield, Hale and Wilkinson (2005) provide the calculations for both parametric and non-parametric tests.

Statistical tests for relationship between variables are determined by the level of data collected. Higher levels of data can be downgraded, but it is impossible to upgrade data to a higher level. This means that the choice of relationship test (or correlation) is dictated by the lowest level of data in the comparison. Table 24.2 shows the statistical procedures that are suitable for specific levels of data.

How statistics can help to make informed decisions

The tests identified in Table 24.2 are applicable in controlled circumstances, such as experiments. However, the implications of applying tests to non-experimental situations need careful consideration to ensure we do not draw inappropriate or incorrect conclusions. Quantitative data in published papers must therefore be read critically. For example, it would be a mistake to collect data from two separate schools through a questionnaire and then analyse the data for differences between the schools through parametric, independent *t*-tests or non-parametric Mann–Whitney tests. The tests are appropriate for the structure of the data, but are *not* suited to the data collection method, since it cannot be assumed that those

Table 24.2 Appropriate tests for particular levels of data

Research requirement	Level of data			
	Nominal	*Ordinal*	*Interval/ratio: normally distributed*	*Interval/ratio: but not normally distributed*
Descriptive statistics	Mode	Median and range	Mean and standard deviation	Median and range
Differences between two related groups	–	Wilcoxon test	Paired *t*-test	Wilcoxon test
Difference between two independent groups	–	Mann–Whitney *U* test	Independent *t*-test	Mann–Whitney *U* test
Differences between more than two related groups	–	Friedman test	Within-groups analysis of variance (ANOVA)	Friedman test
Difference between more than two independent groups	–	Kruskal–Wallis test	Between-groups analysis of variance (ANOVA)	Kruskal–Wallis test
Correlation	Chi-squared test of association	Spearman's rank correlation coefficient	Pearson's product moment correlation coefficient	Pearson's product moment correlation coefficient
	Correlation analysis may be followed by regression analysis to investigate the interrelationship between several variables, or to see if it is possible to predict one variable from a group of other related variables.			

who filled in the questionnaire in School A are comparable to those in School B. A common and often quoted rule for making decisions from quantitative data through the use of statistical tests is that we 'must compare like with like'. The tests mentioned could be used if the questionnaires had been given to specific individuals, purposively selected because of the similarity of their roles in each school. The most appropriate analysis if there was no such control would be to use descriptive statistics, graphs and summaries, to provide an overview of the situation in each school.

The focus of a research question should clarify whether an analysis of differences or relationships is required. A difference test could be applied to an evaluation of two different groups, such as the effect of a circuit training session on the heart rate recovery (HRR) of a 16–18-year-old hockey squad and a 16–18-year-old rugby squad. In this circumstance, the two squads could attend the same training session and the HRR for each participant could be measured at the end. A test of difference between rugby and hockey could be conducted to evaluate whether the HRR of rugby players differs from that of hockey players in that particular age group. Alternatively, if the research question demands evaluation of whether intensity of circuit training is related to HRR, data need to be collected after exercise on different activities around the circuit that have been predetermined to require differing exercise intensities. In this context, whether a participant plays rugby or hockey is irrelevant. Of importance is how each participant's recovery rate is related to the levels of exercise intensity, and correlation analysis should be employed. Consider the research questions you developed in response to Chapter 1 to identify the type of statistical analysis that could be used to evaluate them.

Once the particular statistical procedure has been selected, there are many texts that explain how to conduct the test. Some provide instructions for analysis with computer software, which makes it easy to handle large data sets. Fallowfield, Hale and Wilkinson (2005), and Thomas, Nelson and Silverman (2005) provide information about the most commonly used statistical procedures for PE and sport, without reference to particular statistical packages. Field (2009) uses the computer software program SPSS (PASW) as a vehicle to explain statistical procedures, but also includes readable explanations of the applications of tests and the interpretation of results.

The role of probability in decision making

Statistical tests work with probability to determine the likelihood of seeing similar outcomes again. Probability is measured on a scale from 0 (zero – an event is impossible) to 1 (an event is certain). The difficult part of the interpretation process is that the probability relates to the situation known as a *null hypothesis*, that is, the chance of *nothing* happening. If we have tested rugby and hockey players' HRR because we think it should differ, and we get a result from a statistical test that provides a probability very close to 0 (zero), the interpretation is that it is very unlikely that HRR is the same; it is therefore probably different: a rather complicated process!

One of the tricks of reading statistical data is to be alert to misleading interpretations. If a very small sample is discussed in terms of percentages, it is worthwhile considering how many people equate to 1 per cent. In a sample of 10 pupils, 20 per cent could be reported as inactive if two of them habitually avoid PE lessons. Over a class of 30 pupils, the same two pupils become approximately 7 per cent, a seemingly more acceptable figure, yet the situation which gave rise to both percentages could be the same. Where the size of reported standard deviations is half or more of the mean, summary statistics indicate that data are not normally distributed. Scrutinize any graphs closely – these are often a source of illumination about the true nature of data – but do not forget to check scales carefully. Very small differences can look bigger if a scale is altered to give that impression. Histograms and boxplots are particularly useful to identify outliers, which could have an undue impact on outcomes. Look at the strength of correlations as well as the probability, to make sure you appreciate the full situation. These are some examples of ways in which results can be misinterpreted in published papers.

Case study 1 The use of notational analysis to determine whether there is a relationship between pitch surface and the frequency of different pass shots in hockey

Performance analysis is always carried out in the field, to investigate real situations. Research purists have criticized the approach because of the lack of control exercised over the performance, and because 'performance' can be viewed as very personal. However, PE teachers and sports coaches, including those of youth teams, probably view these as positive attributes. O'Donoghue (2010) is a useful introductory text. This case study indicates how statistical testing of data derived from a notational analysis of performance data can inform the professional practices of those engaged in PE or youth sports.

In recent years, many schools and sports clubs in the UK have installed artificial hockey pitches, either sand or water based, in order to circumvent the wet weather conditions that make traditional turf pitches too muddy for matches for much of the season. Knowledge of how the playing surface affects performance is invaluable to those teaching children to play on a mixture of surfaces, in order to be able to cope with away matches on the pitches of other schools or clubs. Video footage of hockey matches on grass, water-based and sand-based pitches were obtained by filming six interschool hockey matches at three different locations, two matches at each location. All of the games were within the same school league and were deemed to be at the same level of play.

Two teachers analysed the videos, looking at the frequency of different types of passes made by the home team only (because those children were familiar with the surface). The aim was to see if there was evidence that different pitch surfaces generated different frequencies of the three main pass types, flicks, pushes and hits. The teachers checked at the end of the videos that they agreed about the numbers of each type of pass. A chi-squared test was appropriate to analyse the data because this test can identify association between different categories – in this case the pass categories with the surface types. The teachers filled in a table, similar to that shown in Table 24.3, with the number of each shot they saw on each type of surface.

The probability of a result is said to be 'significant' if it falls below a pre-decided 'significance level'. This is usually 0.05 for PE and sport-related research, and is taken to mean that the probability is close enough to 0 (zero) if it is 0.05 or below. Such a result suggests that the association between pass and pitch surface will happen again and again, although it does not *prove* that it will. The interpretation of the findings and the application to coaching strategies require care. The players must not be coached to expect certain passes to the exclusion of others. However, the findings can be used to help players adapt to different surface types when they travel to schools where the pitch surfaces differ from their own.

Table 24.3 Table to record the frequencies of each type of shot on each pitch

Pass/surface	Grass	Water-based	Sand-based	Total
Flick				
Push				
Hit				
Total				

Case study 2 Selection of statistical analysis procedures for a study of female students' participation in physical activity

Young females' participation in physical activity has been a focus of research in previous years and has generated vast amounts of numerical data. Examination of curriculum time and extracurricular club registers for 14–16-year-old females could reveal whether physical activity patterns in a school reflect the national trend and identify activities that would motivate further participation.

A second, experimental, phase could be the design and implementation of an intervention programme aimed to improve female participation rates. Measurement of the impact of the programme would require statistical analysis. Questionnaire responses from female pupils might help a PE department provide a range of 'female-focused' activities, the impact of which could be measured across a term. Registers of attendance, potential health and perceptual benefits of the intervention and pre- and post-intervention measures could be recorded, such as body composition and physical self-perception profiling (Fox, 1990). These measures could be used to track changes and evaluate the need for female-focused extracurricular clubs.

This research follows a repeated measures design, where the same participants (control and experimental) are measured in this case from pre- to post-intervention regardless of whether they attend extracurricular sessions (see Figure 24.3).

From this experimental design, a number of research questions can be examined. One example is provided in Table 24.4.

In addition to the above suggestions, a more complex analysis of the physiological variables could be undertaken to compare the pre- and post-intervention measurements within the groups. A mixed design analysis of variance (ANOVA) would fulfil that function because there is more than one independent variable: pre- and post-intervention within the same group of pupils and participation groups of different pupils.

Parallels can be drawn between this case study and the second case study in Chapter 8. Look at that case study and try to determine the analysis you think should be applied before reading the next paragraph.

Data were collected from the same children, so a within-group analysis of a repeated measures design with two groups and some degree of experimental control are appropriate. The mean mathematics test scores for the pupils will follow a normal distribution (the central limit theorem states that means are always normally distributed), so paired *t*-tests are appropriate to evaluate differences between mean test scores to see whether there is evidence that PE prior to mathematics tests improves marks. The Strengths and Difficulties Questionnaire subscales can be taken as ratio-level data for the same reason applied to the PSPP data in the case study above. Normal distribution checks would determine whether further paired samples *t*-tests could be used, or if Wilcoxon tests would be more appropriate to evaluate whether PE lessons affect behaviour in subsequent mathematics lessons.

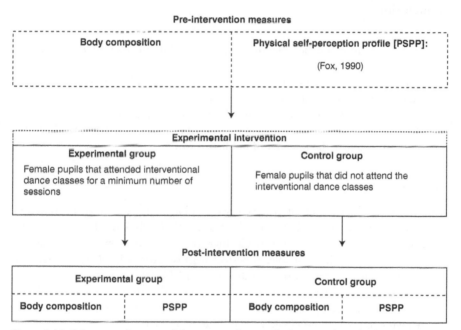

Figure 24.3 Schematic diagram of the proposed research design and methods to investigate female pupils' participation

Table 24.4 Increased participation in extracurricular programme and physical self-perception profiles in 14–16-year-old females

Does increased participation in an extracurricular programme improve physical self-perception profiles in 14–16-year-old females?

Considerations and statistical analysis:

a) Experimental vs control pre-intervention physical self-perception profile analysis (independent / between groups design: independent *t*-test / Mann–Whitney);

b) Experimental pre- to post-intervention physical self-perception profile analysis (repeated measures design: paired *t*-test / Wilcoxon);

c) Control pre- to post-intervention physical self-perception profile analysis (repeated measures design: paired *t*-test / Wilcoxon);

d) Experimental vs control post-intervention physical self-perception profile analysis (independent / between groups design: independent *t*-test / Mann–Whitney).

Conclusions

• There is a strong link between the research question, the research design and the choice of analysis.
• The analysis is limited by the sensitivity of the data collected. The type of data required to answer a particular research question needs careful consideration.
• Inferences for data analysis are limited by the research design.
• Read statistics intelligently to avoid potential mistakes in research work, and to critically evaluate the integrity of published work.

Key terms

Correlation   The relationship between two or more variables. This is measured on a scale from −1 to +1. Zero (0) indicates no relationship at all, +1 is a perfect positive relationship: as one variable increases the second variable increases in proportion to the first variable. A perfect negative correlation (−1) is where one variable decreases in proportion to the other variable.

Levels of data   The characteristics that can be attached to the numeric data collected as part of a research project. There is increasing numeric power attached to the following four levels: nominal, ordinal, interval and ratio.

Probability   The chance of seeing similar results if the statistical test were to be repeated on similar data collected from the same population. Probability is measured on a scale from 0 (zero – impossible) to 1 (absolutely certain).

Regression   A procedure which follows a correlation analysis if there is a suggestion that relationships are sufficiently strong to be able to predict one variable from others included in the analysis.

Statistical test   A procedure that enables probability to influence decisions of generalizability based on the data collected.

References

Fallowfield, J. L., Hale, B. J. and Wilkinson, D. M. (2005) *Using Statistics in Sport and Exercise Research*, Chichester: Lotus Publishing (2nd edn available in 2011).

Field, A. (2009) *Discovering Statistics Using SPSS*, 3rd edn, London: Sage.

Fox, K. R. (1990) *The Physical Self-perception Profile Manual*, DeKalb, IL: Office for Health Promotion, Northern Illinois University.

O'Donoghue, P. (2010) *Research Methods for Sports Performance Analysis*, Oxford: Routledge.

Thomas, J. R., Nelson, J. K. and Silverman, S. J. (2005) *Research Methods in Physical Activity*, 5th edn, Champaign, IL: Human Kinetics.

Part V

Communicating your research

25 Effective research writing

David Kirk and Ashley Casey

> Good writing isn't forged by magic or hatched out of thin air. Good writing happens when human beings take particular steps to take control of their sentences, to make their words do what they want them to do.
>
> (Fletcher, 2000: 5)

Introduction

This chapter explores ways in which research writing can be most effective for its intended audiences. Research is time consuming and sometimes expensive, but this considerable investment could be undermined if researchers cannot articulate their findings. Unfortunately, as Cuthbert, Spark and Burke (2009) recently wrote, there is a clear gulf between the writing that people are asked to do in their school and undergraduate programmes and the often highly specialized ways in which they are required and expected to write as post-graduate, doctoral, early career and established researchers. The process described by Fletcher (2000) in the opening quote may arguably be applicable to all forms of written communication. But because research is a 'truth-seeking' process (however we understand the term 'truth'), researchers have a special responsibility when they write to carefully construct and articulate their arguments and present their work in a manner that is credible and accessible to readers.

We think effective writing is an integral part of the research process, rather than something that is separate and occurs only once all of the fieldwork, experiments or interviews have been completed and the data analysed. This is so, regardless of whether an author writes in the first or the third person, because we continue to develop insights as we engage in a process of making our own personal knowledge public. One important implication of this perspective on effective research writing is for researchers to be aware of the variety of contexts for writing and how their understanding of both their target audience and the type and genre of 'publication' influences the writing process. While different writing skills are required by different readerships, including other researchers, professional colleagues and students, we propose nevertheless that there are generic technical aspects of writing that apply in all contexts. We conclude the chapter with an example of writing for research journals in physical education to illustrate the importance of considering contexts and the 'basics' of effective research writing.

About us

David: I've probably written hundreds of thousands of words on physical education and related topics over the past 30 years, many of them published in books and journals. I can't say whether these have been good or useful or helpful words; whether when strung together into sentences and paragraphs and sections and papers or chapters or books or reports they have been meaningful or obscure; a pleasure or a chore to read. It is for you, the reader, to decide these matters. What I do believe, though, is that while writing well is an art, every one of us can learn to write better.

Ashley: As the junior author, I was intrigued to see how I might write in a manner that would challenge my peers to challenge their readers. This aim was made even more complex, and potentially unattainable, when I acknowledged that my experiences are those of a beginner 'insider' teacher-researcher striving to turn his first bits of research into meaningful research papers and then publish them. However, I felt that having experienced the dichotomy between writing personal accounts and trying to generalize from them, I had something to offer. I have brought one question with me to this writing process: how do I maximize the impact of my work without sacrificing quality for quantity?

Writing as inquiry and author position

Even the most rigorous and scholarly research on an important research topic might be considered unsuccessful if it fails to engage the intended audience. In their account, 'Writing: A method of inquiry', Richardson and St Pierre (2005) confess that they have yawned their way through many supposedly exemplary research studies and even abandoned some, half read. It was this that led these researchers to develop the idea of writing as an integral part of the research process, rather than as a process outside and separate from research. Richardson (2000) argues that this is the case regardless of how authors position themselves, whether they write themselves into the text (as in narrative research), or out of the text (as in some scientific disciplines).

Effective writing can be in either the first or the third person. Whichever author position is chosen, it is important that authors maintain consistency. This isn't always as easy as it might seem. Ellis and Bochner (2000: 734) note that even in work on self-writing, where writing as 'I' is highly appropriate, authors sometimes struggle to be consistent:

> [T]he 'I' usually disappeared after the introduction and then reappeared abruptly in the conclusion ... and the authors almost never became characters in the stories they wrote ... Why should we take it for granted that the authors' personal feelings and thoughts should be omitted in a handbook chapter? After all, who is the person collecting the evidence, drawing the inferences, and reaching the conclusions?

Richardson (2000) suggests that, whichever author position is adopted, there is still an underlying need for quality. Indeed, she argues that 'how we are expected to write affects what we can write about' (Richardson, 2000: 7). She supports the idea that writing can be both literary *and* factual. It can include various devices that promote effective communication, such as 'dramatic recall, strong imagery, fleshed-out characters, unusual phrasing, puns, subtexts, allusions, flashbacks, flash-forwards, tone shifts, synecdoche, dialogue and interior monologue' (2000: 11). She argues that, regardless of the topic, the genre of research or the discipline of the researcher, effective writing is a form of inquiry itself and is therefore a part of the research process.

The notion of writing as inquiry suggests, then, that research writing is never a neutral process. The data researchers include in written texts – whether they be results from a questionnaire, voices from an interview or observations from the field – are typically selected from a larger bank of data. Selection of data for inclusion in a text is the outcome of an intentional process of reporting findings and evidencing arguments. At the heart of effective research writing is a process of selection, of what to include and what to omit, a process that ultimately reflects what it is authors believe to be worth saying about a topic (Ryan and Bernard, 2000).

Contexts for effective writing

There are a number of possible motives for a researcher to write. While some researchers' motives might legitimately include the desire to influence policy and practice, enhance one's career, or possibly just to stay employed ('publish or perish'), arguably the most obvious motive for writing is the desire to communicate the outcomes of a process of research activity. Research is a highly social activity, and researchers typically belong to at least one intellectual community, organized around a learned society or a professional association and perhaps identified with one or more journals.

In this context, effective writing is essential, because without it there would be little point in going through the effort of doing research if no one else is going to learn from it (Kitchin and Fuller, 2005). Writing involves the passage of what is originally personal knowledge into a form that is publicly accessible. Part of the skill of effective research writing, then, is to understand the various forms of 'publication' and the ways in which they influence – indeed, define – what will count as effective writing.

Books, journal papers, conferences, theses and reports are some of the ways in which what was personal knowledge becomes publicly accessible. Each of these forms of publication has its own requirements for effective writing. One of the primary considerations when seeking to identify these requirements is the intended audience for the writing. Most academic writing will have at least one of three audiences: fellow researchers, other professionals (such as teachers and coaches), and university students. Each of these groups will determine the form effective research writing can take

When writing primarily for fellow researchers, whether in the form of books and book chapters, reports, journal or conference papers, a peer-review process is often used to determine the newsworthiness, rigour and scholarship of the writing. Writing for peers is invariably highly valued within the academy, as an indicator of the quality of research. It is worth noting, at the same time, that such writing may be highly specialized and may be read by only a small number of peers (Kitchin and Fuller, 2005).

Writing for a professional audience typically involves a different approach, often requiring the omission of highly specialized language or 'jargon', using practical examples to illustrate concepts and adopting a less formal tone (Epstein et al., 2005). These characteristics often mislead inexperienced writers to believe that it is easier to write for a professional audience than for a readership of fellow researchers. This is not so. To write effectively for a professional audience is a specialized skill in itself. An effectively written text in this context can benefit from the fact that the readership can often be quite large, with the potential for high impact of research. To write effectively for a professional readership, the writer must report research findings accurately and in sufficient detail so that practitioners can judge the usefulness or otherwise to them of the research.

Writing for students often takes the form of textbooks. Effective writing in this context is another specialized skill. The best textbooks are pedagogical in their approach, seeking to introduce students to a topic or a field of research in a carefully structured and progressive process. In some respects, textbook writers are writing to support their peers in their teaching, and the effectiveness of the writing in this context will be judged not just in terms of its accessibility to students, but also in terms of its usefulness as a teaching tool.

Some technical aspects of effective writing

Each of the contexts for effective writing formed by the audiences discussed above requires, as we have said, specialized skills that are different in each case. Nevertheless, there are some technical aspects of effective research writing that apply, to varying degrees, to each context. Considered within each of these contexts and applied appropriately, attention to these technical aspects of effective writing will pay dividends.

Drafting and redrafting, using technology

A first draft of a text will rarely if ever be the best and final draft. Indeed, if writing is part of the process of inquiry itself, then it is often the case that new insights are gained as we write. With word-processing technology, drafting and redrafting are not the chore they once were. Share your writing with a trusted colleague or friend and invite constructive feedback, and be prepared to act on good advice to improve your writing.

Sentence construction and language – can I say it more clearly?

Consider the length of sentences. Long sentences with many clauses are often tough to read. It is also easy as a writer to lose your train of thought in a long sentence.

Break long sentences up. If used carefully, varying the length of sentences can give the text an interesting rhythm. Ask yourself whether you could say something more clearly, particularly if you are explaining a complex process or an abstract idea.

Headings and subheadings – creating a conceptual map

Headings and subheadings well deployed in a text can make your writing much more reader friendly than large chunks of undifferentiated material. They also provide a kind of conceptual map for your writing. A reader should be able to grasp the topic and some of the main ideas or arguments from reading the headings and subheadings alone.

Paragraphs and sections

Beginners to research writing often do not know when to create a new paragraph or a new section in a text. Sometimes, it is not a straightforward process. It will depend on the intended audience. But as a rough rule of thumb, a new paragraph signals a new idea or a significant development of an idea. The first sentence of the paragraph should state what that idea is. The rest of the paragraph is then an elaboration of the idea, perhaps providing some examples or some arguments for and against. Sections can be built applying the same principle.

Linking paragraphs and sections

Maintaining continuity in writing is important so that you move logically from one idea to another. It is important to avoid making conceptual leaps that may seem obvious to the writer but that leave the reader floundering. It is sometimes helpful to think of the first sentence in a paragraph and first paragraph in a section as the entry to each respectively. It is an opportunity to draw the reader in. The final sentence or paragraph correspondingly can be thought of as an exit, as a means of propelling the reader to the next main idea or topic.

When to write the conclusion – exiting

Just as we can think of entering and exiting from paragraphs and sections, we can also think of the introduction and conclusion of a piece of writing as an entrance and exit respectively. An inexperienced writer, when asked 'When do you write the conclusion?', might say that it is the last thing that is written. This in most circumstances may be the wrong answer. Often, it is the second to last thing to write.

When to write the introduction – entering

The correct answer in most cases is that the introduction is written last. Why? If writing is part of the inquiry process, then we often literally don't know what we have to say about something until we have written it. To write the introduction first, an author would already have worked out exactly what they plan to say. Some experienced and artful writers are indeed able to do this. The rest of us can't. If the conclusion is an exit that propels the reader into future investigation armed with the insights the writer has provided, then the introduction draws the reader in. It commands their attention, introduces the topic and establishes its importance, before providing an overview of what the reader can expect to encounter.

Blogging

Blogging can be a very helpful way to practise writing skills, as well as providing a useful means of communication in itself. Setting an exact limit on words (say 200, precisely) and writing regularly about a range of topics, helps authors to write clearly and concisely. It also helps to choose your words carefully in order to get your message across.

Read while you write

Effective writing requires extensive reading. Richards (2010: 50) argues that reading is not always given the consideration it deserves: 'If you can't think of anything to write, you don't have writer's block. You have readers' block. You need to stop writing and start reading more about your topic.' Some authors (see Epstein et al., 2005; Kitchin and Fuller, 2005 for examples) also suggest that writers need to read. However, this is not a naive process of passing our eyes over the words (Epstein et al., 2005) but the active process of internalizing and challenging the words that are read. In undertaking this process, writers begin to understand what aspects of other writers' work are relevant, usable and newsworthy.

Writing for journals: An illustrative example

It was noted earlier that there are a number of ways to transfer personal knowledge into a public forum. For each form of publication, there is a range of writing requirements. An illustration can be provided by analysing the requirements of five peer-reviewed journals in one field – physical education – and noting their different aims, scope and mission.

Sport, Education and Society, published by Routledge, invites 'social science research on pedagogy, policy and the body in society'. The *European Physical Education Review*, a Sage journal, publishes papers based on 'scholarly enquiry in the broad field of physical education, including sport and leisure issues and research'. Former Human Kinetics and now Routledge journal, *Quest*'s 'primary purpose is to publish manuscripts that address issues and concerns relevant and meaningful to kinesiology and physical education in higher education'. A long-running research publication, *Journal of Teaching in Physical Education*, which is a Human Kinetics journal, explores 'teaching, teacher education, and curriculum as these fields relate to physical activity in schools, communities, higher education, and sport'. The newest journal of the five, published by Routledge, is *Physical Education and Sport Pedagogy*, which 'promotes the communication of educational research in physical education and youth sport and related fields such as teacher and coach education'.

While these five journals serve the research community in physical education and sport, each occupies a specific niche. *Sport, Education and Society*, for example, emphasizes social science research, while *Quest* mentions higher education as a specific focus, and *Physical Education and Sport Pedagogy* is concerned with pedagogy and educational research. Having considered contexts, audiences and some generic technical aspects of writing, it is also important to target the right journal to match the topic of the written text, in this case a paper, and to ensure that it is appropriate to the aims, mission and scope of the targeted journal. Getting this wrong is one of the main causes of rejection for inexperienced writers, because the first question an editor asks of a paper when it arrives on their desk is, 'Is the topic of this paper appropriate to my journal?' If the answer is no, the paper is immediately rejected, without review.

Targeting the right journal is, then, a very important aspect of effective writing. Having cleared the hurdle of the editor's first question, the subsequent successful passage through the review process to publication will be aided by paying close attention to the 'basics'. These have been defined by Kitchin and Fuller (2005) as appropriate writing style, grammar and punctuation, narrative and structure, clarity, writing within word limits, and having a good title.

Good grammar and punctuation are prerequisites in any form of writing, as both provide the reader with a structure that helps them interpret the author's intended meaning. Readability is made easier when the text is well structured:

> Any text, whether factually based or fiction, should read like a story; there should be a beginning, a middle and an end, with a strong, coherent plot-line running throughout linking all the intervening sentences and sections.
>
> (Kitchin and Fuller, 2005: 19)

Applying these rules brings clarity to the text, so that ideas, arguments and evidence are strongly represented and are comprehensively explained to the reader. All journal articles have a predefined word limit since, in order to stay within budget, publishers set limits on the number of pages that can be included in each issue of a journal.

The title of the article is another very important, but often under-considered, aspect of effective writing. This has become even more important as online searches of library and other databases use precise terms to find relevant material. Many potential readers will use the title as their primary filter for what might be of interest to them, and sometimes a paper might be overlooked simply because its title doesn't engage with the target readership. Or, alternatively, when authors use analogy or colloquialisms in titles, a paper can appear in surprising and unexpected databases.

While it is crucially important to get the basics right, Kitchin and Fuller (2005) also highlight a number of common mistakes beyond poor grammar and punctuation that limit the effectiveness of writing. *Padding* is the inclusion of text that, no matter how well it is written, lends little or nothing to the central arguments of a paper. *Repetition* is often the result of having too few points to make, suggesting superficial or 'thin' analysis. Conversely, *trying to say too much* may leave the author with too little space to communicate effectively all of the key points of the research to the reader. Good ideas can get lost in the crowd and the text can be seen as bitty and confusing. The final avoidable error identified by Kitchin and Fuller (2005) is failing to leave some time between finishing writing, a 'cooling-off' period, and sending the paper to a journal for review. Leaving a suitable gap (measured in days or weeks, not hours) allows writers to return to the text with fresh eyes, to remove any basic errors and have a final start-to-finish read through.

Following the advice in this section and elsewhere in the chapter will assist you to become a more effective writer, but it cannot guarantee that your work will be published. JOPERD (*Journal of Physical Education, Recreation and Dance*), a US-based professional journal, reports a 28 per cent acceptance rate on its website (i.e., only one in four papers submitted are published) (JOPERD, 2011). In the next section, we provide a case study of Ashley and his colleague's attempt to publish from a research project and the importance of persisting in the face of requests to revise and resubmit or rejection.

Case study: Ashley

Following a discussion in 2006, and a follow-up email in 2007, it took the authors nearly two years to decide upon a research study that they thought was both newsworthy and interesting. Once the topic was decided, then the opportunity to undertake the research had to be found. The study, which began in September 2008 explored students' use of games-making in secondary school (pupils aged 11–18). It was a demanding undertaking and the first draft of the paper took several months to prepare. Its reception at review was less than favourable and it was flatly rejected. Why?

We had targeted the journal specifically, knew of its recent content, had written in the style of the journal and created, we thought, a good story and some interesting conclusions. The story was about a teacher's and his students' experiences of games-making. The reviews were quite helpful, even though we didn't agree with everything that was written. The advice we received from the review process was supplemented by some good ideas and suggestions made by colleagues who acted as critical friends and proofreaders of the text. Armed with all of this advice we started again – not from scratch but from a new angle and with a new journal in mind. We submitted and waited.

The results of the new reviews were very helpful but the result was similar to the previous submission. We were asked to make some major revisions and to extract a swathe of new information from our data. One of the reviews in particular was incredibly detailed and allowed us to find the true heart of the paper we wanted to write. Unfortunately, the resulting revision to the paper was over 10,000 words in length and journals tend not to accept such long articles. So we made the decision to approach the journal and propose that we split the paper in two. The editors accepted our suggestion but only if each paper was capable of standing 'on its own two feet'. The first paper would be on participant experience and the second on learning. The two papers went into review once again and both reviewers came back with new suggestions and, eventually, one became a new co-author for paper two (after discussions with the editorial team we invited one of the reviewers to join us as an author). This occurred because of the detailed feedback we received. The input was of such quality that it challenged us to develop our original idea and write a second, stand-alone paper on learning. This is the advantage of good reviewers and it is a model to which I try to adhere when I am reviewing myself. Both papers are now in press and our research around games-making has moved on.

Summary

We have proposed that it is useful to regard writing as an integral part of the research process, rather than as a separate task that is undertaken once a study has been completed and is ready to be published. This is the case regardless of the author position as first or third person, the genre of the writing and the discipline of the researcher. The implication of this perspective is that researchers must consider carefully the process of how knowledge that is initially personal to them becomes public. Awareness of the various contexts for publication is an important part of this process. Specialized and somewhat different skills are required when writing for peers, compared with writing for professionals and students. Nevertheless, there are technical aspects of writing that are relevant to each context in varying degrees. We use the example of writing for specific research journals in physical education to illustrate contextual and technical issues, and finish with a brief case study of Ashley's experience of how persistence and willingness to accept advice in the review process resulted in much-improved papers being eventually published.

Key terms

Effective writing A process of communicating to a target audience so that knowledge that is initially personal becomes public.

Writing as inquiry The process of writing is integral to the entire research process and the act of writing often produces new insights.

Contexts for writing There is a range of contexts for writing such as books, papers and reports targeting specific audiences, each of which requires specialized writing skills.

Technical aspects of writing Regardless of context, genre of research and discipline, there are technical aspects of writing such as drafting and redrafting, use of appropriate grammar, sentence construction, and blogging that can be practised and improved.

References

Cuthbert, D., Spark, C. and Burke, E. (2009) 'Disciplining writing: The case for multidisciplinary writing groups to support writing for publication by higher degree by research candidates in the humanities, arts and social sciences', *Higher Education Research and Development*, 28(2): 137–49.

Ellis, C. and Bochner, A. P. (2000) 'Autoethnography, personal narrative, reflexivity. researcher as subject', in N. K. Denzin and Y. S. Lincoln (eds) *The Sage Handbook of Qualitative Research*, 2nd edn (733–68), London: Sage.

Epstein, D., Kenway, J. and Boden, R. (2005) *Writing for Publication*, London: Sage.

Fletcher, R. (2000) *How Writers Work: Finding a Process that Works for You*, London: HarperCollins.

JOPERD (2011) http://www.aahperd.org/publications/journals/joperd/joperdreprintpermission. cfm.

Kitchin, R. and Fuller, D. (2005) *The Academic's Guide to Publishing*, London: Sage.

Richards, J. (2010) 'Academic writing for publication: Some points of departure for success', *Journal of Reading Education*, 35(3): 50–3.

Richardson, L. (2000) 'New writing practices in qualitative research', *Sociology of Sport Journal*, 17(1): 5–20.

Richardson, L. and St Pierre, E. A. (2005) 'Writing: A method of inquiry', in N. K. Denzin and Y. S. Lincoln (eds) *The SAGE Handbook of Qualitative Research*, 3rd edn (959–78), London: Sage.

Ryan, G. W. and Bernard, H. R. (2000) 'Data management and analysis methods', in N. K. Denzin, and Y. S. Lincoln (eds) *The Sage Handbook of Qualitative Research*, 2nd edn (769–802), Thousand Oaks, CA: Sage.

26 The dissertation

*Lisette Burrows, Fiona McLachlan and
Lucy Spowart*

Alice: Which way should I go?
Cat: That depends on where you are going.
Alice: I don't know where I am going!
Cat: Then it doesn't matter which way you go!

(Lewis Carroll, 1871)

Introduction

The above exchange between Alice and the Cat can be understood in multiple ways. Some would argue that Alice needs to decide where she's headed very soon or she will be lost. Others might relish the opportunity Cat presents to head in any direction they choose. Still others might read this exchange as a kind of 'anything goes' approach to finding one's way. We foreground this quote to remind ourselves that dissertation writing, like peering through a looking glass, can yield and draw on an array of perspectives. Each of us writing this chapter brings different resources and experiences to the process. Our chapter reflects this; nevertheless, we aim to tease out some shared commitments to what a sound dissertation might look and feel like.

About us

Associate Professor Lisette Burrows: I have been doing socio-critical research in physical education for over 15 years. After completing a doctorate that deconstructed developmental discourses in physical education, I have continued to draw on post-structural theoretical resources to investigate questions around the place and meaning of health and physical culture in young people's lives. After years of examining honours, master's and doctoral dissertations in physical education, I've come to the conclusion that an outstanding thesis ticks all the 'must have' boxes in terms of scholarship and it 'feels' good. It is what constitutes that 'feel good' sensation that preoccupies me in this chapter.

Fiona McLachlan: My writing experiences are relatively limited when compared with those of Lisette and Lucy. However, I have completed a master's thesis and am in the throes of creating a PhD thesis about public swimming pools. I am fortunate to be supervised by two people whose writing I really enjoy. Although quite different in their styles, they take care with language and use it productively. Indeed, they both inspire me to become more political and more beautiful in my writing. This is especially important for my current thesis because I am making commentary about the 'power' particular forms of knowledge take. Therefore, to subscribe to an institutionalized formula to present my arguments would contradict the very point of my thesis.

Lucy Spowart: I am a self-confessed 'planner'. The desire to know where I am heading from the outset is strong. Having taught in the broad field of sport development for over a decade, my supervision experiences lead me to believe that *most* students also find it helpful to have an overall framework in mind. Much like climbers embarking on a summit bid of Everest, I consider that preparation and the mapping of a route to the end are crucial. That said, no matter how well one prepares, it is impossible to predict every eventuality that life may throw at us. Those that survive to reach the summit are those that are able to adapt, make good decisions, and possibly alter their course, in the most challenging of circumstances. Inevitably, the direction and timeline of any dissertation journey are also likely to shift.

The dissertation?

'What makes a fine dissertation?' is the question driving this chapter. No matter what epistemological orientation you embrace, what methodological repertoires you draw on or which disciplinary boundaries you subscribe to, there is no escaping the 'dissertation' – the culmination of years of work, the make or break of that scholarly toil. We believe there is no singular, fail-safe recipe that guarantees a fine dissertation and, indeed, we suggest that the existence of such a thing would seriously mess with what for us are two key principles undergirding academic enquiry – passion and creativity. In so saying, it *is* important to have some idea of *what* a dissertation looks like and what writing one might require. The 'doing it' section represents our collective efforts to address these two thorny questions.

Motivations to write a dissertation will be as diverse as those people who do it. There are students who *have* to do postgraduate study to keep their jobs; those who are doing it for someone else (e.g., a proud mum); those for whom an honours dissertation is a mandatory part of their undergraduate course work; those who are motivated to study because they have no idea what else to do yet; people who are driven by a passion for a particular research problem born of their own experience or the experience of those close to them; and those who find genuine pleasure in engaging with ideas and literature, driven by a thirst for new knowledge. The initial motivation for study will inevitably contour not only what you do, but also how you choose to display the fruits of your enquiries.

Lucy embarked on her doctoral journey as a mature and somewhat sceptical research student. Having taught sports development in a higher education institution in the UK for nine years, completing a doctoral degree was the furthest thing from her mind. However, changes to the funding of academic institutions meant that Lucy was pressured by her workplace to undertake a PhD. Therefore, from the outset she was driven by a strong motivation to 'get it done' as quickly as possible.

Fiona enjoyed writing her master's thesis about weight-loss reality television shows so much that she wanted to do another project. She is not doing this under duress. Fiona considers researching and writing a luxury and believes that the final product should reflect more than just going through the motions. Rather, she views the thesis as a form of expression that, like other creative enterprises, should produce an affective response.

Lisette's choice to write a doctoral dissertation was born out of a desire to keep doing what she loved doing – teaching undergraduate physical education students. It quickly morphed, however, to a somewhat surprising affection for researching and writing about something that really 'grabbed' her. While at times it felt like a 'must do' chore, most of the time writing the dissertation felt like a luxurious opportunity to read, think, write – an opportunity, as senior colleagues reminded her, that often comes but once in one's life.

Despite our diverse motivations for study, each of us shares a desire to write in ways that potentially 'move' readers, evoke a sense of why our respective topics are interesting and, perhaps most importantly, honour our commitments to particular world views.

Doing it

There is a hungry market for 'how to write a dissertation' books. Nevertheless, we think that far better and cheaper resources on dissertation writing are readily available. Talking with others – students, supervisors, colleagues – and reading others' work can afford insights that are not necessarily embedded in the 'how to do a thesis' tomes gracing on- and offline book shelves. Attending writing workshops, research workshops, asking questions, quizzing your supervisor about what constitutes 'good' from their perspective are all key strategies. We suggest that accessing these resources (human and textual) at the beginning rather than the end of the dissertation journey is a wise move.

Writing is a very personal thing. Yes, there are literary conventions that can be learnt and that can help but, technicalities aside, styles are as diverse as the people who deploy them. This is a good thing. While perhaps disturbing to those seeking 'the' recipe for dissertation writing, a proliferation of writing styles in the academy affords many more kinds of students the opportunity to envisage themselves as postgraduate students.

Dissertations written in narrative style, as dramas with 'acts' instead of chapters, autobiographical work, poetry, visual images and co-constructed stories are just a few of the options (many more are described in this book). Suffice to say that the traditional format – introduction, literature review, methodology, findings, discussion and conclusion – is no longer the orthodoxy for physical education research. Some sub-disciplines do still favour this style, however. Assessing the availability of examiners who think outside the conventional thesis 'square' will be crucial for those wanting to break free from tradition. That is, assessing your examiners' palate is important.

Currently, there is also a growing interest in thesis by publication, where the student submits a series of published, or often 'in press' journal articles supplemented with front (introduction) and back (conclusion) sections that link the articles together as a cohesive whole. While the number of published/in press papers varies for each student, typically three to four papers is considered appropriate. Some would argue that completing several relatively short papers is a more manageable task than one enormous dissertation, while others might find that writing short pieces for journals constrains their ability to develop a coherent and detailed argument. One of the perceived advantages of approaching a dissertation in this way is the capacity to publish as you go, thereby building your academic profile en route rather than post thesis submission. We have no experience in examining or completing a dissertation in this mode, yet feel it is important to signal this emergent trend.

The techniques we refer to below are drawn from our collective experiences as dissertation examiners and postgraduate students, and as voracious readers of others' work. We have no desire to present these as fail-safe, generic recipes for success with dissertation writing. Each of us has encountered enough instances of wonderful writing being negatively assessed and poor writing celebrated to recognize that, like beauty, a great thesis is to some extent in the eye of the beholder. Nevertheless, we hope our thoughts may be helpful on some level to both emerging researchers and seasoned proponents of the trade. First, we present *two key 'process' strategies*. Next, we suggest *six key tips* about what a dissertation should look and feel like.

Our first suggestion regarding the process of writing a dissertation is to search and *absorb as many theses as you can that are (at least tangentially) related to your sphere of study*. Which ones did you like? Why? What did they do that appeals? The rationale behind this is not to copy, but to be inspired and provoked. Like music, there will be some pieces you adore, some that leave you cold and others that fail to connect with who you think you are or what you want to be. Finding a couple of star theses – that turn your wheels, that make you want to be a groupie – is a fine start. If nothing else, this random roaming of the thesis library will reassure you that many styles of work qualify as theses, that many kinds of people become PhDs; and hopefully, among the rabble you'll find one or two that help you feel 'I can do that!' or 'I *want* to do it like that'.

Fiona says:

> When I started my master's thesis, I really had no idea what was expected of me in terms of processing the written document. I took Lisette's advice and read several different theses. Finding ones that I did and did not like was the easy part. What it took me a long time to realize was that we only ever read highly polished pieces of writing. In articles, books and theses. Very rarely do we witness others' writing in progress – so we don't get to see or feel the pain of their blank pages, or the destruction of a draft that has been covered in track changes. I got into a fairly bad habit of hating my writing unless it seemed like it was on its way to being of thesis standard. Often this became paralysing because I didn't know why I couldn't 'just write'. So while the absorption method is helpful, try not to get stuck in the same trap that I did – first thoughts do not have to be polished!

Our second technique relates to what helps and/or hinders the writing process. As with all aspects of the dissertation experience, the day-to-day doing of it will be shaped by why you're doing it, what else is going on in your life at the time, your work habits, your environment (physical, social, emotional) and, of course, the nature of your supervision. Some dissertation supervisors will have fixed notions about how to write, when to write and what that writing should look like. I know supervisors who require their students to write 200 words a day, no matter what the words are; others who encourage students to refrain from writing until data are collected; and still others who are happy to wait until students are ready, willing and able to write – within or outside any fixed schedule. The key here is to *ensure your processes gel with, or at least are accepted as viable by, your supervisor*. A deadline-fixated supervisor and a floppy student are not a fine match. Whatever the case, beginning to write early on and getting comfortable with letting others read and review your scribblings are crucial.

Lucy says:

> While it is a generally accepted fact that dissertations will grow and alter as they are developed, this can be disturbing for someone like me who likes to plan. Despite some rather major changes to my own original plans, I am still of the firm belief that outlining a basic framework of what your dissertation will look like, from the outset, is helpful. It is difficult to fully imagine the end product, but I always worked with a chapter outline taped to the wall, and amended it as I went. Alongside the chapter framework, I set myself deadlines. Keeping my dissertation framework 'public', on my office wall at university had a number of benefits. First, it generated my weekly work plan: it kept me focused, and meant that there was always a deadline to be striving towards. Second, it meant that other students and staff were able to see my thesis plan, and this prompted discussions about its content and form.

Writing and organizational habits aside, there *are* a few things that a good thesis should display. In our view there are six 'must dos'.

First, a good thesis must *address the research question/s*. Hold those questions you had at the start of the book tightly. They are the golden thread that will ensure your story makes sense. They should be there at the beginning, be substantially addressed in the main body of the work and take centre stage at the end. Without a consistent focus on these, the dissertation runs a risk of resembling a multi-activity physical education programme – a series of random events bearing little relevance to the underlying purpose. Clearly stated research questions that are visible and engaged with throughout all parts of the dissertation are the cornerstone of a good and a great dissertation.

Second, it is crucial that readers understand, as you presumably do, *why these research questions are interesting and/or relevant*. This may be obvious to you, but without a context, a critical review of what else has been said (or not) about them, how will anyone else be persuaded? For some, this bit is the 'literature review', while for others the context will be set in the introductory pages, or integrated into another chapter going by some other name.

Related to the issue of clearly establishing and addressing research questions is the third matter: *what theoretical drivers inform the work and why?* In some disciplines, simply acknowledging a debt to prior work in the field will suffice, while for others clearly establishing what ontological and/or epistemological assumptions underpin your thesis will be vital. Once again, here your supervisors' perspectives may influence your decisions. Some will want you to frame your study around an established theoretical framework, insisting that the questions you ask, your methodology and modes of analysis must 'fit' with this theoretical frame. Others will happily encourage an exploration of multiple theories, promoting a pick-and-mix approach to theory. The latter style of enquiry permits students to pragmatically draw on theoretical approaches that help explain the data, or advance an argument, whether or not they are, at first blush, commensurate. There is no hard and fast rule regarding the wisdom of either approach, yet what *is* important here is selecting examiners who are open to the particular take on theoretical drivers you embrace.

Fourth, and somewhat obviously, a good thesis should *tell the reader what you did, what you found out and why it is important.* For some these missions are encoded in methodology (e.g., What did you do? Why? How did your methods help you address the question?), results (What did you find out?), discussion (What sense do you make of what you found? How did the findings relate to prior literature? How did your theoretical drivers help you interpret what you've found?) and conclusion chapters (So what for future research, the profession, the people/things at the centre of your enquiry?). For others, they are not necessarily segregated but rather interwoven in chapters that go by other names. Whatever the case, the reader *does* need to know the answers to these questions.

Fifth, *a good thesis needs to be grammatically correct.* There is nothing more distracting to an examiner than pages of mechanical errors (e.g., spelling, grammatical errors, inconsistency of citation style etc.). A 'clean' dissertation is a crucial precursor to ensuring your examiner engages with your ideas, your argument – your dissertation.

Finally, the most profound ideas in the world cannot make an impact if they don't reach the reader. Some dissertations are rich with fabulous ideas, but not necessarily represented in a way that allows readers to follow the argument. *Signposts* can help here. Signposts signal to the reader what is coming up next. They can also be a useful tool to help you write. Signposts can take the form of chapter headings, subheadings and paragraph headers or leading statements. Much like signs on a roadside, the detail needs to be accurate. Once you commit your reader to a certain direction, they will be lost if your writing does not take them there.

With the six cornerstones of a good thesis so simply articulated above, it is tempting to regard the process as a relatively straightforward one; yet, it is our experience that nothing much in life is straightforward. Yes, there are some students who seemingly have it all worked out. They approach the thesis like a giant jigsaw, squeezing pieces into the puzzle at appointed deadlines, rarely skipping a beat. While pragmatically splendid, we are not convinced that ideas are like this. Ideas don't always come 'on deadline', the writing doesn't come 'on target', things (life events; reading tangents; exposure to fresh ideas) get in the way – and so they should. Writing a dissertation is a messy affair, and pieces that come together like clockwork are rare finds. Taking time to savour ideas, random and strange as they may initially appear, is time well spent. Changing your mind and feeling uncertain are good things. These interruptions to the process are indicators that you're prepared to think 'otherwise' – to *think*, full stop. And examiners are interested in this thinking.

For some, the thesis will come together in what we like to call a 'whoosh' at the end of the study period. For others, this seemingly chaotic possibility is too risky and knowing precisely what one will say at the end before one begins is important. For those undertaking a thesis by publication there are particular milestones (publications) to be met along the way. In our view, it doesn't really matter how one works. Both organized and dishevelled modes of operating can produce good and great theses.

Next we share some personal stories about the dissertation writing process: what pleased, irked and drove us during the process.

Lisette

I got besotted with post-structural theory in 1995 during a postgraduate course. The theory helped me understand what pleased and challenged me as a physical education teacher in the early 1990s. It afforded a lens through which to interrogate my experience and wonder about the experiences of others en route to becoming physically educated. Squeezing study time amidst full-time duties as a lecturer, I needed supervisors who didn't want weekly meetings or reports, supervisors who didn't bug me about my 'progress', yet were there when time permitted conversations about the work. I found two of these. One with an intellectual curiosity and passion born in an era when doctoral work was viewed as the penultimate opportunity to think otherwise; a person who wanted me to not only engage with Foucault, but 'be' Foucault – challenge the orthodoxy, write as a free-thinking spirit, with little regard for academic conventions regarding what a thesis should look or feel like. My other supervisor was no less bereft of intellectual rigour, yet displayed a more pragmatic attitude to the process of dissertation writing. With multiple thesis examinations in her wake, she never dissuaded me from my idiosyncratic thoughts, but consistently pushed for a more pragmatic approach to doing the thesis, an approach designed to get it done relatively timeously, rather than one that potentially could have seen me gulping down books in the library for multiple years. I can see merits in both approaches, and again, it depends on what you're doing and why you're doing it.

I ended up writing a thesis about developmental discourses in school physical education, drawing on post-structural theory. It was okay, yet I remain conflicted about the contradictions my thesis displays. While the driver for the work was post-structural theory, my thesis format – its chapters, its linear 'development', its adherence to what was then an 'orthodox' manner of displaying one's research – belied the post-structural commitments I avowedly embraced. That is, the theory didn't match the product. Ten years post submission, I would now take more risks, dare to organize my thoughts in ways that don't necessarily cohere with traditional expectations. In so saying, I was one of those students who wanted to keep her job, needed to get it done quickly, and wanted to pass. Thankfully, there are many more style options for 21st-century students that *are* palatable to contemporary thesis examiners.

Fiona

To the outside observer, my writing process might appear quite chaotic. I have bakery wrappers with handwritten scribbles of endless revisions to my thesis and chapter outlines scattered across my office. My desk is littered with books and articles seemingly bearing no order or system. I do not work in a chronological or linear fashion and jump from working on the beginning to the end and all the bits in between, sometimes within the same hour. However, amidst this chaos my approach to the thesis itself is actually quite exacting – I firmly believe that every word counts.

Sometimes, I like to pretend that I am one of the chefs on the reality TV show *Iron Chef*. The premise of this show rests on two chefs competing against each other in a cook-off, using a selected core ingredient as their focus. Using this ingredient, the chefs each have to produce six elegant and delicious dishes; success lies in ensuring that the main ingredient remains the 'hero' on the plate.

While I am not competing against my fellow chefs, I think the process is very similar to thesis writing. My main ingredient is swimming pools and my research questions and theoretical orientations provide me with ideas for each dish. I think of each plate as a chapter in the thesis – while distinct in its own right, each chapter should connect with each of the others to achieve a coherent meal. Like the iron chefs, I have to start with information in bulk and the final thesis will reflect a long process of refinement. While the final product might demonstrate finesse, the process itself is not so elegant – chaos, mess and mistakes abound!

I think the end product should produce an affective response, much like when tasting food. Personally, I like to read, and write, imaginative theses – those that are more like a piece of art than a quarterly business report. This is because it is these types of theses that are more likely to upset me, make me laugh or change my mind about something. Regardless of style, at the very least I think a thesis should be thoughtfully presented. An iron chef wouldn't figure out an amazing new method for cooking roast lamb and then serve it to you in its messy roasting dish; the same logic applies with thesis writing. However, the aesthetic of the thesis should also reflect the aims and theoretical orientations of the project. A visually stunning plate of food may offer a favourable first impression but unless it has substance the critic will score it low. Finally, a coherent thesis needs to have a point. The iron chefs are sometimes criticized for overcomplicating their dishes or for losing the essence of their main ingredient. These are things that I am careful about as I try to inject a dash of creativity into my thesis.

So, in my ongoing process of chaotic refinement, I am guided by a feeling for what I want to say about public swimming pools, and am committed to putting my mark on my dish. I hope that my critics will recognize and appreciate that my plate reflects my thought that knowledge-making is an artistic and creative pursuit. What will your plate say about you?

Lucy

Not uncommonly, my personal experiences have to a large extent driven my research (Cresswell, 1994), and also played a substantial part in shaping my thesis. While I was pregnant, I experienced a significant amount of disapproval from friends, family, work colleagues and, perhaps most frustratingly, from relative strangers, in connection with my leisure choices. The focus of this condemnation was the alleged risks that I was taking by continuing to participate in a range of physical (some would say high-risk) activities, including snowboarding. This sense of disapproval continued once I became a mother.

After a cursory look at the literature related to leisure and motherhood, I discovered that there are very few in-depth studies of motherhood and sport, and no studies that looked at mothers' participation in so-called 'lifestyle sports'. This gave me the perfect opportunity to study something I was passionate about. My research project is undeniably, and I might add, unapologetically, a personal quest to understand and challenge the status that motherhood currently holds.

Rather than study a range of 'risky' activities, I chose to hone in on snowboarding. This also reflected my own interests, and assisted greatly when it came to conversing with other female snowboarders. My thesis, then, was an exploration of the experiences of mothers who returned to snowboarding within the first year of having children, and who remain regularly active in the sport. The key question that orientated my research project was: How do female snowboarders, who are mothers, constitute their selves in the context of discourses around motherhood and snowboarding which currently circulate in Aotearoa/New Zealand? This was my golden thread, and each chapter of my thesis aimed to shed some light on this question.

I set out to give voice to mothers who would not normally be heard and in so doing, I intended to raise the profile of nonconformist gender performances. Like Lisette, I drew on post-structural theory to assist me. This theory was helpful because of the central concepts of discourse and subjectivity. To explain these concepts in detail here would serve no purpose. Suffice to say that you will need to discuss this with your supervisor, and find a theoretical lens that works for you and your project.

So, what did I find out about snowboarding mothers? In brief, I discovered that snowboarding held a significant place in the lives of my study participants. For them, snowboarding is a time for fun, relaxation, friendship, revitalization and a sense of self. That said, the women cannot escape (at times) strong feelings of guilt, and carefully monitor the amount of time they spend away from their children, as well as the level of risk taking they engage in. 'Is that it?' I hear you say. Three years of reading, gathering data, analysing data, and that is what you came up with? Clearly, I do not have the space here to go into my study in detail, but, yes, essentially, that's it! So, whatever it is that you decide to study, it is as much about the process as the findings. Of course, I hope that my research will in some way impact upon the lives of other women, but I now have the skills to go on and research other things. It has opened up new doors, as I hope that your research will open doors for you.

End thought

As the vignettes above have hopefully conveyed, what each of us shares is a dissertation drawn from personal and professional passion – a dissertation focused on something that grabbed us, sustained us, meant something to us at a visceral level. For each of us, the dissertation, eventually, was recognized as a privilege, an apprenticeship, a rare opportunity to read, think, talk and engage with ideas and people and tell a story that may be of interest to others. How and why that story is told is not something a chapter in a textbook can prescribe. What we have tried to do is share our experiences of writing a thesis – our motivations for doing it, the process and the outcomes.

We anticipate there will be some readers who rail against Fiona's 'left-of-centre' ideas or Lisette's 'floppy' processes. There will be those who take comfort in the more pragmatic approach to writing a dissertation embraced by Lucy, and others who wonder why bother writing a chapter on this at all if the authors can't agree on a 'right' way to do it! If nothing else, we hope the diversity of our experience prompts lively debate among emergent physical education and youth sport researchers – conversations that mess up the orthodoxy and challenge us to examine what counts in scholarship, and life.

Key terms

Dissertation   A document representing a degree candidate's research and findings.
Thesis   A word used interchangeably with 'dissertation,' depending on one's geographic location.
Post-structuralism   A school of thought that affirms the socially constructed nature of reality.
Creativity   The process of producing novel and/or unexpected insights.

References

Carroll, L. (1871) *Through the Looking-Glass and What Alice Found There*, London: Macmillan.
Cresswell, J. (1994) *Research Design: Qualitative and Quantitative Approaches*, London: Sage.

Further reading

Dunleavy, P. (2003) *Authoring a PhD: How to Plan, Draft, Write and Finish a Doctoral Thesis or Dissertation*, Basingstoke: Palgrave Macmillan.

Index